UNTOUCHABLES™

JOE PRUETT
WRITER/LETTERER

JOHN KISSEE
PENCILER

CHRIS DREIER
INKER

GALEN SHOWMAN
COVER ARTIST

DEVELOPED AND CREATED BY
JOE PRUETT AND GARY REED

JOE PRUETT
COLLECTION EDITOR/BOOK DESIGNER

JAMES PRUETT
JOE PRUETT
GARY REED
ORIGINAL SERIES EDITORS

NATE PRIDE
LOGO DESIGN

FIRST EDITION:
OCTOBER 2006

10 9 8 7 6 5 4 3 2 1

WITHDRAWN

DESPERADO
www.desperadopublishing.com

Joe Pruett
Publisher

April Doster
Creative Director

Gary Reed
Business Development

Malcolm Bourne
Special Projects Coordinator

Ian Feller
Media Liaison
www.813sands.com

Ryan Crissey
Production Assistant

Tim Hegarty
Foreign Rights Representative
www.InternationalEnterprise.org

www.imagecomics.com

Erik Larsen
Publisher

Todd McFarlane
President

Marc Silvestri
CEO

Jim Valentino
Vice-President

Eric Stephenson
Executive Director

Jim Demonakos
PR & Marketing Coordinator

Mia MacHatton
Accounts Manager

Traci Hui
Administrative Assistant

Joe Keatinge
Traffic Manager

Allen Hui
Production Manager

Jonathan Chan
Production Artist

Drew Gill
Production Artist

Chris Giarrusso
Production Artist

UNTOUCHABLES

UNTOUCHABLES

"A NEW BEGINNING"

ACT 1

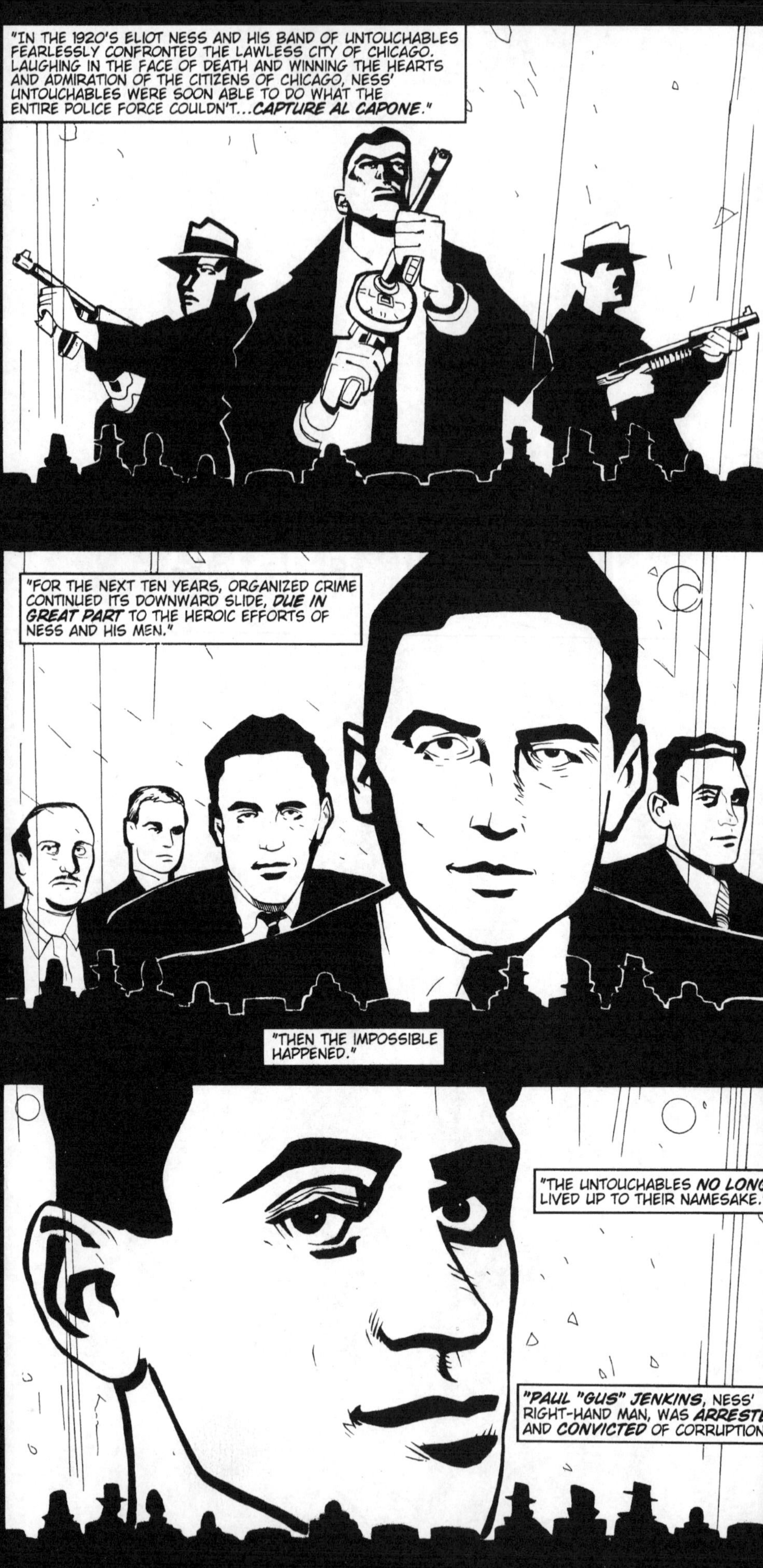
"IN THE 1920'S ELIOT NESS AND HIS BAND OF UNTOUCHABLES FEARLESSLY CONFRONTED THE LAWLESS CITY OF CHICAGO. LAUGHING IN THE FACE OF DEATH AND WINNING THE HEARTS AND ADMIRATION OF THE CITIZENS OF CHICAGO, NESS' UNTOUCHABLES WERE SOON ABLE TO DO WHAT THE ENTIRE POLICE FORCE COULDN'T...***CAPTURE AL CAPONE***."
"FOR THE NEXT TEN YEARS, ORGANIZED CRIME CONTINUED ITS DOWNWARD SLIDE, ***DUE IN GREAT PART*** TO THE HEROIC EFFORTS OF NESS AND HIS MEN."
"THEN THE IMPOSSIBLE HAPPENED."
"THE UNTOUCHABLES ***NO LONGER*** LIVED UP TO THEIR NAMESAKE."
"***PAUL "GUS" JENKINS***, NESS' RIGHT-HAND MAN, WAS ***ARRESTED*** AND ***CONVICTED*** OF CORRUPTION."

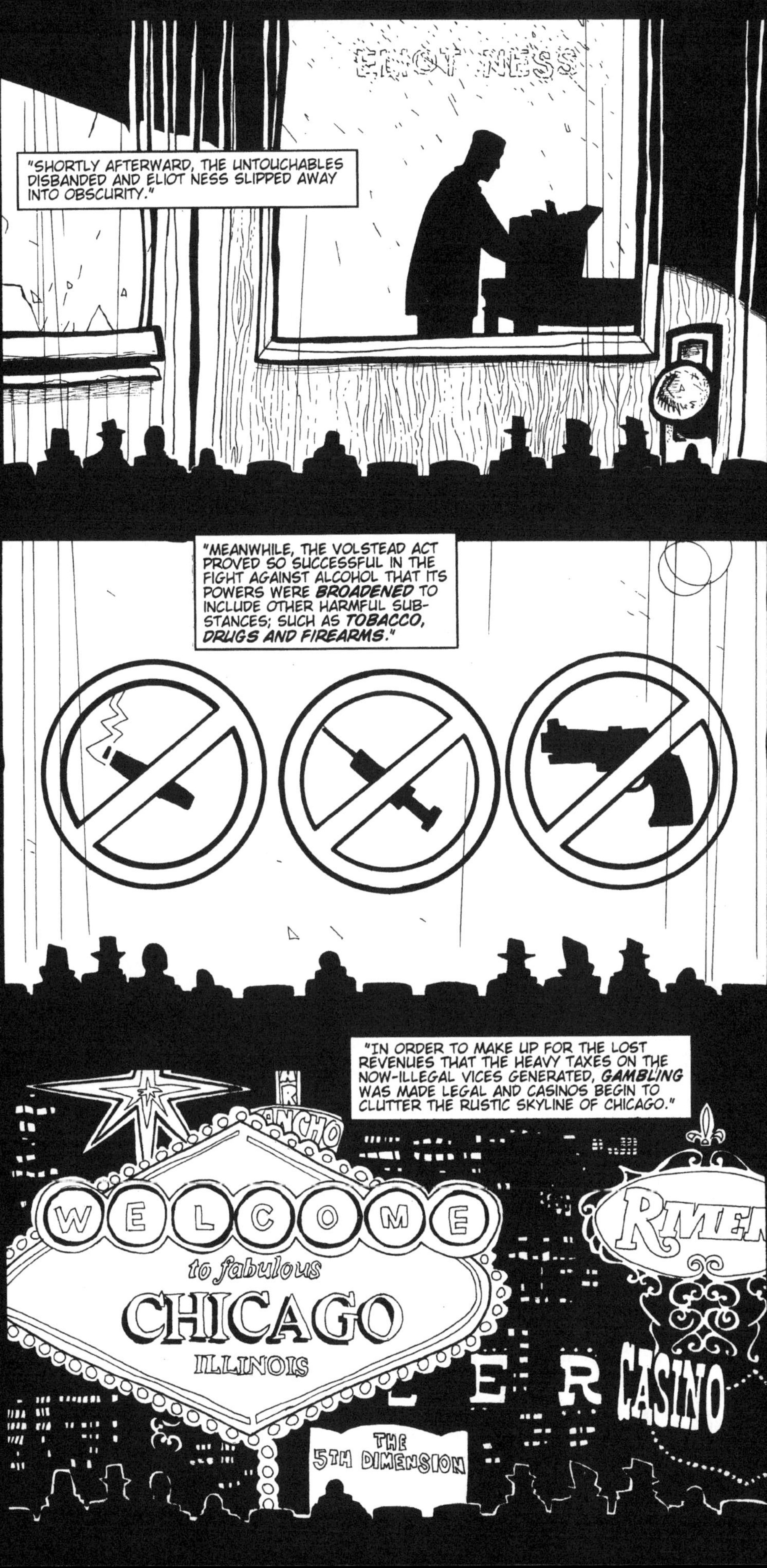
"SHORTLY AFTERWARD, THE UNTOUCHABLES DISBANDED AND ELIOT NESS SLIPPED AWAY INTO OBSCURITY."
"MEANWHILE, THE VOLSTEAD ACT PROVED SO SUCCESSFUL IN THE FIGHT AGAINST ALCOHOL THAT ITS POWERS WERE *BROADENED* TO INCLUDE OTHER HARMFUL SUBSTANCES; SUCH AS *TOBACCO, DRUGS AND FIREARMS.*"
"IN ORDER TO MAKE UP FOR THE LOST REVENUES THAT THE HEAVY TAXES ON THE NOW-ILLEGAL VICES GENERATED, *GAMBLING* WAS MADE LEGAL AND CASINOS BEGIN TO CLUTTER THE RUSTIC SKYLINE OF CHICAGO."
WELCOME
to fabulous
CHICAGO
ILLINOIS
CASINO
THE 5TH DIMENSION

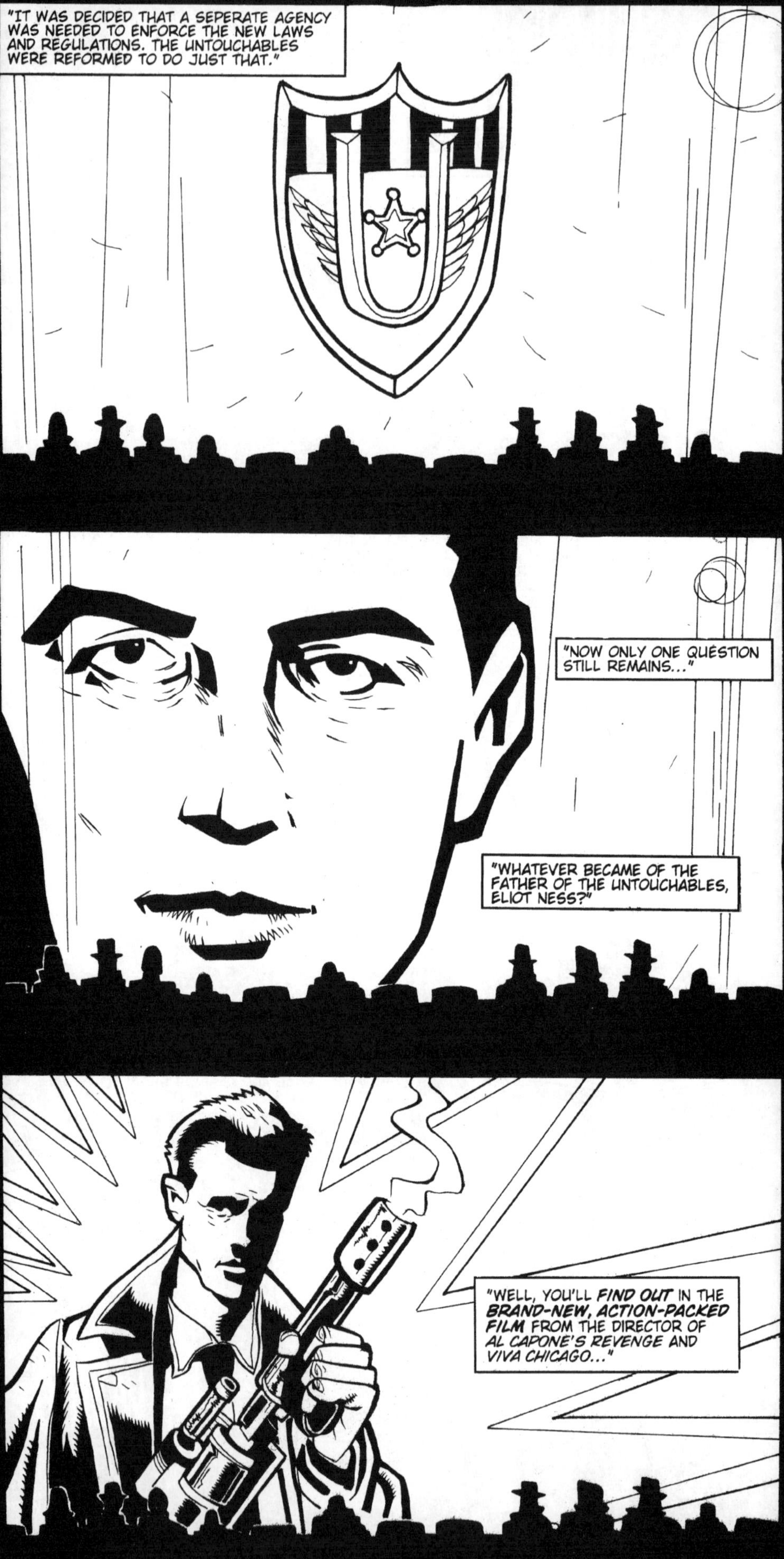
"IT WAS DECIDED THAT A SEPERATE AGENCY WAS NEEDED TO ENFORCE THE NEW LAWS AND REGULATIONS. THE UNTOUCHABLES WERE REFORMED TO DO JUST THAT."
"NOW ONLY ONE QUESTION STILL REMAINS..."
"WHATEVER BECAME OF THE FATHER OF THE UNTOUCHABLES, ELIOT NESS?"
"WELL, YOU'LL ***FIND OUT*** IN THE ***BRAND-NEW, ACTION-PACKED FILM*** FROM THE DIRECTOR OF ***AL CAPONE'S REVENGE*** AND ***VIVA CHICAGO...***"

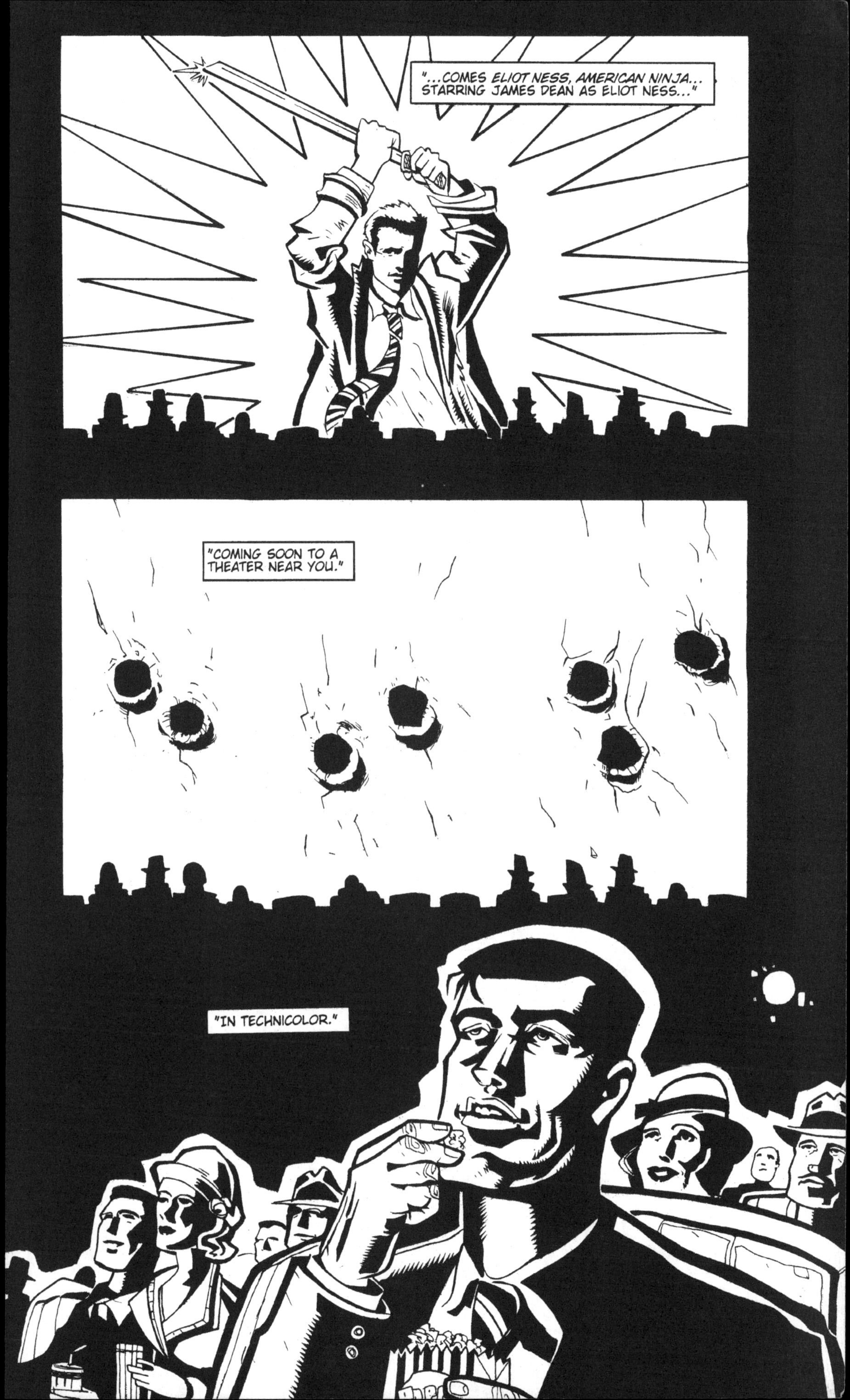
"...COMES ELIOT NESS, AMERICAN NINJA... STARRING JAMES DEAN AS ELIOT NESS..."
"COMING SOON TO A THEATER NEAR YOU."
"IN TECHNICOLOR."

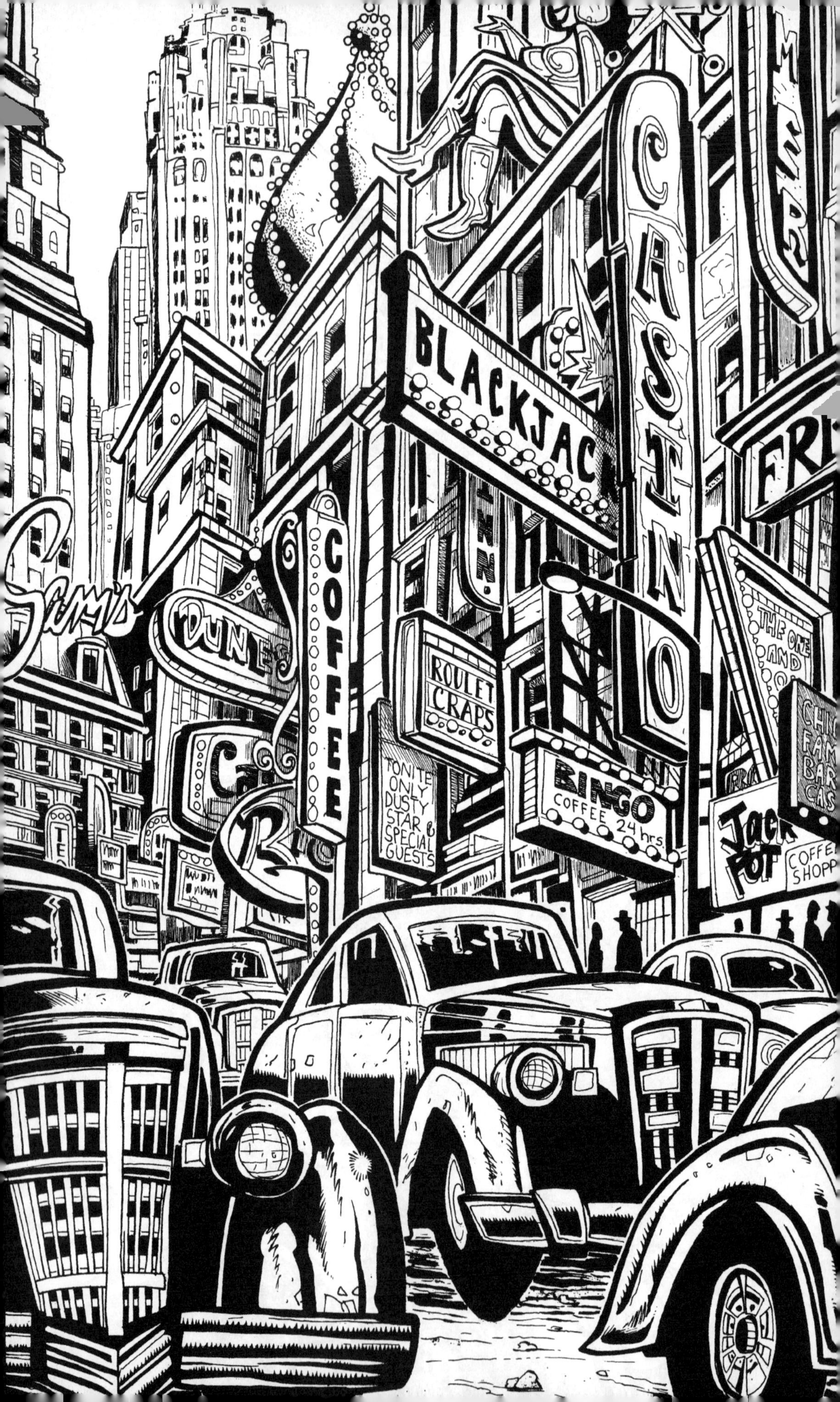

BLACKJAC
CASINO
COFFEE
Sam's
DUNES
ROULET
CRAPS
TONITE ONLY DUSTY STAR & SPECIAL GUESTS
BINGO
COFFEE 24 hrs.
THE ONE AND
Jack Pot

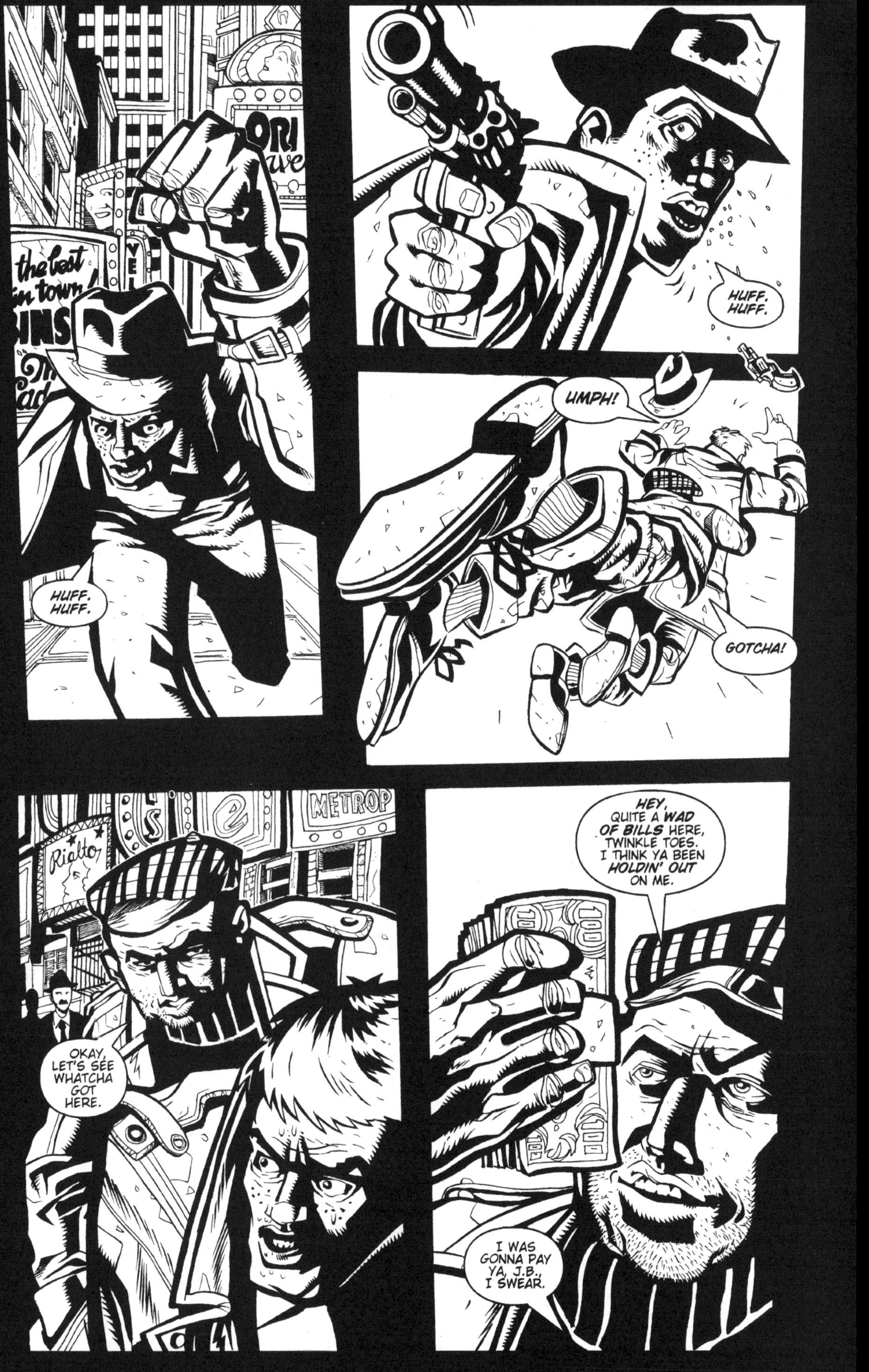

the best in town!
HUFF. HUFF.
HUFF. HUFF.
UMPH!
GOTCHA!
METROP
Rialto
OKAY, LET'S SEE WHATCHA GOT HERE.
HEY, QUITE A WAD OF BILLS HERE, TWINKLE TOES. I THINK YA BEEN HOLDIN' OUT ON ME.
I WAS GONNA PAY YA, J.B., I SWEAR.

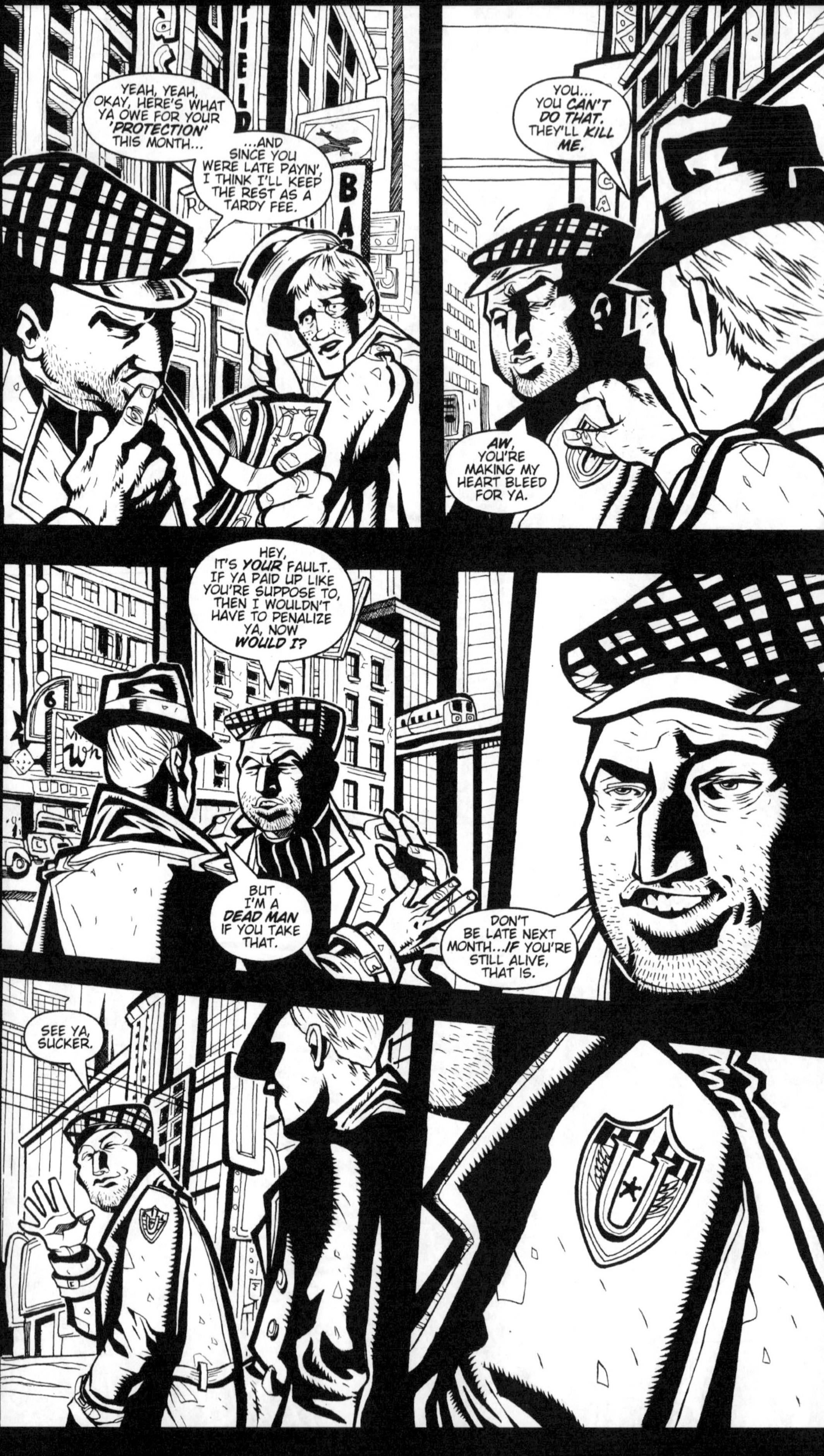
YEAH, YEAH, OKAY, HERE'S WHAT YA OWE FOR YOUR 'PROTECTION' THIS MONTH...
...AND SINCE YOU WERE LATE PAYIN', I THINK I'LL KEEP THE REST AS A TARDY FEE.
YOU... YOU CAN'T DO THAT. THEY'LL KILL ME.
AW, YOU'RE MAKING MY HEART BLEED FOR YA.
HEY, IT'S YOUR FAULT. IF YA PAID UP LIKE YOU'RE SUPPOSE TO, THEN I WOULDN'T HAVE TO PENALIZE YA, NOW WOULD I?
BUT I'M A DEAD MAN IF YOU TAKE THAT.
DON'T BE LATE NEXT MONTH...IF YOU'RE STILL ALIVE, THAT IS.
SEE YA, SUCKER.

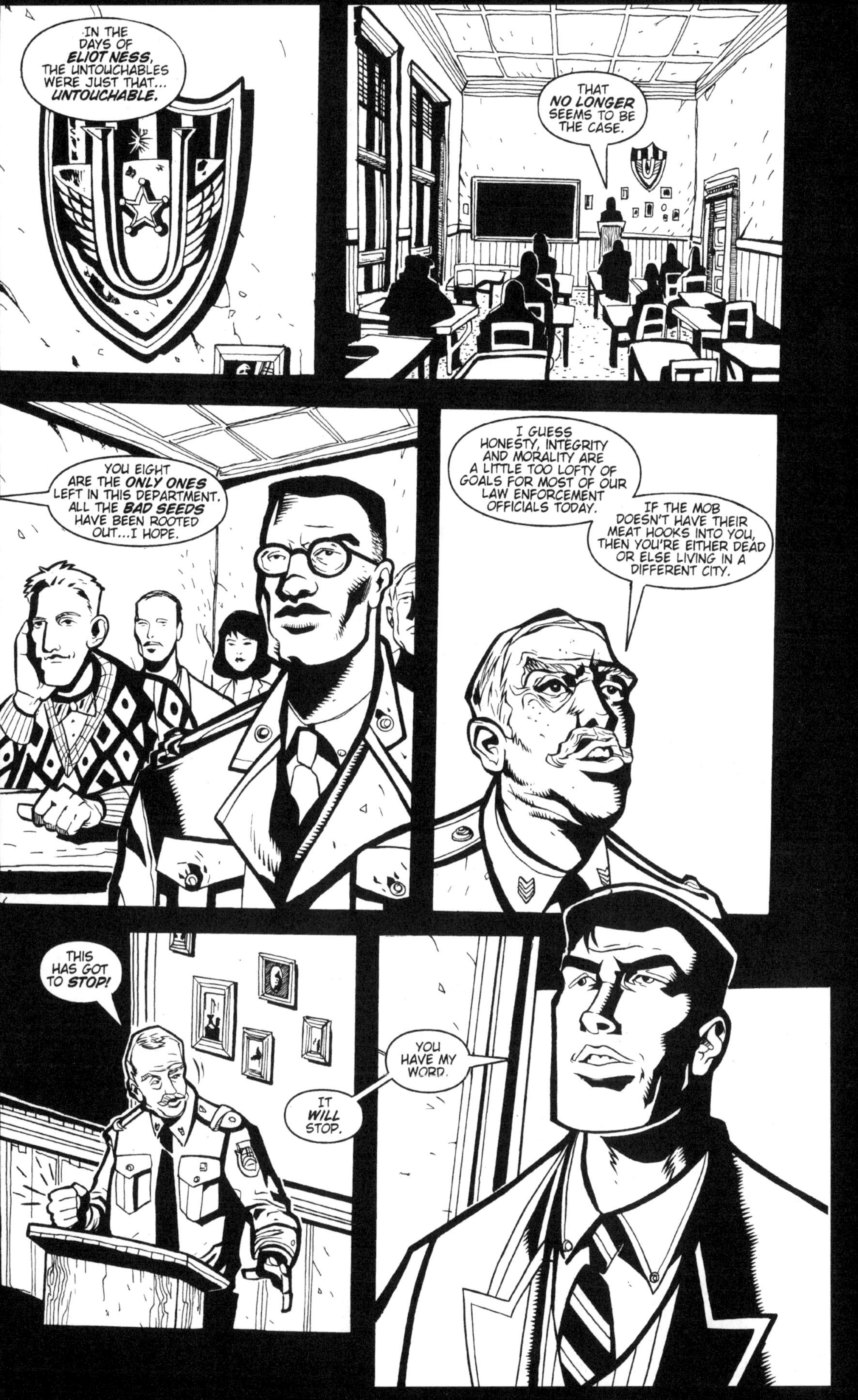
IN THE DAYS OF ELIOT NESS, THE UNTOUCHABLES WERE JUST THAT... UNTOUCHABLE.
THAT NO LONGER SEEMS TO BE THE CASE.
YOU EIGHT ARE THE ONLY ONES LEFT IN THIS DEPARTMENT. ALL THE BAD SEEDS HAVE BEEN ROOTED OUT...I HOPE.
I GUESS HONESTY, INTEGRITY AND MORALITY ARE A LITTLE TOO LOFTY OF GOALS FOR MOST OF OUR LAW ENFORCEMENT OFFICIALS TODAY.
IF THE MOB DOESN'T HAVE THEIR MEAT HOOKS INTO YOU, THEN YOU'RE EITHER DEAD OR ELSE LIVING IN A DIFFERENT CITY.
THIS HAS GOT TO STOP!
YOU HAVE MY WORD.
IT WILL STOP.

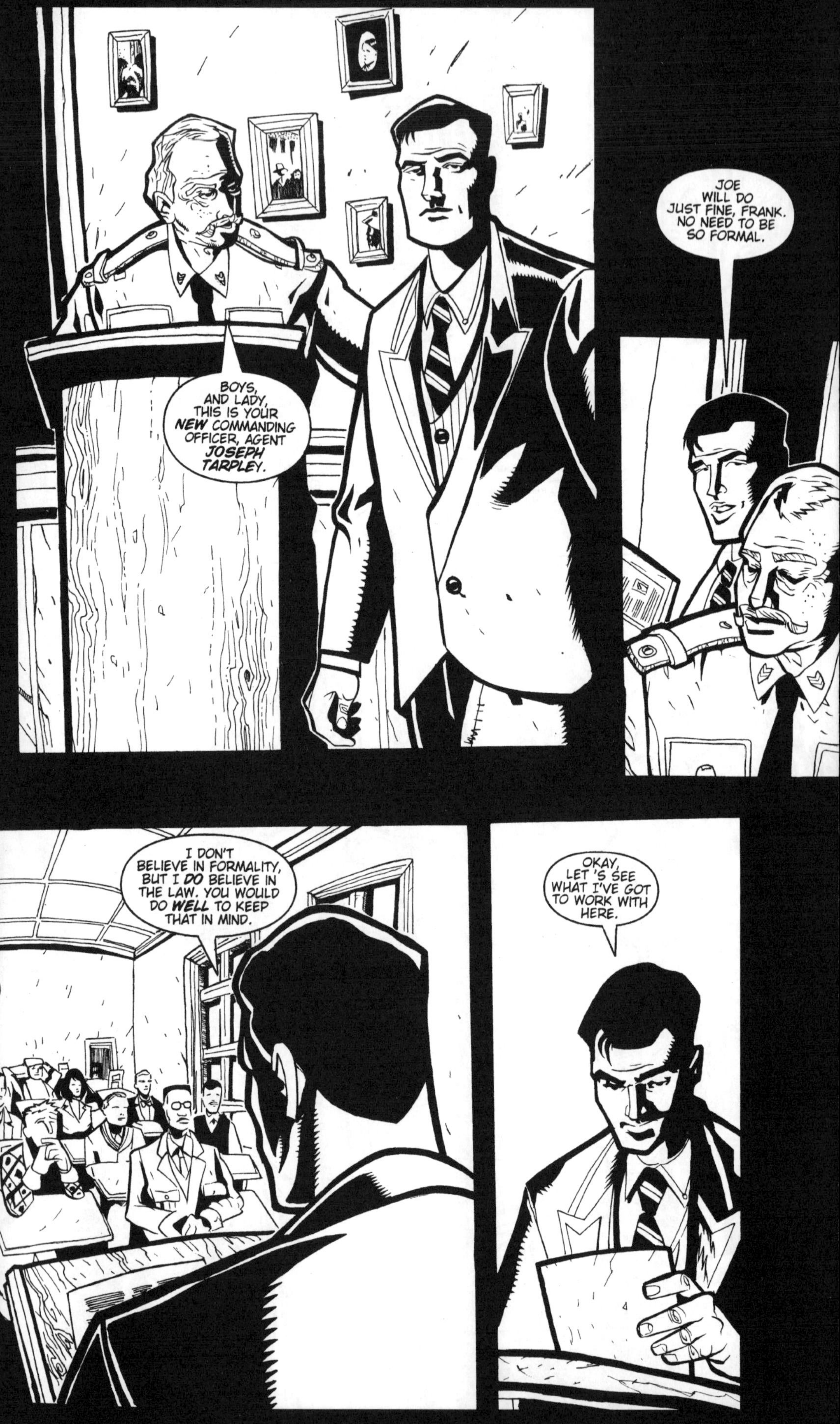

BOYS, AND LADY, THIS IS YOUR NEW COMMANDING OFFICER, AGENT JOSEPH TARPLEY.
JOE WILL DO JUST FINE, FRANK. NO NEED TO BE SO FORMAL.
I DON'T BELIEVE IN FORMALITY, BUT I DO BELIEVE IN THE LAW. YOU WOULD DO WELL TO KEEP THAT IN MIND.
OKAY, LET'S SEE WHAT I'VE GOT TO WORK WITH HERE.

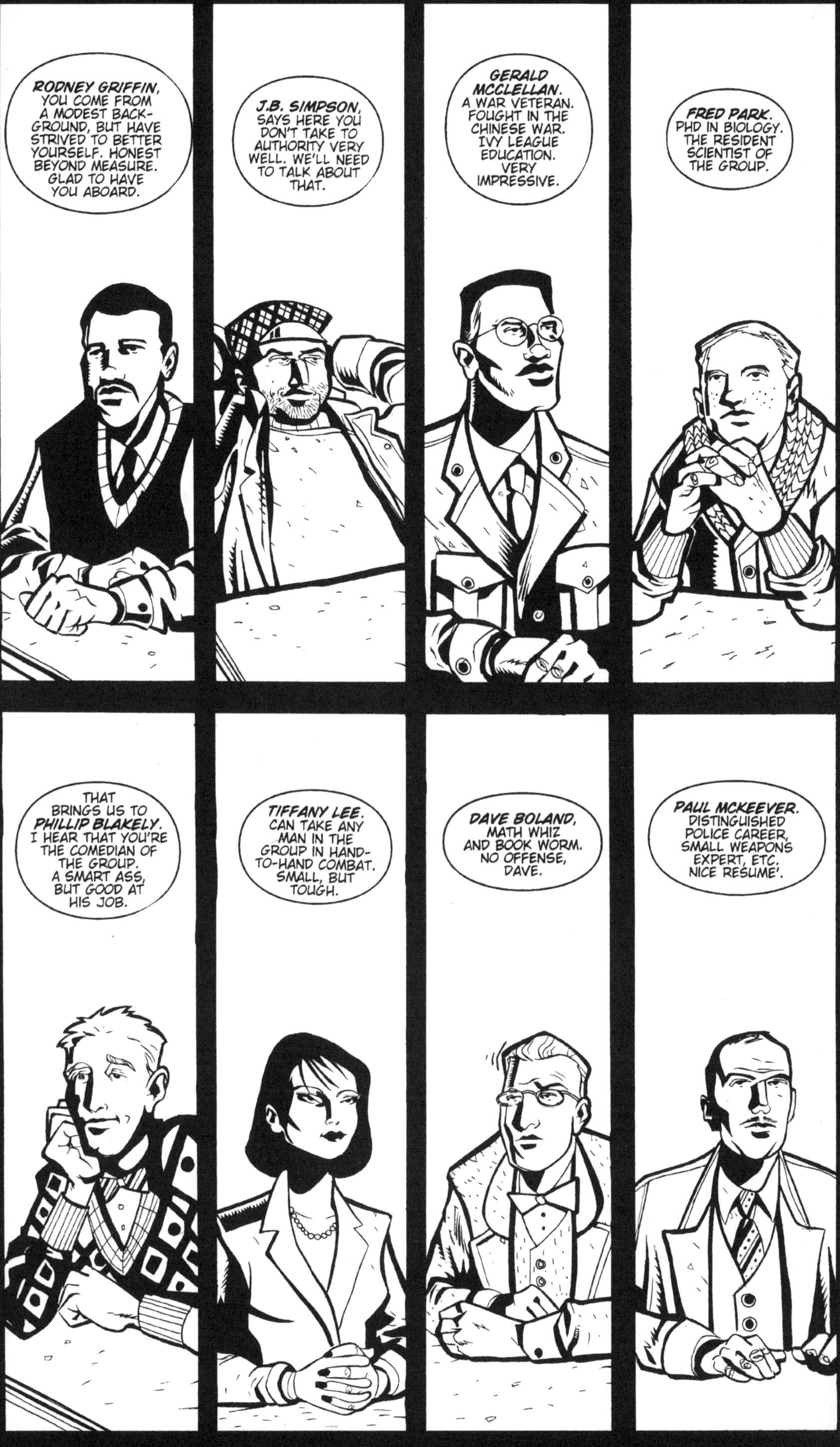
RODNEY GRIFFIN, YOU COME FROM A MODEST BACK-GROUND, BUT HAVE STRIVED TO BETTER YOURSELF. HONEST BEYOND MEASURE. GLAD TO HAVE YOU ABOARD.
J.B. SIMPSON, SAYS HERE YOU DON'T TAKE TO AUTHORITY VERY WELL. WE'LL NEED TO TALK ABOUT THAT.
GERALD MCCLELLAN. A WAR VETERAN. FOUGHT IN THE CHINESE WAR. IVY LEAGUE EDUCATION. VERY IMPRESSIVE.
FRED PARK. PHD IN BIOLOGY. THE RESIDENT SCIENTIST OF THE GROUP.
THAT BRINGS US TO PHILLIP BLAKELY. I HEAR THAT YOU'RE THE COMEDIAN OF THE GROUP. A SMART ASS, BUT GOOD AT HIS JOB.
TIFFANY LEE. CAN TAKE ANY MAN IN THE GROUP IN HAND-TO-HAND COMBAT. SMALL, BUT TOUGH.
DAVE BOLAND, MATH WHIZ AND BOOK WORM. NO OFFENSE, DAVE.
PAUL MCKEEVER. DISTINGUISHED POLICE CAREER, SMALL WEAPONS EXPERT, ETC. NICE RESUME'.

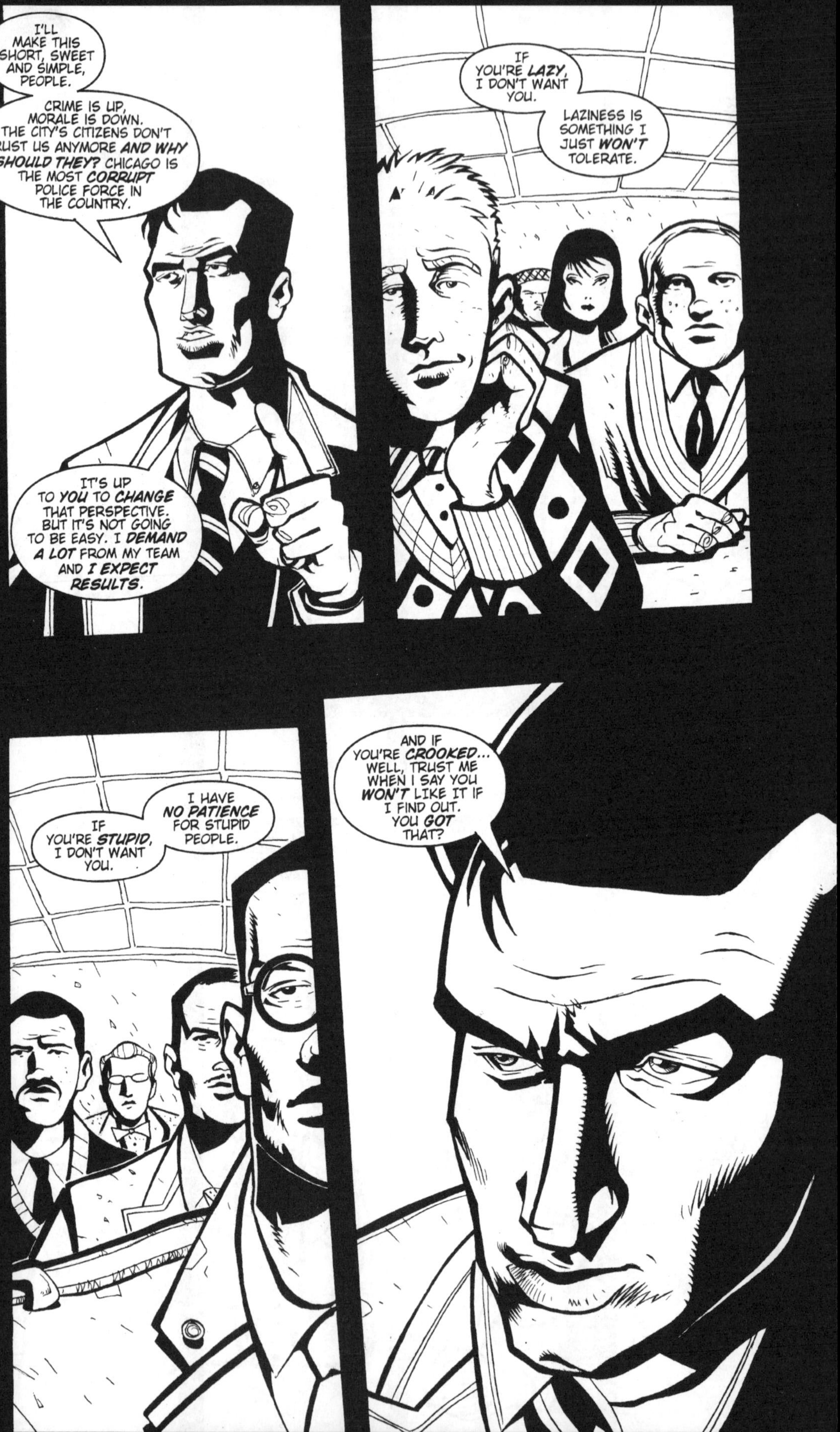
I'LL MAKE THIS SHORT, SWEET AND SIMPLE, PEOPLE.
CRIME IS UP, MORALE IS DOWN. THE CITY'S CITIZENS DON'T TRUST US ANYMORE AND WHY SHOULD THEY? CHICAGO IS THE MOST CORRUPT POLICE FORCE IN THE COUNTRY.
IT'S UP TO YOU TO CHANGE THAT PERSPECTIVE. BUT IT'S NOT GOING TO BE EASY. I DEMAND A LOT FROM MY TEAM AND I EXPECT RESULTS.
IF YOU'RE LAZY, I DON'T WANT YOU.
LAZINESS IS SOMETHING I JUST WON'T TOLERATE.
IF YOU'RE STUPID, I DON'T WANT YOU.
I HAVE NO PATIENCE FOR STUPID PEOPLE.
AND IF YOU'RE CROOKED... WELL, TRUST ME WHEN I SAY YOU WON'T LIKE IT IF I FIND OUT. YOU GOT THAT?

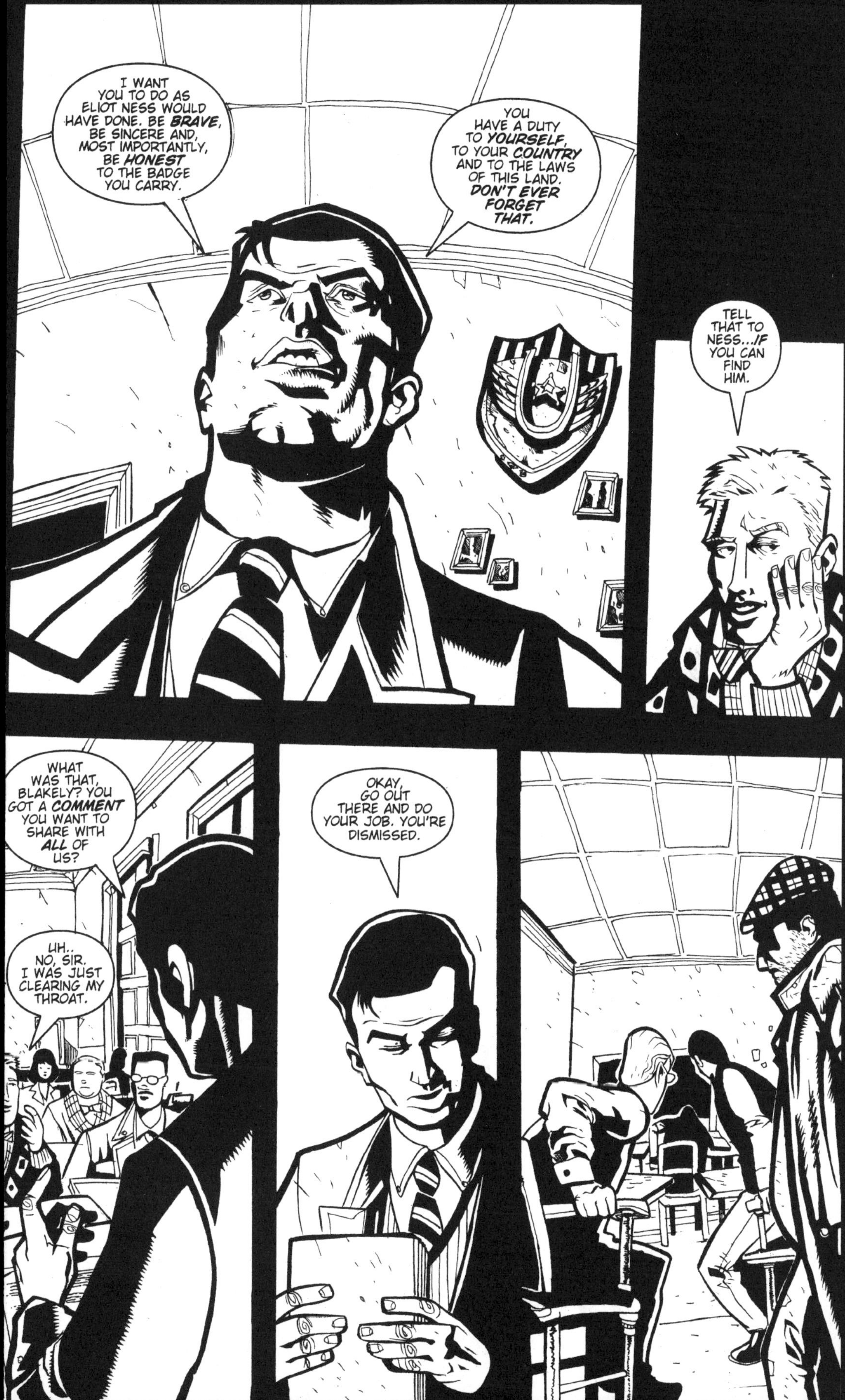
I WANT YOU TO DO AS ELIOT NESS WOULD HAVE DONE. BE BRAVE, BE SINCERE AND, MOST IMPORTANTLY, BE HONEST TO THE BADGE YOU CARRY.
YOU HAVE A DUTY TO YOURSELF, TO YOUR COUNTRY AND TO THE LAWS OF THIS LAND. DON'T EVER FORGET THAT.
TELL THAT TO NESS...IF YOU CAN FIND HIM.
WHAT WAS THAT, BLAKELY? YOU GOT A COMMENT YOU WANT TO SHARE WITH ALL OF US?
UH.. NO, SIR. I WAS JUST CLEARING MY THROAT.
OKAY, GO OUT THERE AND DO YOUR JOB. YOU'RE DISMISSED.

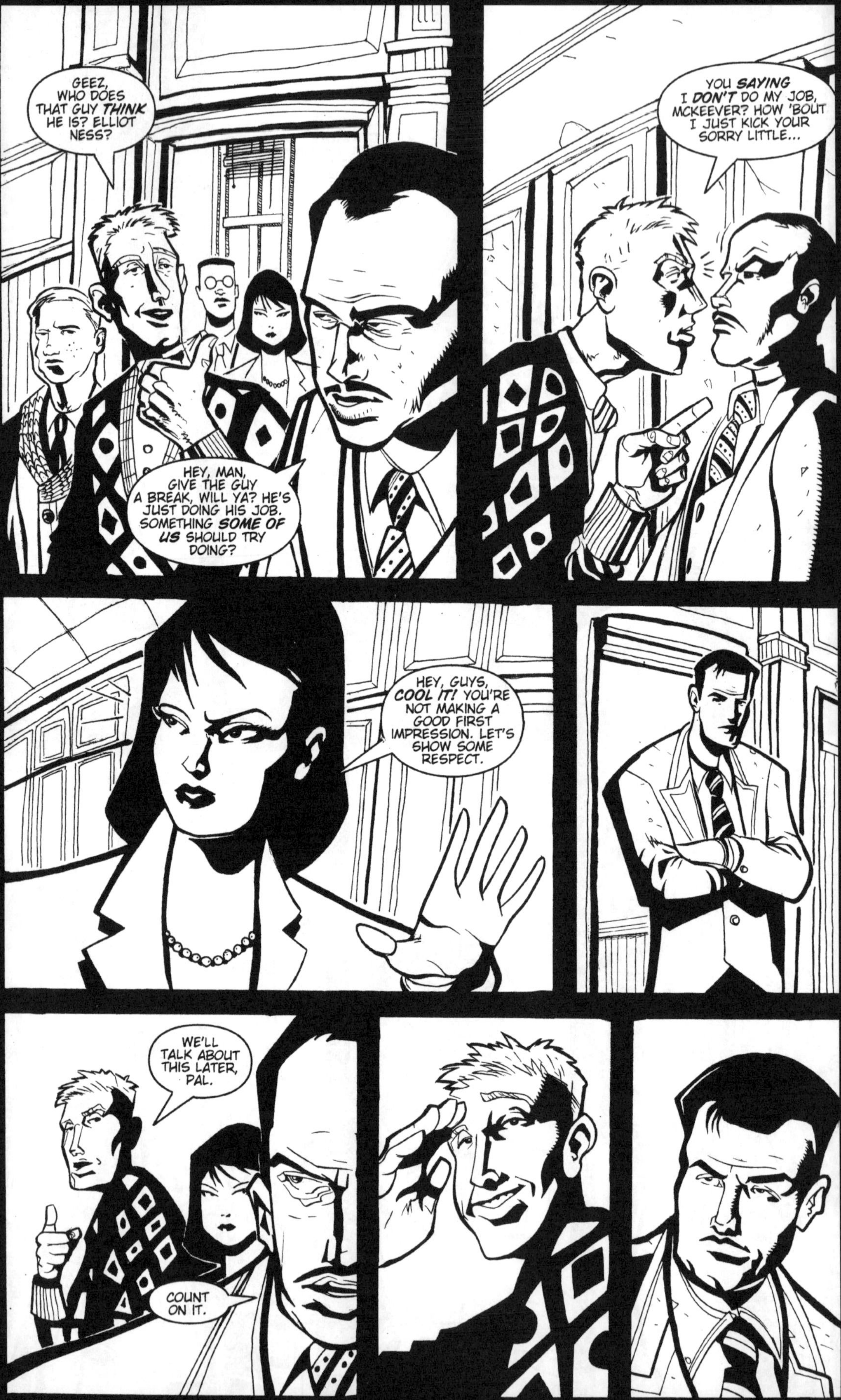
GEEZ, WHO DOES THAT GUY *THINK* HE IS? ELLIOT NESS?
HEY, MAN, GIVE THE GUY A BREAK, WILL YA? HE'S JUST DOING HIS JOB. SOMETHING *SOME OF US* SHOULD TRY DOING?
YOU *SAYING* I *DON'T* DO MY JOB, MCKEEVER? HOW 'BOUT I JUST KICK YOUR SORRY LITTLE...
HEY, GUYS, *COOL IT!* YOU'RE NOT MAKING A GOOD FIRST IMPRESSION. LET'S SHOW SOME RESPECT.
WE'LL TALK ABOUT THIS LATER, PAL.
COUNT ON IT.

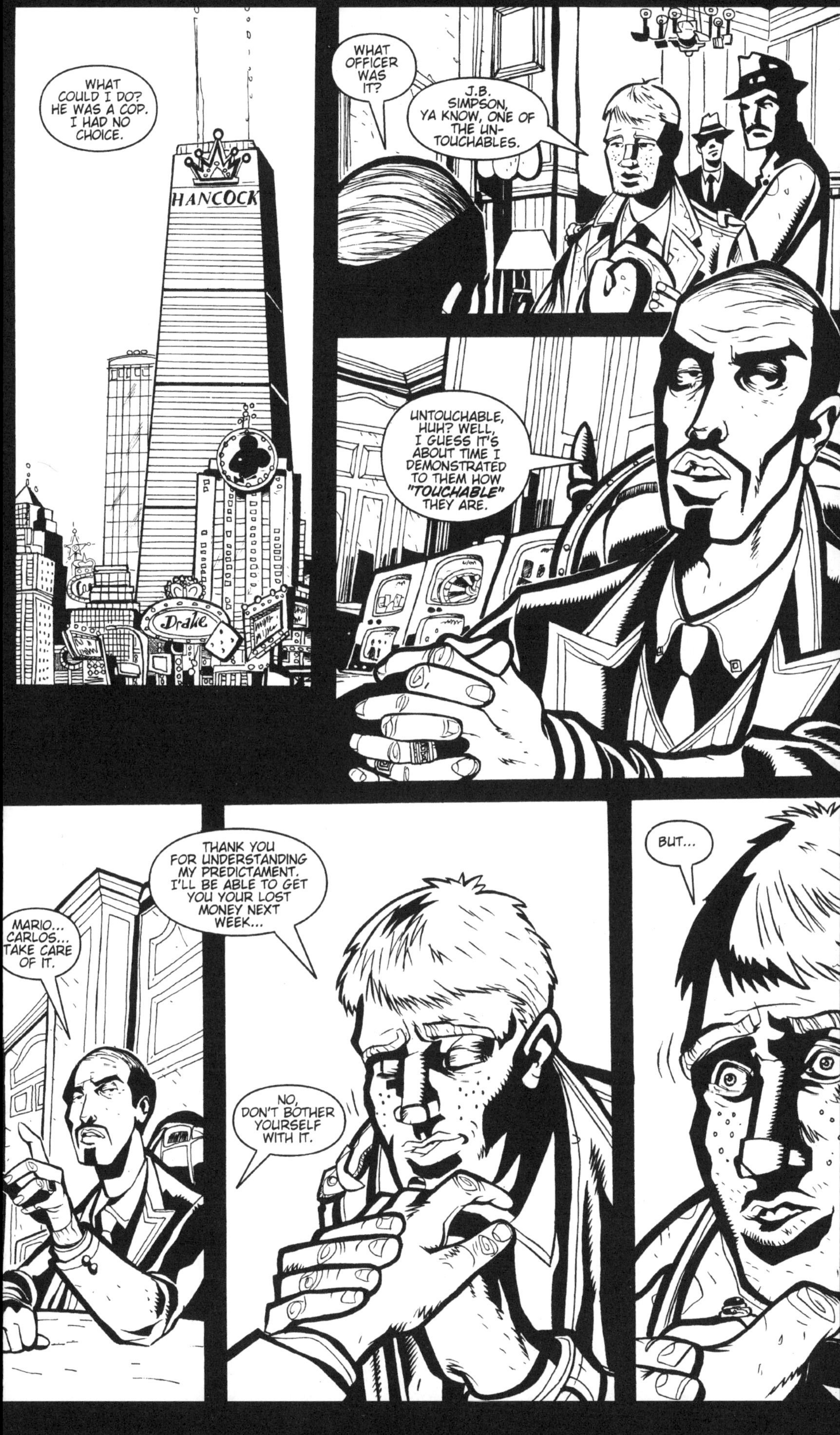
WHAT COULD I DO? HE WAS A COP. I HAD NO CHOICE.
HANCOCK
Drake
WHAT OFFICER WAS IT?
J.B. SIMPSON, YA KNOW, ONE OF THE UN-TOUCHABLES.
UNTOUCHABLE, HUH? WELL, I GUESS IT'S ABOUT TIME I DEMONSTRATED TO THEM HOW "TOUCHABLE" THEY ARE.
MARIO... CARLOS... TAKE CARE OF IT.
THANK YOU FOR UNDERSTANDING MY PREDICTAMENT. I'LL BE ABLE TO GET YOU YOUR LOST MONEY NEXT WEEK...
NO, DON'T BOTHER YOURSELF WITH IT.
BUT...

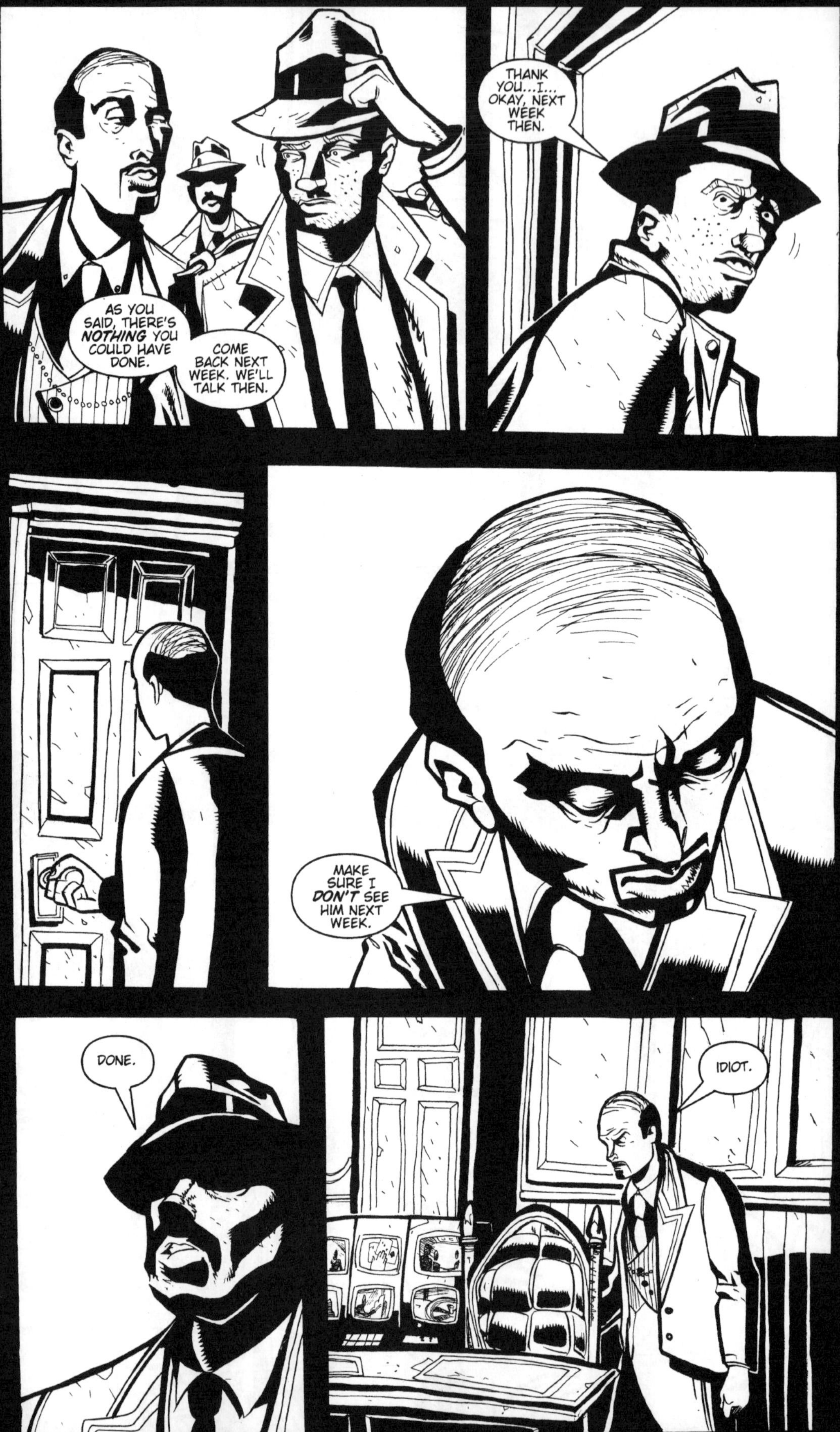
AS YOU SAID, THERE'S NOTHING YOU COULD HAVE DONE.
COME BACK NEXT WEEK. WE'LL TALK THEN.
THANK YOU...I... OKAY, NEXT WEEK THEN.
MAKE SURE I DON'T SEE HIM NEXT WEEK.
DONE.
IDIOT.

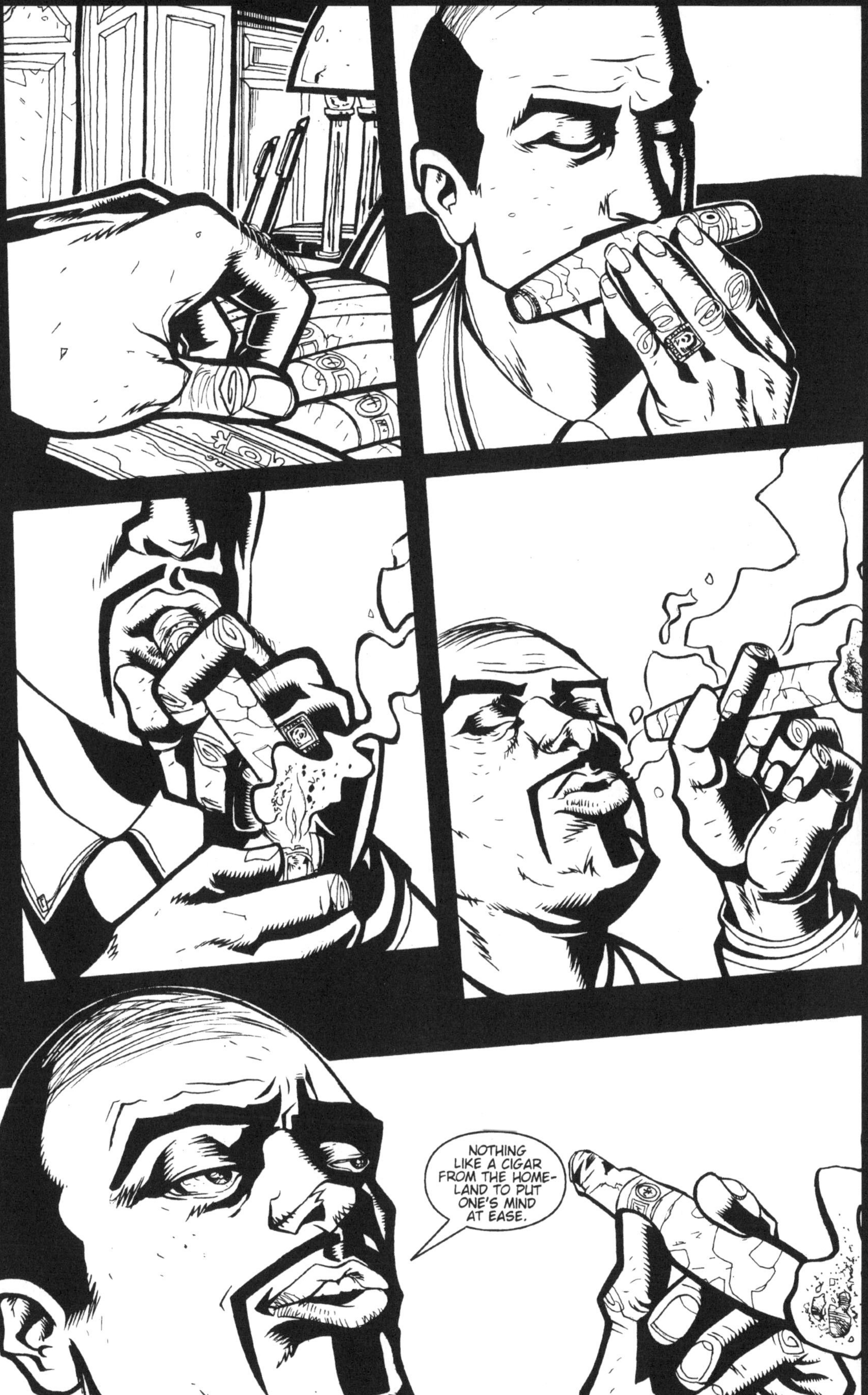
NOTHING LIKE A CIGAR FROM THE HOME-LAND TO PUT ONE'S MIND AT EASE.

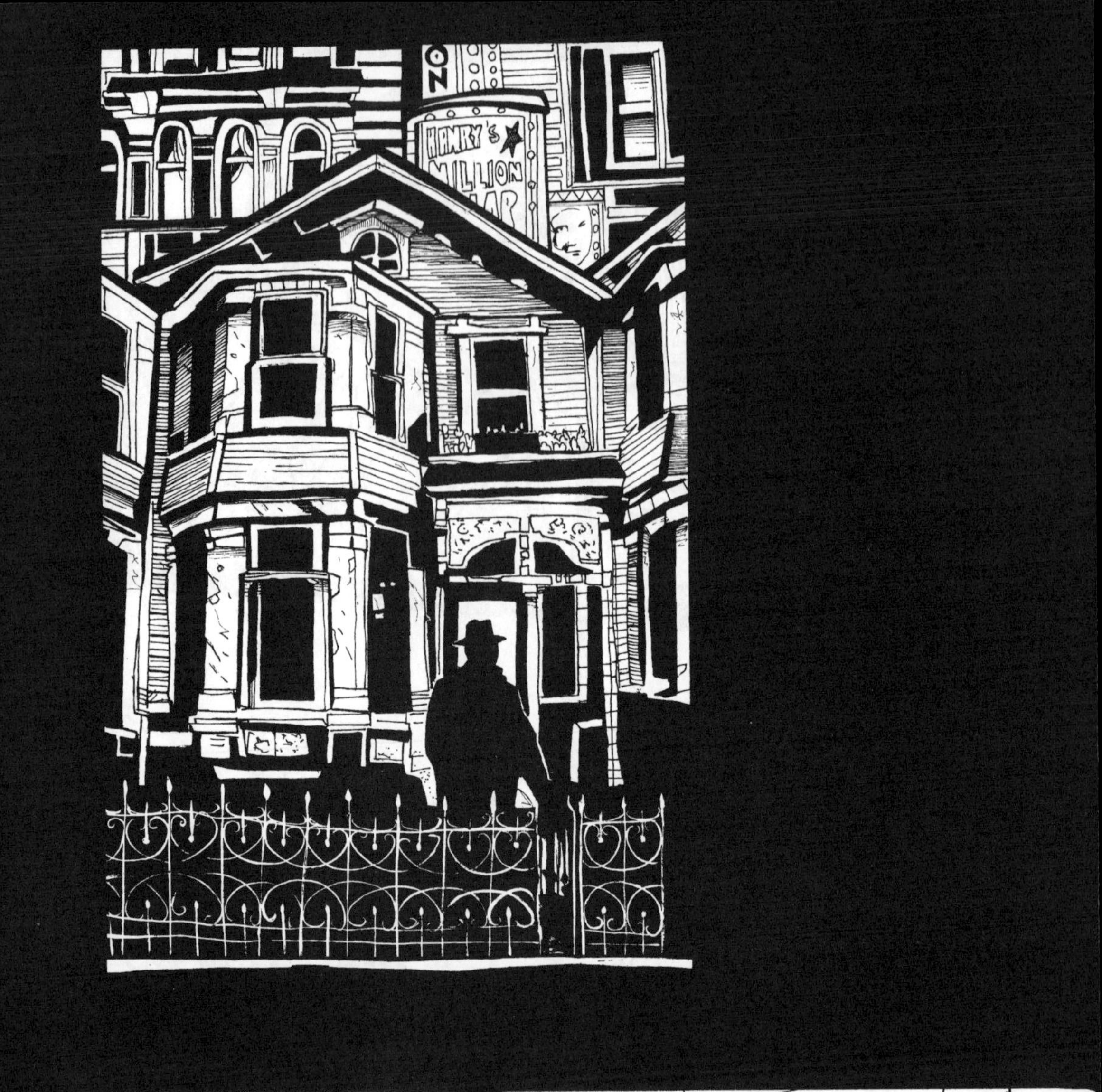
HENRY'S
MILLION
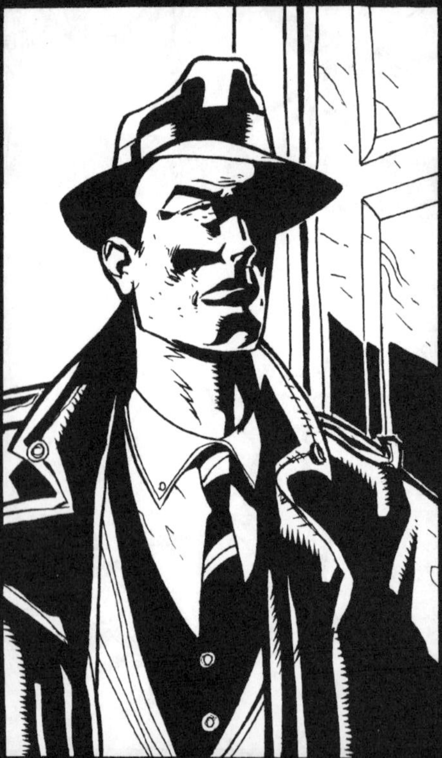
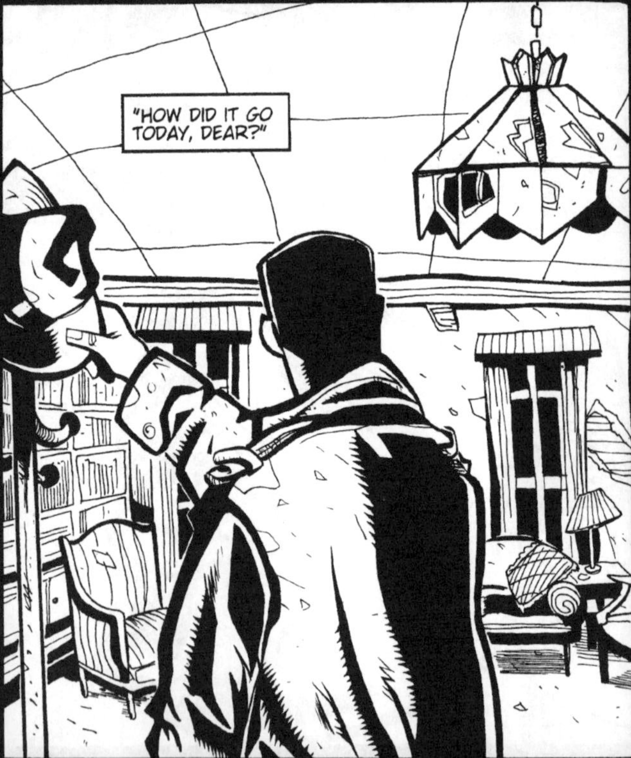
"HOW DID IT GO TODAY, DEAR?"

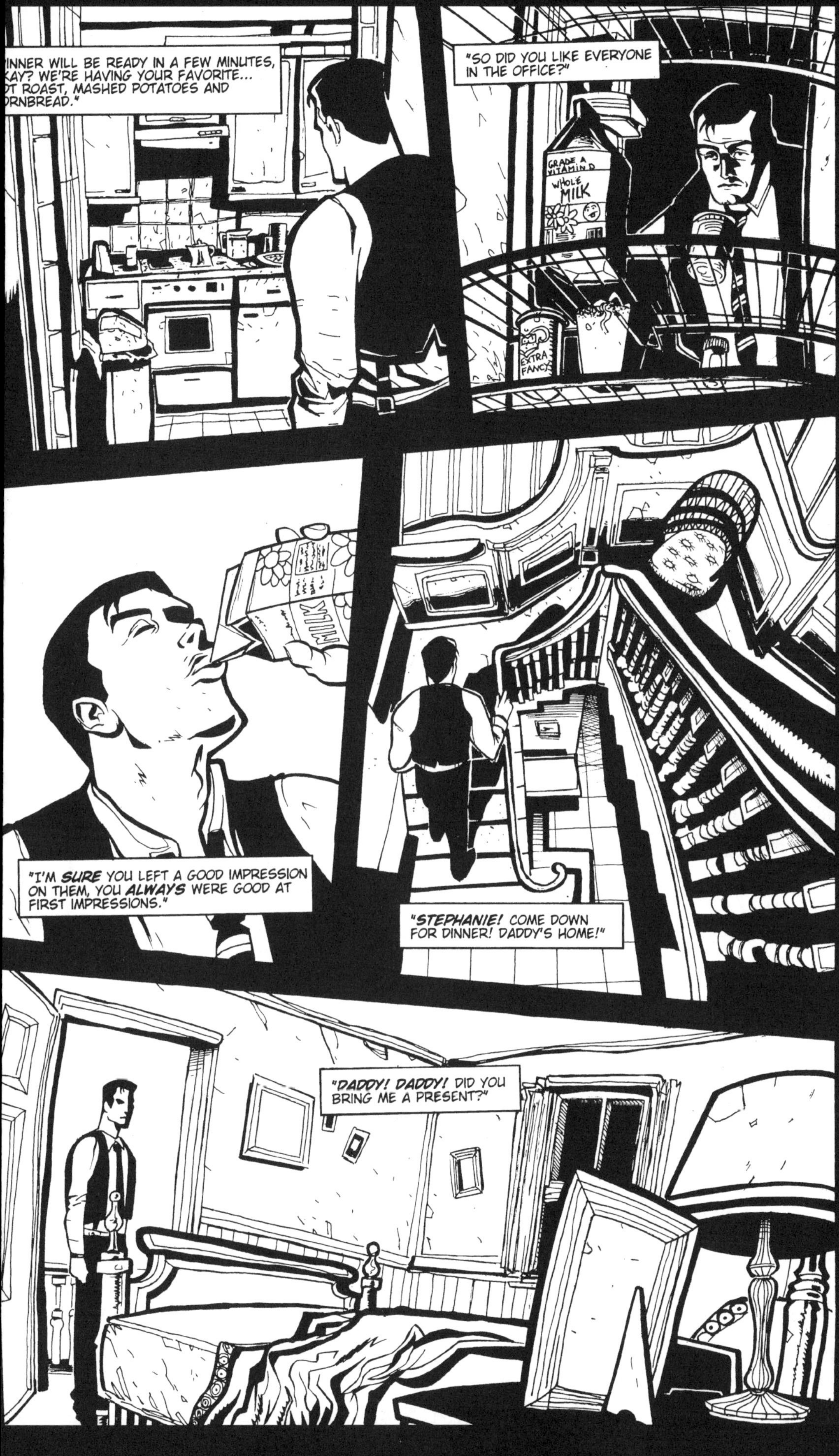
INNER WILL BE READY IN A FEW MINUTES, KAY? WE'RE HAVING YOUR FAVORITE... OT ROAST, MASHED POTATOES AND ORNBREAD."
"SO DID YOU LIKE EVERYONE IN THE OFFICE?"
GRADE A VITAMIN D
WHOLE MILK
EXTRA FANCY
MILK
"I'M SURE YOU LEFT A GOOD IMPRESSION ON THEM, YOU ALWAYS WERE GOOD AT FIRST IMPRESSIONS."
"STEPHANIE! COME DOWN FOR DINNER! DADDY'S HOME!"
"DADDY! DADDY! DID YOU BRING ME A PRESENT?"

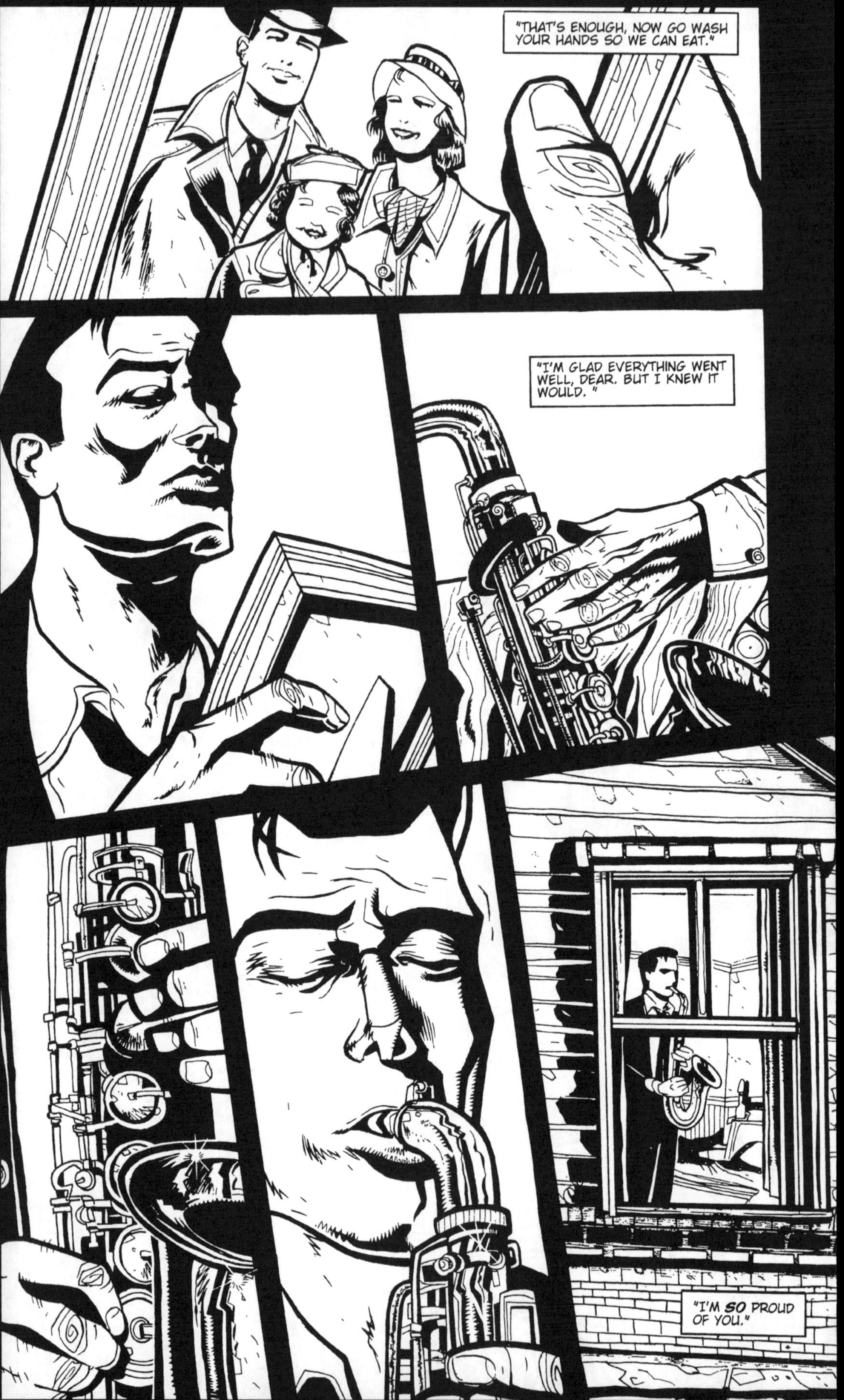
"THAT'S ENOUGH, NOW GO WASH YOUR HANDS SO WE CAN EAT."
"I'M GLAD EVERYTHING WENT WELL, DEAR. BUT I KNEW IT WOULD."
"I'M SO PROUD OF YOU."

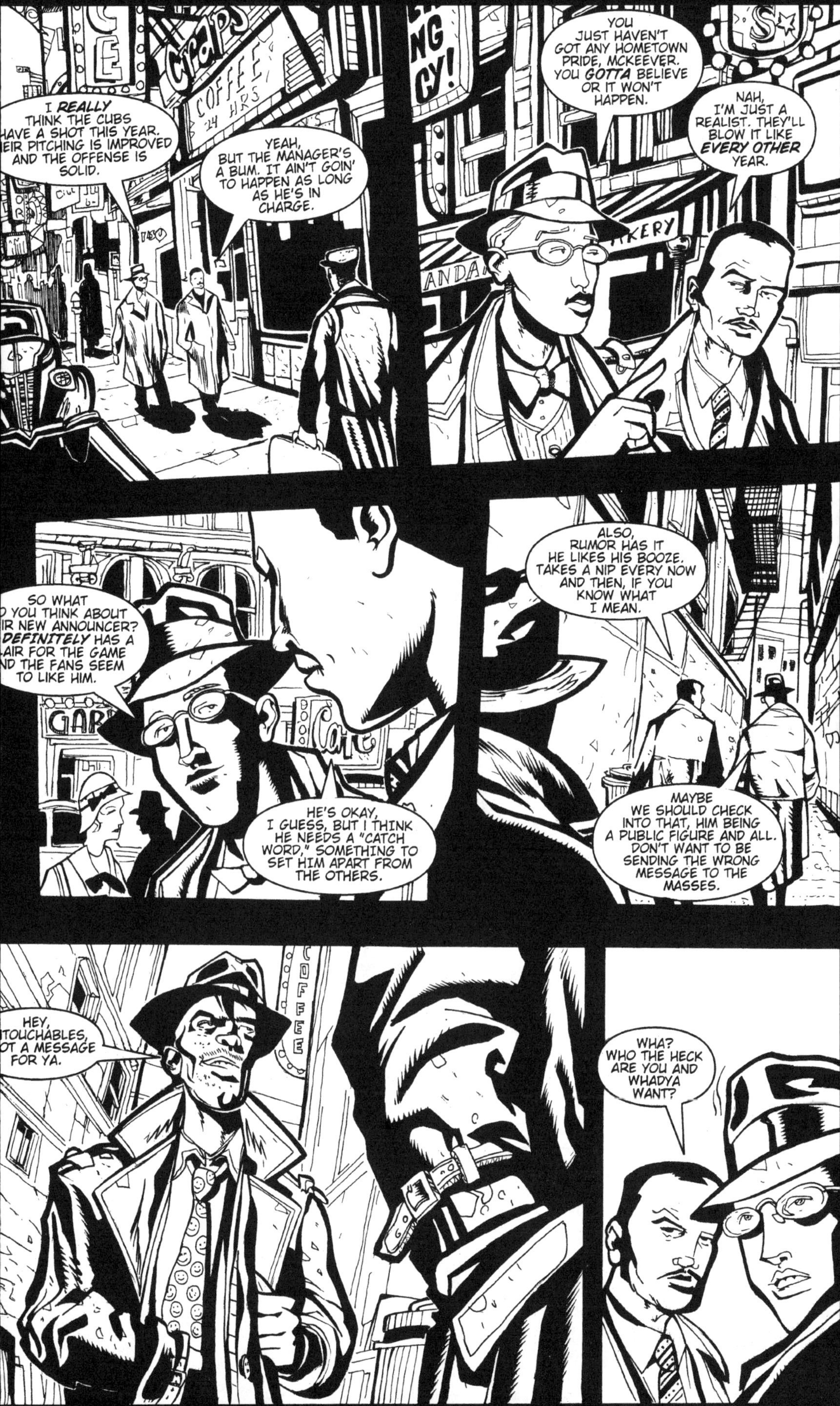
CRAPS
COFFEE 24 HRS
I *REALLY* THINK THE CUBS HAVE A SHOT THIS YEAR. EIR PITCHING IS IMPROVED AND THE OFFENSE IS SOLID.
YEAH, BUT THE MANAGER'S A BUM. IT AIN'T GOIN' TO HAPPEN AS LONG AS HE'S IN CHARGE.
YOU JUST HAVEN'T GOT ANY HOMETOWN PRIDE, MCKEEVER. YOU *GOTTA* BELIEVE OR IT WON'T HAPPEN.
NAH, I'M JUST A REALIST. THEY'LL BLOW IT LIKE *EVERY OTHER* YEAR.
SO WHAT D YOU THINK ABOUT IR NEW ANNOUNCER? *DEFINITELY* HAS A AIR FOR THE GAME ND THE FANS SEEM TO LIKE HIM.
HE'S OKAY, I GUESS, BUT I THINK HE NEEDS A "CATCH WORD," SOMETHING TO SET HIM APART FROM THE OTHERS.
ALSO, RUMOR HAS IT HE LIKES HIS BOOZE. TAKES A NIP EVERY NOW AND THEN, IF YOU KNOW WHAT I MEAN.
MAYBE WE SHOULD CHECK INTO THAT, HIM BEING A PUBLIC FIGURE AND ALL. DON'T WANT TO BE SENDING THE WRONG MESSAGE TO THE MASSES.
HEY, NTOUCHABLES, OT A MESSAGE FOR YA.
COFFEE
WHA? WHO THE HECK ARE YOU AND WHADYA WANT?

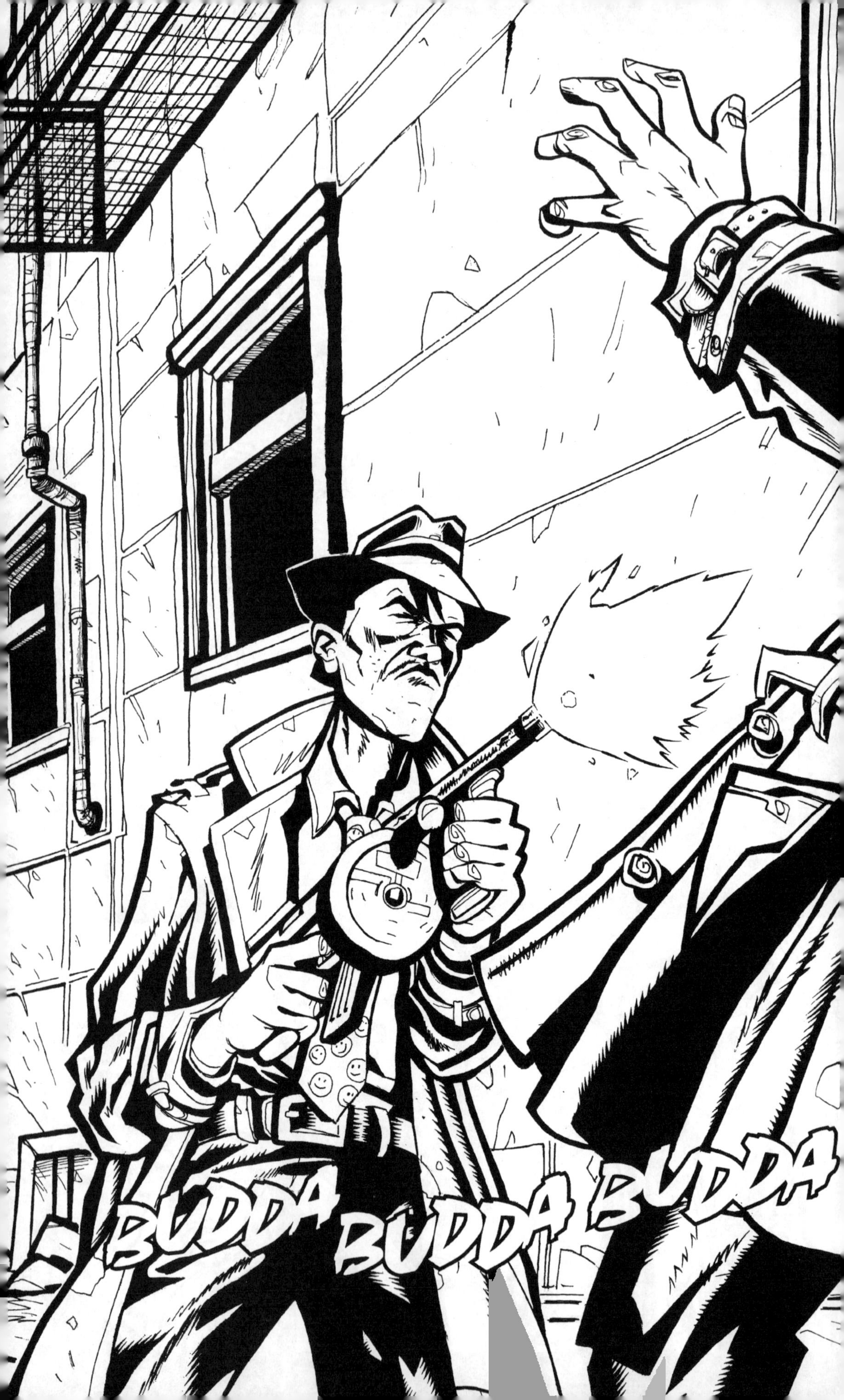
BUDDA BUDDA BUDDA

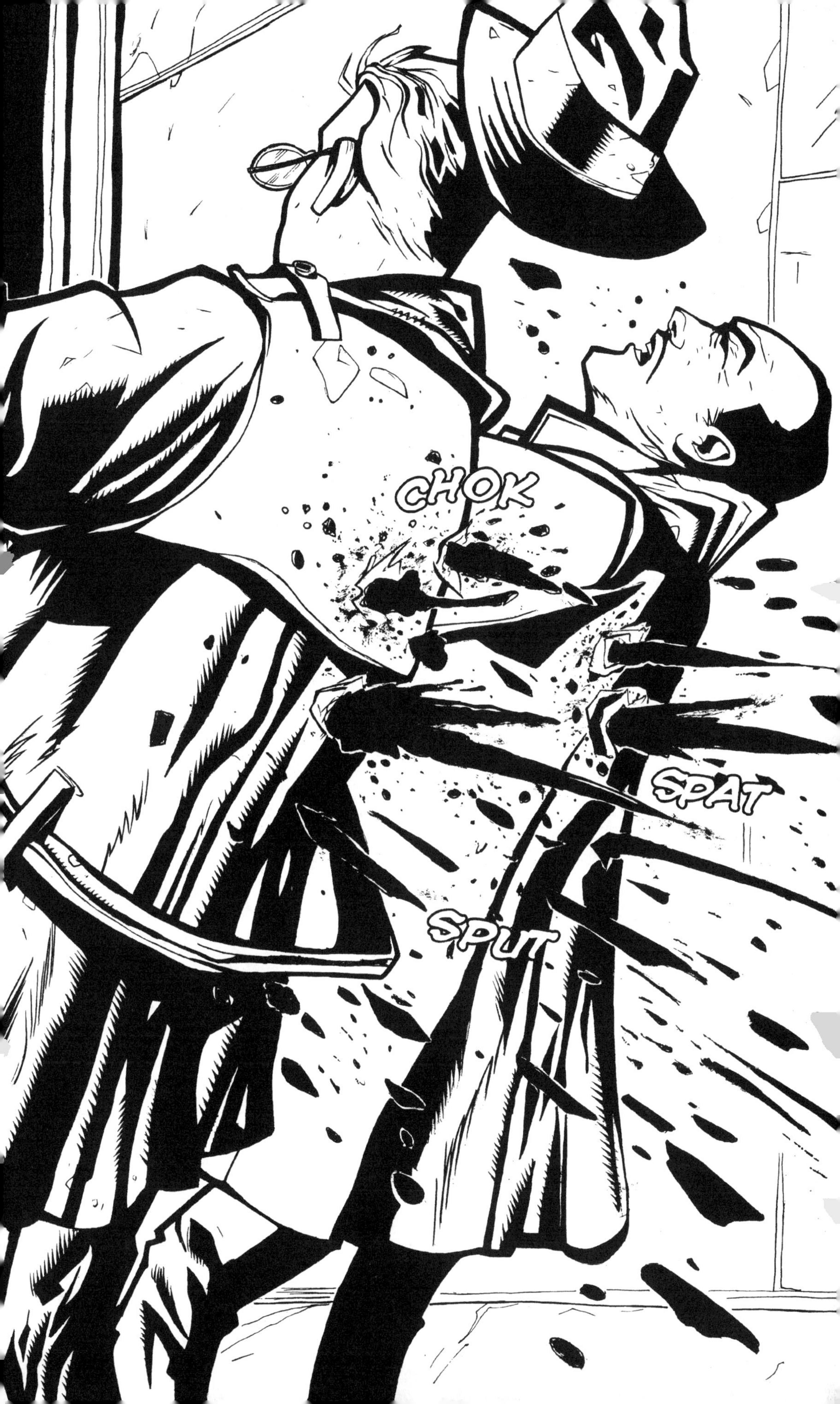
CHOK
SPAT
SPUT

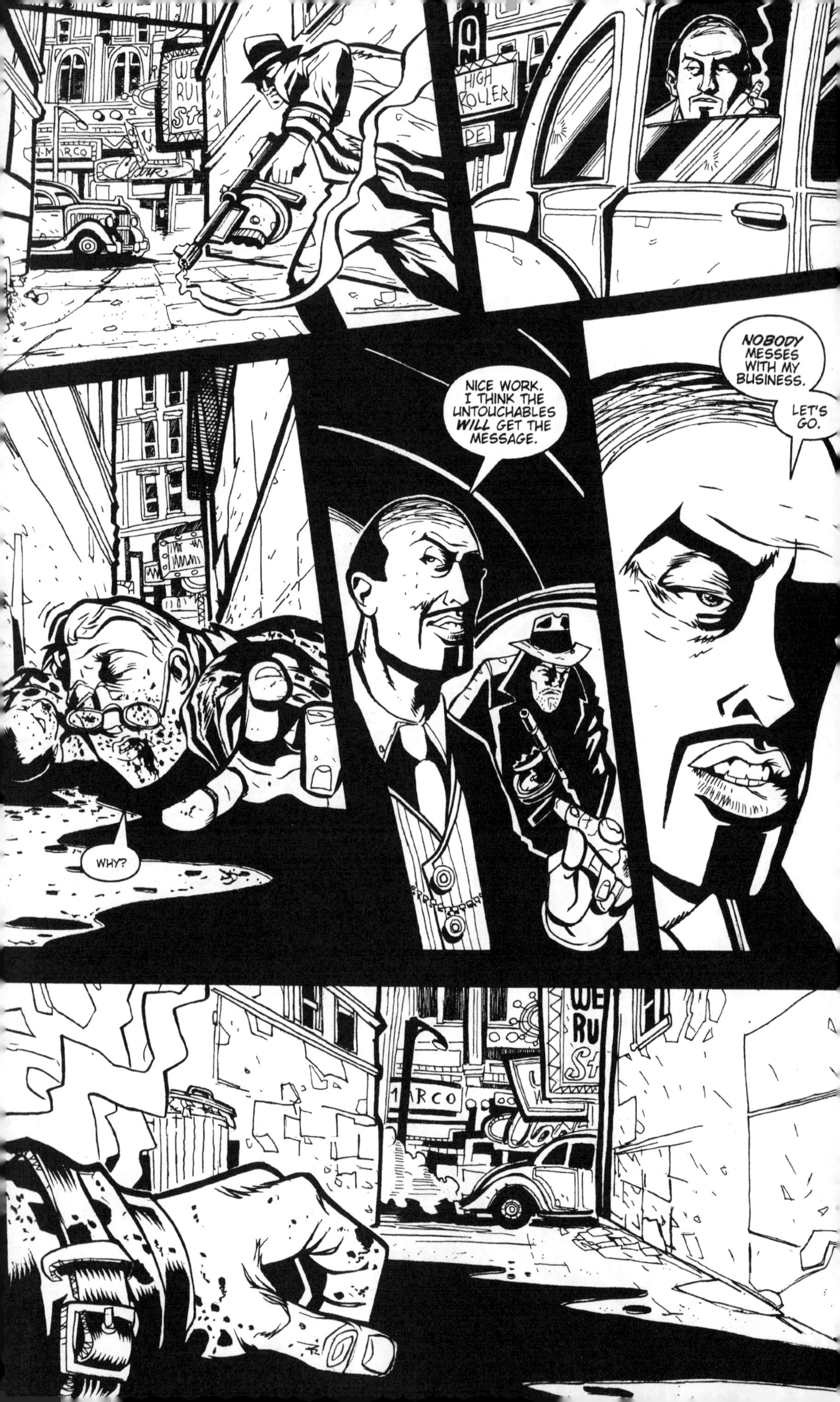

HIGH ROLLER
NICE WORK. I THINK THE UNTOUCHABLES WILL GET THE MESSAGE.
NOBODY MESSES WITH MY BUSINESS.
LET'S GO.
WHY?

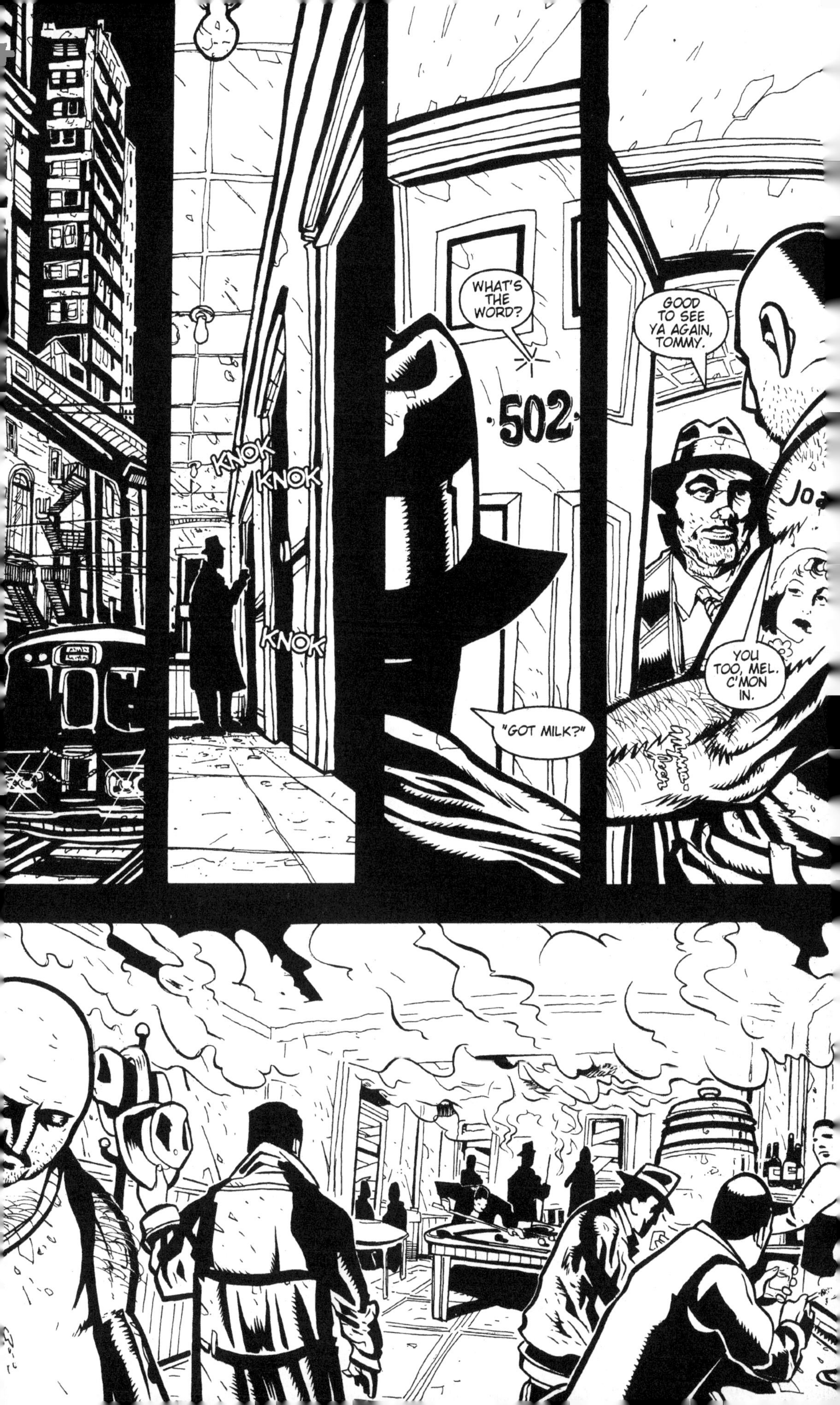
KNOK
KNOK
KNOK
WHAT'S THE WORD?
"GOT MILK?"
GOOD TO SEE YA AGAIN, TOMMY.
YOU TOO, MEL. C'MON IN.

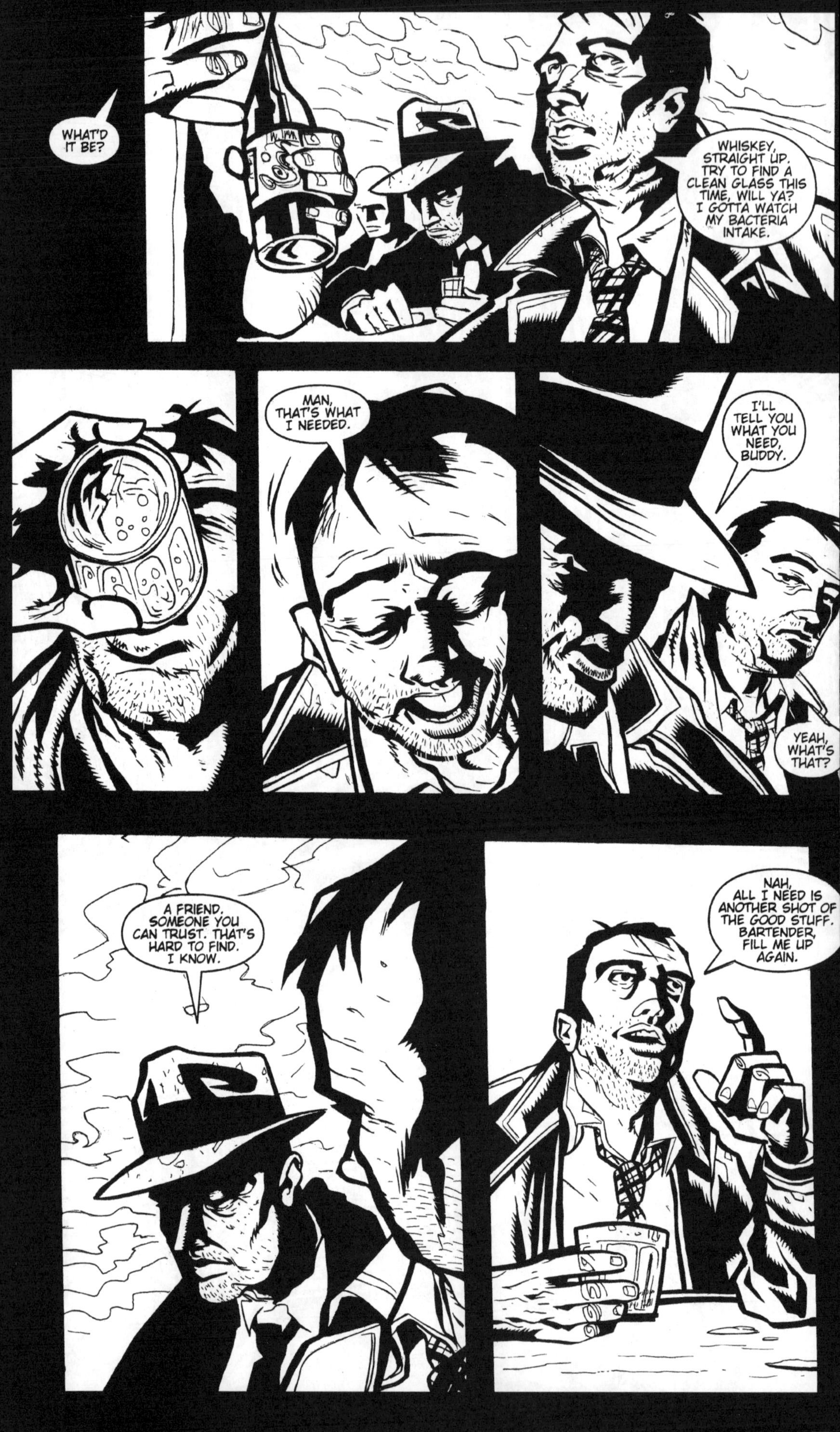
WHAT'D IT BE?
WHISKEY, STRAIGHT UP. TRY TO FIND A CLEAN GLASS THIS TIME, WILL YA? I GOTTA WATCH MY BACTERIA INTAKE.
MAN, THAT'S WHAT I NEEDED.
I'LL TELL YOU WHAT YOU NEED, BUDDY.
YEAH, WHAT'S THAT?
A FRIEND. SOMEONE YOU CAN TRUST. THAT'S HARD TO FIND. I KNOW.
NAH, ALL I NEED IS ANOTHER SHOT OF THE GOOD STUFF. BARTENDER, FILL ME UP AGAIN.

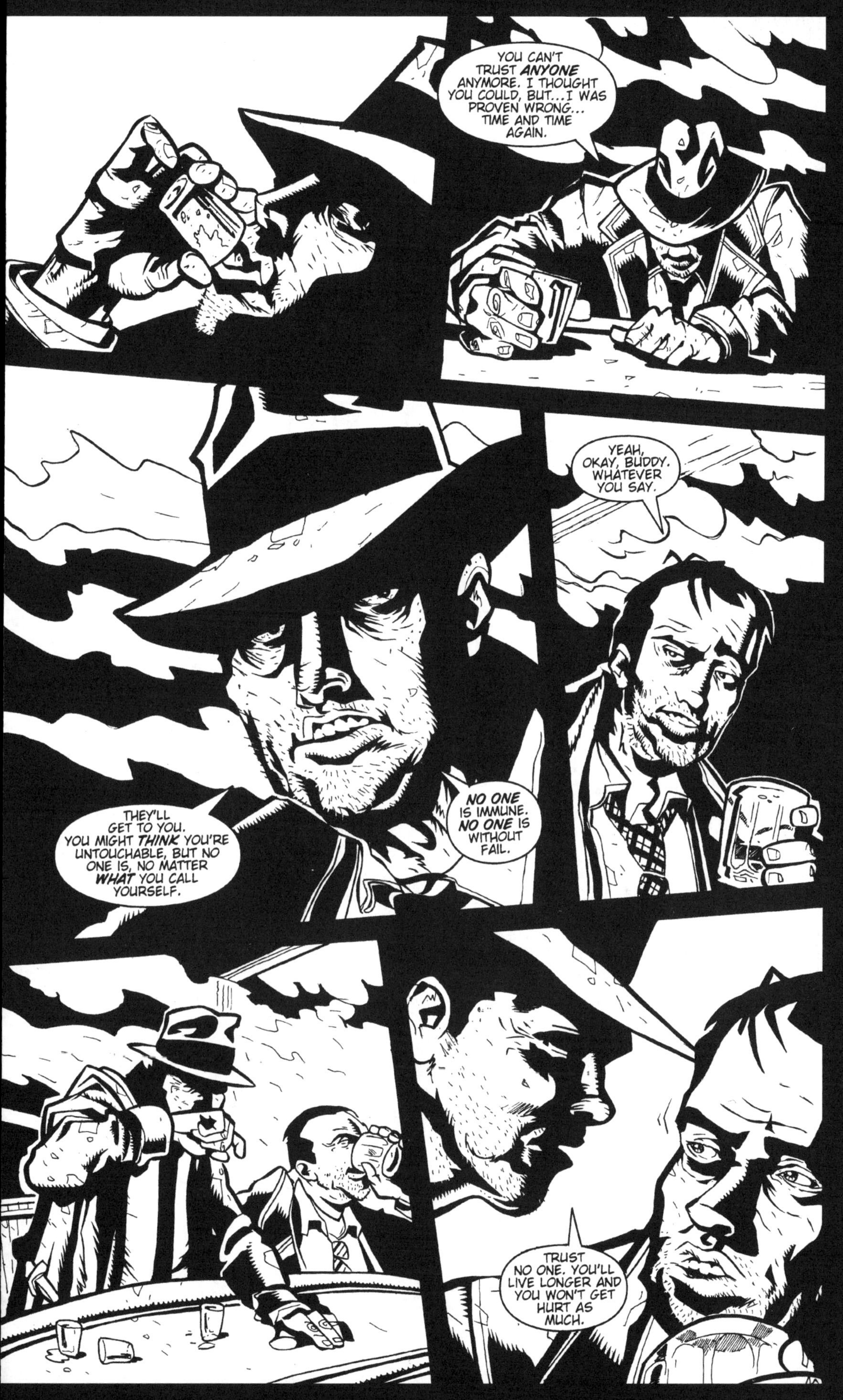
YOU CAN'T TRUST ANYONE ANYMORE. I THOUGHT YOU COULD, BUT...I WAS PROVEN WRONG... TIME AND TIME AGAIN.
YEAH, OKAY, BUDDY. WHATEVER YOU SAY.
THEY'LL GET TO YOU. YOU MIGHT THINK YOU'RE UNTOUCHABLE, BUT NO ONE IS, NO MATTER WHAT YOU CALL YOURSELF.
NO ONE IS IMMUNE. NO ONE IS WITHOUT FAIL.
TRUST NO ONE. YOU'LL LIVE LONGER AND YOU WON'T GET HURT AS MUCH.

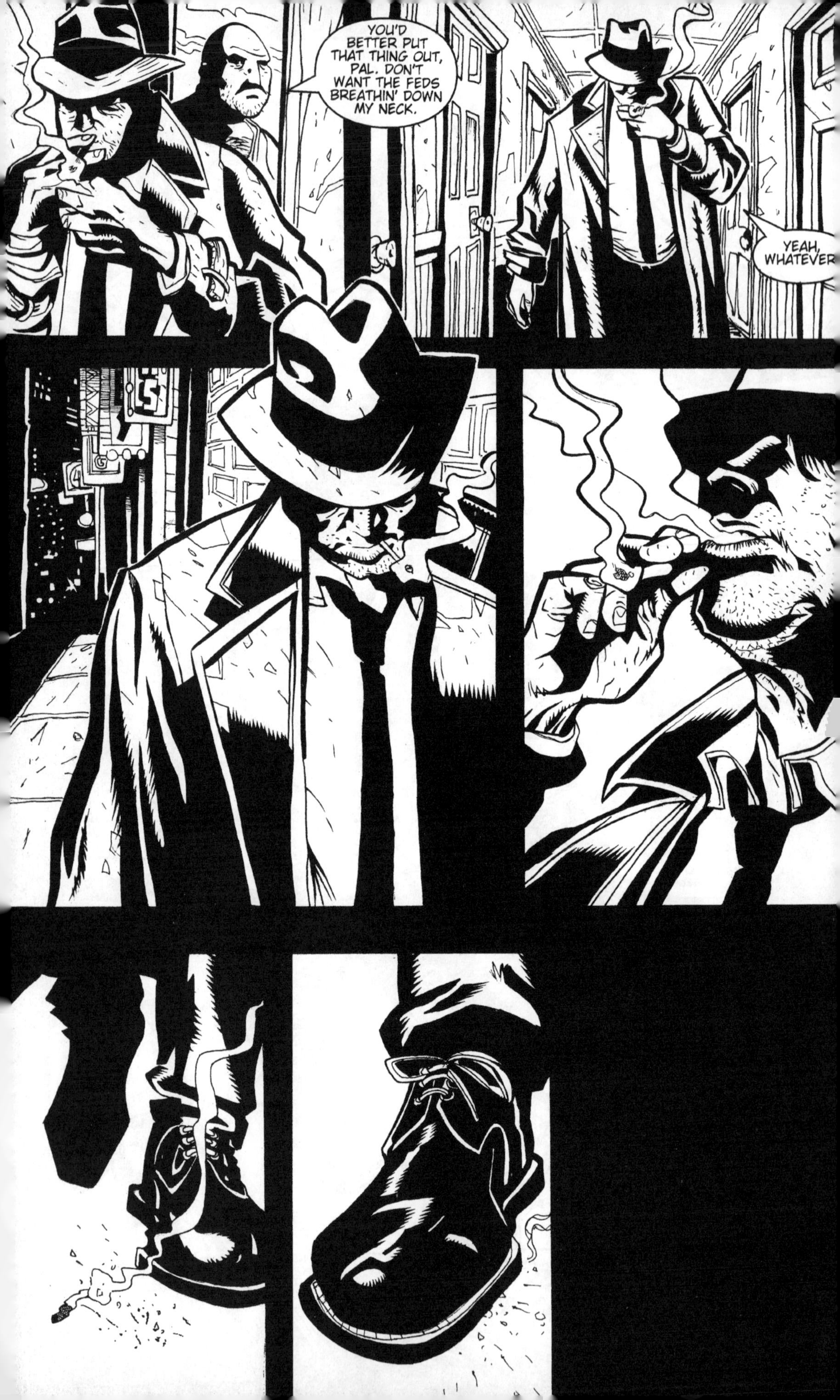
YOU'D BETTER PUT THAT THING OUT, PAL. DON'T WANT THE FEDS BREATHIN' DOWN MY NECK.
YEAH, WHATEVER

UNTOUCHABLES

"A NEW BEGINNING"

ACT 2

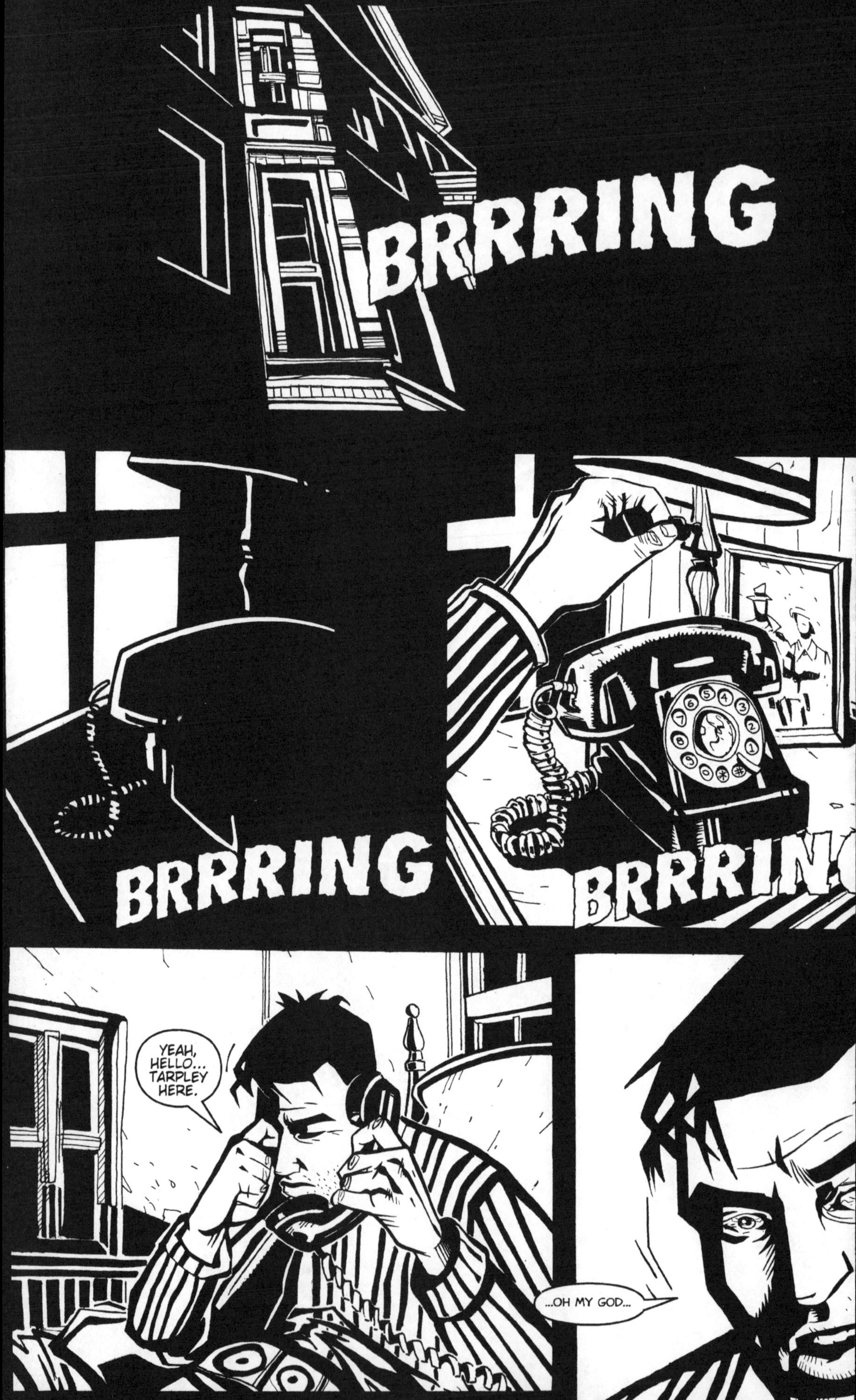
BRRRING
BRRRING
BRRRIN
YEAH, HELLO... TARPLEY HERE.
...OH MY GOD...

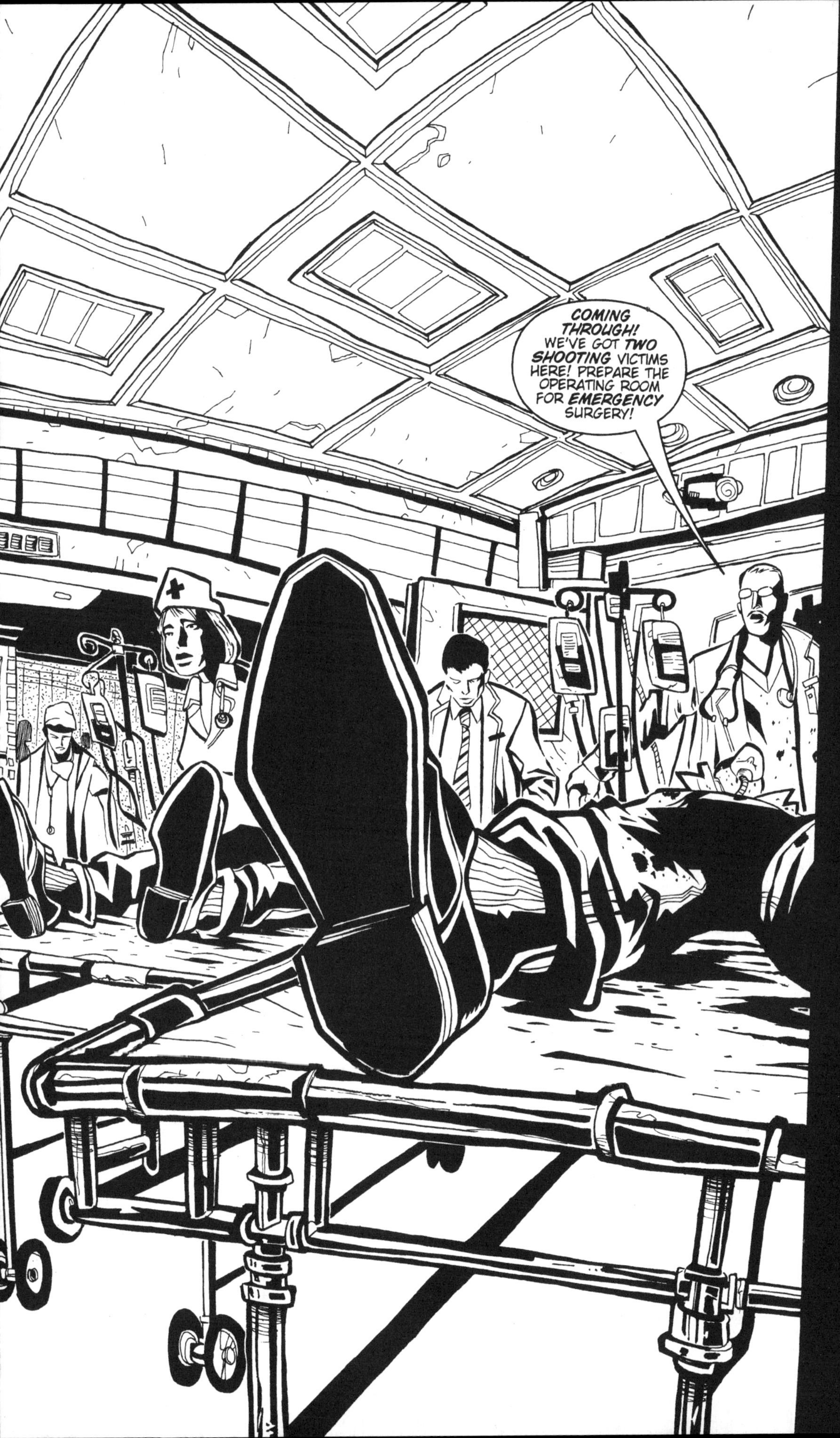
COMING THROUGH! WE'VE GOT TWO SHOOTING VICTIMS HERE! PREPARE THE OPERATING ROOM FOR EMERGENCY SURGERY!

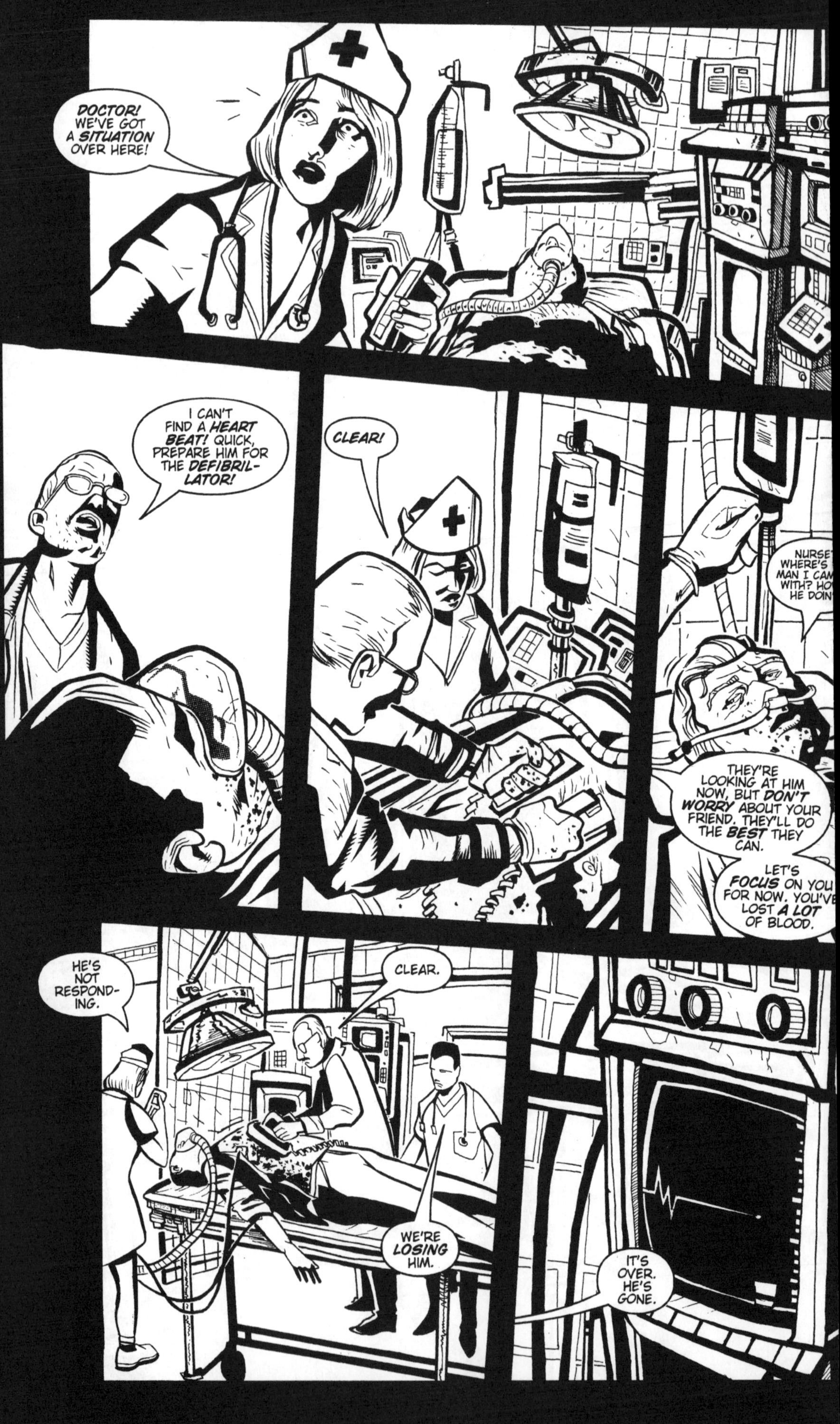
DOCTOR! WE'VE GOT A SITUATION OVER HERE!
I CAN'T FIND A HEART BEAT! QUICK, PREPARE HIM FOR THE DEFIBRIL-LATOR!
CLEAR!
NURSE WHERE'S MAN I CAM WITH? HO HE DOIN
THEY'RE LOOKING AT HIM NOW, BUT DON'T WORRY ABOUT YOUR FRIEND. THEY'LL DO THE BEST THEY CAN.
LET'S FOCUS ON YOU FOR NOW. YOU'V LOST A LOT OF BLOOD.
HE'S NOT RESPOND-ING.
CLEAR.
WE'RE LOSING HIM.
IT'S OVER. HE'S GONE.

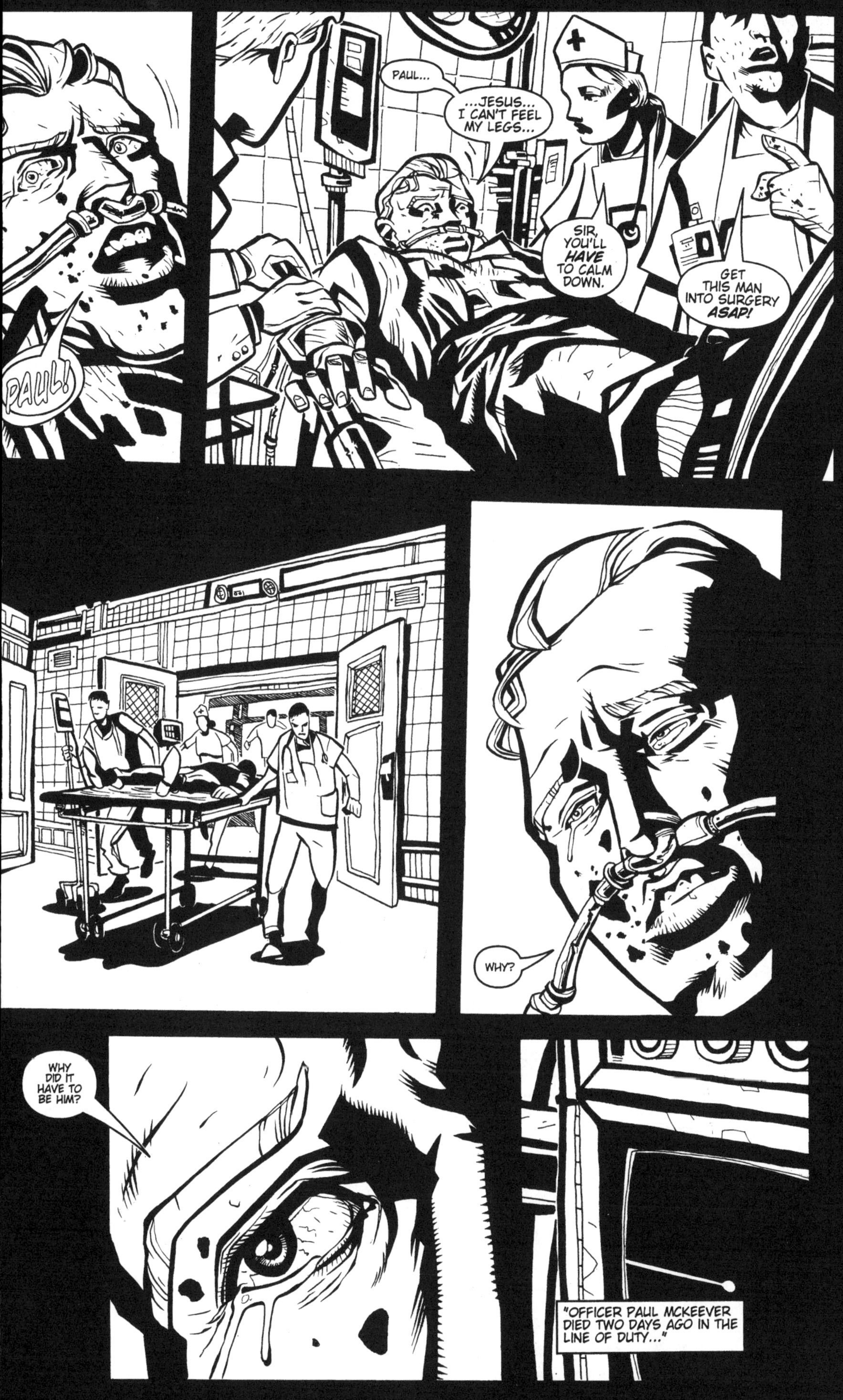
PAUL!
PAUL...
...JESUS... I CAN'T FEEL MY LEGS...
SIR, YOU'LL HAVE TO CALM DOWN.
GET THIS MAN INTO SURGERY ASAP!
WHY?
WHY DID IT HAVE TO BE HIM?
"OFFICER PAUL MCKEEVER DIED TWO DAYS AGO IN THE LINE OF DUTY..."

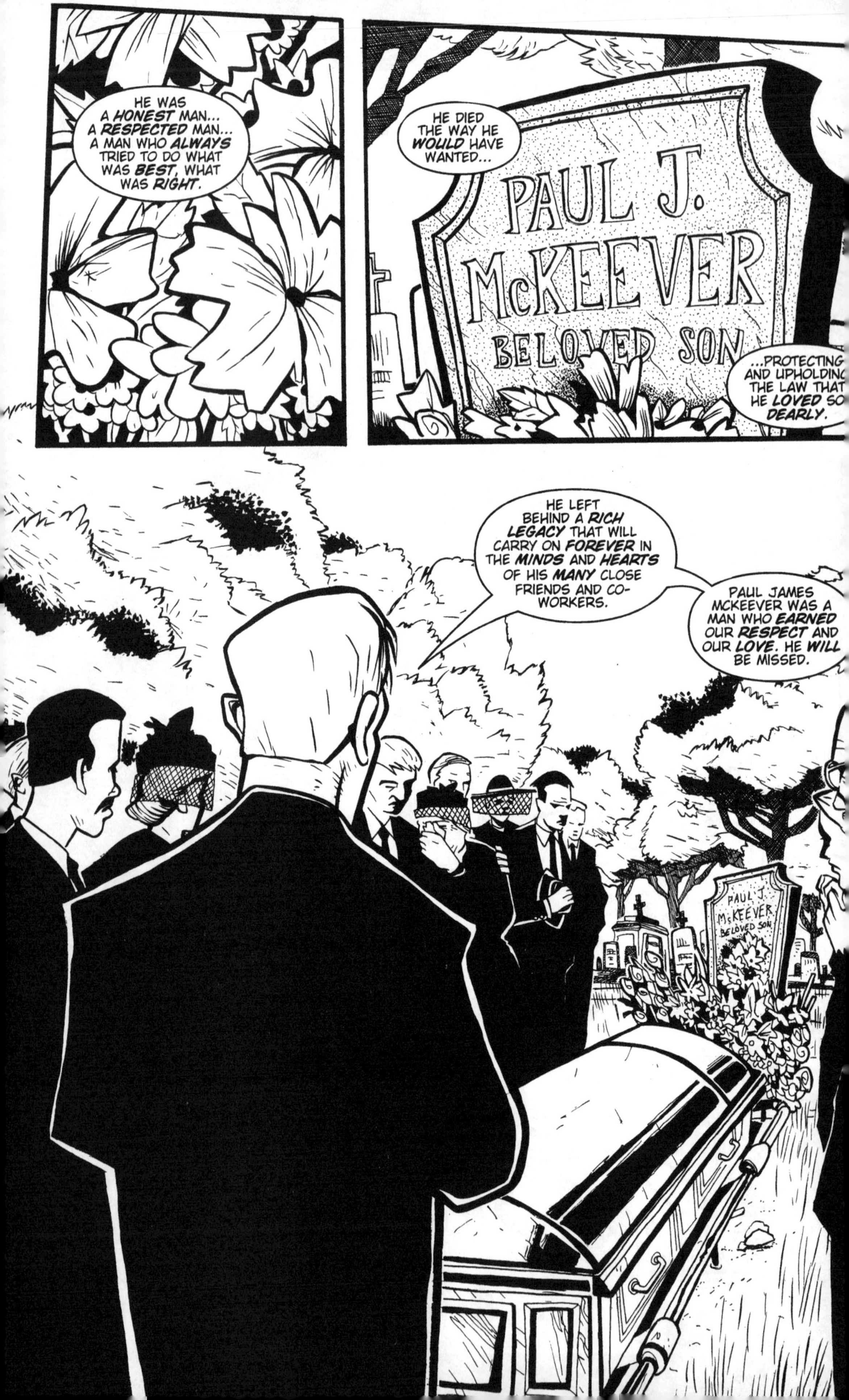

HE WAS A HONEST MAN... A RESPECTED MAN... A MAN WHO ALWAYS TRIED TO DO WHAT WAS BEST, WHAT WAS RIGHT.
HE DIED THE WAY HE WOULD HAVE WANTED...
PAUL J. McKEEVER
BELOVED SON
...PROTECTING AND UPHOLDING THE LAW THAT HE LOVED SO DEARLY.
HE LEFT BEHIND A RICH LEGACY THAT WILL CARRY ON FOREVER IN THE MINDS AND HEARTS OF HIS MANY CLOSE FRIENDS AND CO-WORKERS.
PAUL JAMES MCKEEVER WAS A MAN WHO EARNED OUR RESPECT AND OUR LOVE. HE WILL BE MISSED.

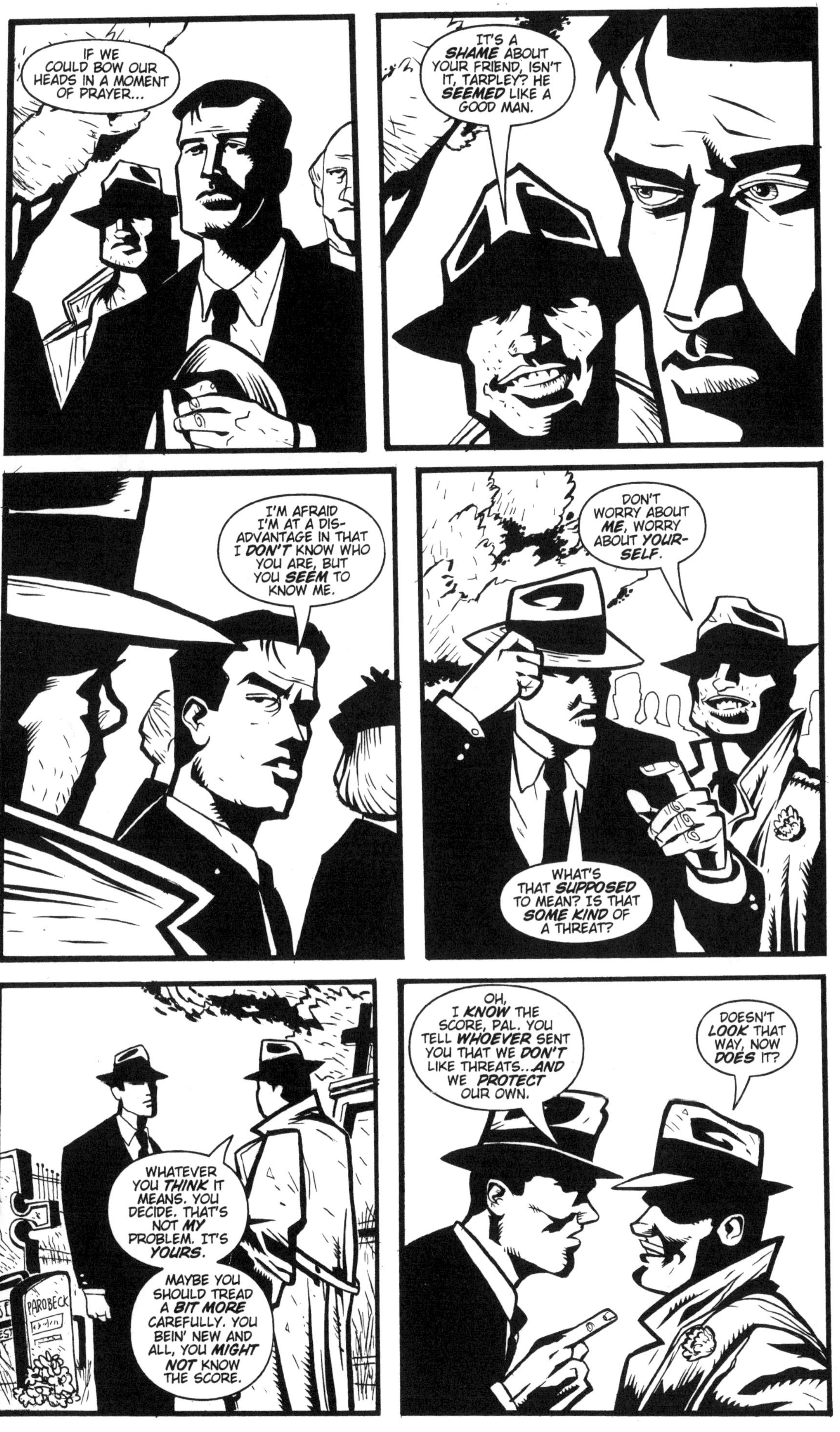
IF WE COULD BOW OUR HEADS IN A MOMENT OF PRAYER...
IT'S A SHAME ABOUT YOUR FRIEND, ISN'T IT, TARPLEY? HE SEEMED LIKE A GOOD MAN.
I'M AFRAID I'M AT A DIS-ADVANTAGE IN THAT I DON'T KNOW WHO YOU ARE, BUT YOU SEEM TO KNOW ME.
DON'T WORRY ABOUT ME, WORRY ABOUT YOUR-SELF.
WHAT'S THAT SUPPOSED TO MEAN? IS THAT SOME KIND OF A THREAT?
WHATEVER YOU THINK IT MEANS. YOU DECIDE. THAT'S NOT MY PROBLEM. IT'S YOURS.
MAYBE YOU SHOULD TREAD A BIT MORE CAREFULLY. YOU BEIN' NEW AND ALL, YOU MIGHT NOT KNOW THE SCORE.
PAROBECK
OH, I KNOW THE SCORE, PAL. YOU TELL WHOEVER SENT YOU THAT WE DON'T LIKE THREATS...AND WE PROTECT OUR OWN.
DOESN'T LOOK THAT WAY, NOW DOES IT?

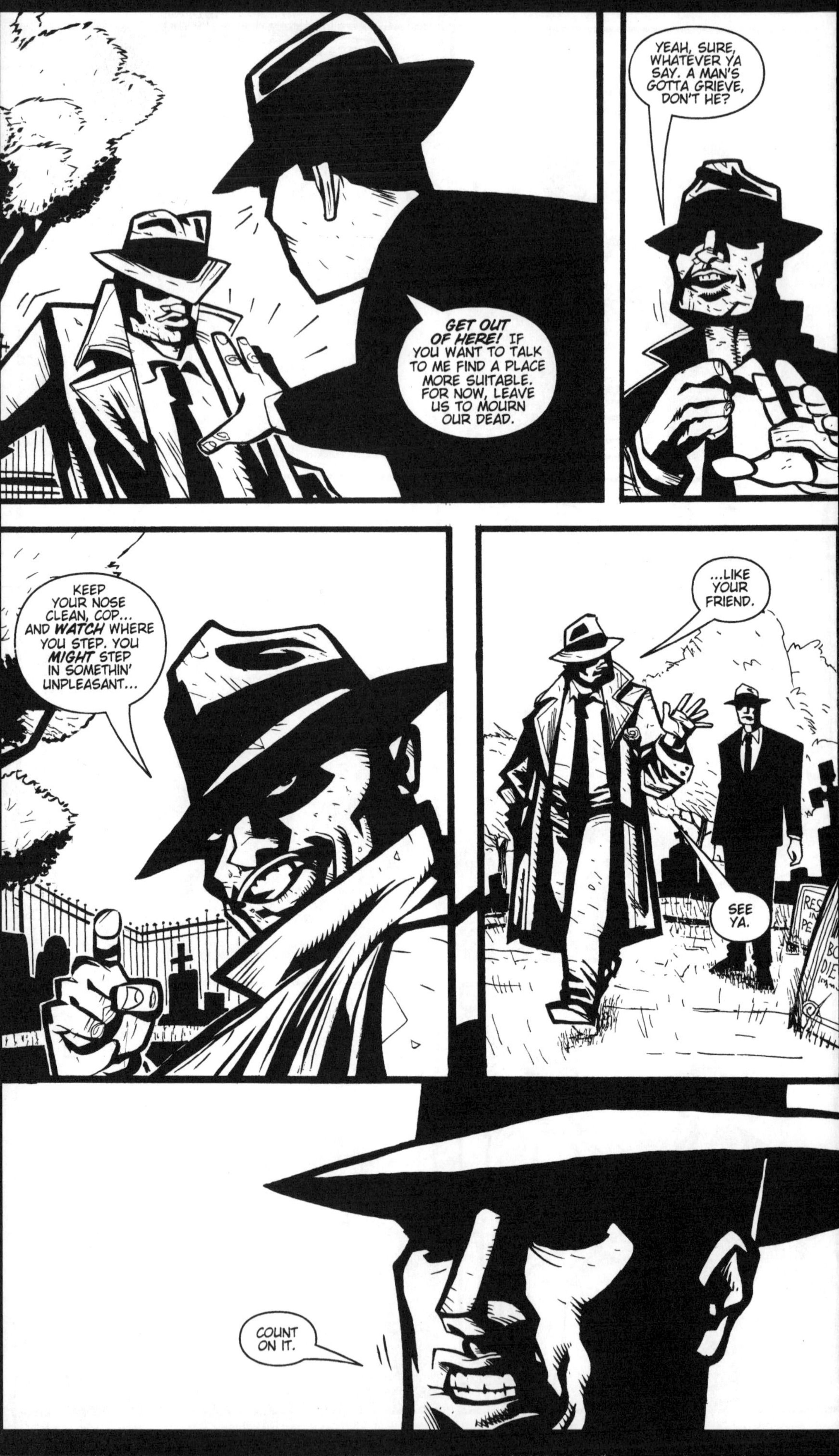

GET OUT OF HERE! IF YOU WANT TO TALK TO ME FIND A PLACE MORE SUITABLE. FOR NOW, LEAVE US TO MOURN OUR DEAD.
YEAH, SURE, WHATEVER YA SAY. A MAN'S GOTTA GRIEVE, DON'T HE?
KEEP YOUR NOSE CLEAN, COP... AND WATCH WHERE YOU STEP. YOU MIGHT STEP IN SOMETHIN' UNPLEASANT...
...LIKE YOUR FRIEND.
SEE YA.
COUNT ON IT.

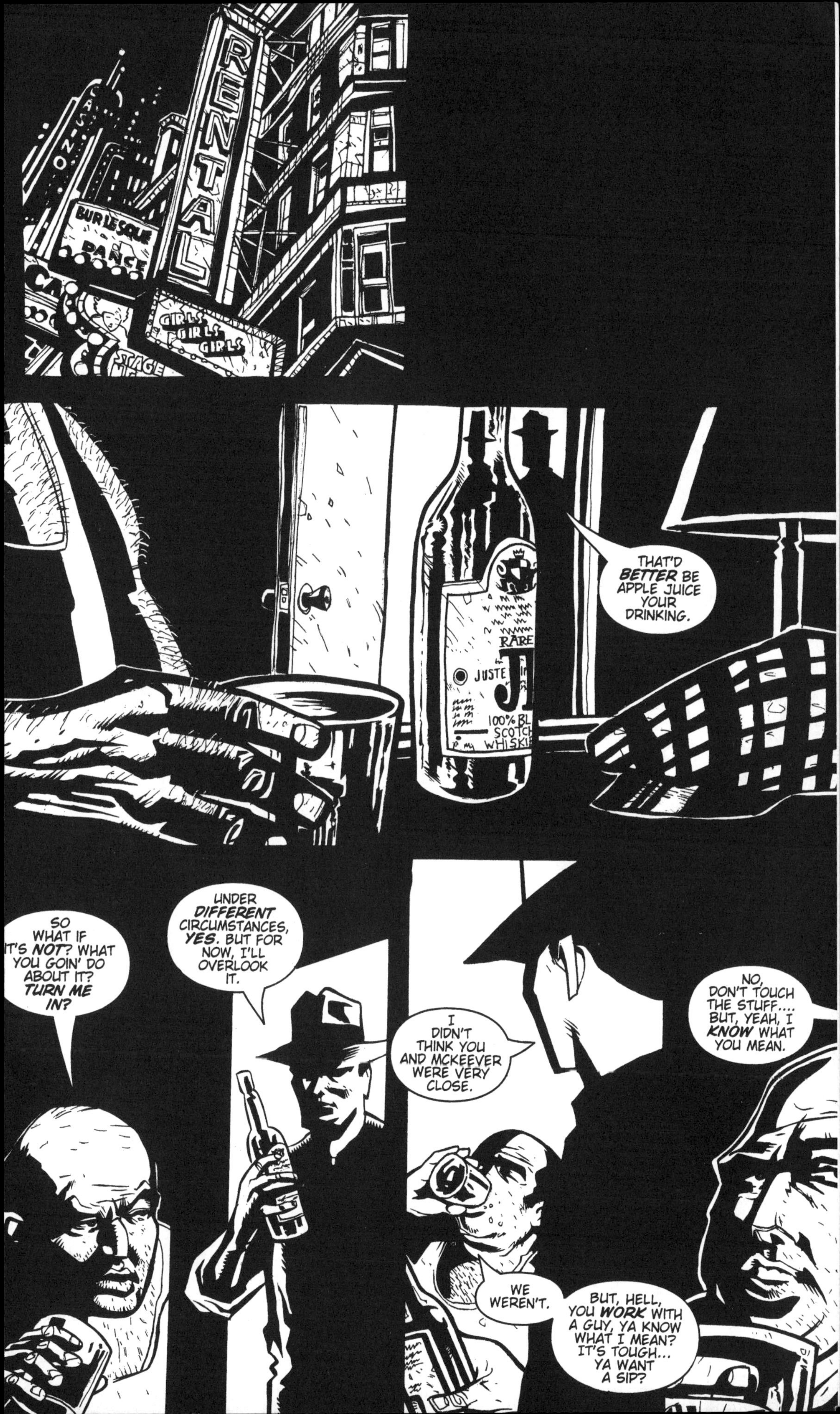
RENTAL
BURLESQUE DANCE
GIRLS GIRLS GIRLS
STAGE
RARE
JUSTE
J
100% BL
SCOTCH
WHISKI
THAT'D BETTER BE APPLE JUICE YOUR DRINKING.
SO WHAT IF IT'S NOT? WHAT YOU GOIN' DO ABOUT IT? TURN ME IN?
UNDER DIFFERENT CIRCUMSTANCES, YES. BUT FOR NOW, I'LL OVERLOOK IT.
I DIDN'T THINK YOU AND MCKEEVER WERE VERY CLOSE.
WE WEREN'T.
BUT, HELL, YOU WORK WITH A GUY, YA KNOW WHAT I MEAN? IT'S TOUGH... YA WANT A SIP?
NO, DON'T TOUCH THE STUFF.... BUT, YEAH, I KNOW WHAT YOU MEAN.

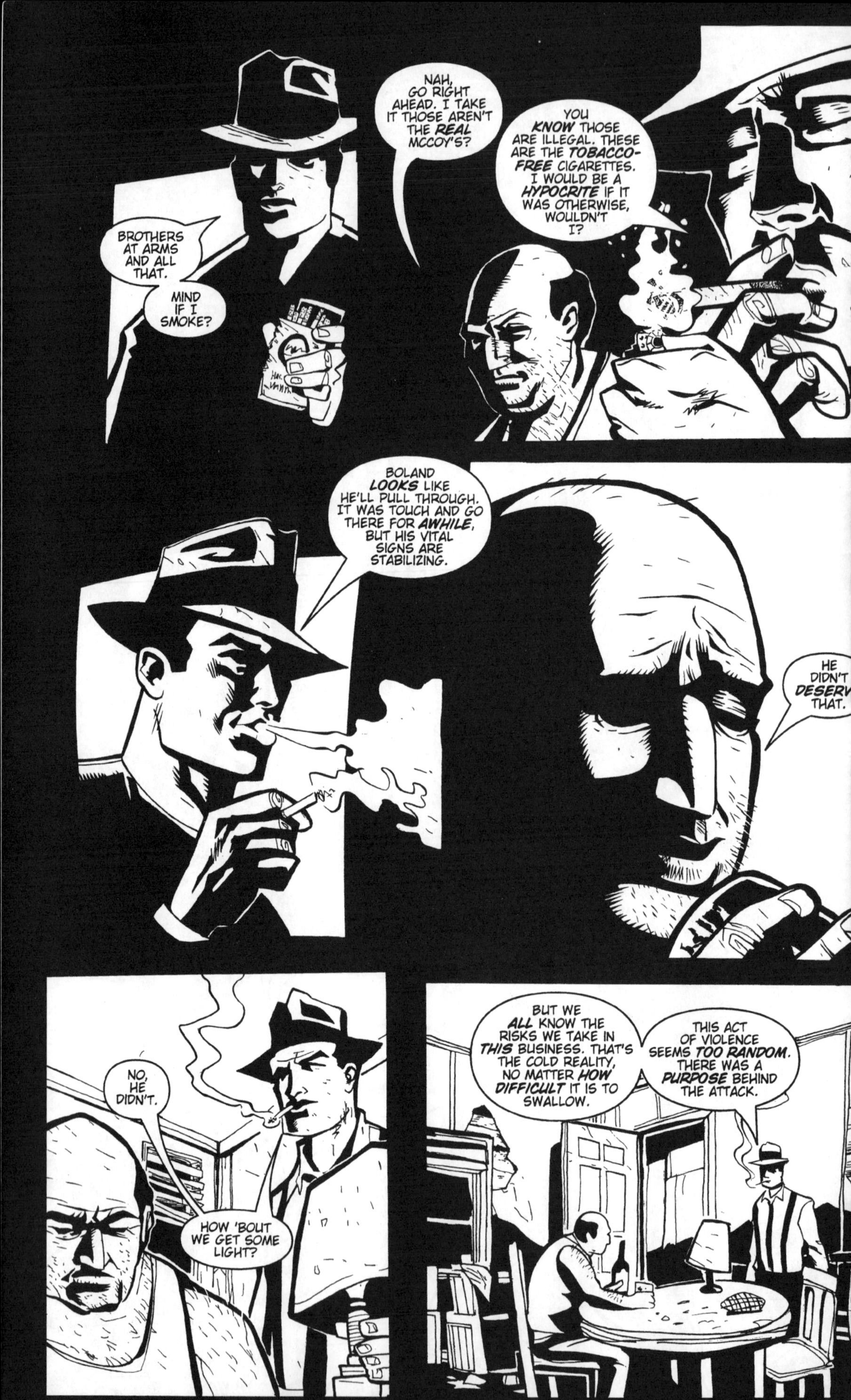
BROTHERS AT ARMS AND ALL THAT.
MIND IF I SMOKE?
NAH, GO RIGHT AHEAD. I TAKE IT THOSE AREN'T THE REAL MCCOY'S?
YOU KNOW THOSE ARE ILLEGAL. THESE ARE THE TOBACCO-FREE CIGARETTES. I WOULD BE A HYPOCRITE IF IT WAS OTHERWISE, WOULDN'T I?
BOLAND LOOKS LIKE HE'LL PULL THROUGH. IT WAS TOUCH AND GO THERE FOR AWHILE, BUT HIS VITAL SIGNS ARE STABILIZING.
HE DIDN'T DESERV THAT.
NO, HE DIDN'T.
HOW 'BOUT WE GET SOME LIGHT?
BUT WE ALL KNOW THE RISKS WE TAKE IN THIS BUSINESS. THAT'S THE COLD REALITY, NO MATTER HOW DIFFICULT IT IS TO SWALLOW.
THIS ACT OF VIOLENCE SEEMS TOO RANDOM. THERE WAS A PURPOSE BEHIND THE ATTACK.

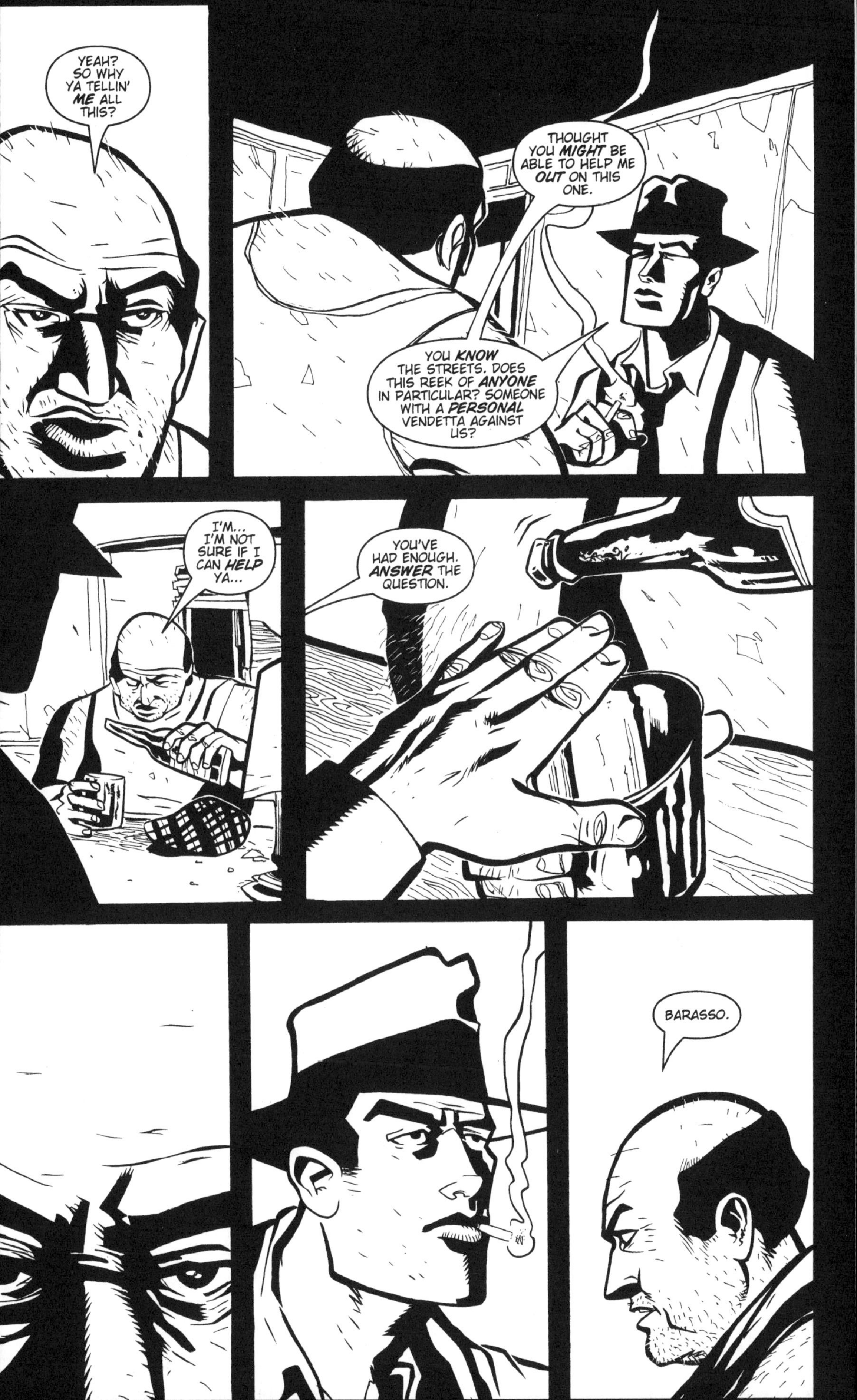
YEAH? SO WHY YA TELLIN' *ME* ALL THIS?
THOUGHT YOU *MIGHT* BE ABLE TO HELP ME *OUT* ON THIS ONE.
YOU *KNOW* THE STREETS. DOES THIS REEK OF *ANYONE* IN PARTICULAR? SOMEONE WITH A *PERSONAL* VENDETTA AGAINST US?
I'M... I'M NOT SURE IF I CAN *HELP* YA...
YOU'VE HAD ENOUGH. *ANSWER* THE QUESTION.
BARASSO.

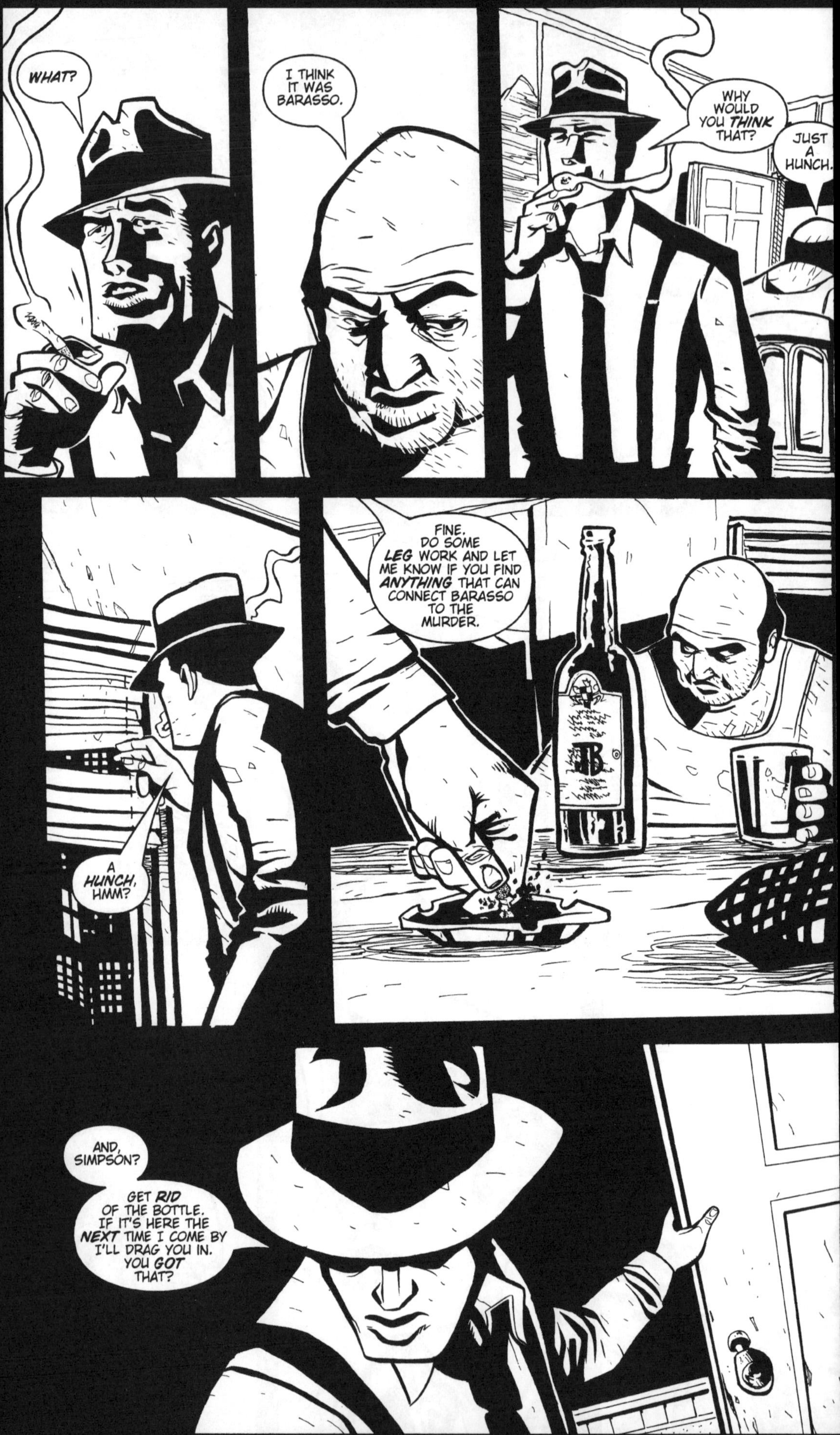
WHAT?
I THINK IT WAS BARASSO.
WHY WOULD YOU THINK THAT?
JUST A HUNCH.
A HUNCH, HMM?
FINE. DO SOME LEG WORK AND LET ME KNOW IF YOU FIND ANYTHING THAT CAN CONNECT BARASSO TO THE MURDER.
AND, SIMPSON?
GET RID OF THE BOTTLE. IF IT'S HERE THE NEXT TIME I COME BY I'LL DRAG YOU IN. YOU GOT THAT?

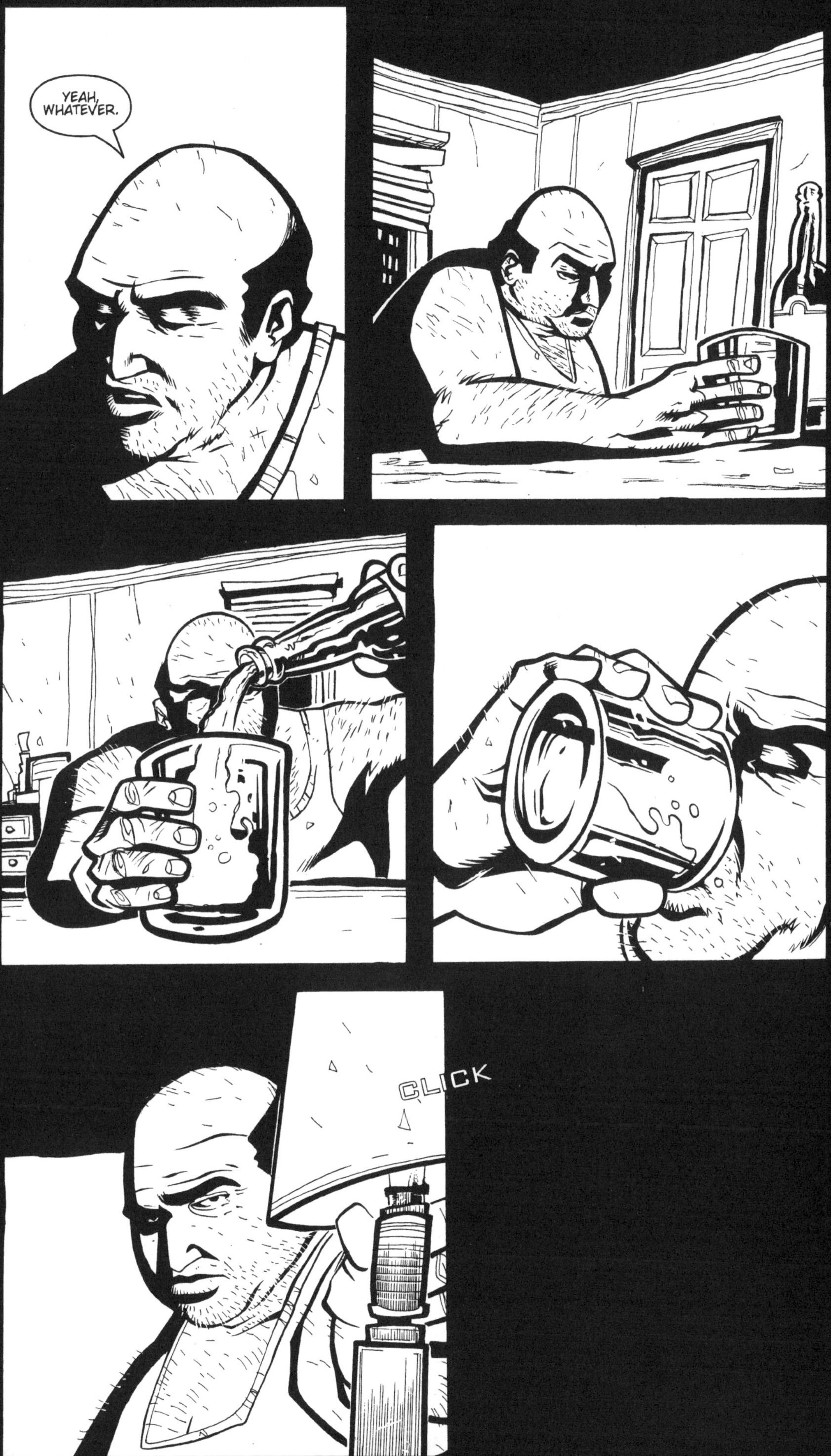
YEAH, WHATEVER.
CLICK

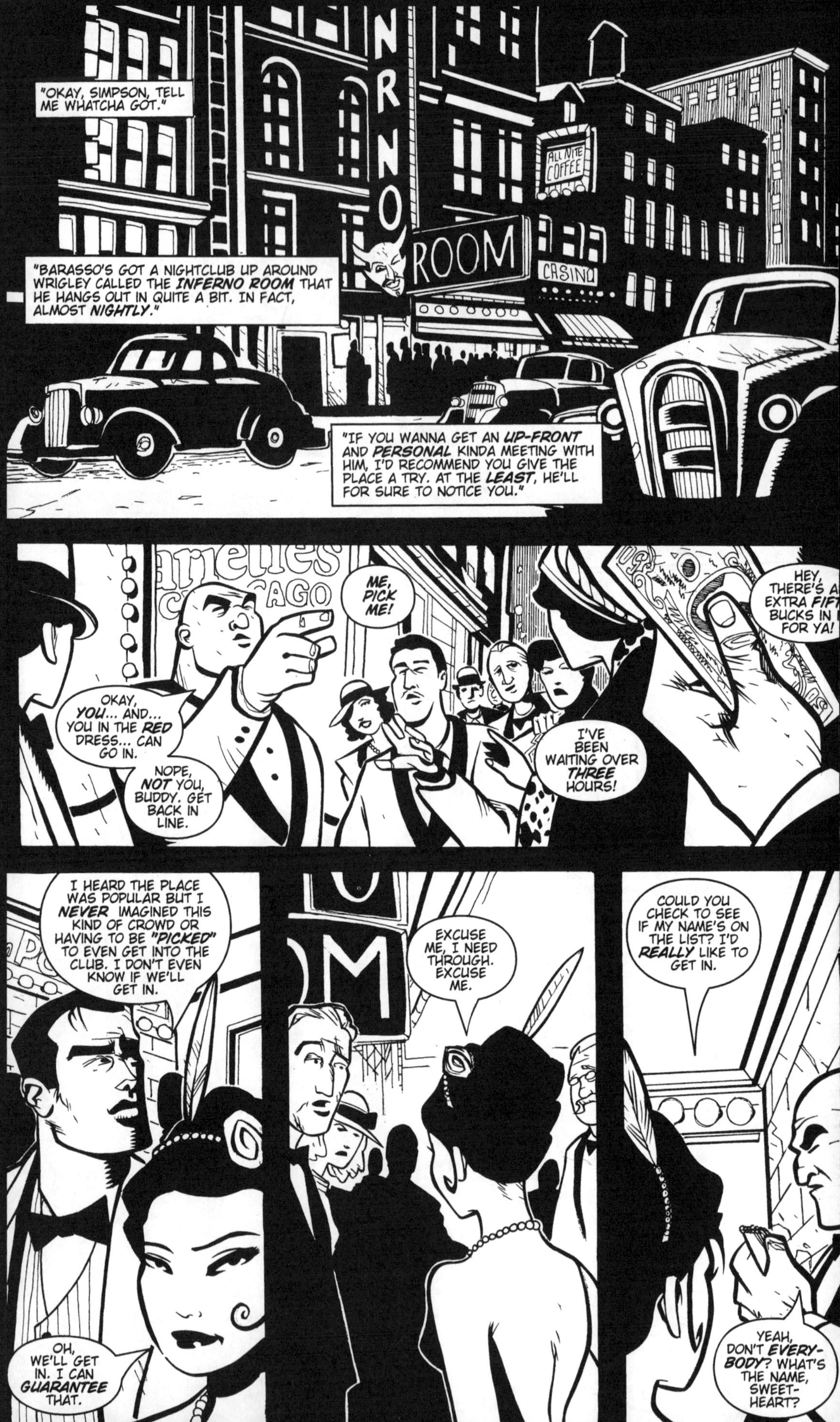
"OKAY, SIMPSON, TELL ME WHATCHA GOT."
ALL NITE COFFEE
ROOM
CASINO
"BARASSO'S GOT A NIGHTCLUB UP AROUND WRIGLEY CALLED THE *INFERNO ROOM* THAT HE HANGS OUT IN QUITE A BIT. IN FACT, ALMOST *NIGHTLY*."
"IF YOU WANNA GET AN *UP-FRONT* AND *PERSONAL* KINDA MEETING WITH HIM, I'D RECOMMEND YOU GIVE THE PLACE A TRY. AT THE *LEAST*, HE'LL FOR SURE TO NOTICE YOU."
ME, PICK ME!
HEY, THERE'S A EXTRA *FIFT* BUCKS IN I FOR YA!
OKAY, *YOU*... AND... YOU IN THE *RED* DRESS... CAN GO IN.
NOPE, *NOT* YOU, BUDDY. GET BACK IN LINE.
I'VE BEEN WAITING OVER *THREE* HOURS!
I HEARD THE PLACE WAS POPULAR BUT I *NEVER* IMAGINED THIS KIND OF CROWD OR HAVING TO BE *"PICKED"* TO EVEN GET INTO THE CLUB. I DON'T EVEN KNOW IF WE'LL GET IN.
OH, WE'LL GET IN. I CAN *GUARANTEE* THAT.
EXCUSE ME, I NEED THROUGH. EXCUSE ME.
COULD YOU CHECK TO SEE IF MY NAME'S ON THE LIST? I'D *REALLY* LIKE TO GET IN.
YEAH, DON'T *EVERY-BODY*? WHAT'S THE NAME, SWEET-HEART?

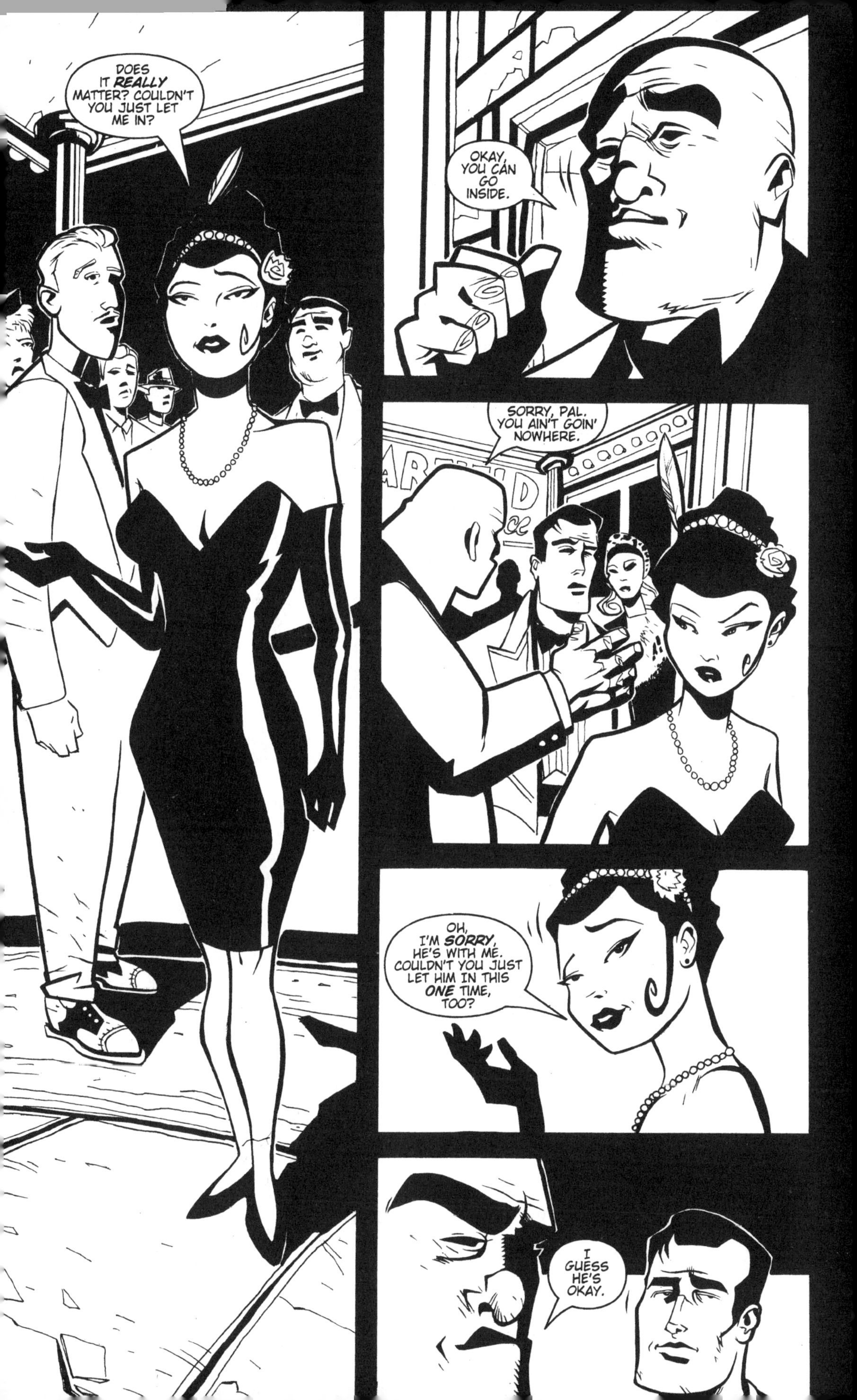
DOES IT *REALLY* MATTER? COULDN'T YOU JUST LET ME IN?
OKAY, YOU CAN GO INSIDE.
SORRY, PAL. YOU AIN'T GOIN' NOWHERE.
OH, I'M *SORRY*, HE'S WITH ME. COULDN'T YOU JUST LET HIM IN THIS *ONE* TIME, TOO?
I GUESS HE'S OKAY.

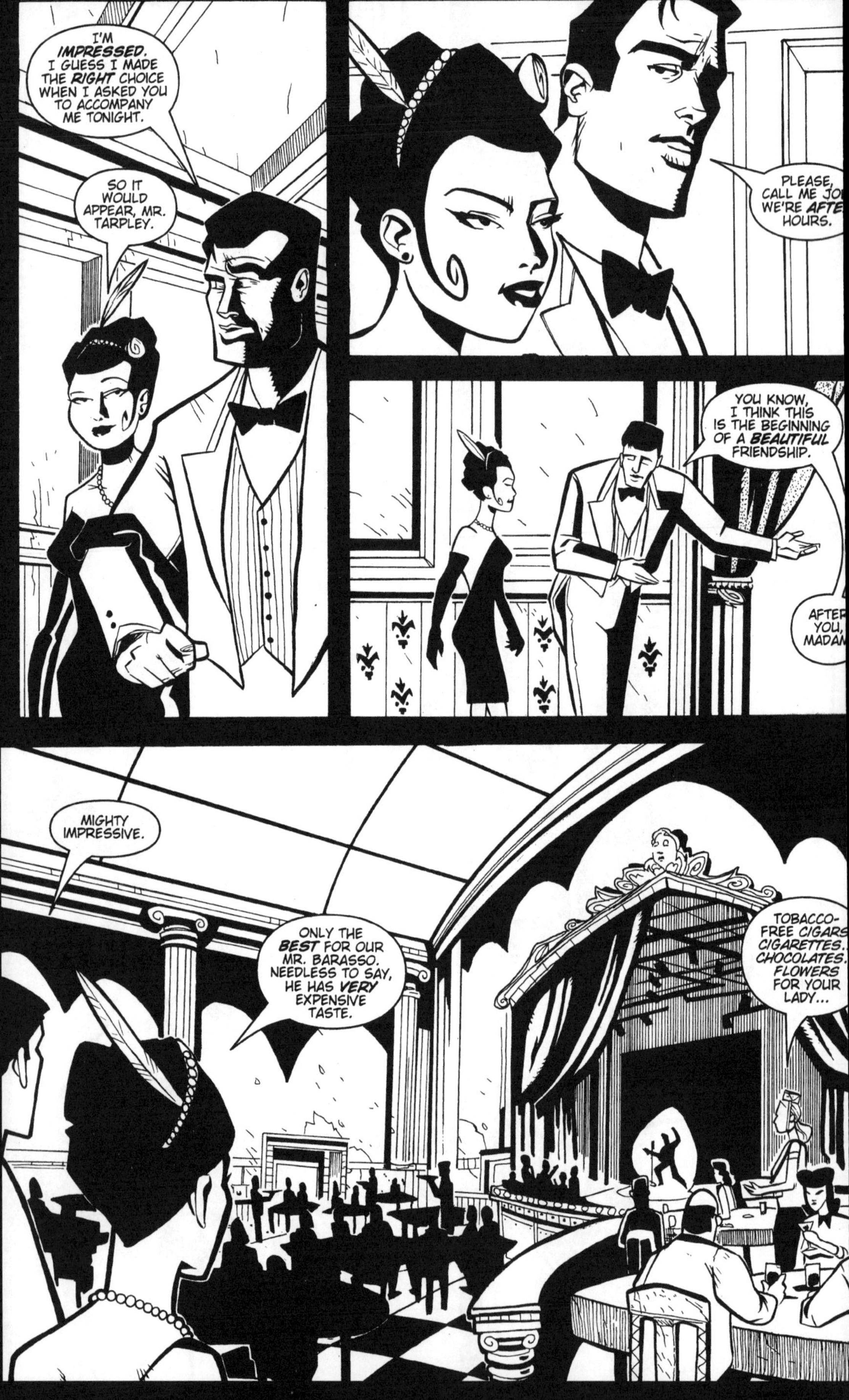
I'M *IMPRESSED.* I GUESS I MADE THE *RIGHT* CHOICE WHEN I ASKED YOU TO ACCOMPANY ME TONIGHT.
SO IT WOULD APPEAR, MR. TARPLEY.
PLEASE, CALL ME JO WE'RE *AFTE* HOURS.
YOU KNOW, I THINK THIS IS THE BEGINNING OF A *BEAUTIFUL* FRIENDSHIP.
AFTER YOU, MADAM
MIGHTY IMPRESSIVE.
ONLY THE *BEST* FOR OUR MR. BARASSO. NEEDLESS TO SAY, HE HAS *VERY* EXPENSIVE TASTE.
TOBACCO-FREE *CIGARS CIGARETTES. CHOCOLATES. FLOWERS* FOR YOUR LADY...

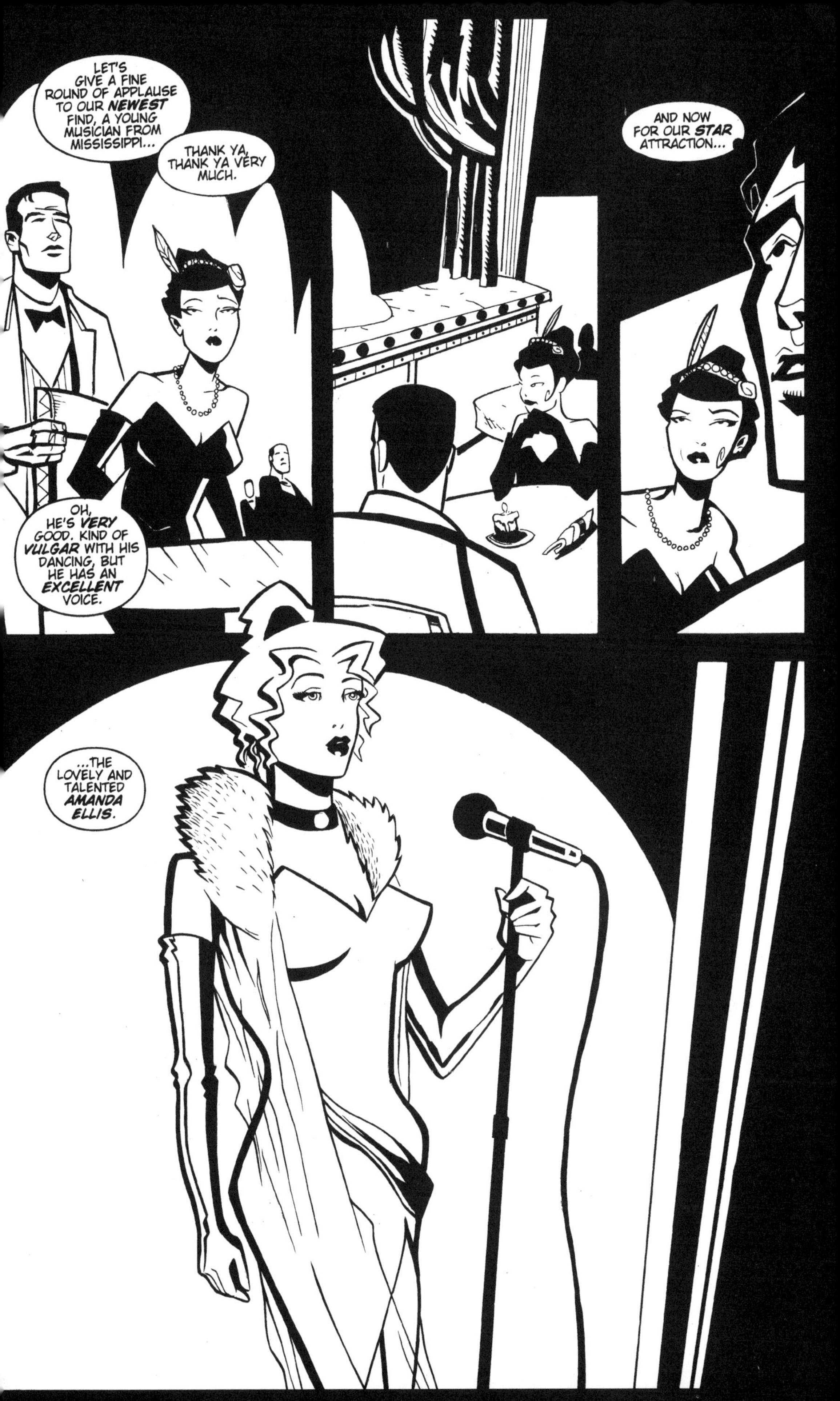
LET'S GIVE A FINE ROUND OF APPLAUSE TO OUR NEWEST FIND, A YOUNG MUSICIAN FROM MISSISSIPPI...
THANK YA, THANK YA VERY MUCH.
OH, HE'S VERY GOOD. KIND OF VULGAR WITH HIS DANCING, BUT HE HAS AN EXCELLENT VOICE.
AND NOW FOR OUR STAR ATTRACTION...
...THE LOVELY AND TALENTED AMANDA ELLIS.

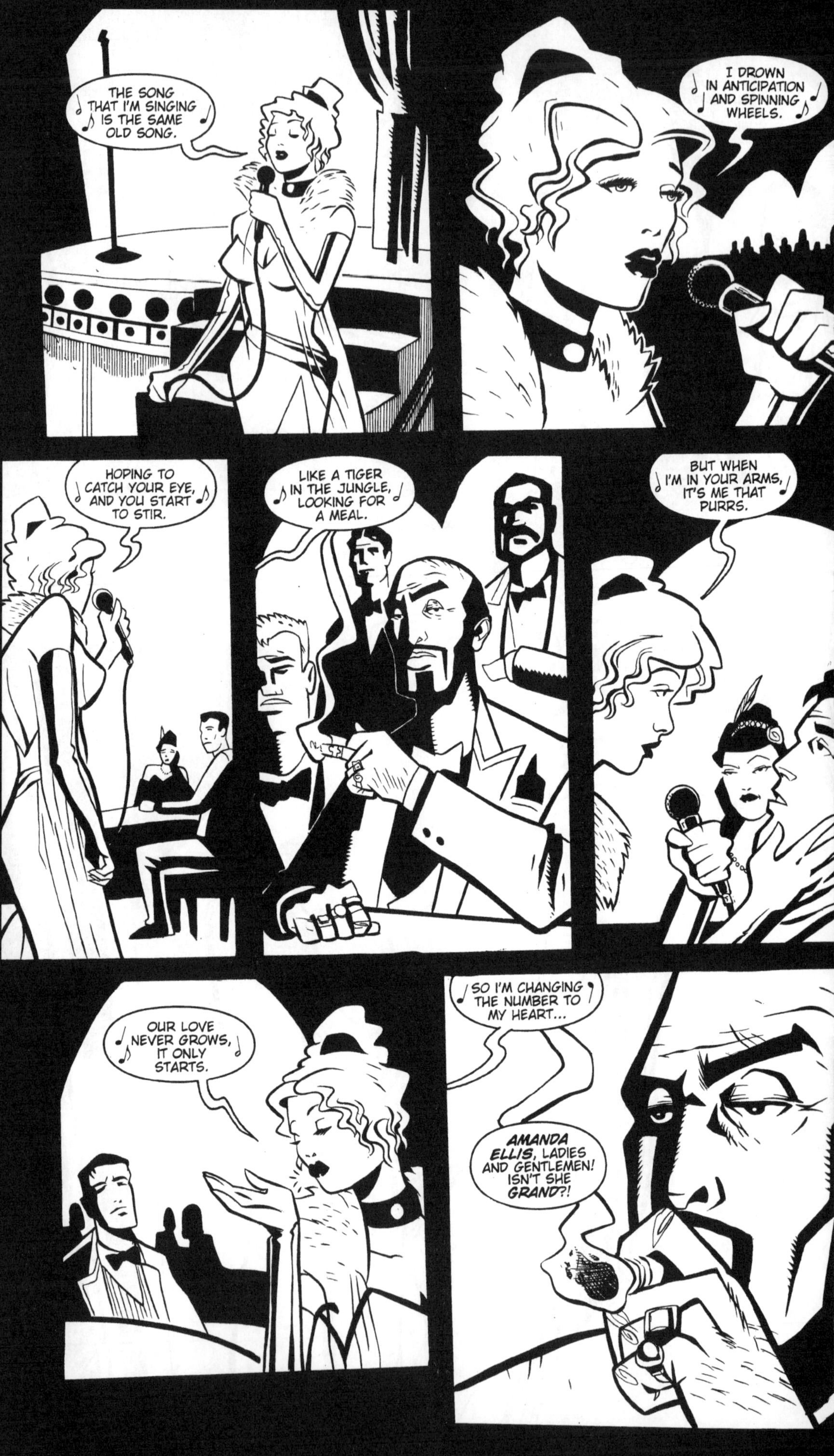
THE SONG THAT I'M SINGING IS THE SAME OLD SONG.
I DROWN IN ANTICIPATION AND SPINNING WHEELS.
HOPING TO CATCH YOUR EYE, AND YOU START TO STIR.
LIKE A TIGER IN THE JUNGLE, LOOKING FOR A MEAL.
BUT WHEN I'M IN YOUR ARMS, IT'S ME THAT PURRS.
OUR LOVE NEVER GROWS, IT ONLY STARTS.
SO I'M CHANGING THE NUMBER TO MY HEART...
AMANDA ELLIS, LADIES AND GENTLEMEN! ISN'T SHE GRAND?!

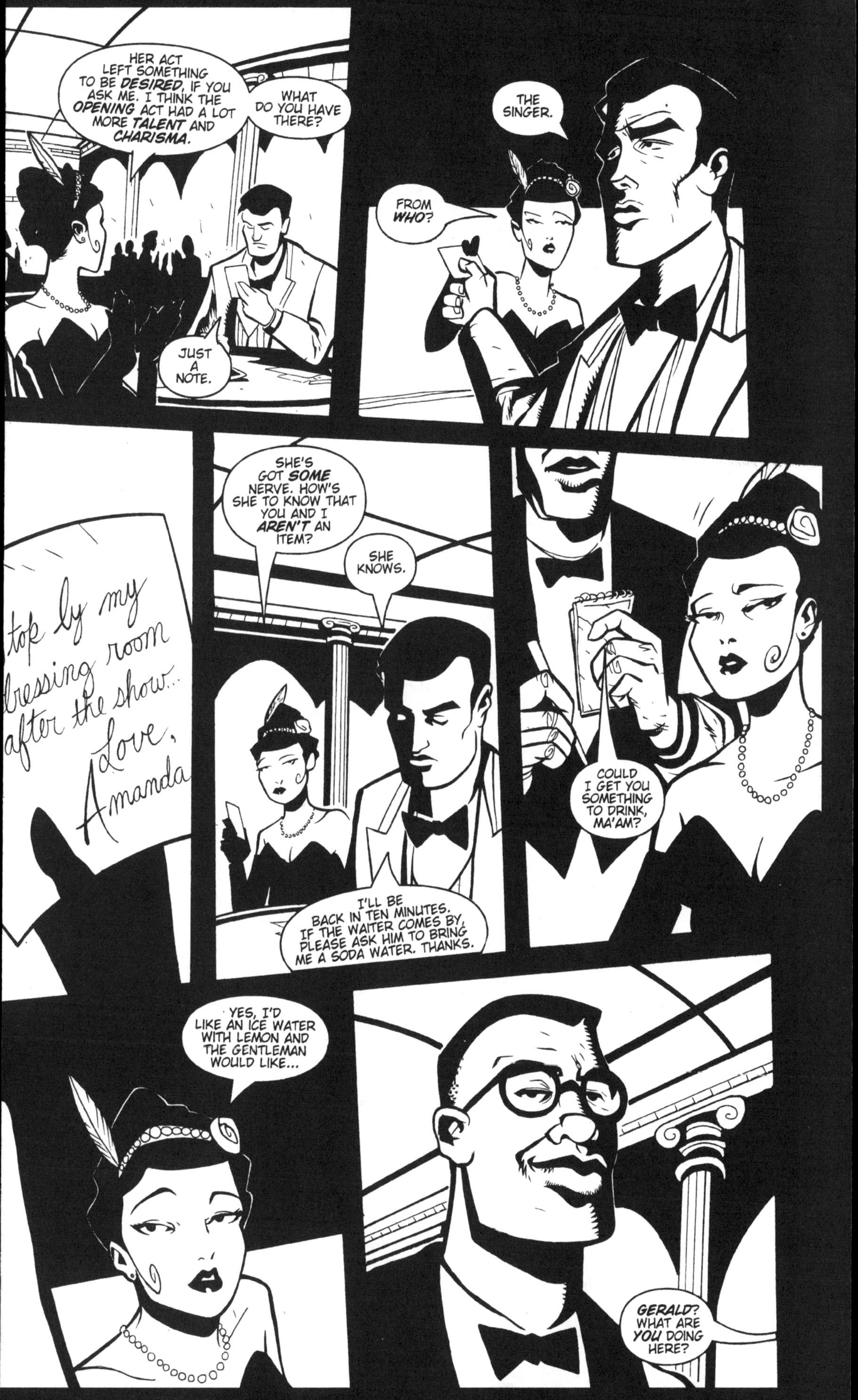
HER ACT LEFT SOMETHING TO BE DESIRED, IF YOU ASK ME. I THINK THE OPENING ACT HAD A LOT MORE TALENT AND CHARISMA.
WHAT DO YOU HAVE THERE?
JUST A NOTE.
THE SINGER.
FROM WHO?
...top by my dressing room after the show... Love, Amanda
SHE'S GOT SOME NERVE. HOW'S SHE TO KNOW THAT YOU AND I AREN'T AN ITEM?
SHE KNOWS.
I'LL BE BACK IN TEN MINUTES. IF THE WAITER COMES BY, PLEASE ASK HIM TO BRING ME A SODA WATER. THANKS.
COULD I GET YOU SOMETHING TO DRINK, MA'AM?
YES, I'D LIKE AN ICE WATER WITH LEMON AND THE GENTLEMAN WOULD LIKE...
GERALD? WHAT ARE YOU DOING HERE?

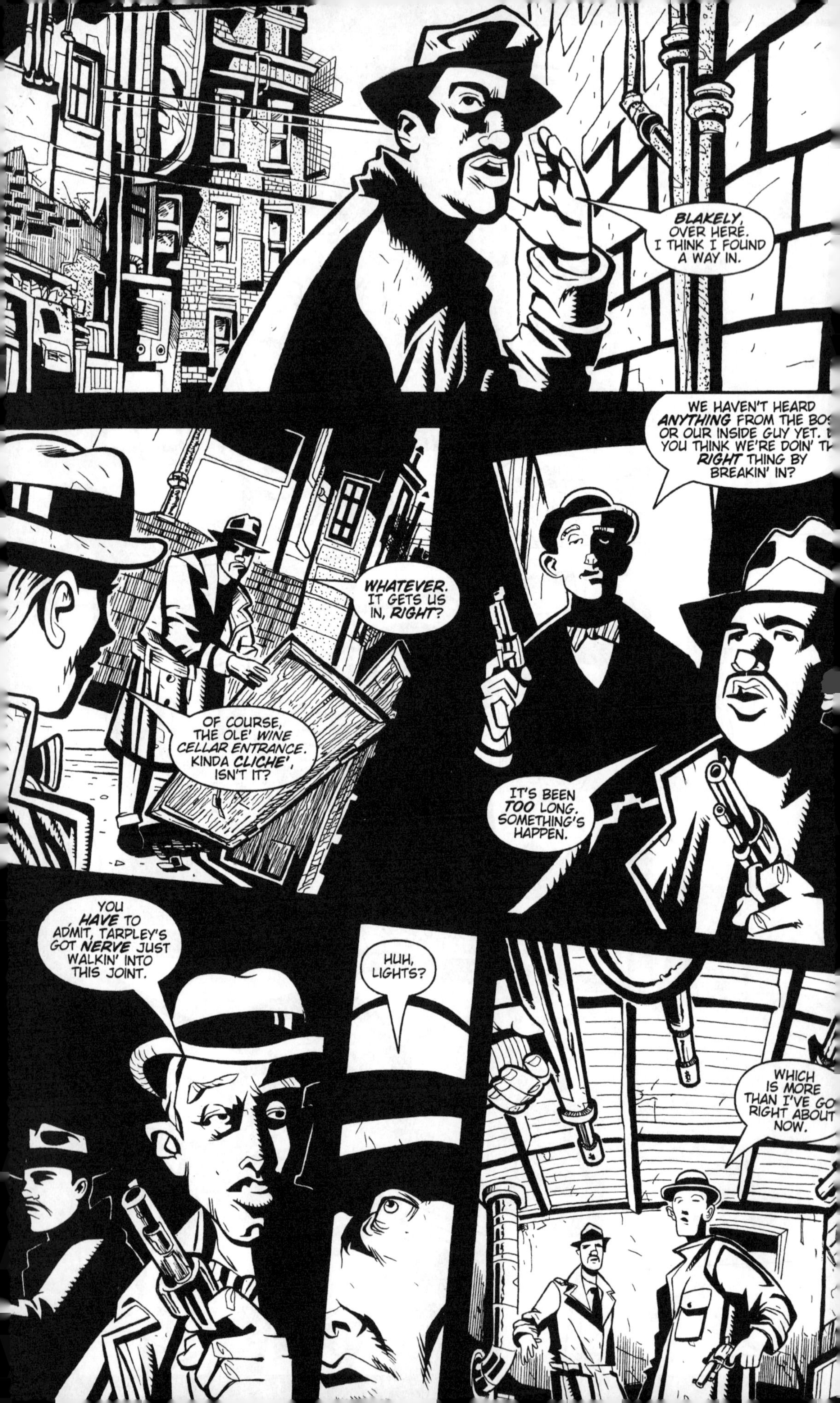
BLAKELY, OVER HERE. I THINK I FOUND A WAY IN.
OF COURSE, THE OLE' WINE CELLAR ENTRANCE. KINDA CLICHE', ISN'T IT?
WHATEVER. IT GETS US IN, RIGHT?
WE HAVEN'T HEARD ANYTHING FROM THE BOS OR OUR INSIDE GUY YET. YOU THINK WE'RE DOIN' T RIGHT THING BY BREAKIN' IN?
IT'S BEEN TOO LONG. SOMETHING'S HAPPEN.
YOU HAVE TO ADMIT, TARPLEY'S GOT NERVE JUST WALKIN' INTO THIS JOINT.
HUH, LIGHTS?
WHICH IS MORE THAN I'VE GO RIGHT ABOUT NOW.

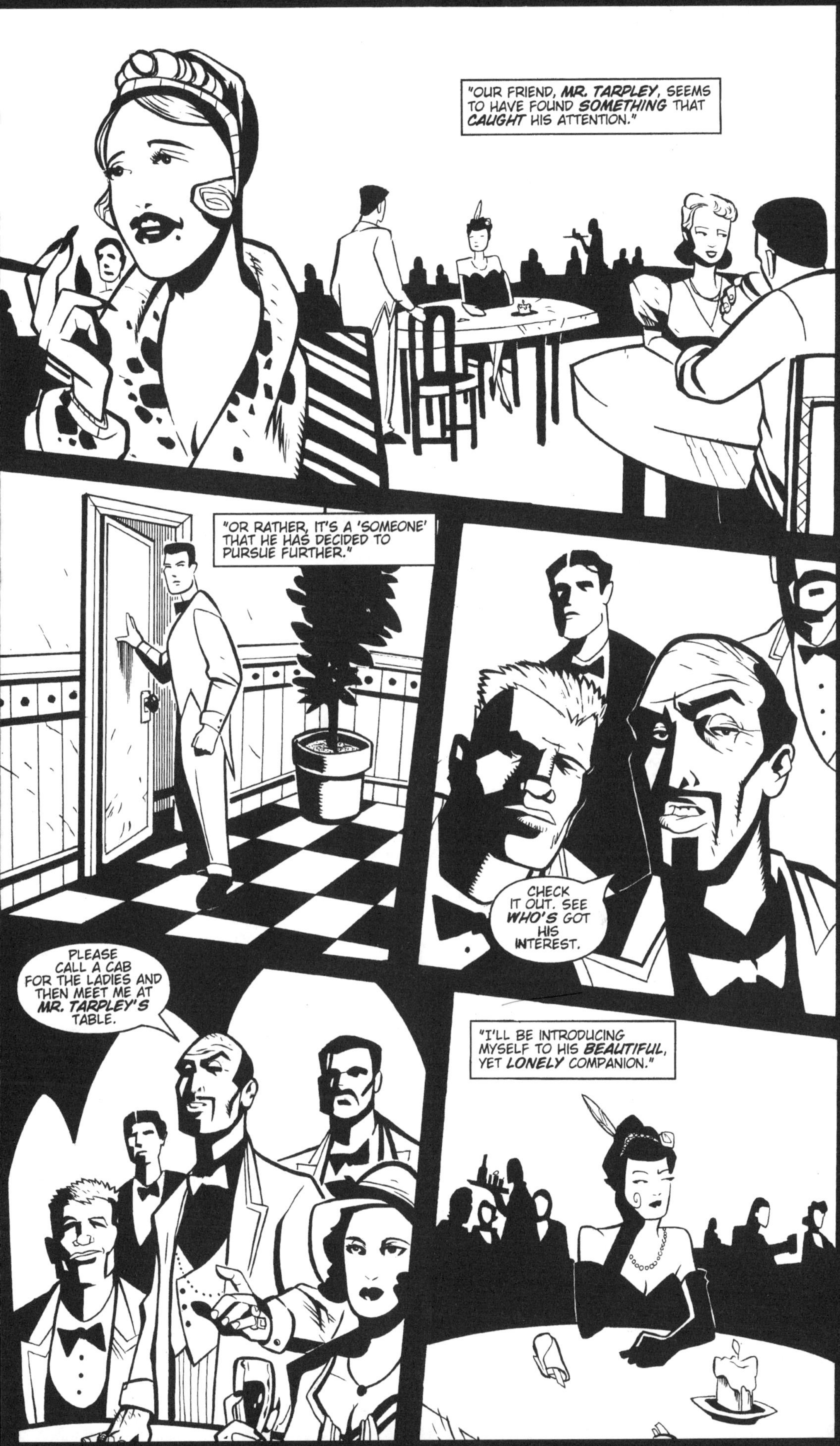
"OUR FRIEND, MR. TARPLEY, SEEMS TO HAVE FOUND SOMETHING THAT CAUGHT HIS ATTENTION."
"OR RATHER, IT'S A 'SOMEONE' THAT HE HAS DECIDED TO PURSUE FURTHER."
CHECK IT OUT. SEE WHO'S GOT HIS INTEREST.
PLEASE CALL A CAB FOR THE LADIES AND THEN MEET ME AT MR. TARPLEY'S TABLE.
"I'LL BE INTRODUCING MYSELF TO HIS BEAUTIFUL, YET LONELY COMPANION."

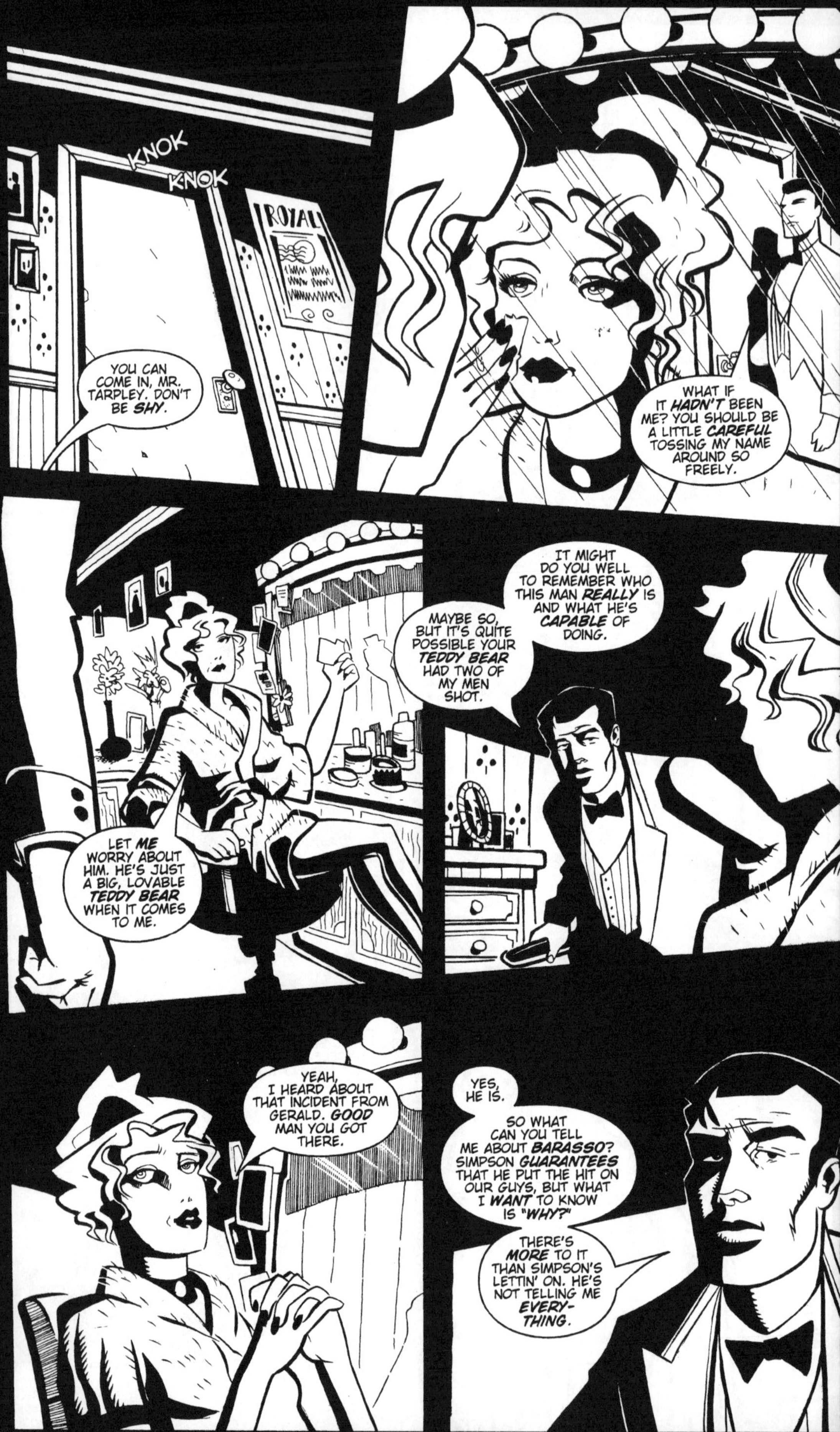
KNOK
KNOK
ROYAL
YOU CAN COME IN, MR. TARPLEY. DON'T BE SHY.
WHAT IF IT HADN'T BEEN ME? YOU SHOULD BE A LITTLE CAREFUL TOSSING MY NAME AROUND SO FREELY.
LET ME WORRY ABOUT HIM. HE'S JUST A BIG, LOVABLE TEDDY BEAR WHEN IT COMES TO ME.
IT MIGHT DO YOU WELL TO REMEMBER WHO THIS MAN REALLY IS AND WHAT HE'S CAPABLE OF DOING.
MAYBE SO, BUT IT'S QUITE POSSIBLE YOUR TEDDY BEAR HAD TWO OF MY MEN SHOT.
YEAH, I HEARD ABOUT THAT INCIDENT FROM GERALD. GOOD MAN YOU GOT THERE.
YES, HE IS.
SO WHAT CAN YOU TELL ME ABOUT BARASSO? SIMPSON GUARANTEES THAT HE PUT THE HIT ON OUR GUYS, BUT WHAT I WANT TO KNOW IS "WHY?"
THERE'S MORE TO IT THAN SIMPSON'S LETTIN' ON. HE'S NOT TELLING ME EVERYTHING.

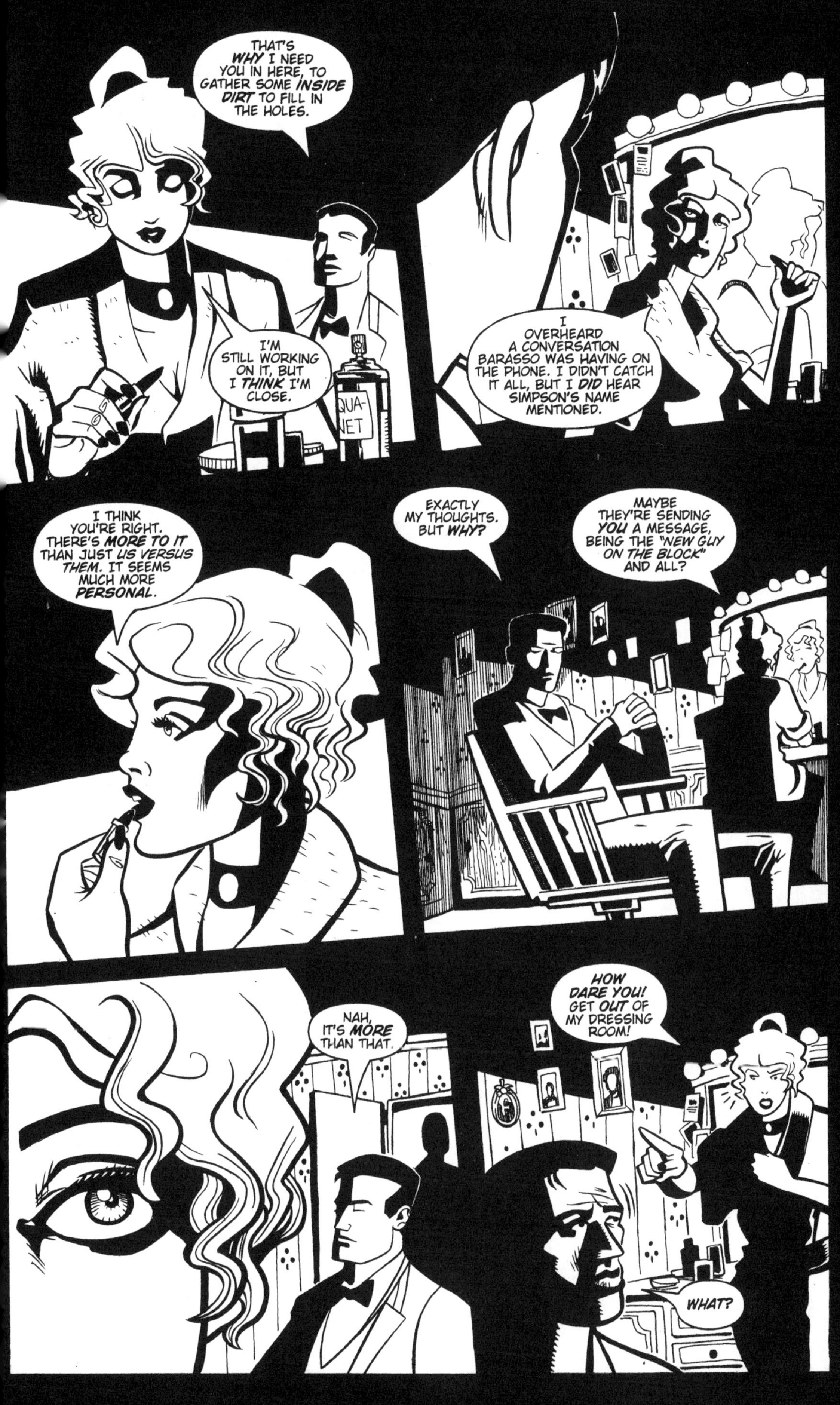

THAT'S WHY I NEED YOU IN HERE, TO GATHER SOME INSIDE DIRT TO FILL IN THE HOLES.
I'M STILL WORKING ON IT, BUT I THINK I'M CLOSE.
QUA-NET
I OVERHEARD A CONVERSATION BARASSO WAS HAVING ON THE PHONE. I DIDN'T CATCH IT ALL, BUT I DID HEAR SIMPSON'S NAME MENTIONED.
I THINK YOU'RE RIGHT. THERE'S MORE TO IT THAN JUST US VERSUS THEM. IT SEEMS MUCH MORE PERSONAL.
EXACTLY MY THOUGHTS. BUT WHY?
MAYBE THEY'RE SENDING YOU A MESSAGE, BEING THE "NEW GUY ON THE BLOCK" AND ALL?
NAH, IT'S MORE THAN THAT.
HOW DARE YOU! GET OUT OF MY DRESSING ROOM!
WHAT?

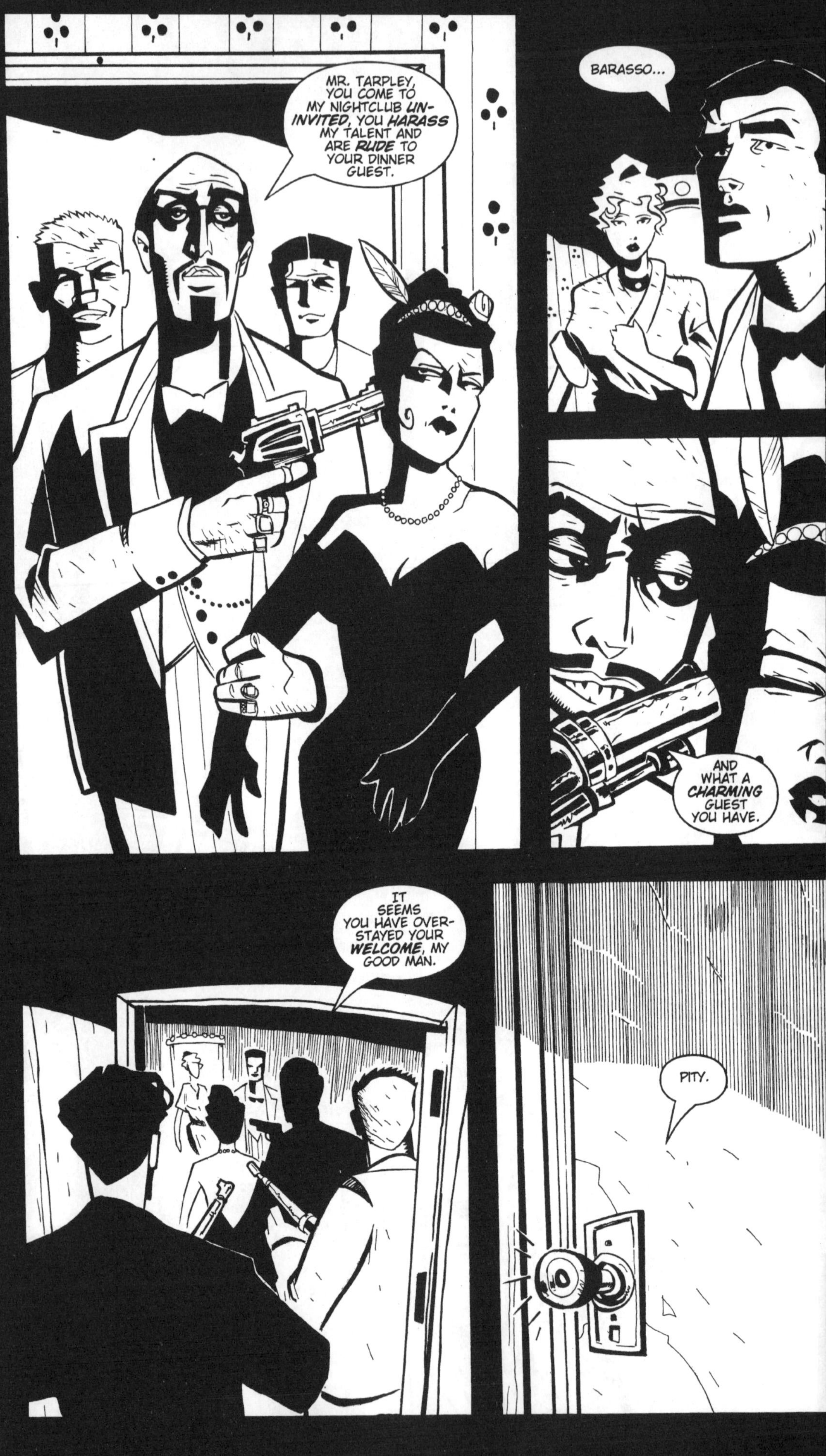
MR. TARPLEY, YOU COME TO MY NIGHTCLUB UN-INVITED, YOU HARASS MY TALENT AND ARE RUDE TO YOUR DINNER GUEST.
BARASSO...
AND WHAT A CHARMING GUEST YOU HAVE.
IT SEEMS YOU HAVE OVER-STAYED YOUR WELCOME, MY GOOD MAN.
PITY.

I'VE GOT THE *LATEST* UPDATE REGARDING YOUR FRIEND, *MR. BOLLAND.*

NCENT ORIAL SPITAL

WELL, WHAT IS IT, DOC? WE CAN *TAKE* IT.

I'M AFRAID WE'VE *DONE* ALL WE CAN. THE OPERATION *WAS* A SUCCESS. HE'LL *LIVE.*

THAT'S *GREAT* NEWS, ISN'T IT, DOC?

YEAH, WHY THE *GLUM* FACE. WHAT *ELSE* YOU GOTTA TELL US?

WELL...

ONE OF THE BULLETS PASSED THROUGH HIS SPINAL CORD, EFFECTIVELY *SEVERING* IT.

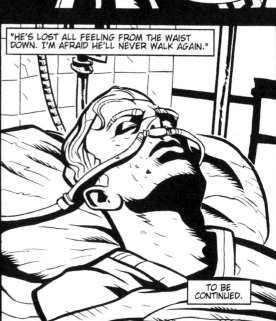

"HE'S LOST ALL FEELING FROM THE WAIST DOWN. I'M AFRAID HE'LL NEVER WALK AGAIN."

TO BE CONTINUED.

UNTOUCHABLES

"A NEW BEGINNING"

ACT 3

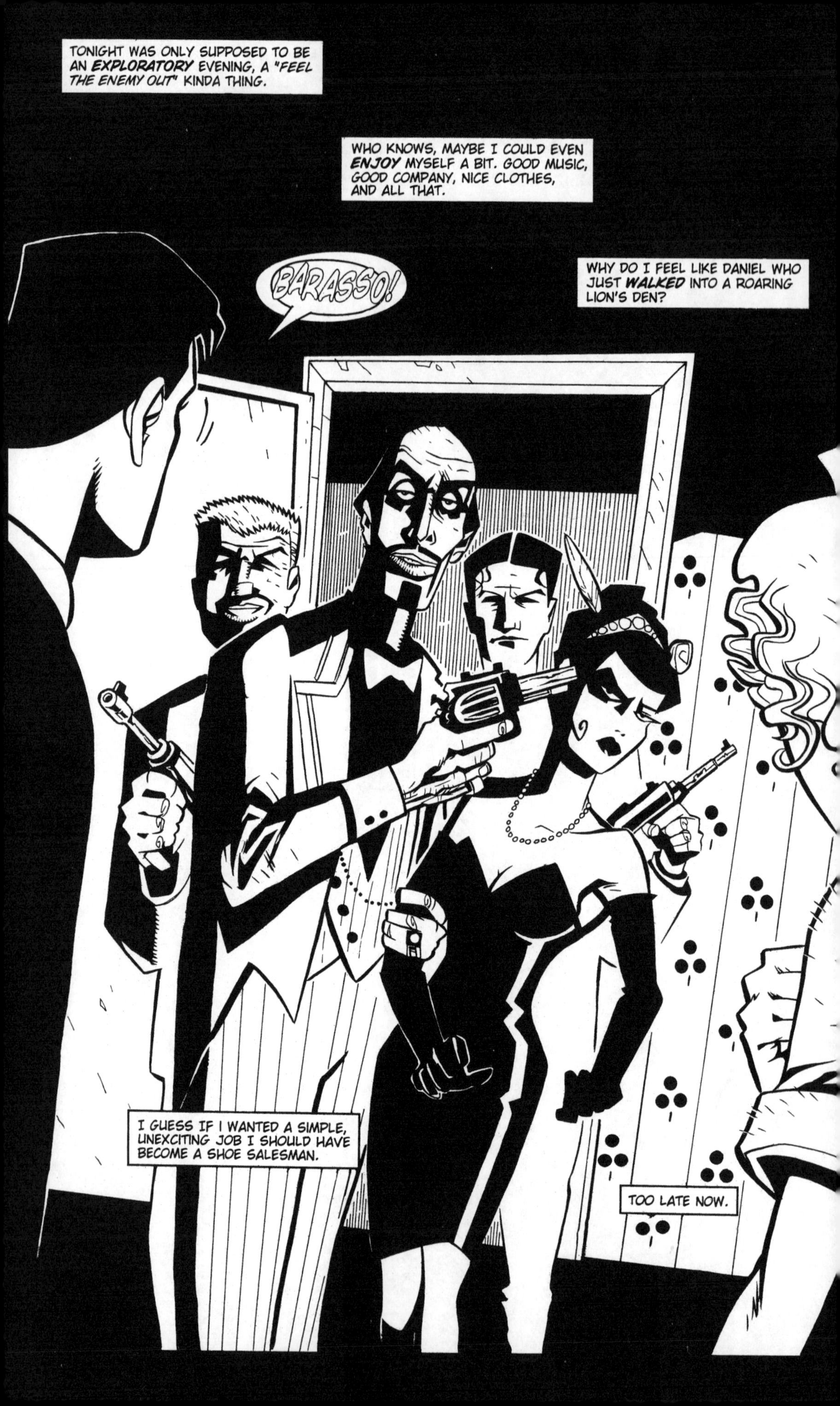

TONIGHT WAS ONLY SUPPOSED TO BE AN **EXPLORATORY** EVENING, A *"FEEL THE ENEMY OUT"* KINDA THING.
WHO KNOWS, MAYBE I COULD EVEN **ENJOY** MYSELF A BIT. GOOD MUSIC, GOOD COMPANY, NICE CLOTHES, AND ALL THAT.
BARASSO!
WHY DO I FEEL LIKE DANIEL WHO JUST **WALKED** INTO A ROARING LION'S DEN?
I GUESS IF I WANTED A SIMPLE, UNEXCITING JOB I SHOULD HAVE BECOME A SHOE SALESMAN.
TOO LATE NOW.

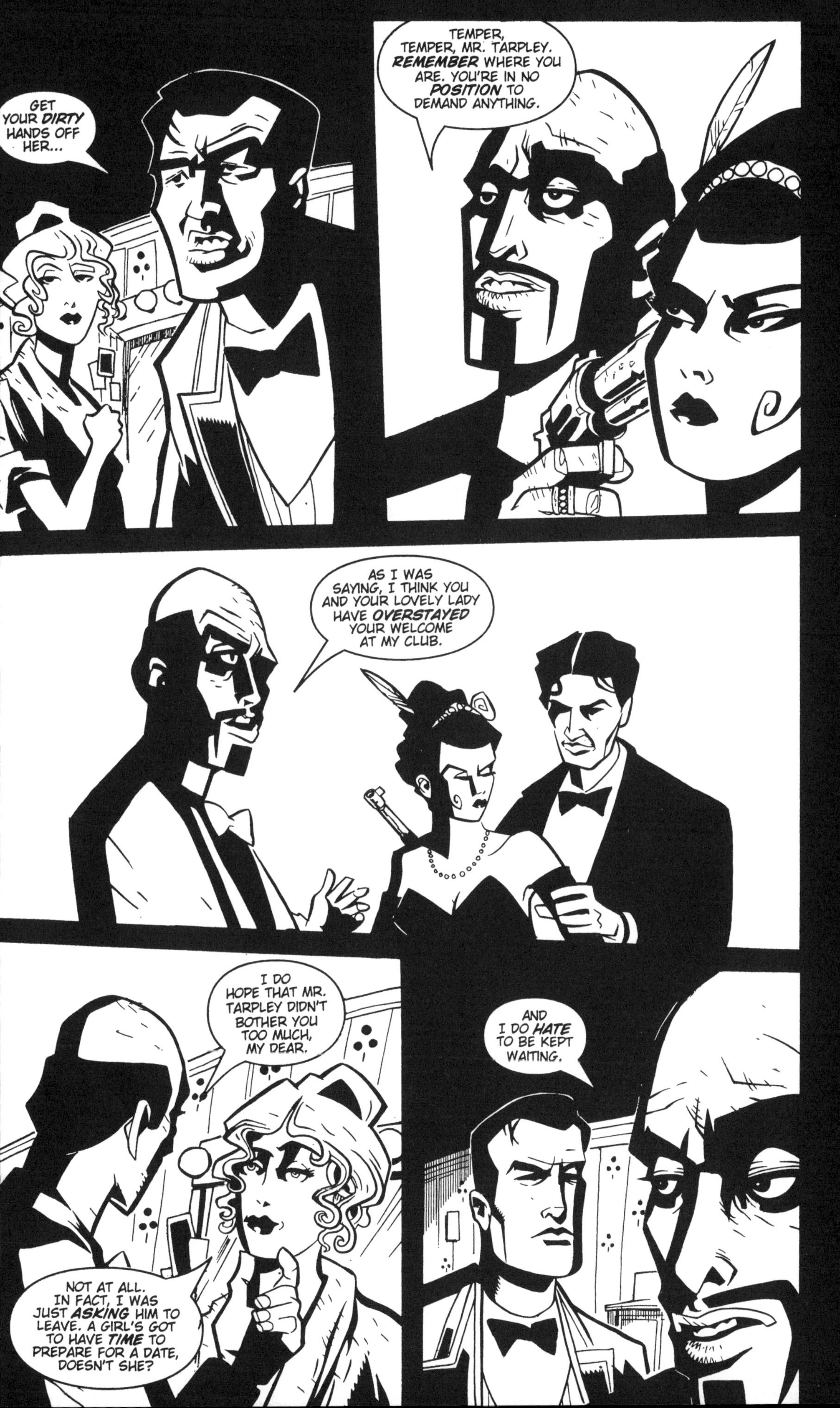

GET YOUR DIRTY HANDS OFF HER...
TEMPER, TEMPER, MR. TARPLEY. REMEMBER WHERE YOU ARE. YOU'RE IN NO POSITION TO DEMAND ANYTHING.
AS I WAS SAYING, I THINK YOU AND YOUR LOVELY LADY HAVE OVERSTAYED YOUR WELCOME AT MY CLUB.
I DO HOPE THAT MR. TARPLEY DIDN'T BOTHER YOU TOO MUCH, MY DEAR.
NOT AT ALL. IN FACT, I WAS JUST ASKING HIM TO LEAVE. A GIRL'S GOT TO HAVE TIME TO PREPARE FOR A DATE, DOESN'T SHE?
AND I DO HATE TO BE KEPT WAITING.

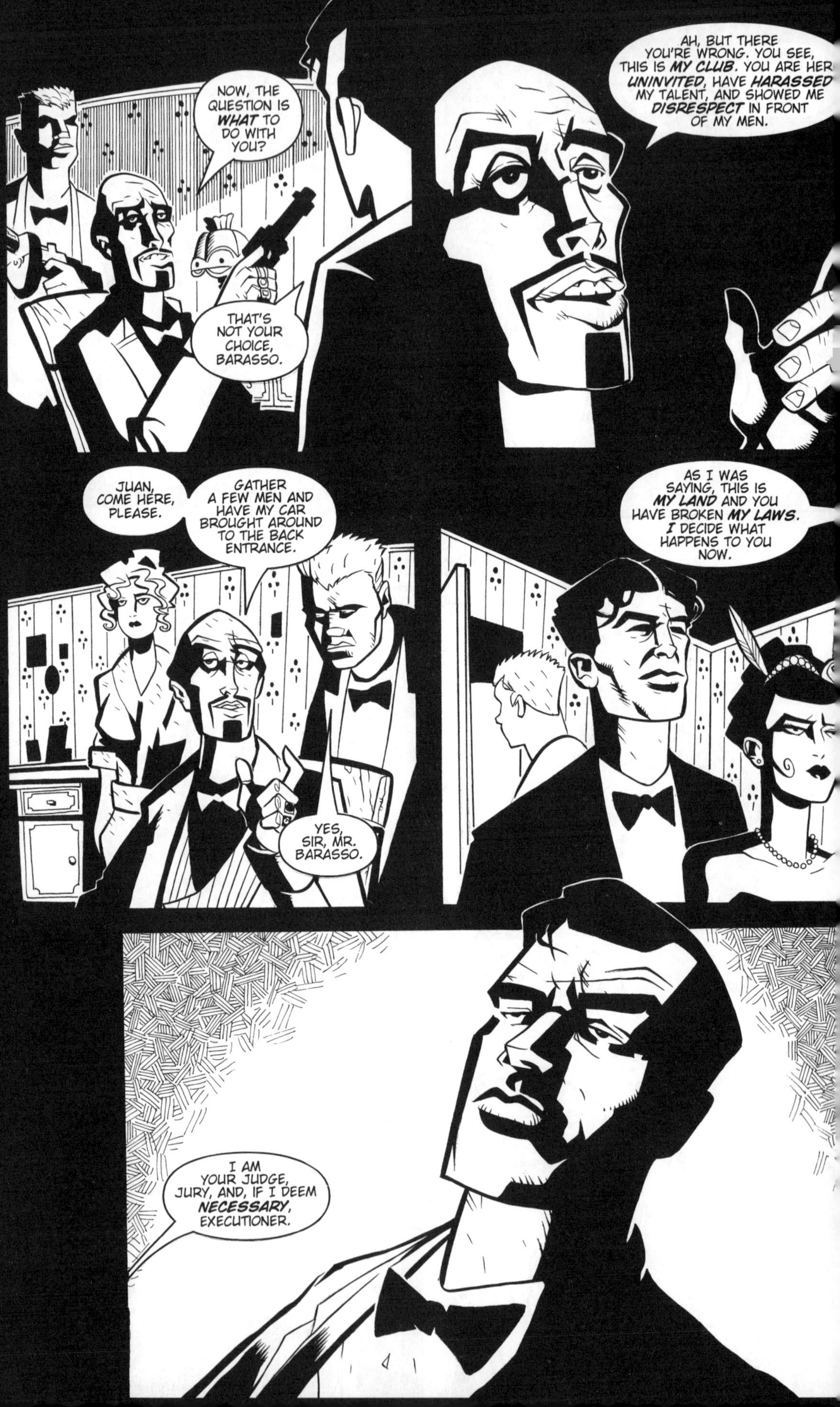
NOW, THE QUESTION IS WHAT TO DO WITH YOU?
THAT'S NOT YOUR CHOICE, BARASSO.
AH, BUT THERE YOU'RE WRONG. YOU SEE, THIS IS MY CLUB. YOU ARE HER UNINVITED, HAVE HARASSED MY TALENT, AND SHOWED ME DISRESPECT IN FRONT OF MY MEN.
JUAN, COME HERE, PLEASE.
GATHER A FEW MEN AND HAVE MY CAR BROUGHT AROUND TO THE BACK ENTRANCE.
YES, SIR, MR. BARASSO.
AS I WAS SAYING, THIS IS MY LAND AND YOU HAVE BROKEN MY LAWS. I DECIDE WHAT HAPPENS TO YOU NOW.
I AM YOUR JUDGE, JURY, AND, IF I DEEM NECESSARY, EXECUTIONER.

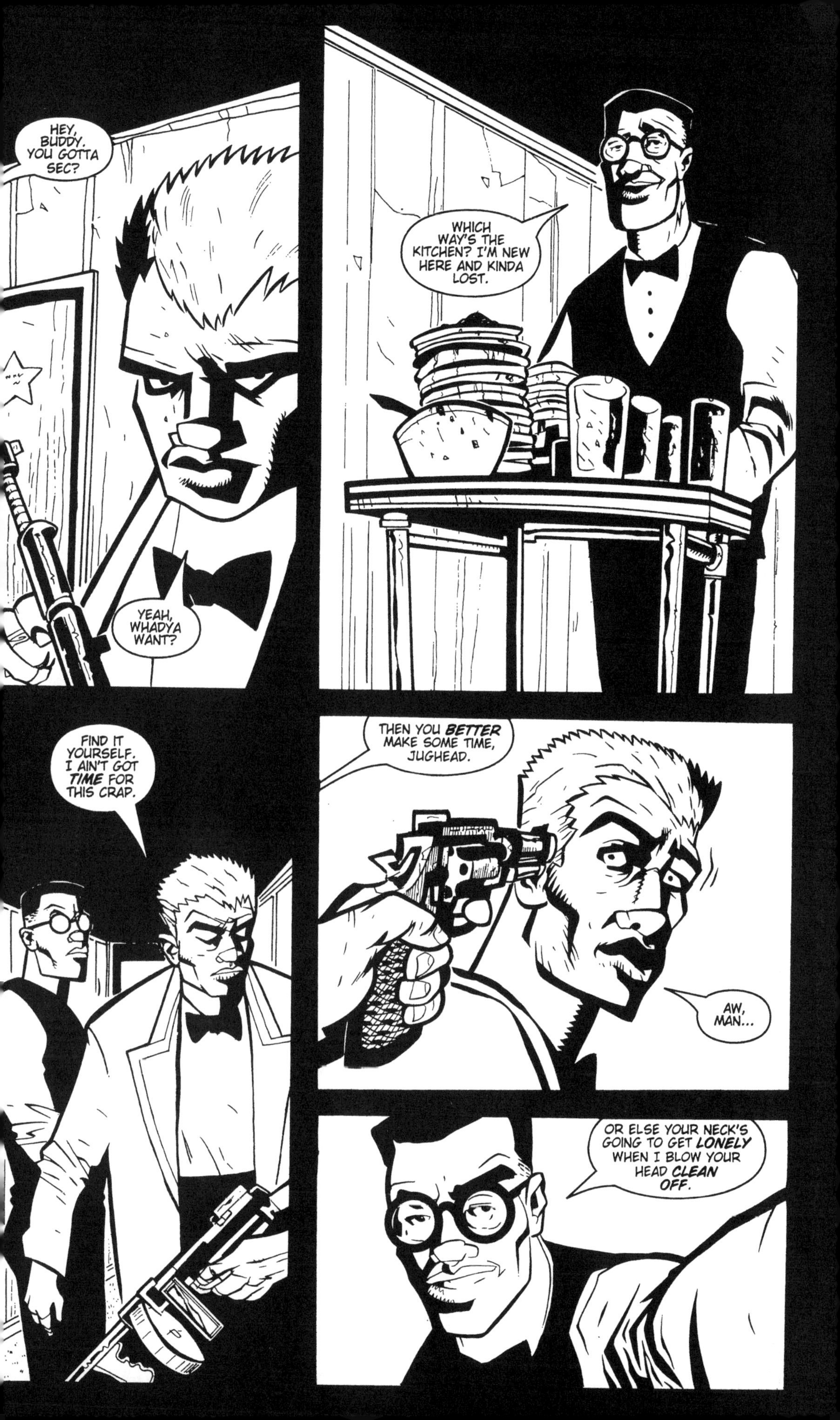
HEY, BUDDY. YOU GOTTA SEC?
YEAH, WHADYA WANT?
WHICH WAY'S THE KITCHEN? I'M NEW HERE AND KINDA LOST.
FIND IT YOURSELF. I AIN'T GOT TIME FOR THIS CRAP.
THEN YOU BETTER MAKE SOME TIME, JUGHEAD.
AW, MAN...
OR ELSE YOUR NECK'S GOING TO GET LONELY WHEN I BLOW YOUR HEAD CLEAN OFF.

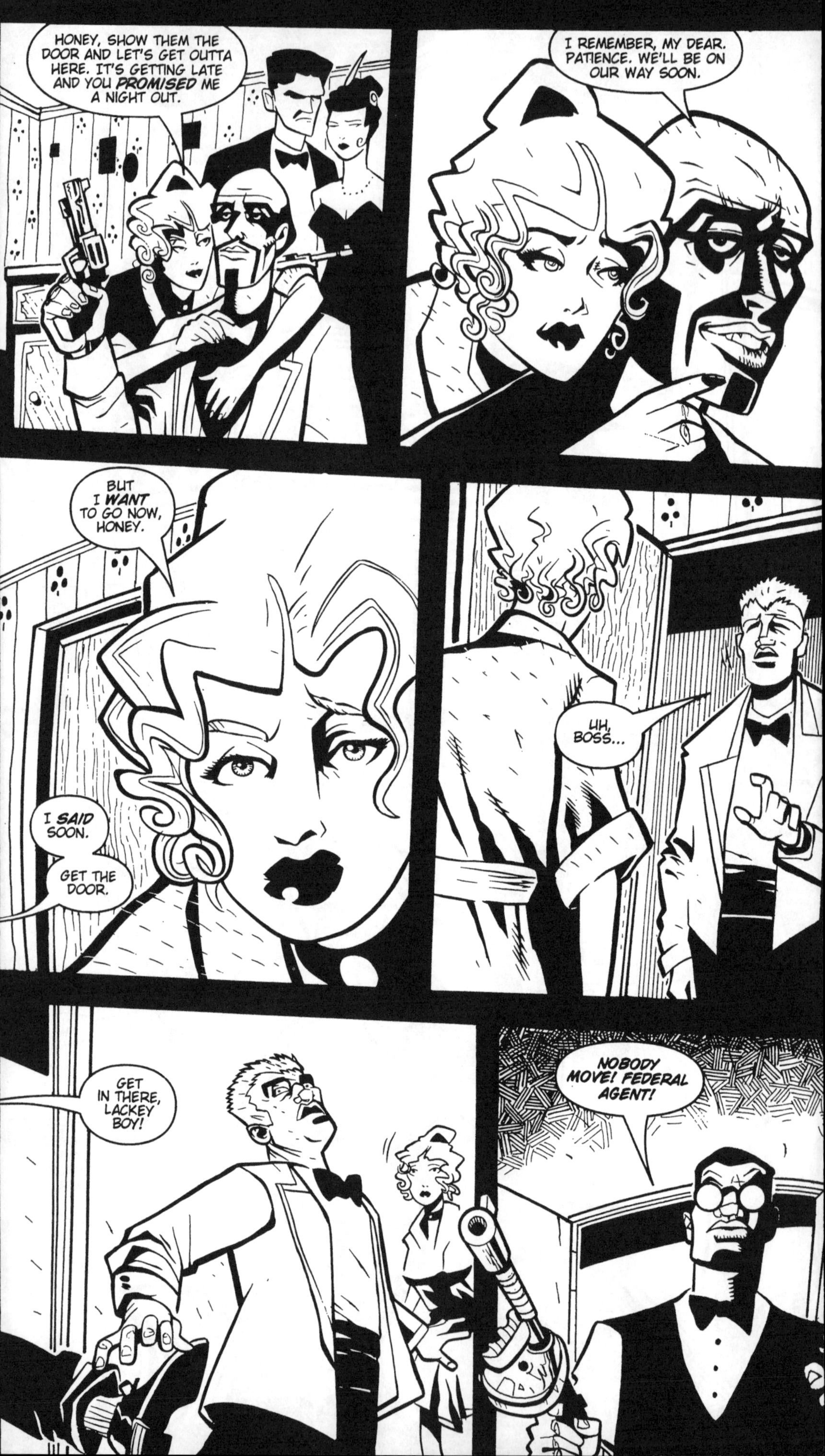
HONEY, SHOW THEM THE DOOR AND LET'S GET OUTTA HERE. IT'S GETTING LATE AND YOU *PROMISED* ME A NIGHT OUT.
I REMEMBER, MY DEAR. PATIENCE. WE'LL BE ON OUR WAY SOON.
BUT I *WANT* TO GO NOW, HONEY.
I *SAID* SOON.
GET THE DOOR.
UH, BOSS...
GET IN THERE, LACKEY BOY!
NOBODY MOVE! FEDERAL AGENT!

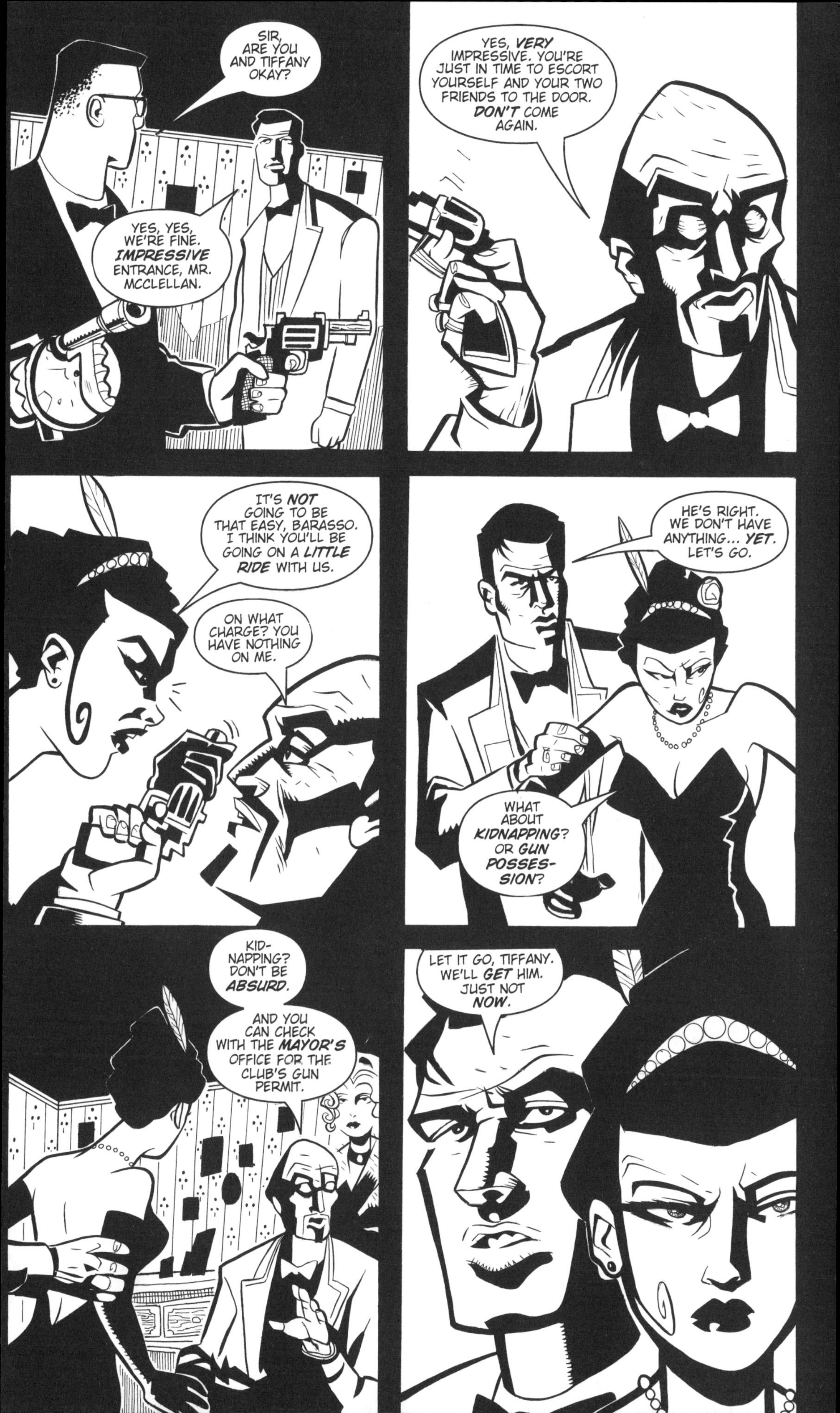
SIR, ARE YOU AND TIFFANY OKAY?
YES, YES, WE'RE FINE. IMPRESSIVE ENTRANCE, MR. MCCLELLAN.
YES, VERY IMPRESSIVE. YOU'RE JUST IN TIME TO ESCORT YOURSELF AND YOUR TWO FRIENDS TO THE DOOR. DON'T COME AGAIN.
IT'S NOT GOING TO BE THAT EASY, BARASSO. I THINK YOU'LL BE GOING ON A LITTLE RIDE WITH US.
ON WHAT CHARGE? YOU HAVE NOTHING ON ME.
HE'S RIGHT. WE DON'T HAVE ANYTHING... YET. LET'S GO.
WHAT ABOUT KIDNAPPING? OR GUN POSSES-SION?
KID-NAPPING? DON'T BE ABSURD.
AND YOU CAN CHECK WITH THE MAYOR'S OFFICE FOR THE CLUB'S GUN PERMIT.
LET IT GO, TIFFANY. WE'LL GET HIM. JUST NOT NOW.

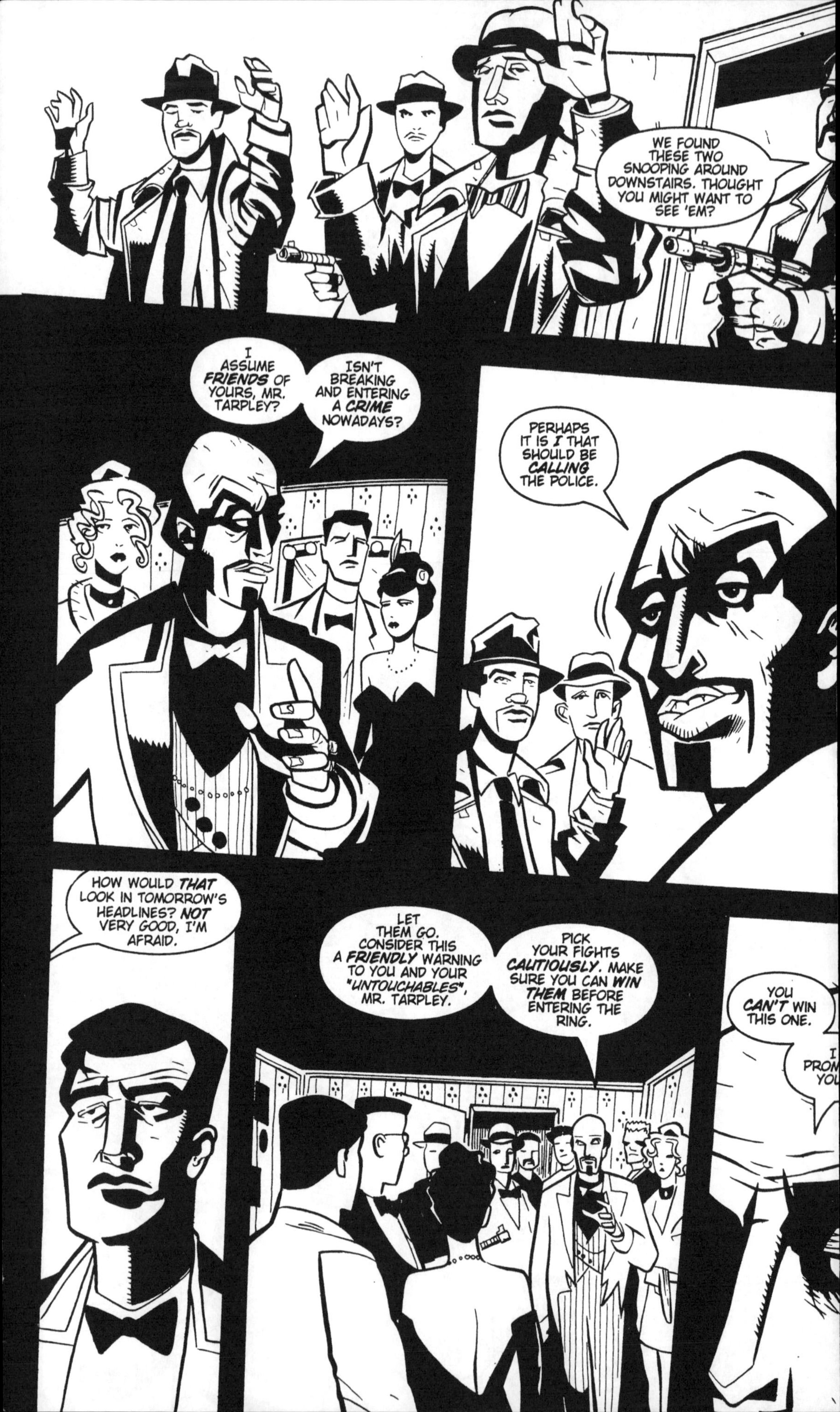
WE FOUND THESE TWO SNOOPING AROUND DOWNSTAIRS. THOUGHT YOU MIGHT WANT TO SEE 'EM?
I ASSUME **FRIENDS** OF YOURS, MR. TARPLEY?
ISN'T BREAKING AND ENTERING A **CRIME** NOWADAYS?
PERHAPS IT IS ***I*** THAT SHOULD BE **CALLING** THE POLICE.
HOW WOULD **THAT** LOOK IN TOMORROW'S HEADLINES? **NOT** VERY GOOD, I'M AFRAID.
LET THEM GO. CONSIDER THIS A **FRIENDLY** WARNING TO YOU AND YOUR "**UNTOUCHABLES**", MR. TARPLEY.
PICK YOUR FIGHTS **CAUTIOUSLY**. MAKE SURE YOU CAN **WIN THEM** BEFORE ENTERING THE RING.
YOU **CAN'T** WIN THIS ONE.

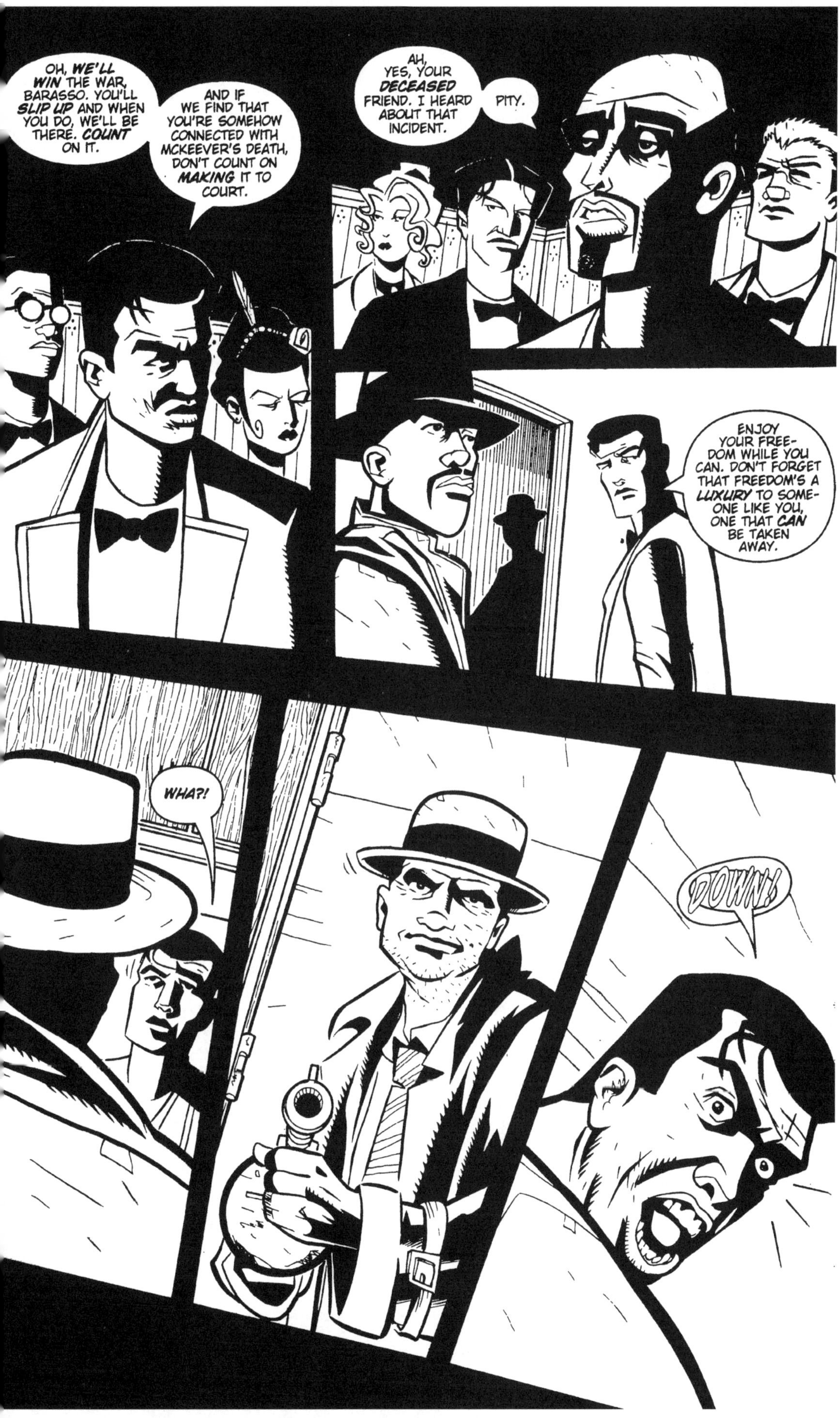
OH, WE'LL WIN THE WAR, BARASSO. YOU'LL SLIP UP AND WHEN YOU DO, WE'LL BE THERE. COUNT ON IT.
AND IF WE FIND THAT YOU'RE SOMEHOW CONNECTED WITH MCKEEVER'S DEATH, DON'T COUNT ON MAKING IT TO COURT.
AH, YES, YOUR DECEASED FRIEND. I HEARD ABOUT THAT INCIDENT.
PITY.
ENJOY YOUR FREE-DOM WHILE YOU CAN. DON'T FORGET THAT FREEDOM'S A LUXURY TO SOME-ONE LIKE YOU, ONE THAT CAN BE TAKEN AWAY.
WHA?!
DOWN!

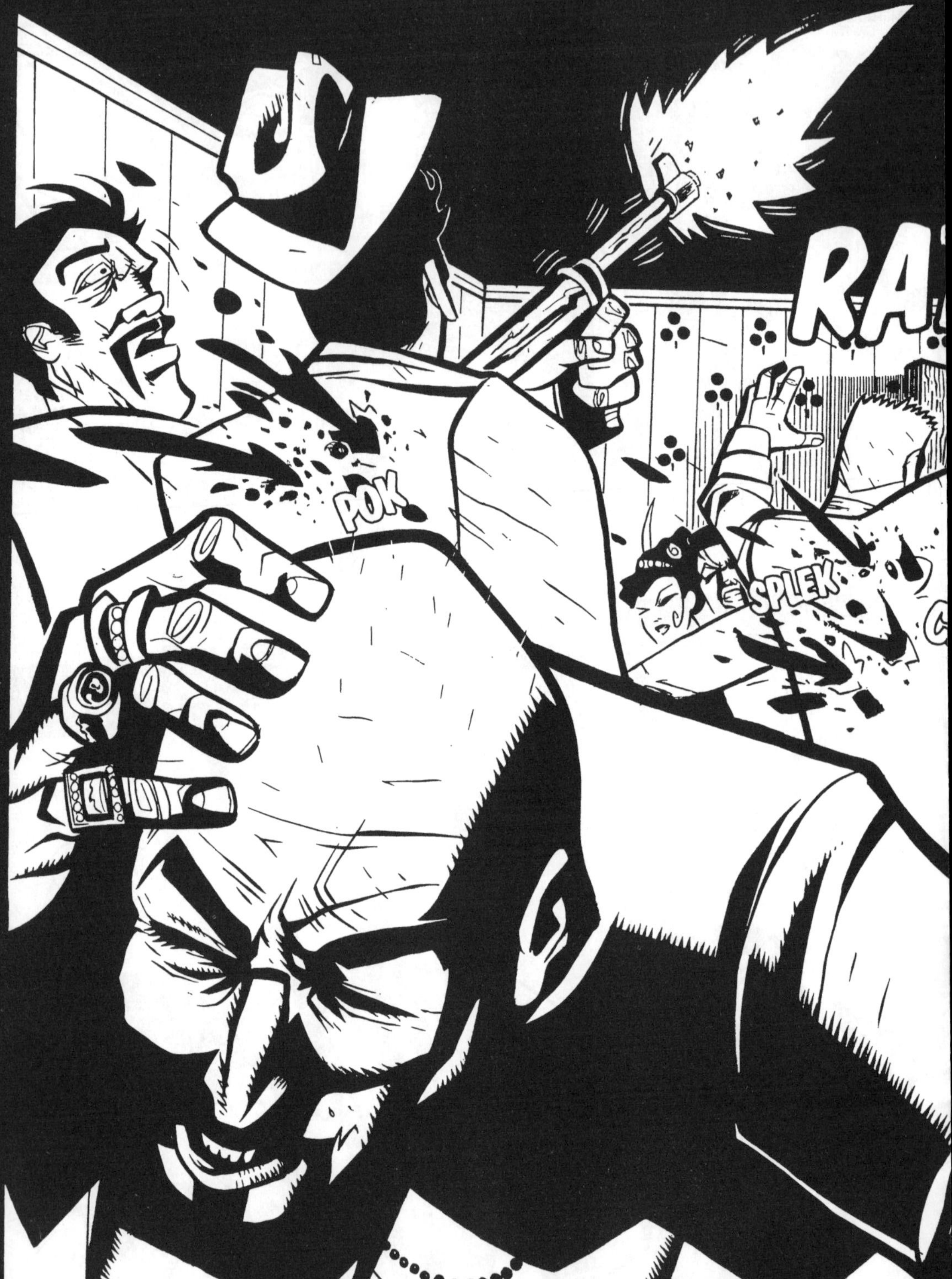
POK
SPLEK

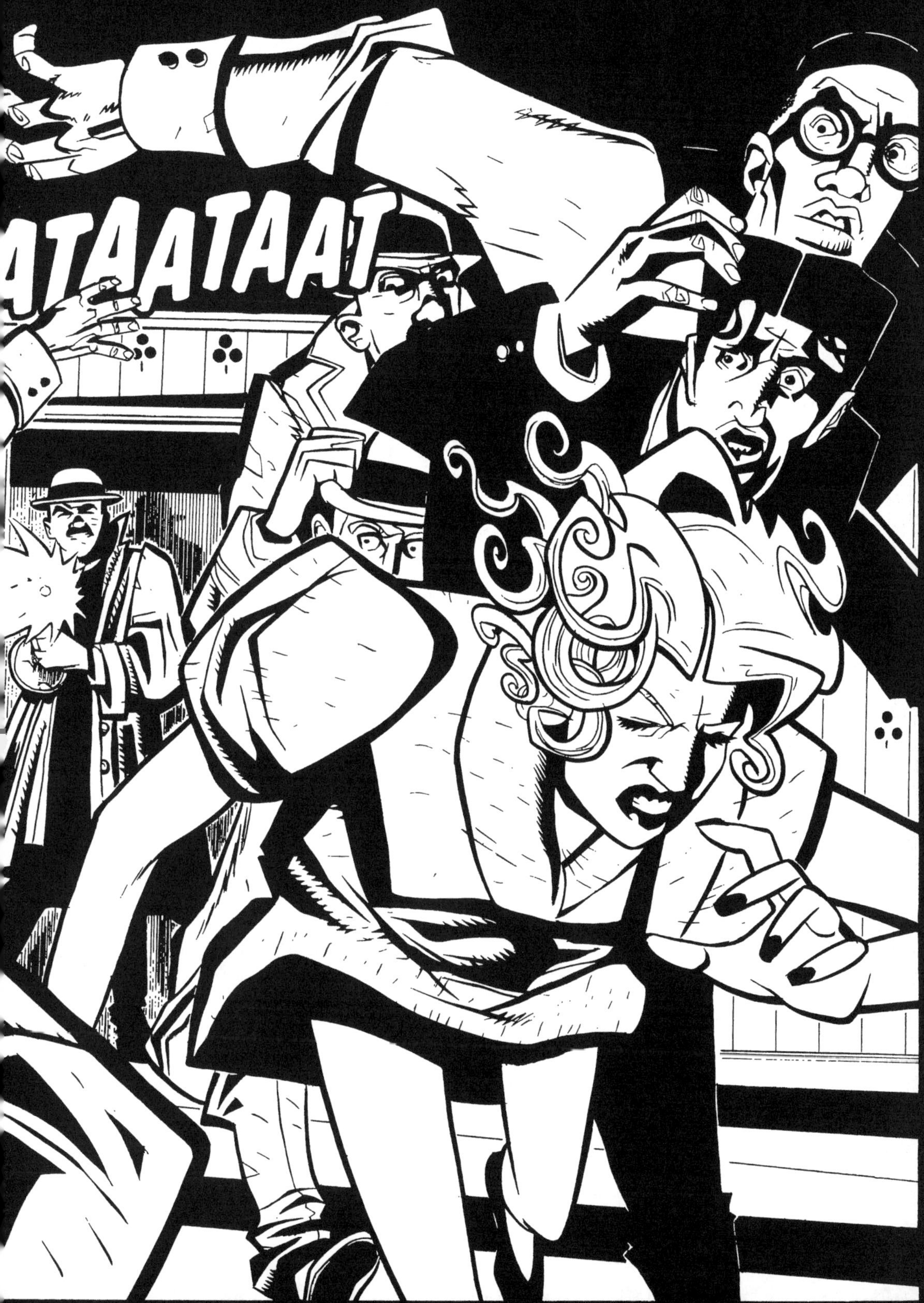
ATAATAAT

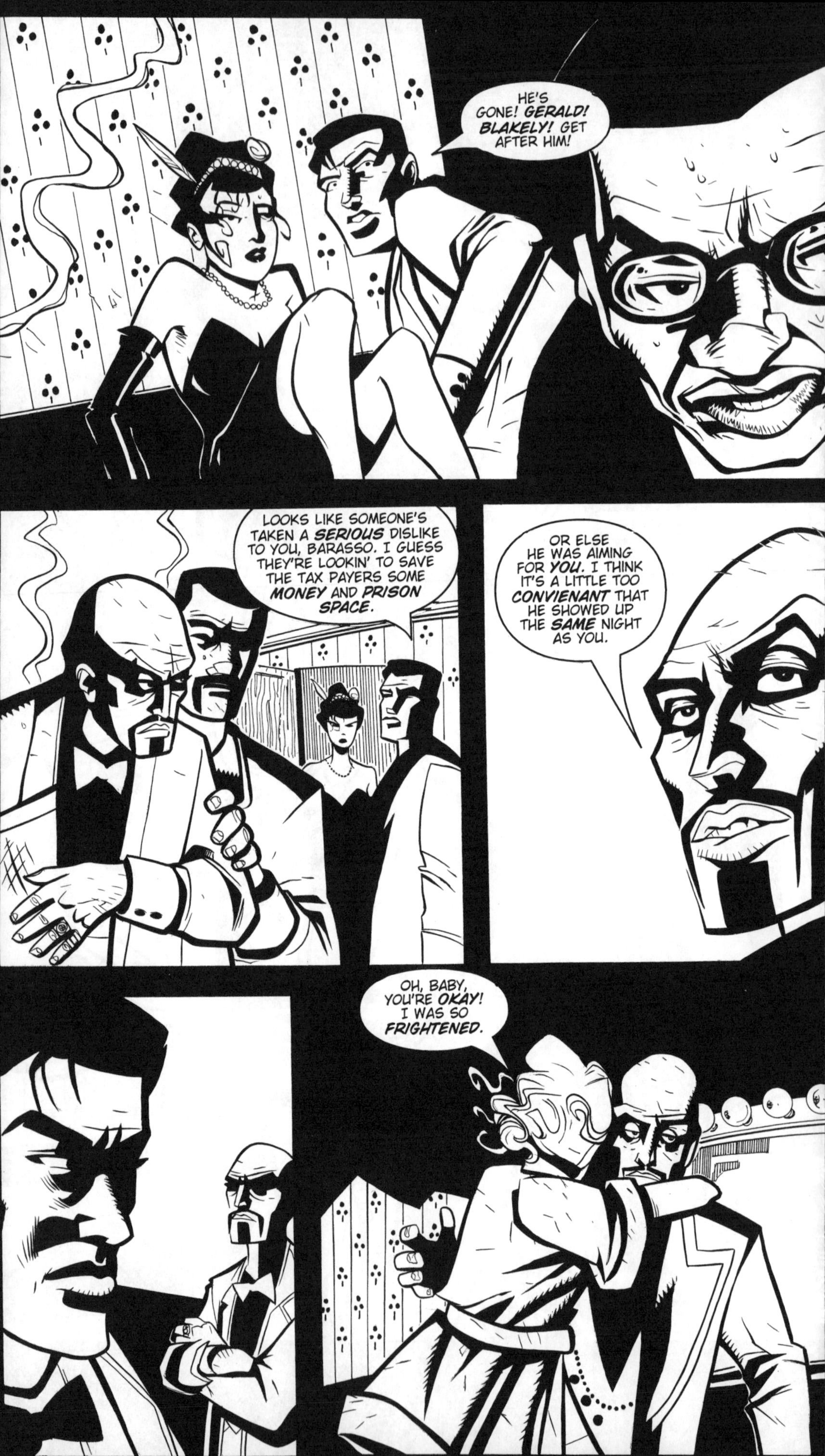
HE'S GONE! GERALD! BLAKELY! GET AFTER HIM!
LOOKS LIKE SOMEONE'S TAKEN A SERIOUS DISLIKE TO YOU, BARASSO. I GUESS THEY'RE LOOKIN' TO SAVE THE TAX PAYERS SOME MONEY AND PRISON SPACE.
OR ELSE HE WAS AIMING FOR YOU. I THINK IT'S A LITTLE TOO CONVIENANT THAT HE SHOWED UP THE SAME NIGHT AS YOU.
OH, BABY, YOU'RE OKAY! I WAS SO FRIGHTENED.

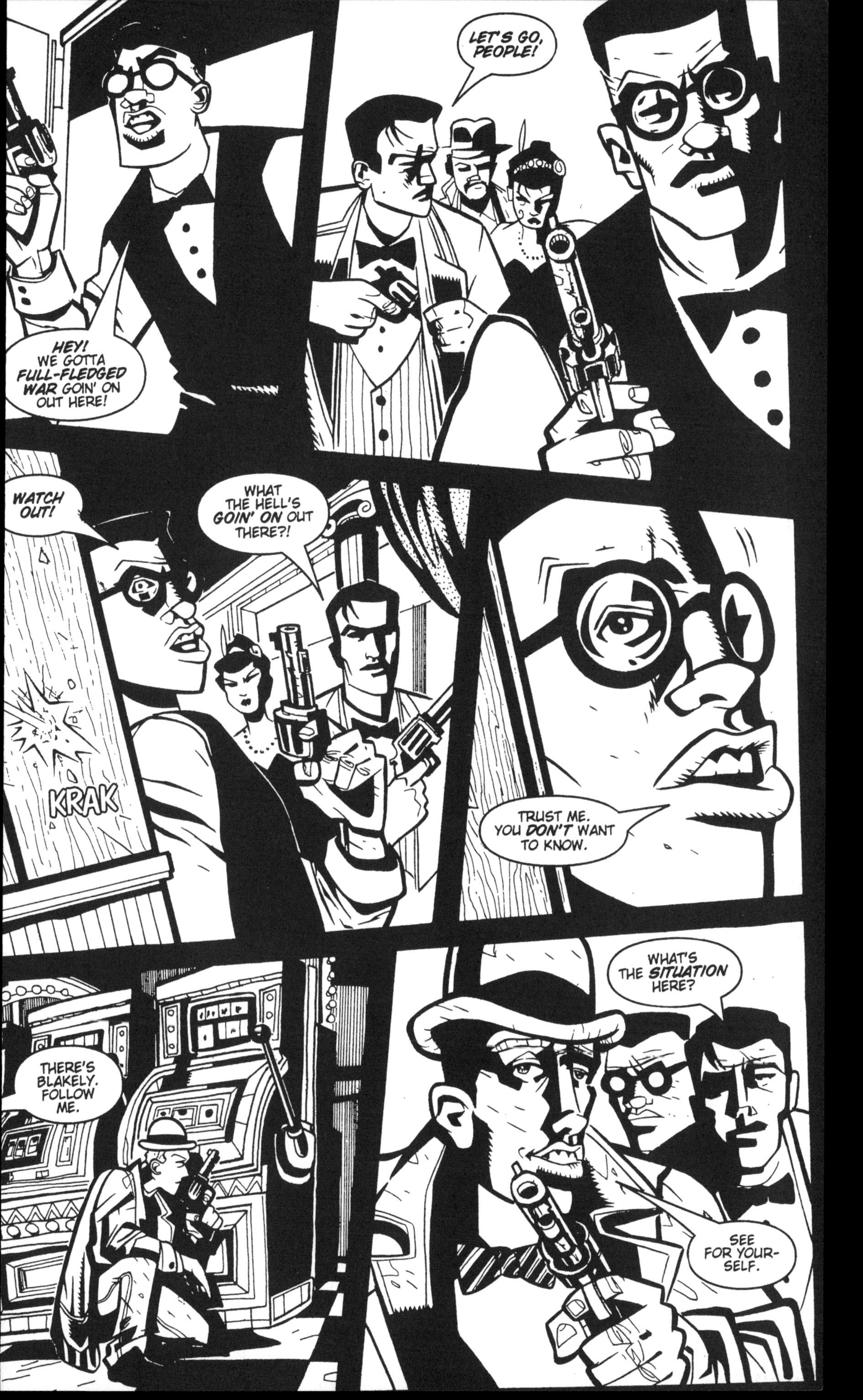
HEY! WE GOTTA FULL-FLEDGED WAR GOIN' ON OUT HERE!
LET'S GO, PEOPLE!
WATCH OUT!
WHAT THE HELL'S GOIN' ON OUT THERE?!
KRAK
TRUST ME. YOU DON'T WANT TO KNOW.
THERE'S BLAKELY. FOLLOW ME.
WHAT'S THE SITUATION HERE?
SEE FOR YOUR-SELF.

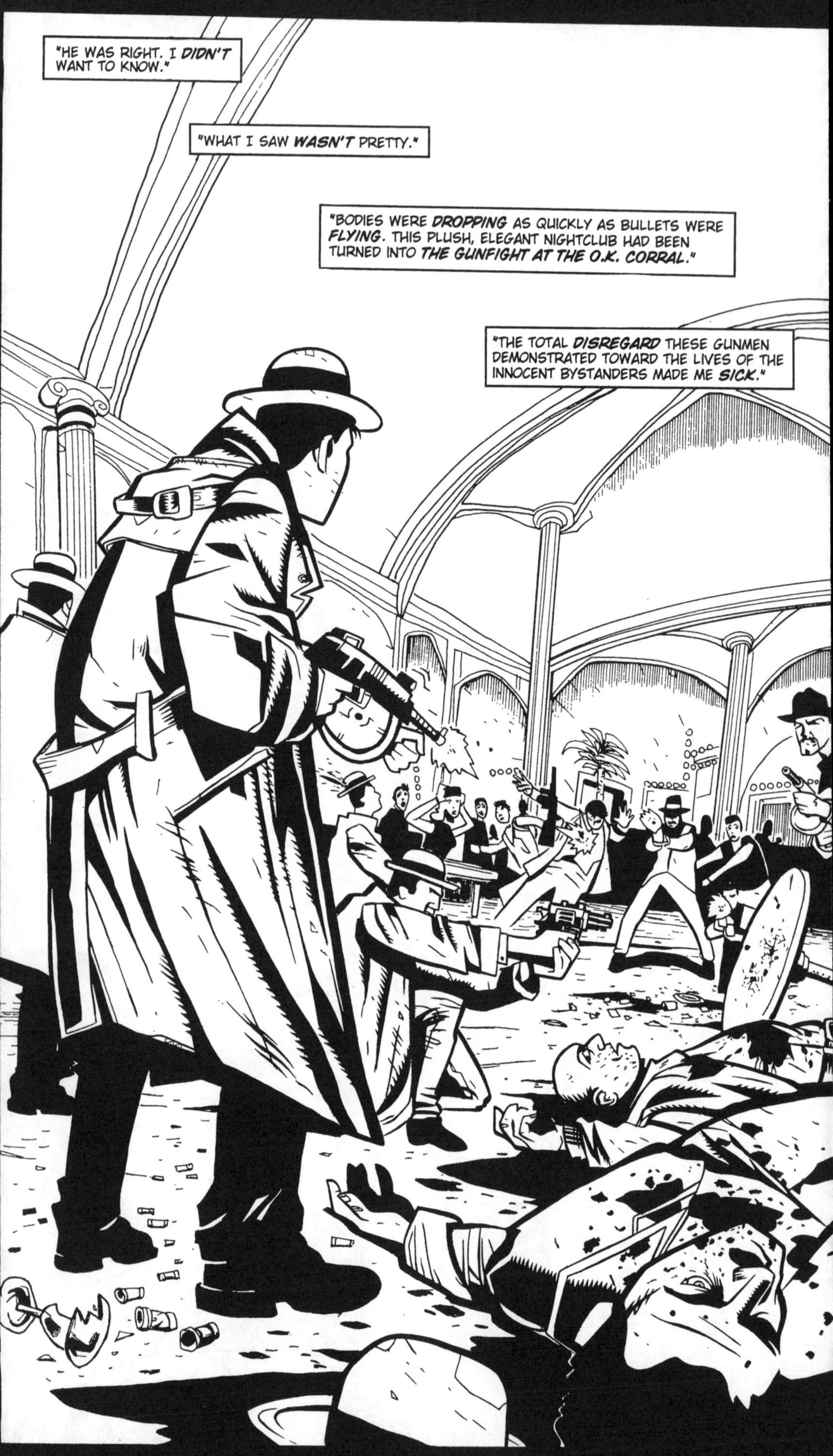
"HE WAS RIGHT. I DIDN'T WANT TO KNOW."
"WHAT I SAW WASN'T PRETTY."
"BODIES WERE DROPPING AS QUICKLY AS BULLETS WERE FLYING. THIS PLUSH, ELEGANT NIGHTCLUB HAD BEEN TURNED INTO THE GUNFIGHT AT THE O.K. CORRAL."
"THE TOTAL DISREGARD THESE GUNMEN DEMONSTRATED TOWARD THE LIVES OF THE INNOCENT BYSTANDERS MADE ME SICK."

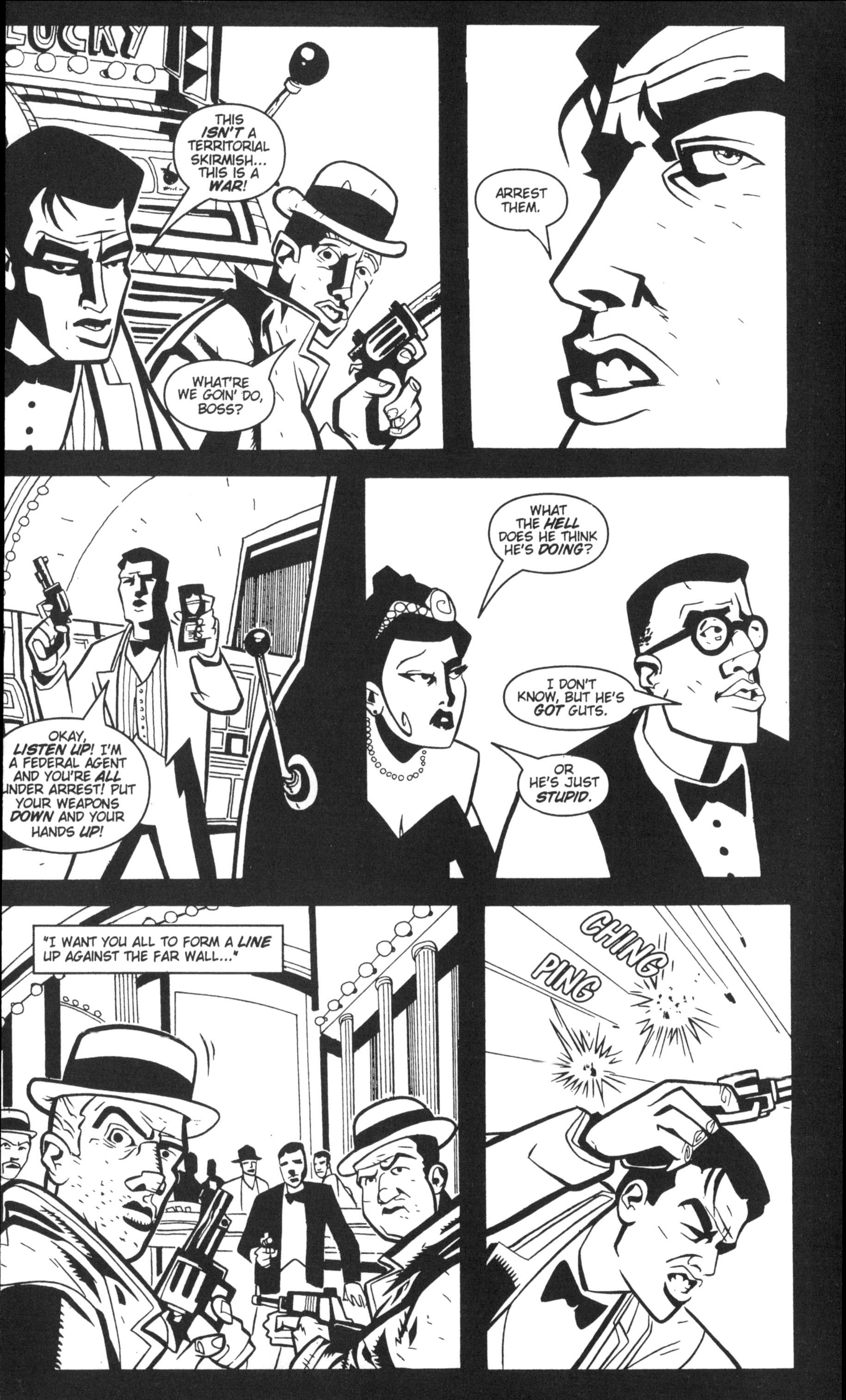
LUCKY
THIS ISN'T A TERRITORIAL SKIRMISH... THIS IS A WAR!
WHAT'RE WE GOIN' DO, BOSS?
ARREST THEM.
OKAY, LISTEN UP! I'M A FEDERAL AGENT AND YOU'RE ALL UNDER ARREST! PUT YOUR WEAPONS DOWN AND YOUR HANDS UP!
WHAT THE HELL DOES HE THINK HE'S DOING?
I DON'T KNOW, BUT HE'S GOT GUTS.
OR HE'S JUST STUPID.
"I WANT YOU ALL TO FORM A LINE UP AGAINST THE FAR WALL..."
CHING
PING

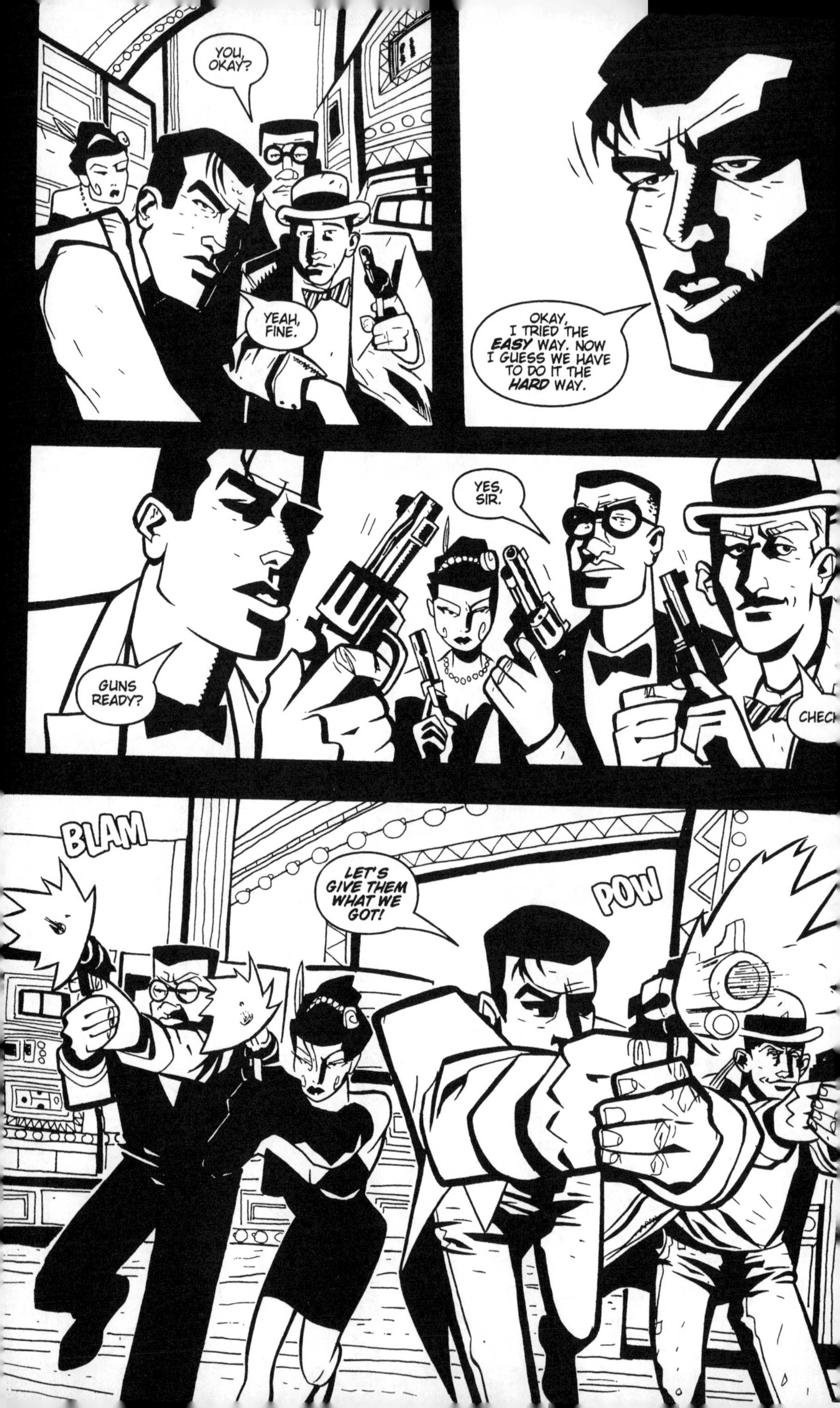

YOU, OKAY?
YEAH, FINE.
OKAY, I TRIED THE *EASY* WAY. NOW I GUESS WE HAVE TO DO IT THE *HARD* WAY.
GUNS READY?
YES, SIR.
CHECK
BLAM
LET'S GIVE THEM WHAT WE GOT!
POW

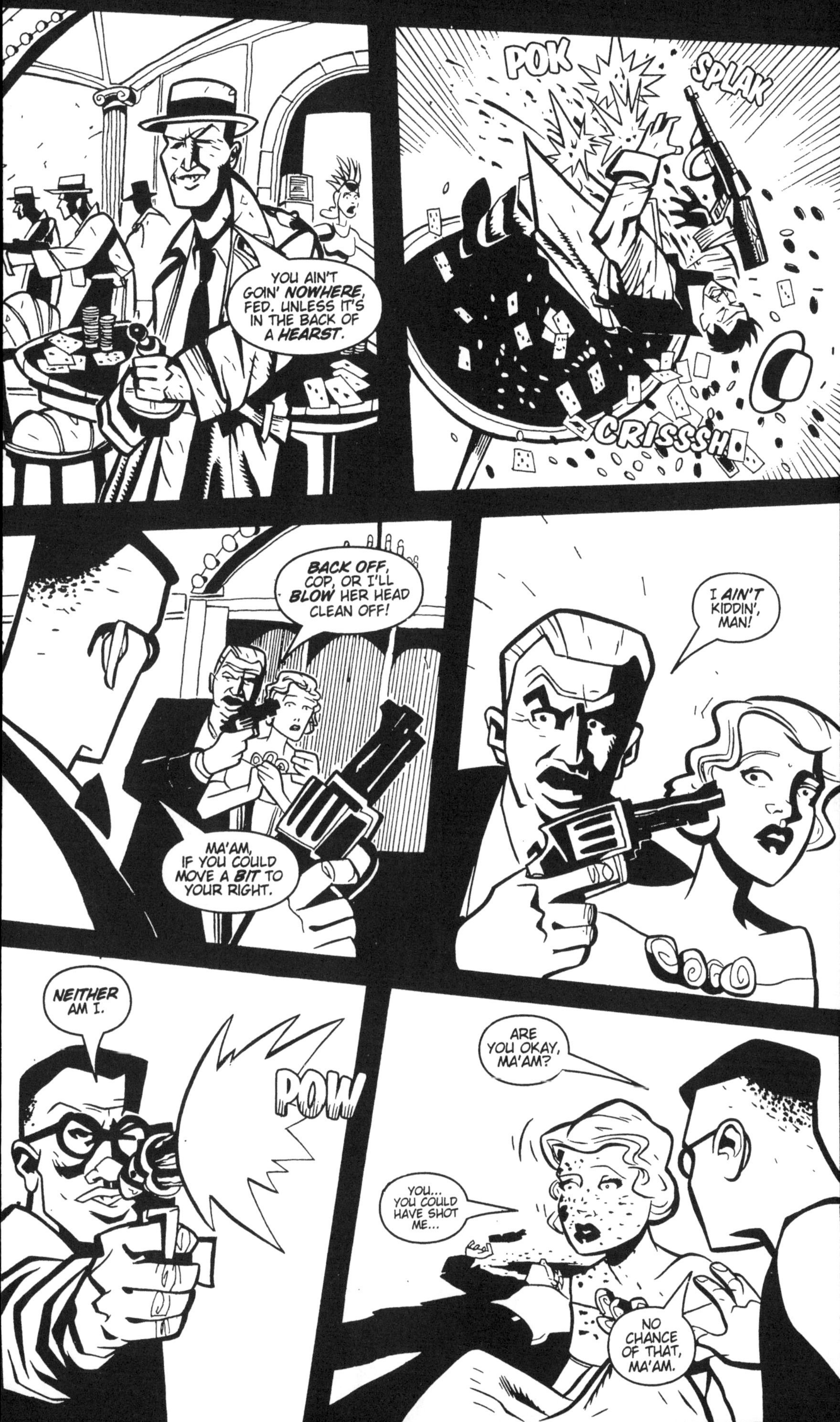
YOU AIN'T GOIN' NOWHERE, FED. UNLESS IT'S IN THE BACK OF A HEARST.
POK
SPLAK
CRISSSH
BACK OFF, COP, OR I'LL BLOW HER HEAD CLEAN OFF!
MA'AM, IF YOU COULD MOVE A BIT TO YOUR RIGHT.
I AIN'T KIDDIN', MAN!
NEITHER AM I.
POW
ARE YOU OKAY, MA'AM?
YOU... YOU COULD HAVE SHOT ME...
NO CHANCE OF THAT, MA'AM.

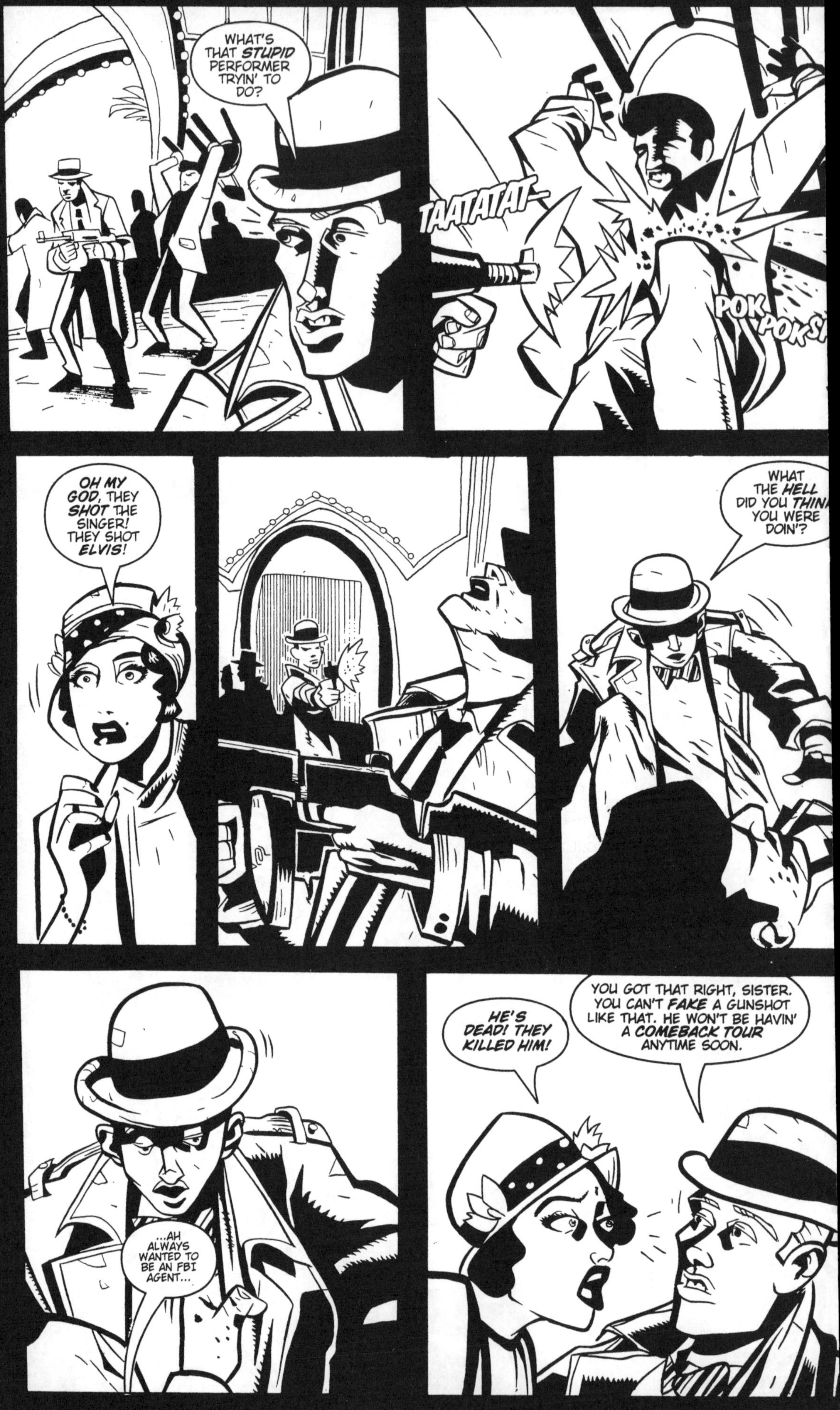

WHAT'S THAT STUPID PERFORMER TRYIN' TO DO?
TAATATAT—
POK POK
OH MY GOD, THEY SHOT THE SINGER! THEY SHOT ELVIS!
WHAT THE HELL DID YOU THINK YOU WERE DOIN'?
...AH ALWAYS WANTED TO BE AN FBI AGENT...
HE'S DEAD! THEY KILLED HIM!
YOU GOT THAT RIGHT, SISTER. YOU CAN'T FAKE A GUNSHOT LIKE THAT. HE WON'T BE HAVIN' A COMEBACK TOUR ANYTIME SOON.

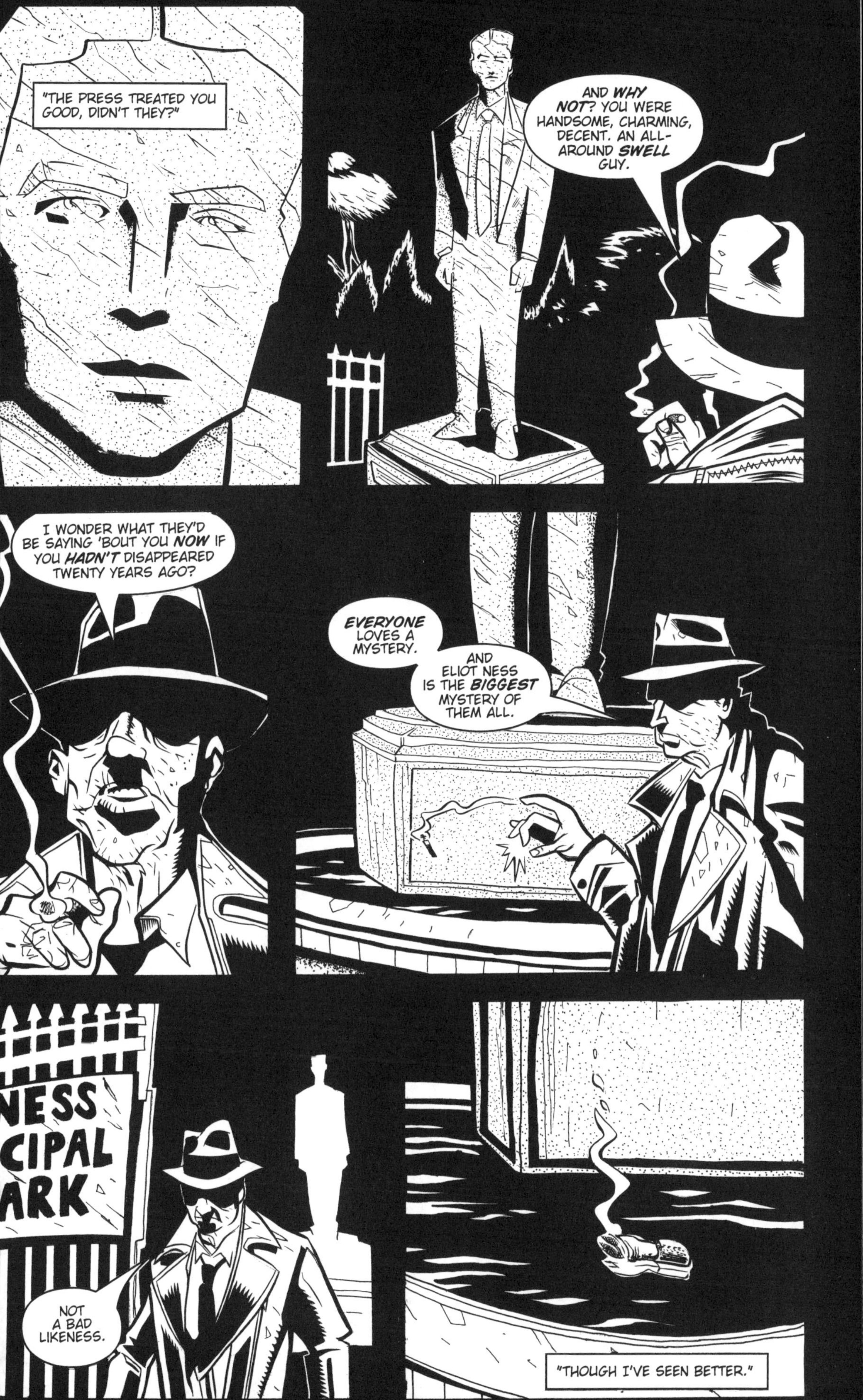
"THE PRESS TREATED YOU GOOD, DIDN'T THEY?"
AND WHY NOT? YOU WERE HANDSOME, CHARMING, DECENT. AN ALL-AROUND SWELL GUY.
I WONDER WHAT THEY'D BE SAYING 'BOUT YOU NOW IF YOU HADN'T DISAPPEARED TWENTY YEARS AGO?
EVERYONE LOVES A MYSTERY.
AND ELIOT NESS IS THE BIGGEST MYSTERY OF THEM ALL.
NESS
CIPAL
ARK
NOT A BAD LIKENESS.
"THOUGH I'VE SEEN BETTER."

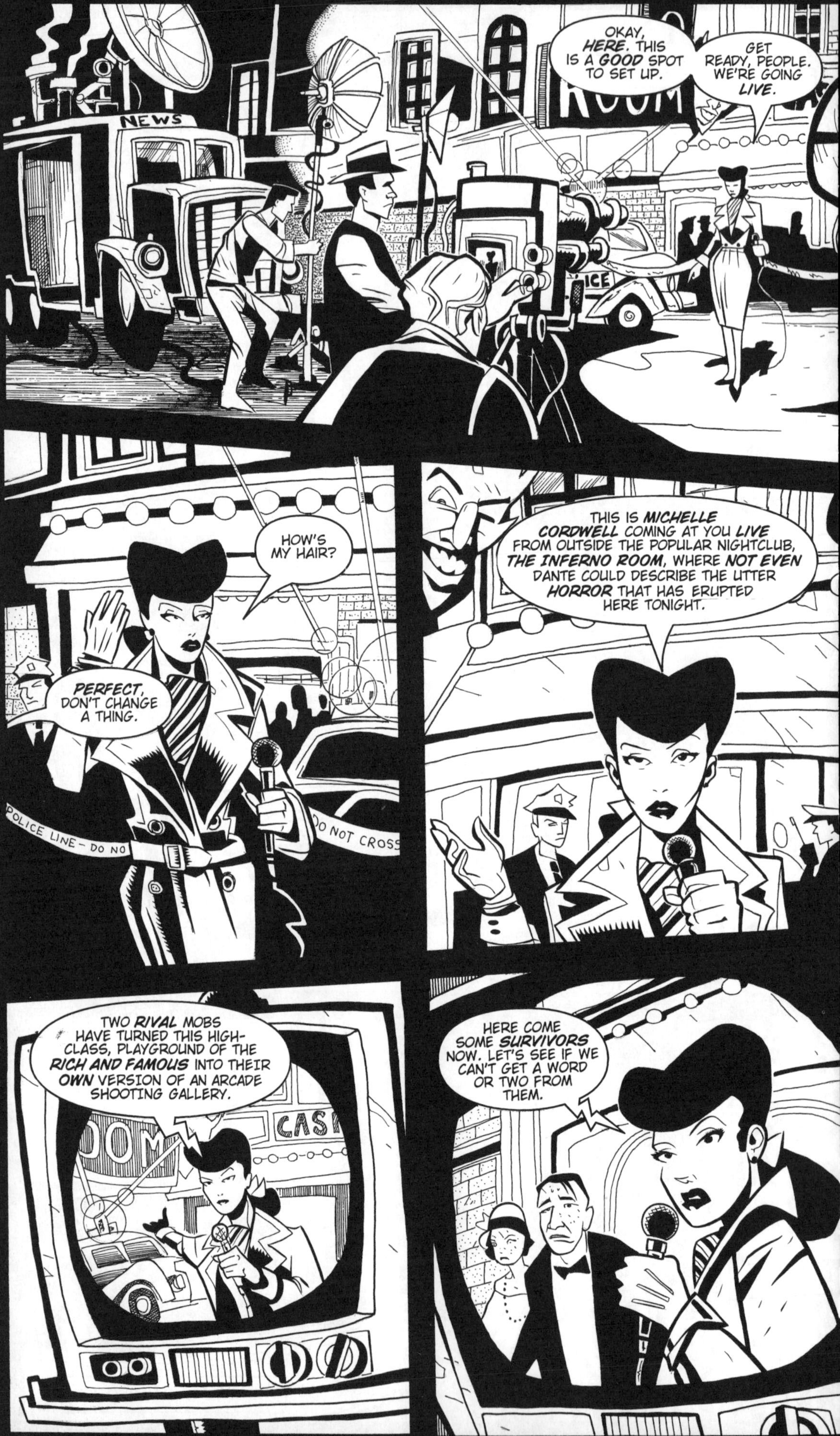
NEWS
ROOM
OKAY, HERE. THIS IS A GOOD SPOT TO SET UP.
GET READY, PEOPLE. WE'RE GOING LIVE.
ICE
HOW'S MY HAIR?
PERFECT, DON'T CHANGE A THING.
POLICE LINE - DO NO
DO NOT CROSS
THIS IS MICHELLE CORDWELL COMING AT YOU LIVE FROM OUTSIDE THE POPULAR NIGHTCLUB, THE INFERNO ROOM, WHERE NOT EVEN DANTE COULD DESCRIBE THE UTTER HORROR THAT HAS ERUPTED HERE TONIGHT.
TWO RIVAL MOBS HAVE TURNED THIS HIGH-CLASS, PLAYGROUND OF THE RICH AND FAMOUS INTO THEIR OWN VERSION OF AN ARCADE SHOOTING GALLERY.
OOM
CAS
HERE COME SOME SURVIVORS NOW. LET'S SEE IF WE CAN'T GET A WORD OR TWO FROM THEM.

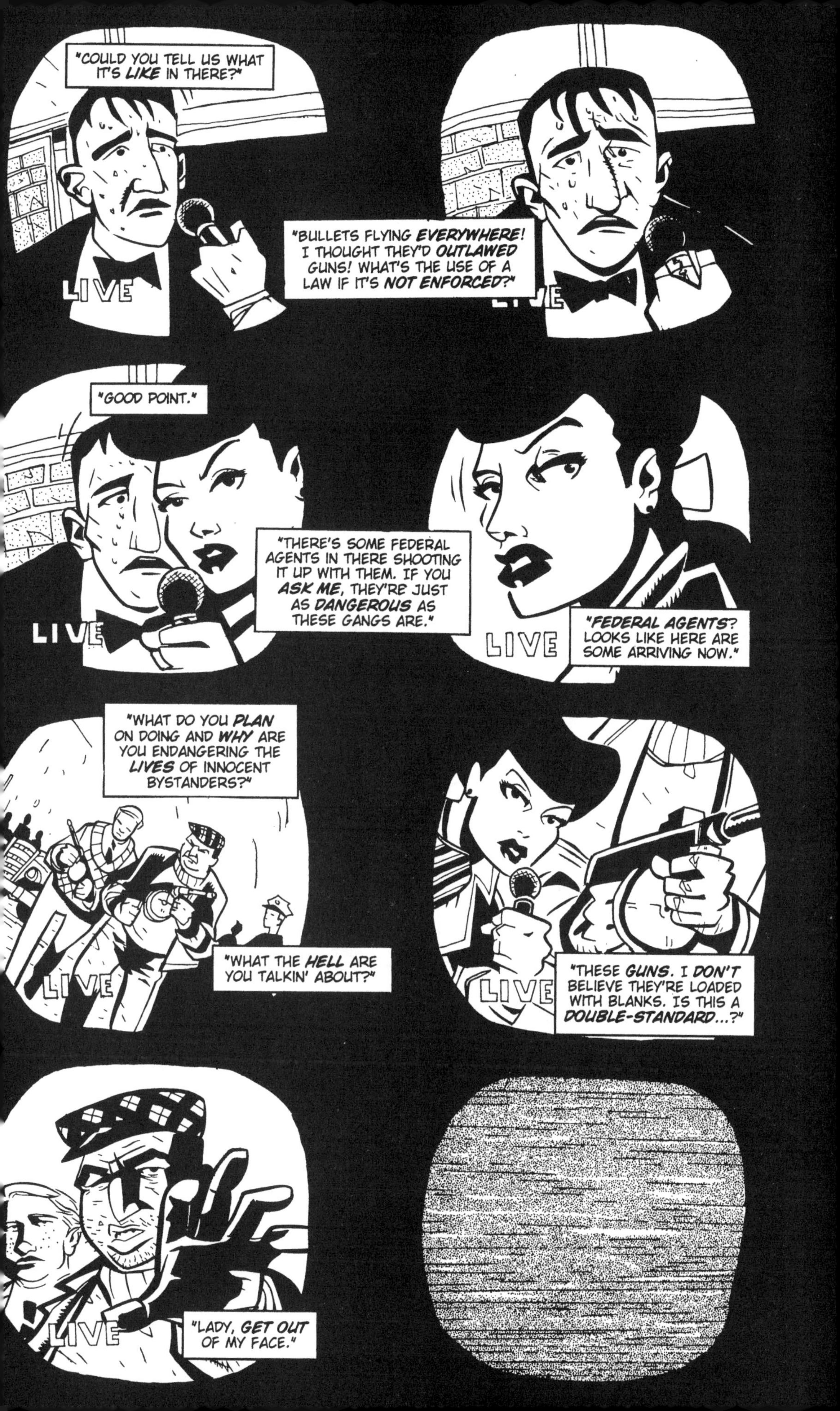

"COULD YOU TELL US WHAT IT'S LIKE IN THERE?"
LIVE
"BULLETS FLYING EVERYWHERE! I THOUGHT THEY'D OUTLAWED GUNS! WHAT'S THE USE OF A LAW IF IT'S NOT ENFORCED?"
"GOOD POINT."
LIVE
"THERE'S SOME FEDERAL AGENTS IN THERE SHOOTING IT UP WITH THEM. IF YOU ASK ME, THEY'RE JUST AS DANGEROUS AS THESE GANGS ARE."
LIVE
"FEDERAL AGENTS? LOOKS LIKE HERE ARE SOME ARRIVING NOW."
"WHAT DO YOU PLAN ON DOING AND WHY ARE YOU ENDANGERING THE LIVES OF INNOCENT BYSTANDERS?"
LIVE
"WHAT THE HELL ARE YOU TALKIN' ABOUT?"
LIVE
"THESE GUNS. I DON'T BELIEVE THEY'RE LOADED WITH BLANKS. IS THIS A DOUBLE-STANDARD...?"
LIVE
"LADY, GET OUT OF MY FACE."

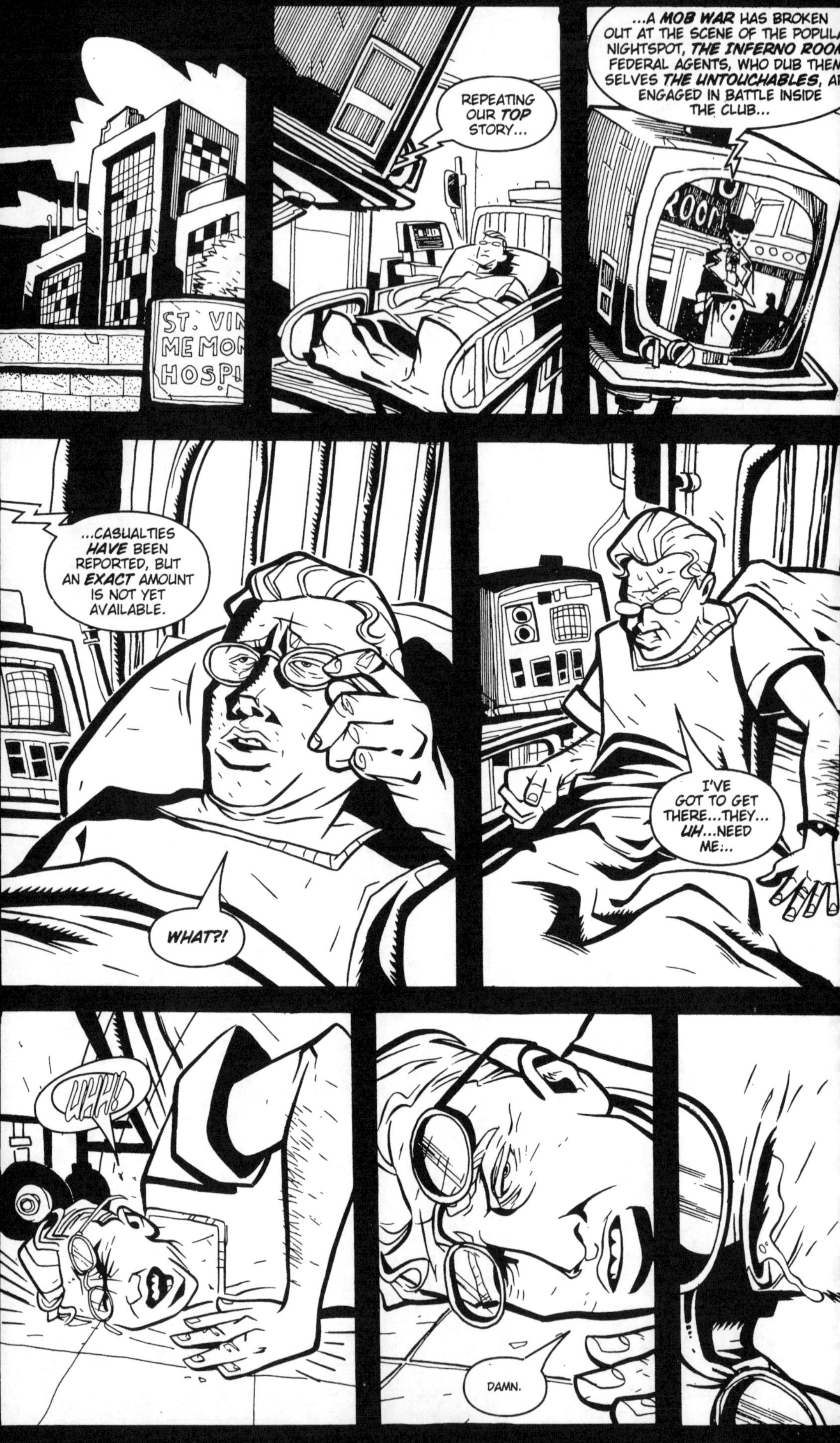

ST. VIN
MEMOR
HOSP
REPEATING OUR TOP STORY...
...A MOB WAR HAS BROKEN OUT AT THE SCENE OF THE POPULA NIGHTSPOT, THE INFERNO ROOM FEDERAL AGENTS, WHO DUB THEM SELVES THE UNTOUCHABLES, A ENGAGED IN BATTLE INSIDE THE CLUB...
ROOM
...CASUALTIES HAVE BEEN REPORTED, BUT AN EXACT AMOUNT IS NOT YET AVAILABLE.
WHAT?!
I'VE GOT TO GET THERE...THEY... UH...NEED ME:..
UHH!
DAMN.

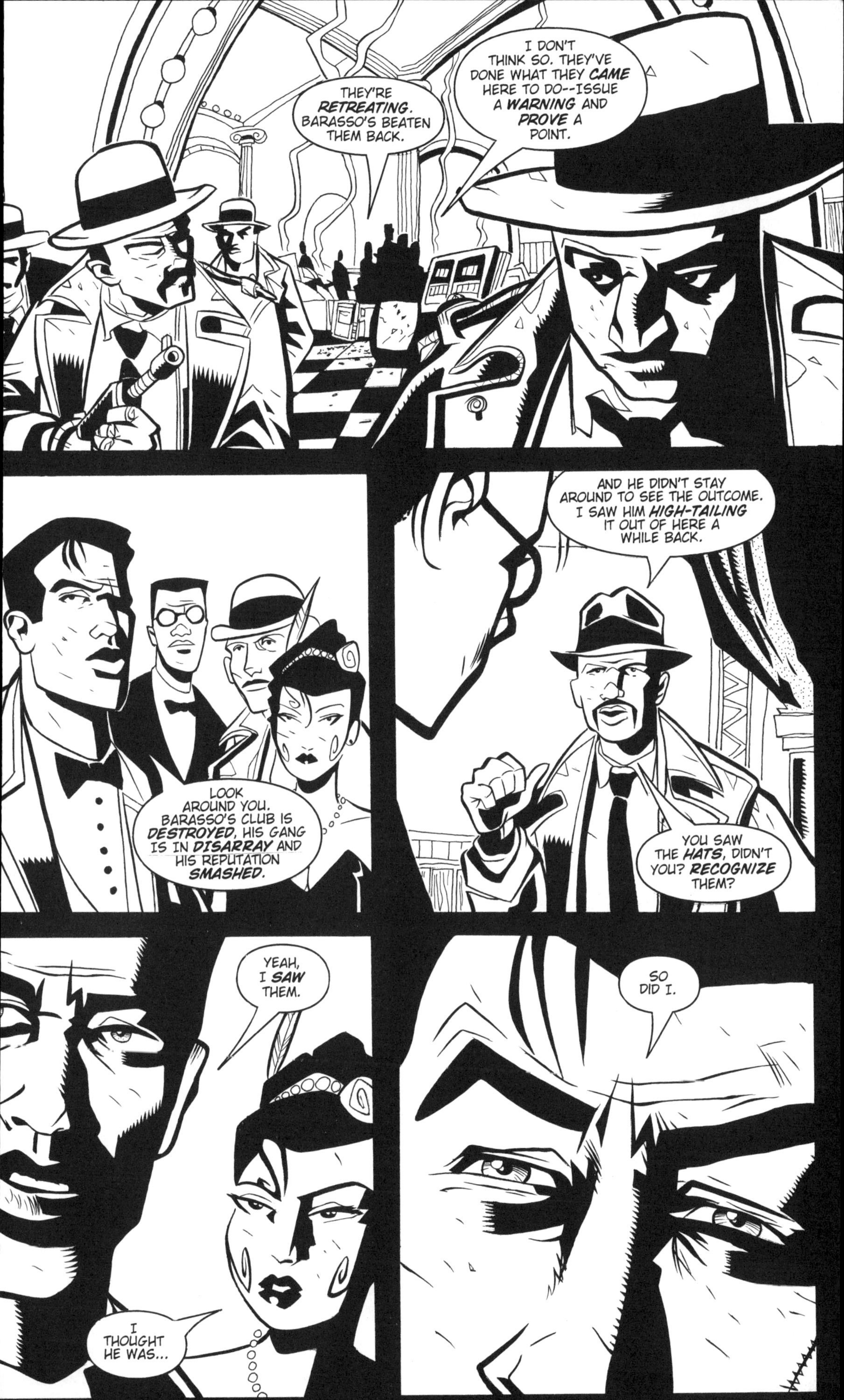
THEY'RE RETREATING. BARASSO'S BEATEN THEM BACK.
I DON'T THINK SO. THEY'VE DONE WHAT THEY CAME HERE TO DO--ISSUE A WARNING AND PROVE A POINT.
LOOK AROUND YOU. BARASSO'S CLUB IS DESTROYED, HIS GANG IS IN DISARRAY AND HIS REPUTATION SMASHED.
AND HE DIDN'T STAY AROUND TO SEE THE OUTCOME. I SAW HIM HIGH-TAILING IT OUT OF HERE A WHILE BACK.
YOU SAW THE HATS, DIDN'T YOU? RECOGNIZE THEM?
YEAH, I SAW THEM.
I THOUGHT HE WAS...
SO DID I.

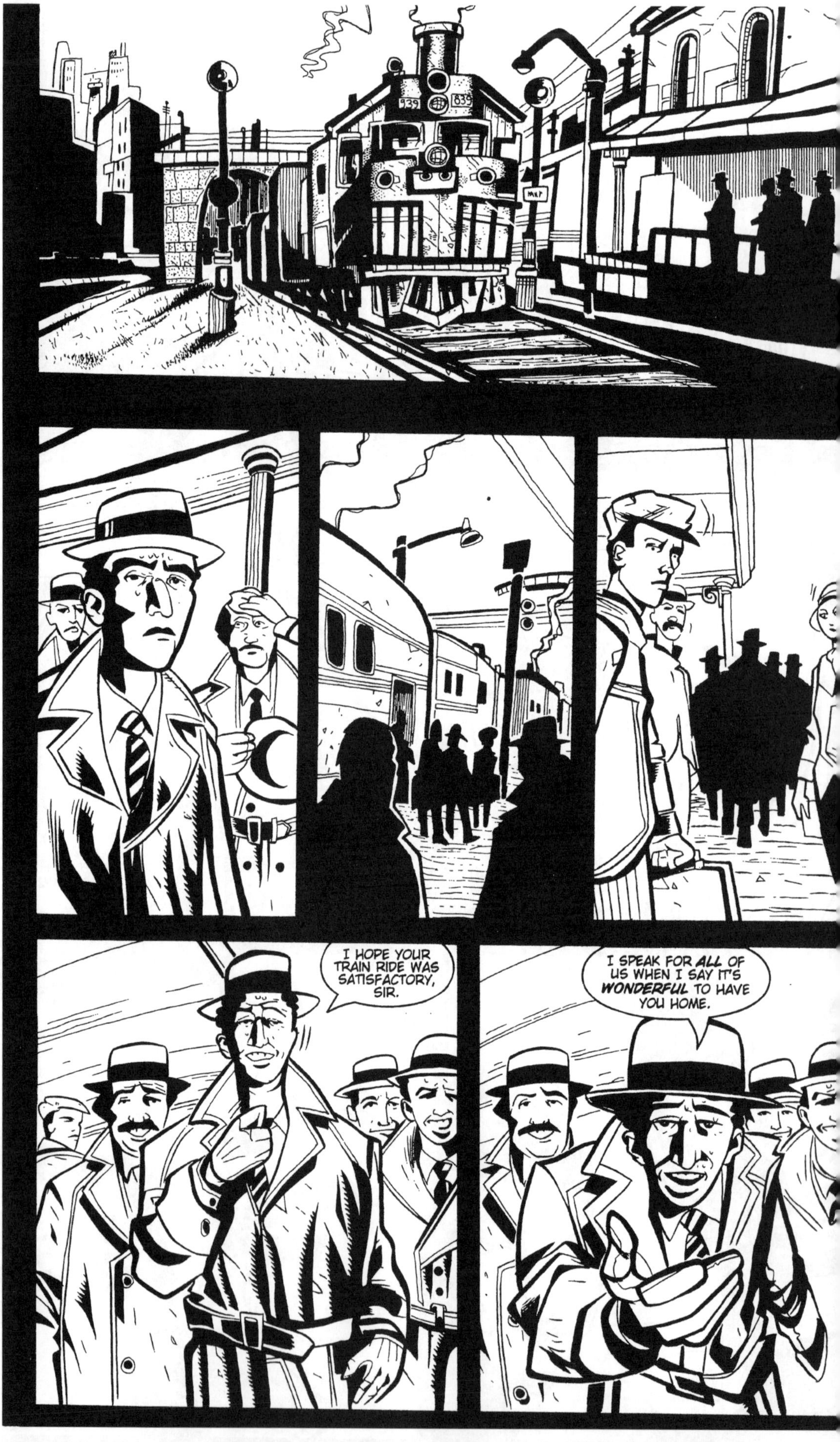
I HOPE YOUR TRAIN RIDE WAS SATISFACTORY, SIR.
I SPEAK FOR ALL OF US WHEN I SAY IT'S WONDERFUL TO HAVE YOU HOME.

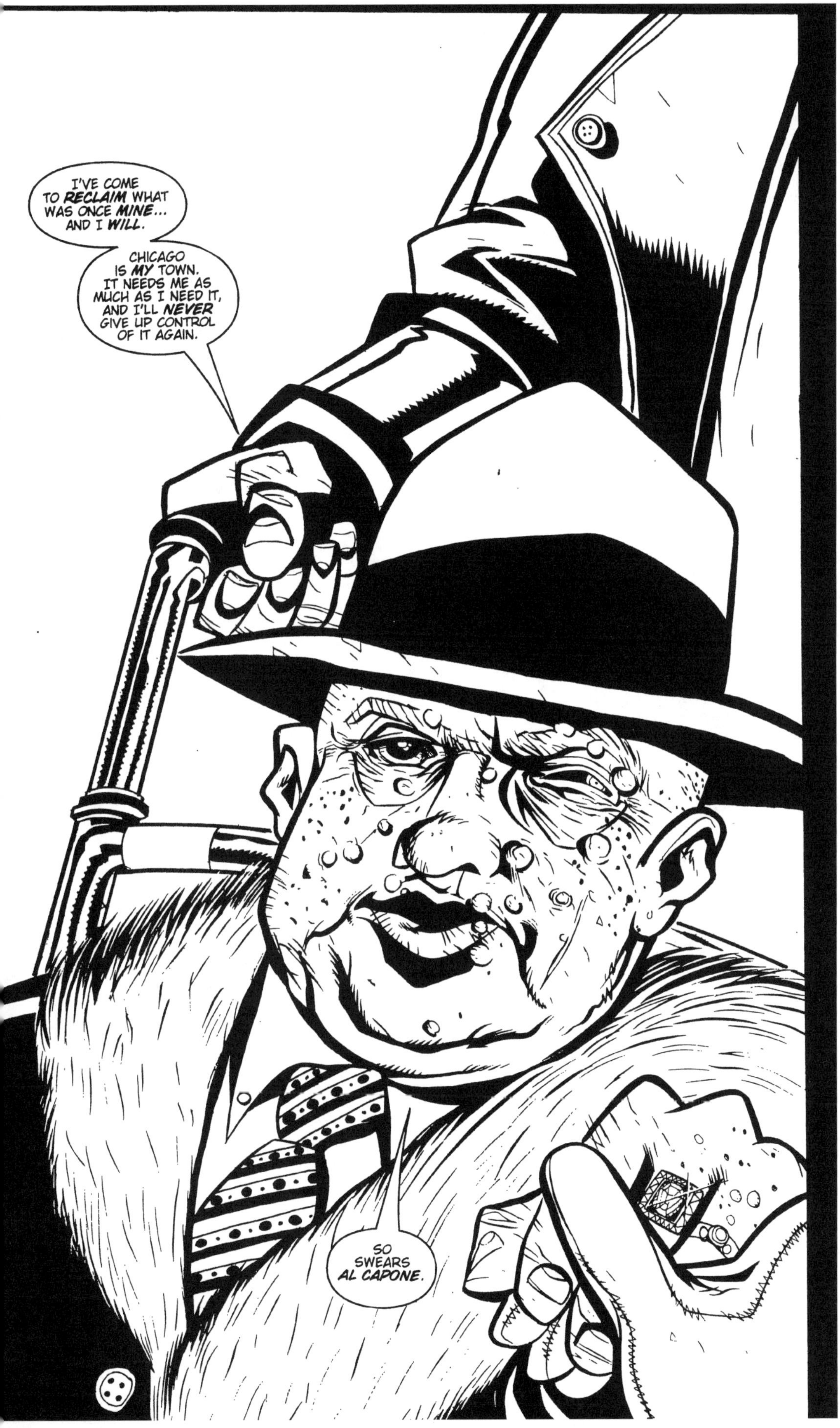

I'VE COME TO RECLAIM WHAT WAS ONCE MINE... AND I WILL.
CHICAGO IS MY TOWN. IT NEEDS ME AS MUCH AS I NEED IT, AND I'LL NEVER GIVE UP CONTROL OF IT AGAIN.
SO SWEARS AL CAPONE.

UNTOUCHABLES

"A NEW BEGINNING"

ACT 4

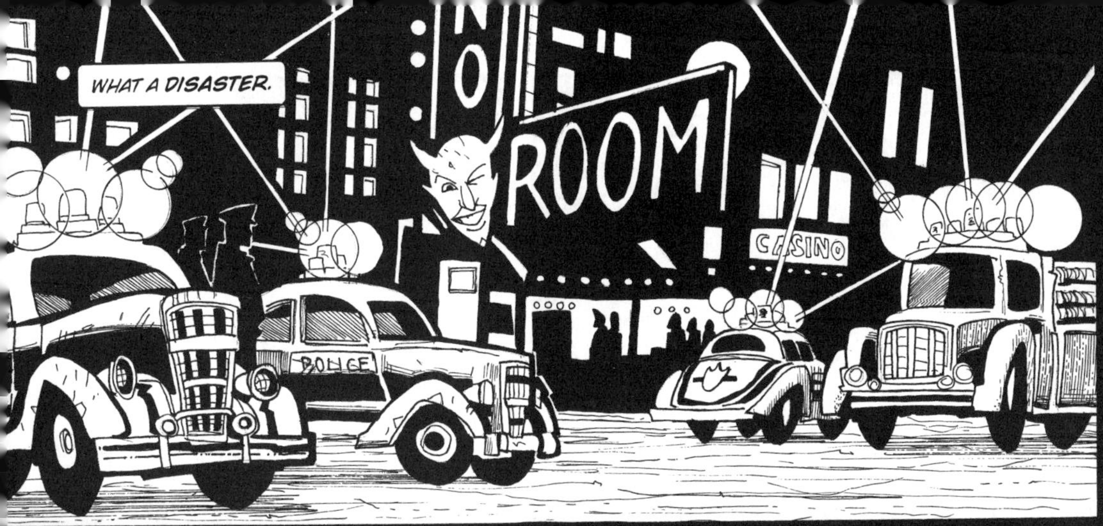
WHAT A DISASTER.
ROOM
CASINO
POLICE

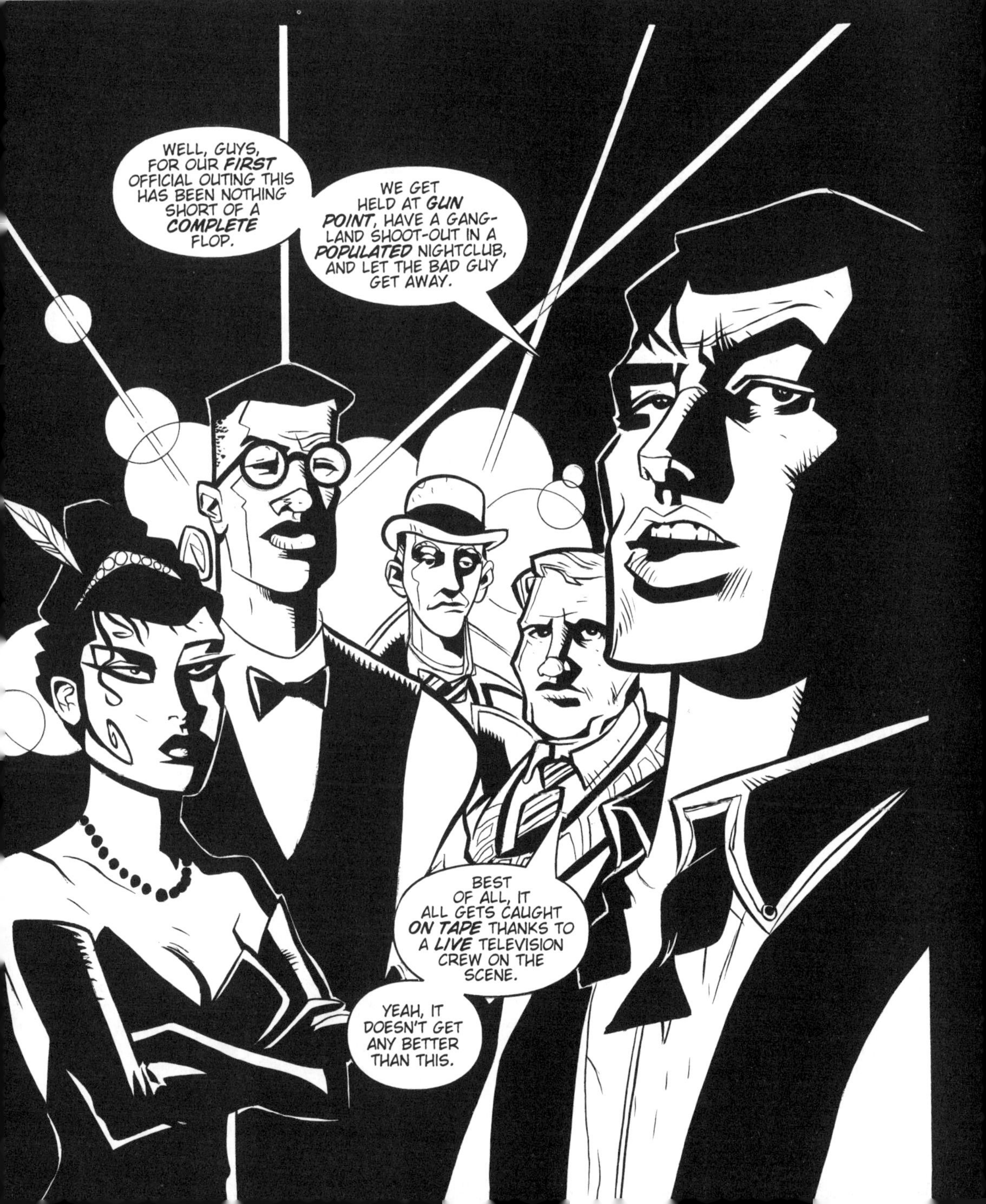
WELL, GUYS, FOR OUR FIRST OFFICIAL OUTING THIS HAS BEEN NOTHING SHORT OF A COMPLETE FLOP.
WE GET HELD AT GUN POINT, HAVE A GANG-LAND SHOOT-OUT IN A POPULATED NIGHTCLUB, AND LET THE BAD GUY GET AWAY.
BEST OF ALL, IT ALL GETS CAUGHT ON TAPE THANKS TO A LIVE TELEVISION CREW ON THE SCENE.
YEAH, IT DOESN'T GET ANY BETTER THAN THIS.

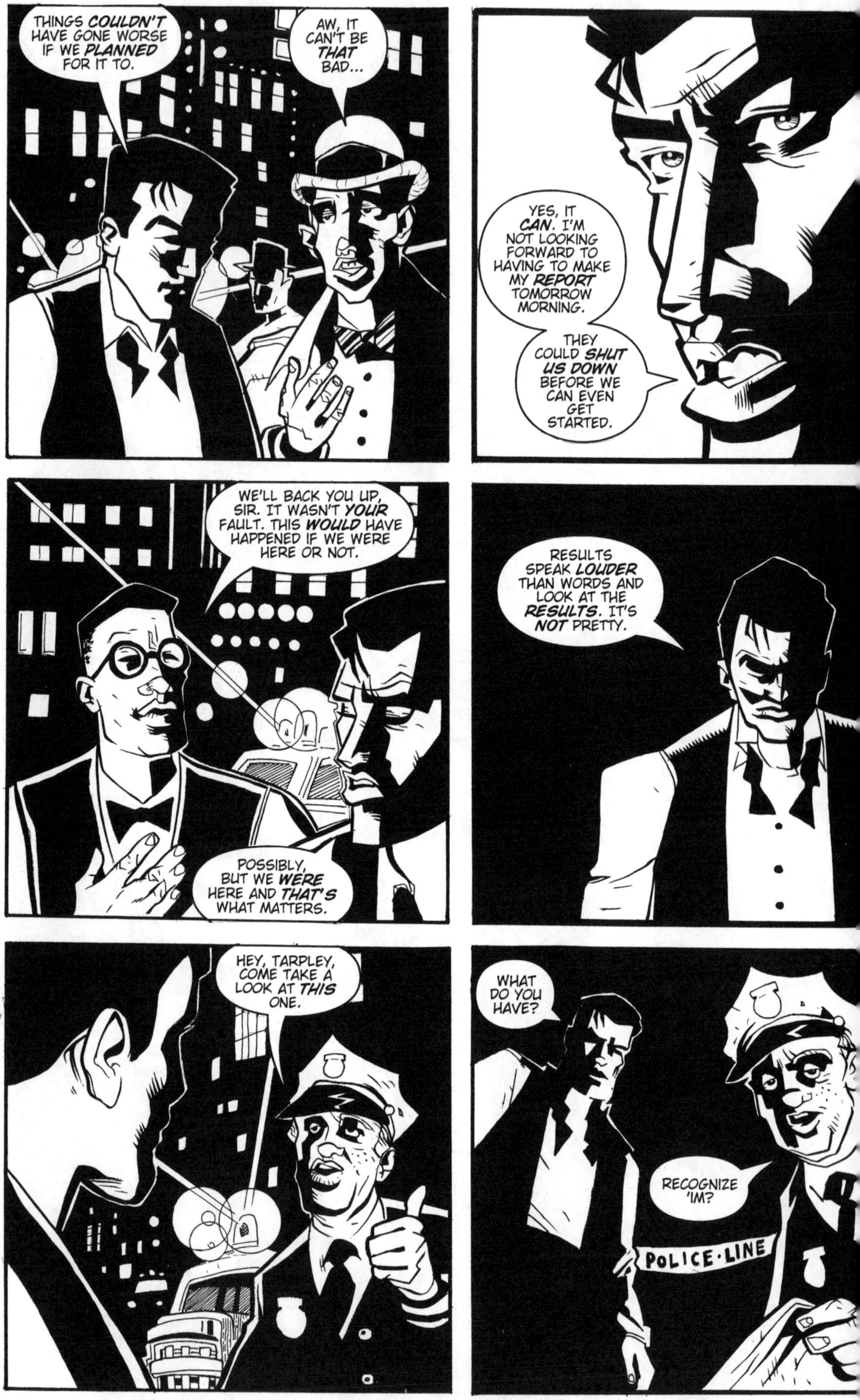
THINGS COULDN'T HAVE GONE WORSE IF WE PLANNED FOR IT TO.
AW, IT CAN'T BE THAT BAD...
YES, IT CAN. I'M NOT LOOKING FORWARD TO HAVING TO MAKE MY REPORT TOMORROW MORNING.
THEY COULD SHUT US DOWN BEFORE WE CAN EVEN GET STARTED.
WE'LL BACK YOU UP, SIR. IT WASN'T YOUR FAULT. THIS WOULD HAVE HAPPENED IF WE WERE HERE OR NOT.
POSSIBLY, BUT WE WERE HERE AND THAT'S WHAT MATTERS.
RESULTS SPEAK LOUDER THAN WORDS AND LOOK AT THE RESULTS. IT'S NOT PRETTY.
HEY, TARPLEY, COME TAKE A LOOK AT THIS ONE.
WHAT DO YOU HAVE?
RECOGNIZE 'IM?
POLICE·LINE

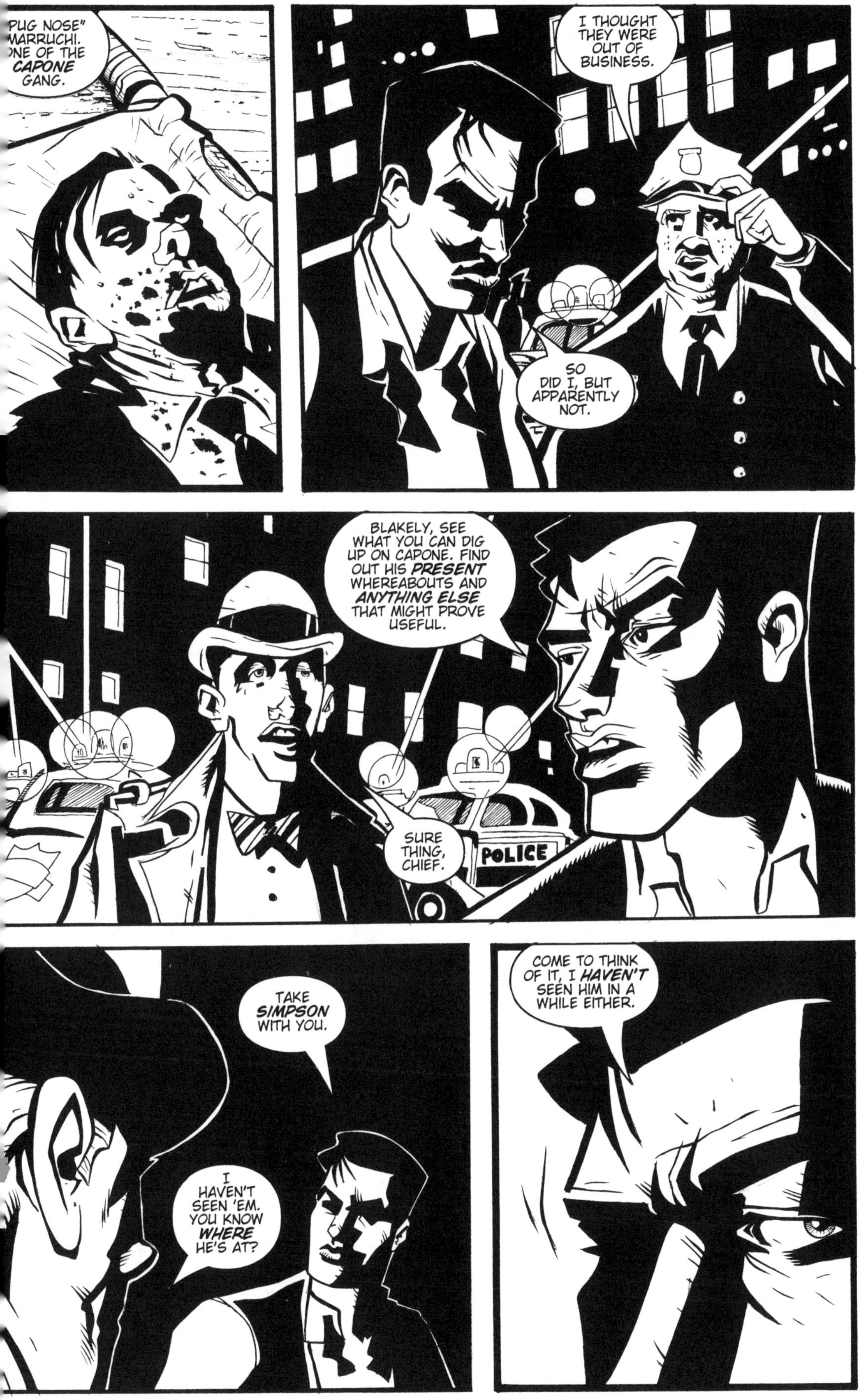
"PUG NOSE" MARRUCHI. ONE OF THE CAPONE GANG.
I THOUGHT THEY WERE OUT OF BUSINESS.
SO DID I, BUT APPARENTLY NOT.
BLAKELY, SEE WHAT YOU CAN DIG UP ON CAPONE. FIND OUT HIS PRESENT WHEREABOUTS AND ANYTHING ELSE THAT MIGHT PROVE USEFUL.
SURE THING, CHIEF.
POLICE
TAKE SIMPSON WITH YOU.
I HAVEN'T SEEN 'EM. YOU KNOW WHERE HE'S AT?
COME TO THINK OF IT, I HAVEN'T SEEN HIM IN A WHILE EITHER.

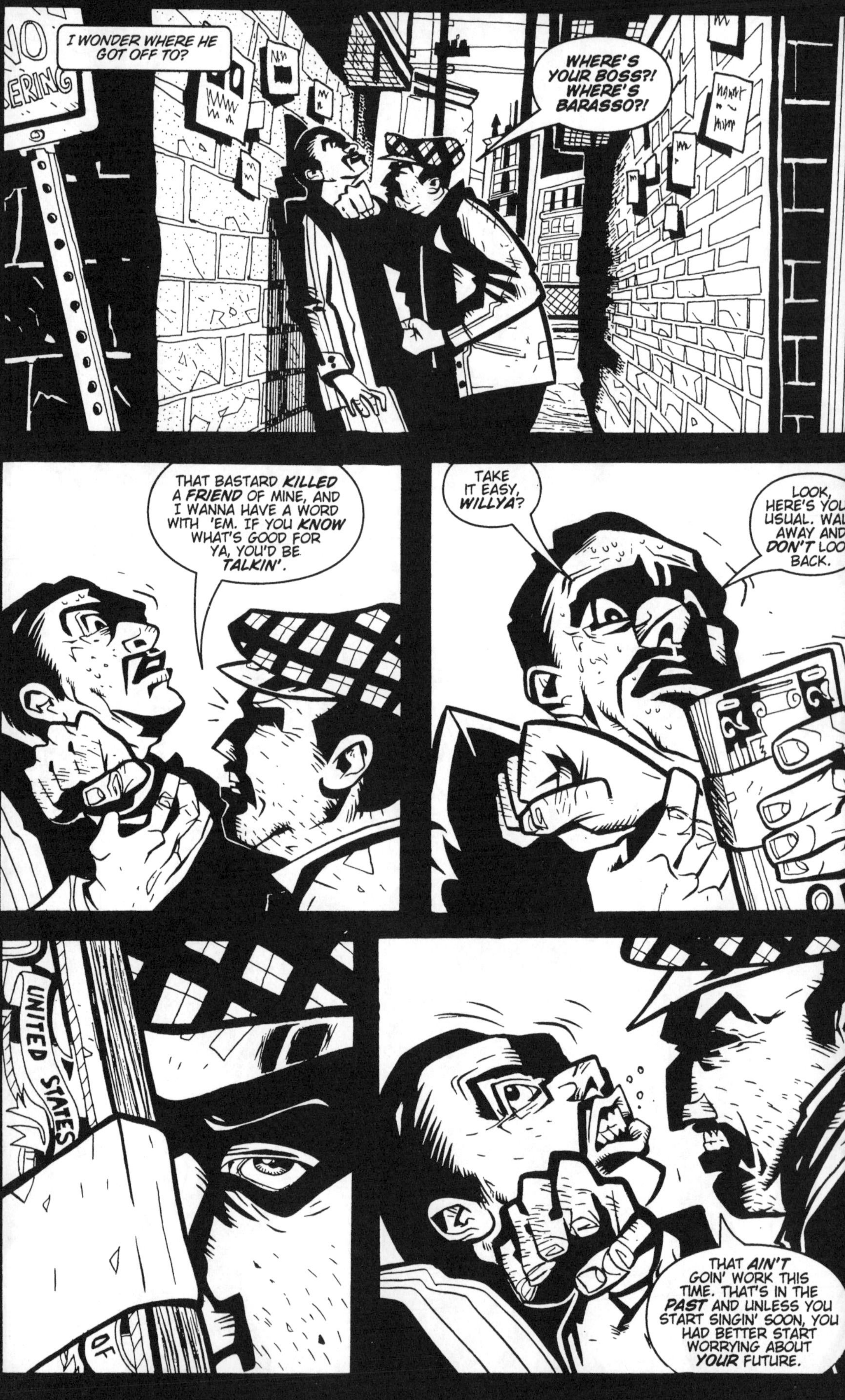
I WONDER WHERE HE GOT OFF TO?
WHERE'S YOUR BOSS?! WHERE'S BARASSO?!
THAT BASTARD KILLED A FRIEND OF MINE, AND I WANNA HAVE A WORD WITH 'EM. IF YOU KNOW WHAT'S GOOD FOR YA, YOU'D BE TALKIN'.
TAKE IT EASY, WILLYA?
LOOK, HERE'S YOU USUAL. WAL AWAY AND DON'T LOO BACK.
UNITED STATES
THAT AIN'T GOIN' WORK THIS TIME. THAT'S IN THE PAST AND UNLESS YOU START SINGIN' SOON, YOU HAD BETTER START WORRYING ABOUT YOUR FUTURE.

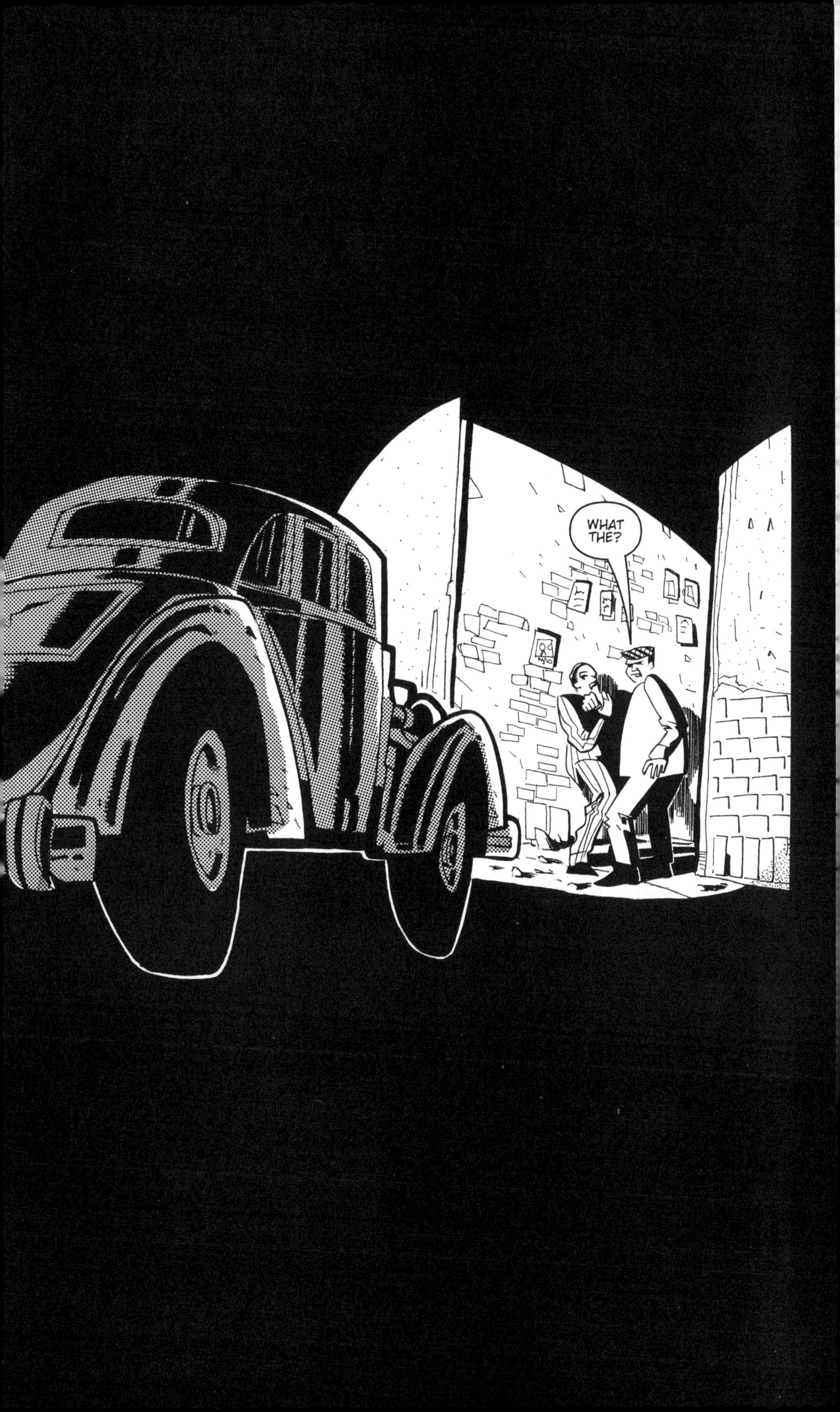
WHAT THE?

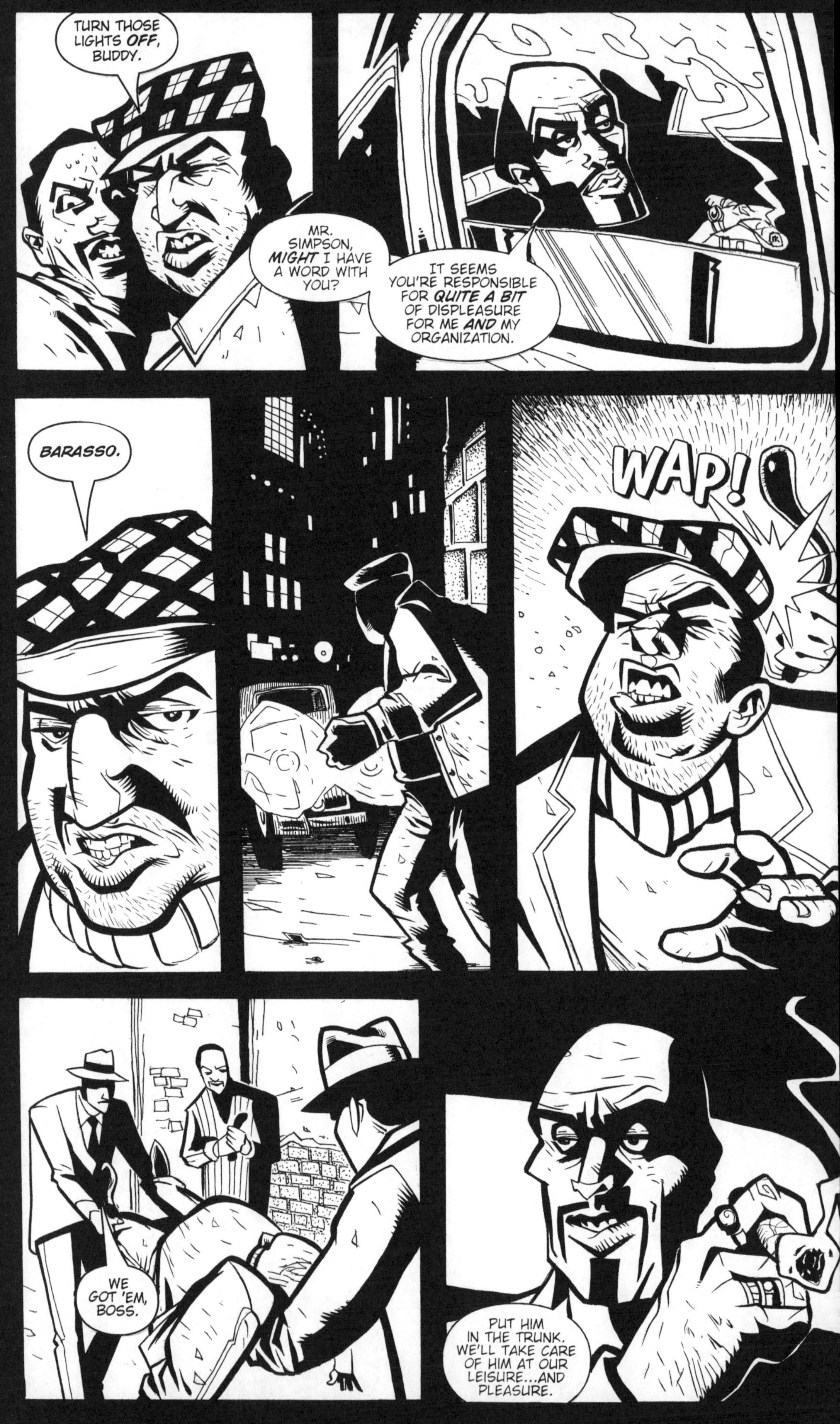

TURN THOSE LIGHTS OFF, BUDDY.
MR. SIMPSON, MIGHT I HAVE A WORD WITH YOU?
IT SEEMS YOU'RE RESPONSIBLE FOR QUITE A BIT OF DISPLEASURE FOR ME AND MY ORGANIZATION.
BARASSO.
WAP!
WE GOT 'EM, BOSS.
PUT HIM IN THE TRUNK. WE'LL TAKE CARE OF HIM AT OUR LEISURE...AND PLEASURE.

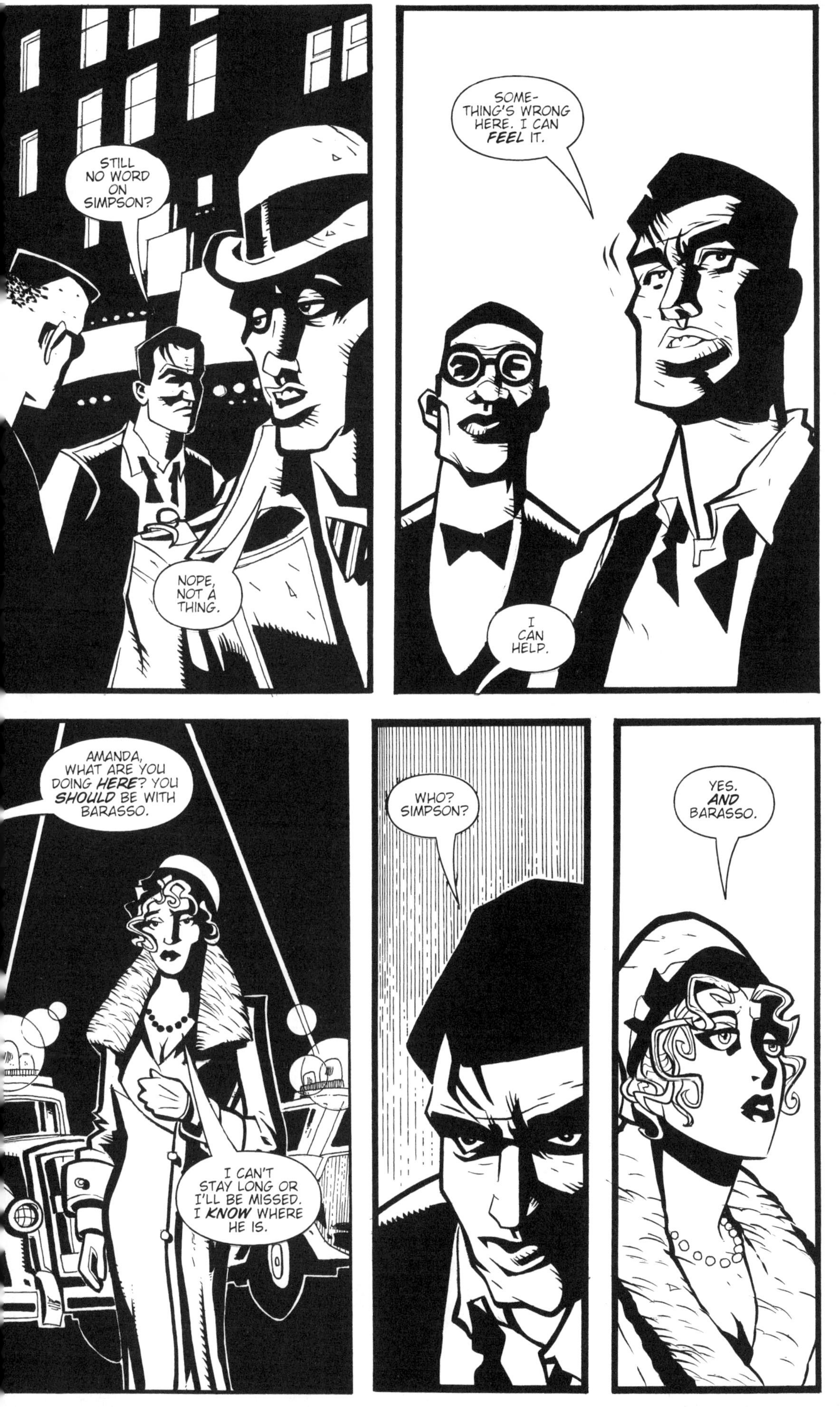
STILL NO WORD ON SIMPSON?
NOPE, NOT A THING.
SOME-THING'S WRONG HERE. I CAN FEEL IT.
I CAN HELP.
AMANDA, WHAT ARE YOU DOING HERE? YOU SHOULD BE WITH BARASSO.
I CAN'T STAY LONG OR I'LL BE MISSED. I KNOW WHERE HE IS.
WHO? SIMPSON?
YES. AND BARASSO.

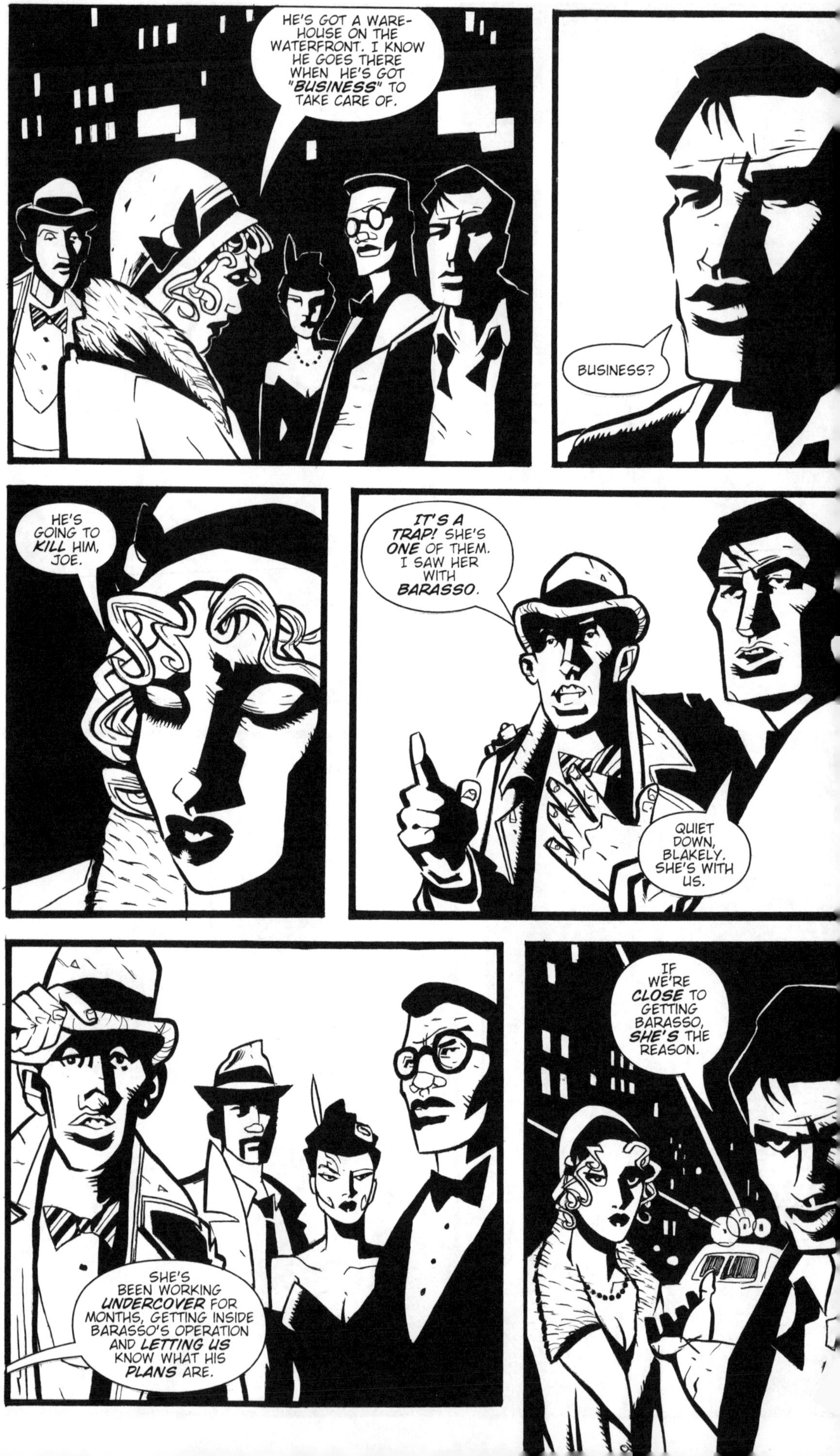
HE'S GOT A WARE-HOUSE ON THE WATERFRONT. I KNOW HE GOES THERE WHEN HE'S GOT "BUSINESS" TO TAKE CARE OF.
BUSINESS?
HE'S GOING TO KILL HIM, JOE.
IT'S A TRAP! SHE'S ONE OF THEM. I SAW HER WITH BARASSO.
QUIET DOWN, BLAKELY. SHE'S WITH US.
SHE'S BEEN WORKING UNDERCOVER FOR MONTHS, GETTING INSIDE BARASSO'S OPERATION AND LETTING US KNOW WHAT HIS PLANS ARE.
IF WE'RE CLOSE TO GETTING BARASSO, SHE'S THE REASON.

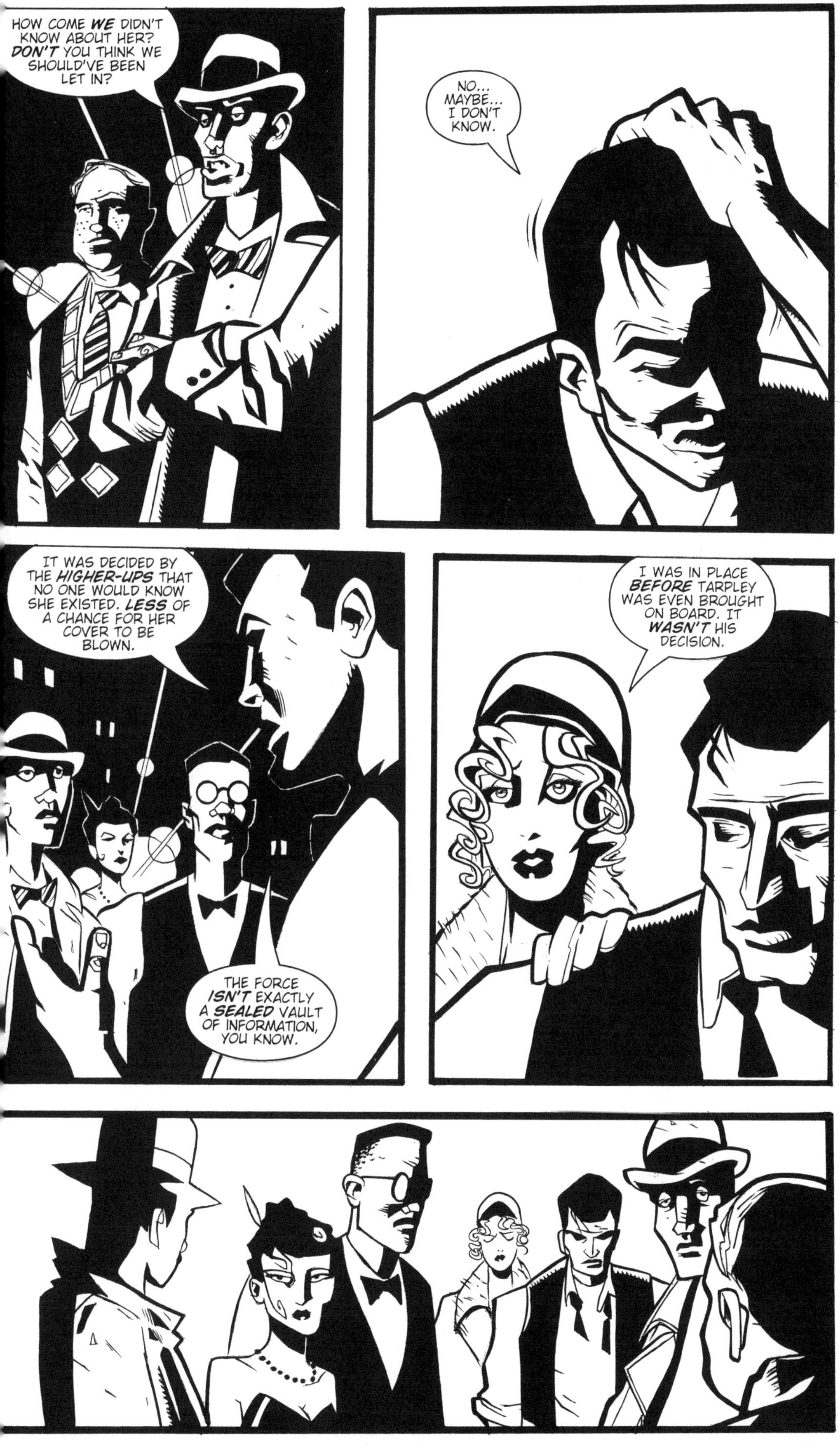
HOW COME **WE** DIDN'T KNOW ABOUT HER? **DON'T** YOU THINK WE SHOULD'VE BEEN LET IN?
NO... MAYBE... I DON'T KNOW.
IT WAS DECIDED BY THE **HIGHER-UPS** THAT NO ONE WOULD KNOW SHE EXISTED. **LESS** OF A CHANCE FOR HER COVER TO BE BLOWN.
THE FORCE **ISN'T** EXACTLY A **SEALED** VAULT OF INFORMATION, YOU KNOW.
I WAS IN PLACE **BEFORE** TARPLEY WAS EVEN BROUGHT ON BOARD. IT **WASN'T** HIS DECISION.

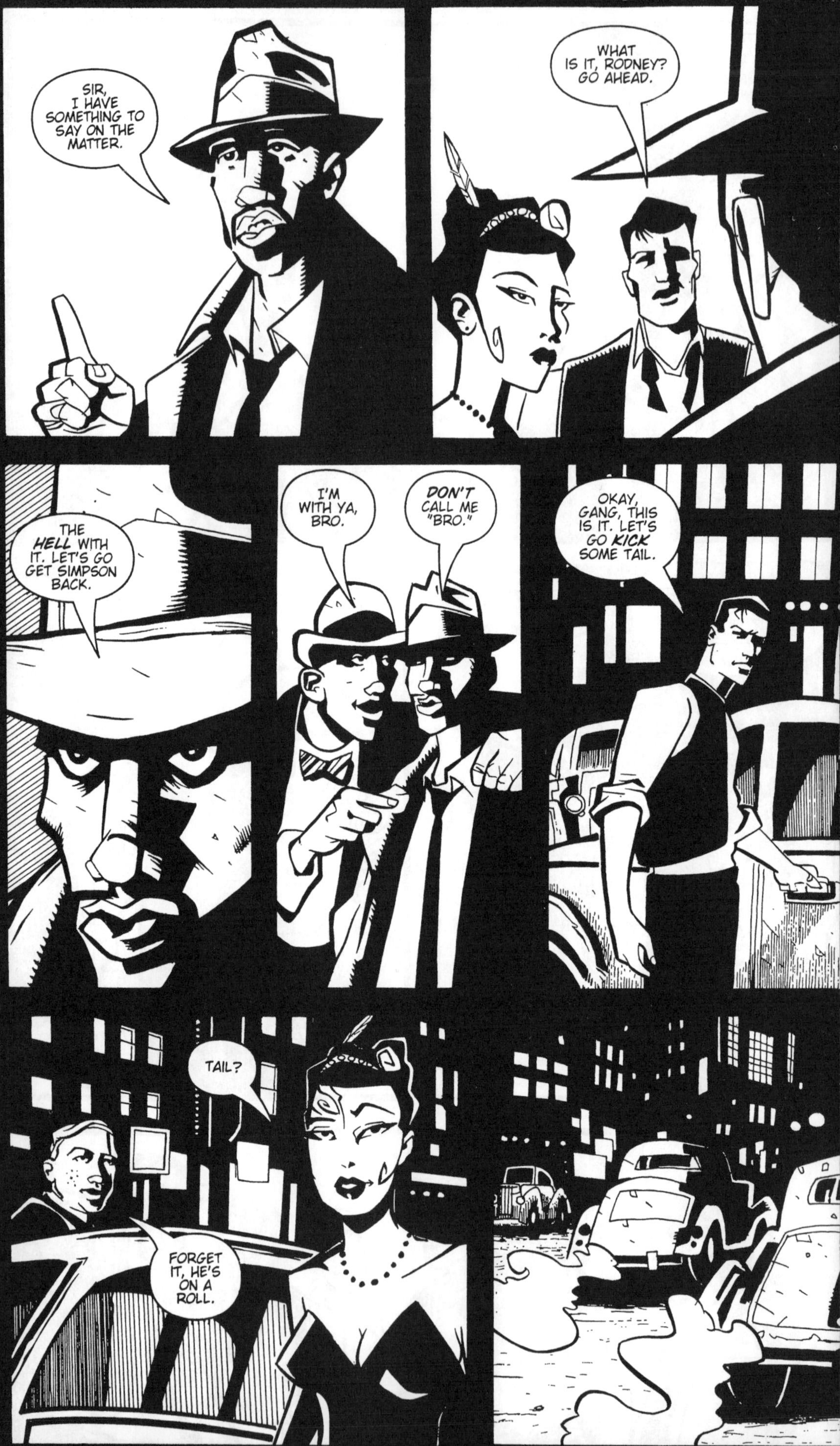
SIR, I HAVE SOMETHING TO SAY ON THE MATTER.
WHAT IS IT, RODNEY? GO AHEAD.
THE HELL WITH IT. LET'S GO GET SIMPSON BACK.
I'M WITH YA, BRO.
DON'T CALL ME "BRO."
OKAY, GANG, THIS IS IT. LET'S GO KICK SOME TAIL.
TAIL?
FORGET IT, HE'S ON A ROLL.

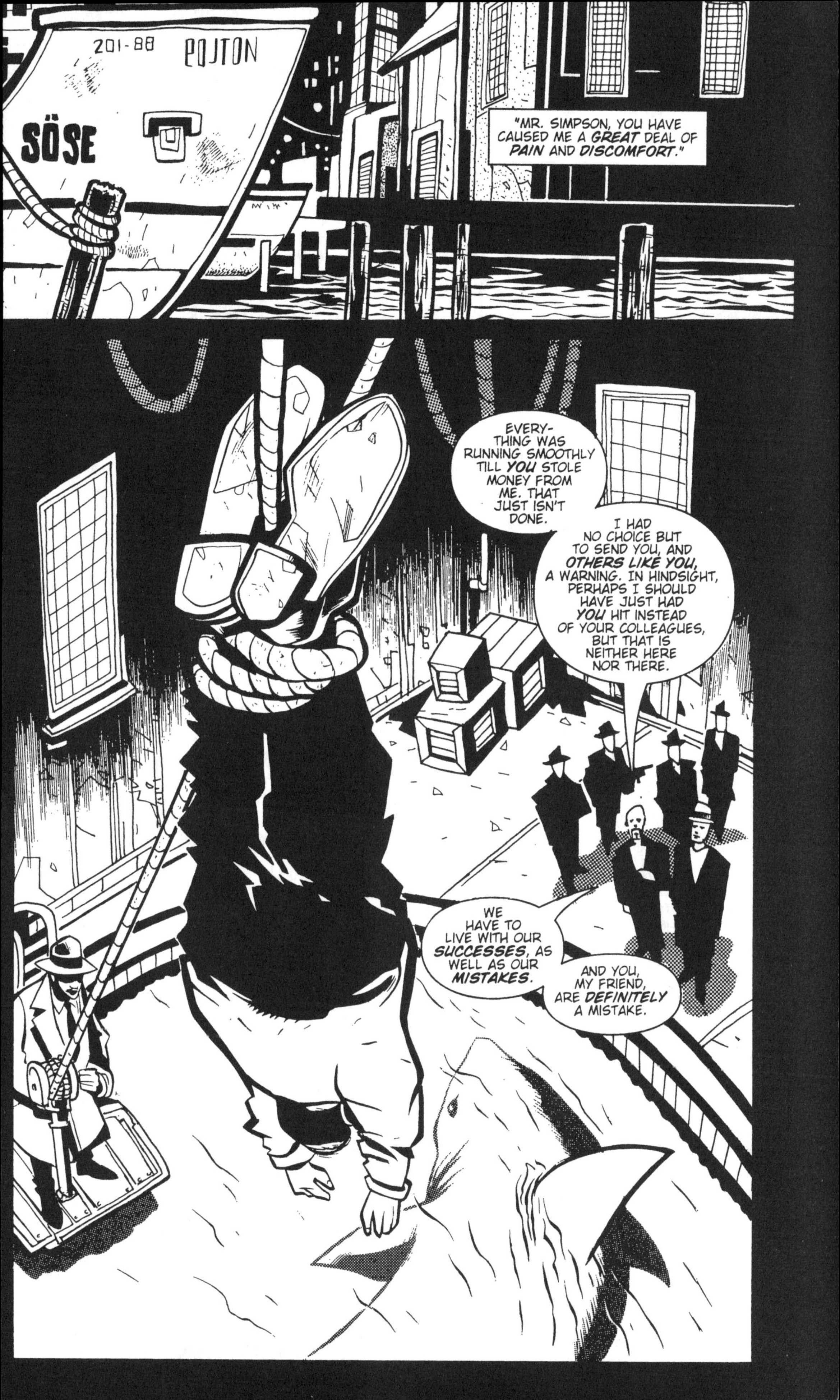
201-88
BOJTON
SÖSE
"MR. SIMPSON, YOU HAVE CAUSED ME A GREAT DEAL OF PAIN AND DISCOMFORT."
EVERY-THING WAS RUNNING SMOOTHLY TILL YOU STOLE MONEY FROM ME. THAT JUST ISN'T DONE.
I HAD NO CHOICE BUT TO SEND YOU, AND OTHERS LIKE YOU, A WARNING. IN HINDSIGHT, PERHAPS I SHOULD HAVE JUST HAD YOU HIT INSTEAD OF YOUR COLLEAGUES, BUT THAT IS NEITHER HERE NOR THERE.
WE HAVE TO LIVE WITH OUR SUCCESSES, AS WELL AS OUR MISTAKES.
AND YOU, MY FRIEND, ARE DEFINITELY A MISTAKE.

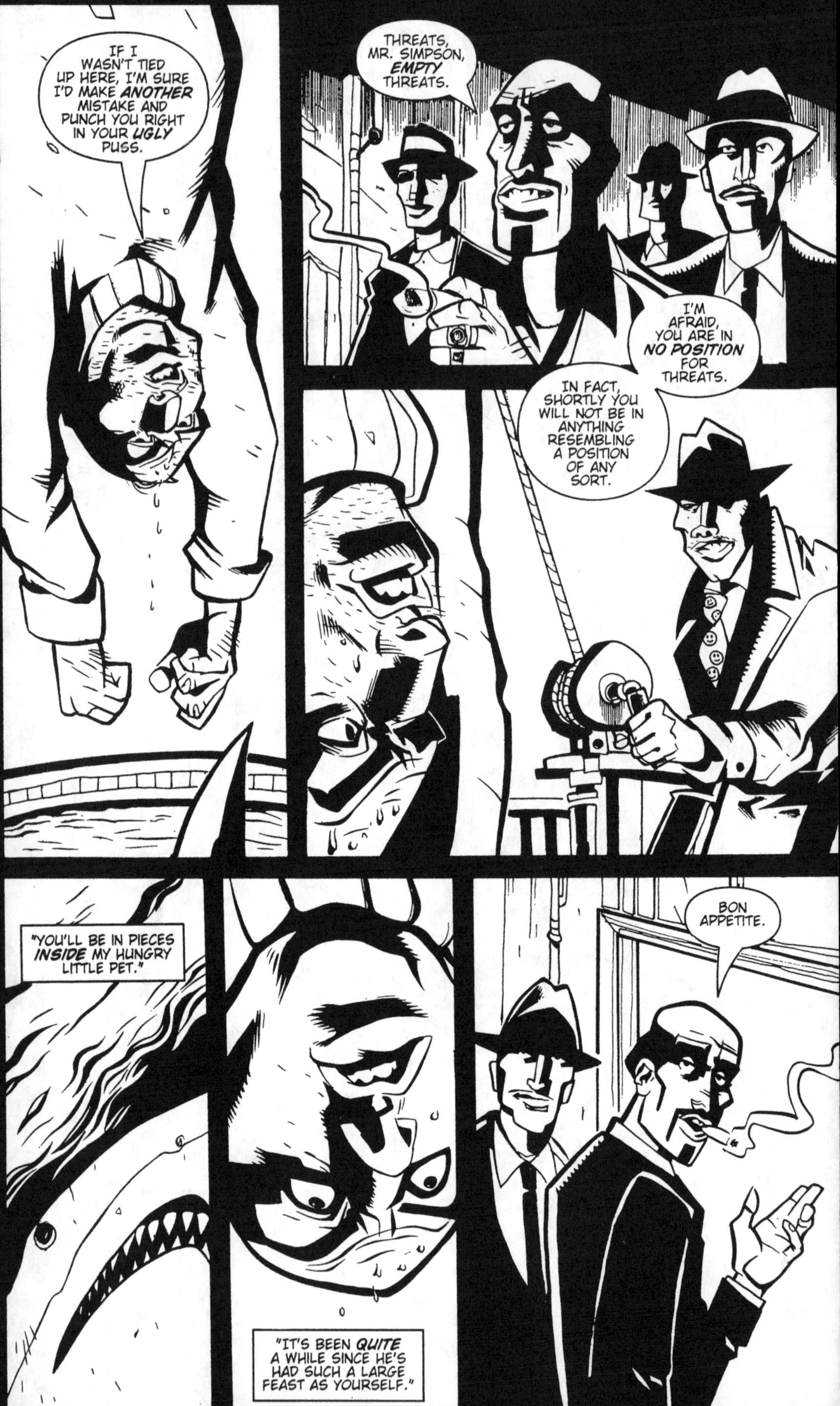
IF I WASN'T TIED UP HERE, I'M SURE I'D MAKE ANOTHER MISTAKE AND PUNCH YOU RIGHT IN YOUR UGLY PUSS.
THREATS, MR. SIMPSON, EMPTY THREATS.
I'M AFRAID, YOU ARE IN NO POSITION FOR THREATS.
IN FACT, SHORTLY YOU WILL NOT BE IN ANYTHING RESEMBLING A POSITION OF ANY SORT.
"YOU'LL BE IN PIECES INSIDE MY HUNGRY LITTLE PET."
"IT'S BEEN QUITE A WHILE SINCE HE'S HAD SUCH A LARGE FEAST AS YOURSELF."
BON APPETITE.

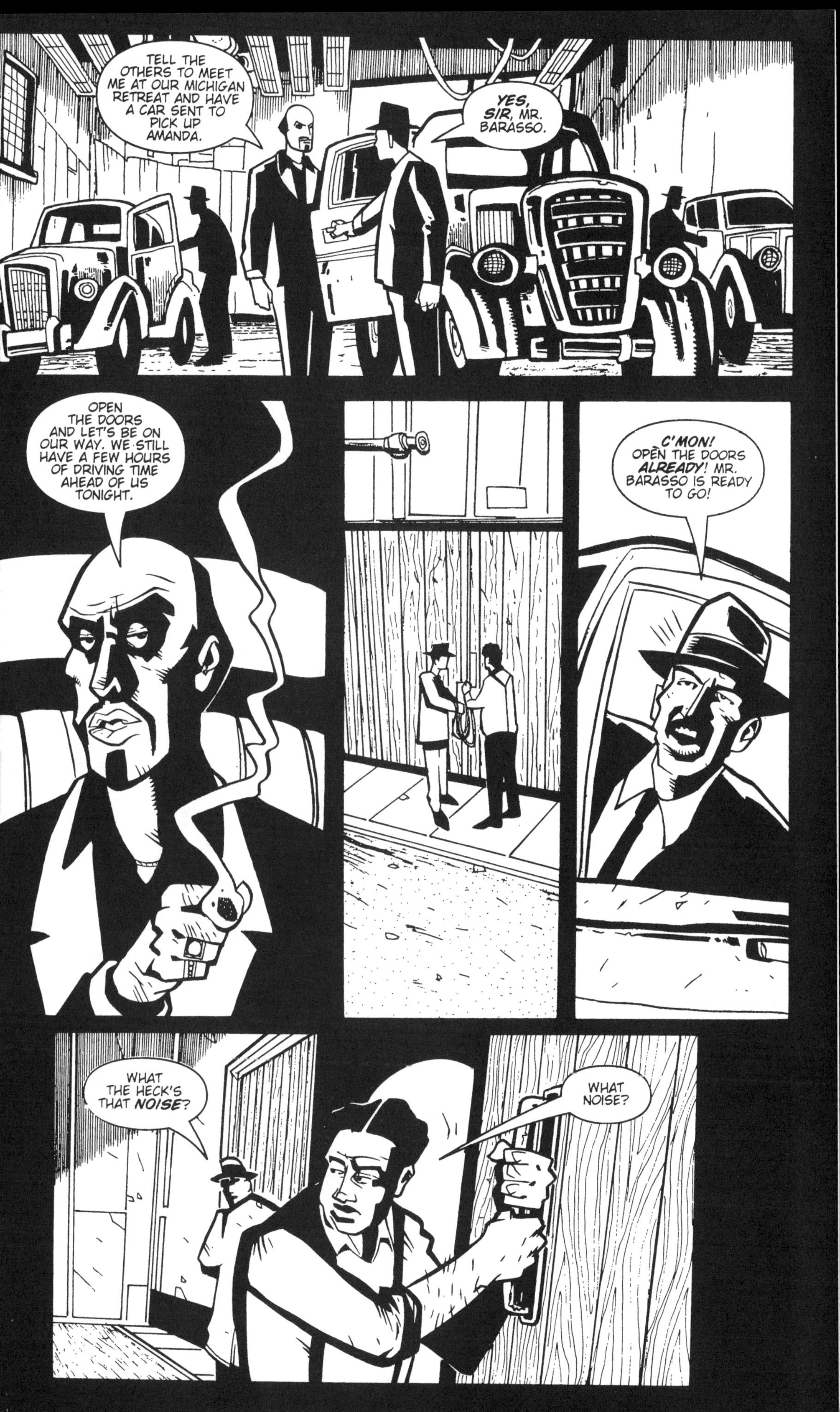
TELL THE OTHERS TO MEET ME AT OUR MICHIGAN RETREAT AND HAVE A CAR SENT TO PICK UP AMANDA.
YES, SIR, MR. BARASSO.
OPEN THE DOORS AND LET'S BE ON OUR WAY. WE STILL HAVE A FEW HOURS OF DRIVING TIME AHEAD OF US TONIGHT.
C'MON! OPEN THE DOORS ALREADY! MR. BARASSO IS READY TO GO!
WHAT THE HECK'S THAT NOISE?
WHAT NOISE?

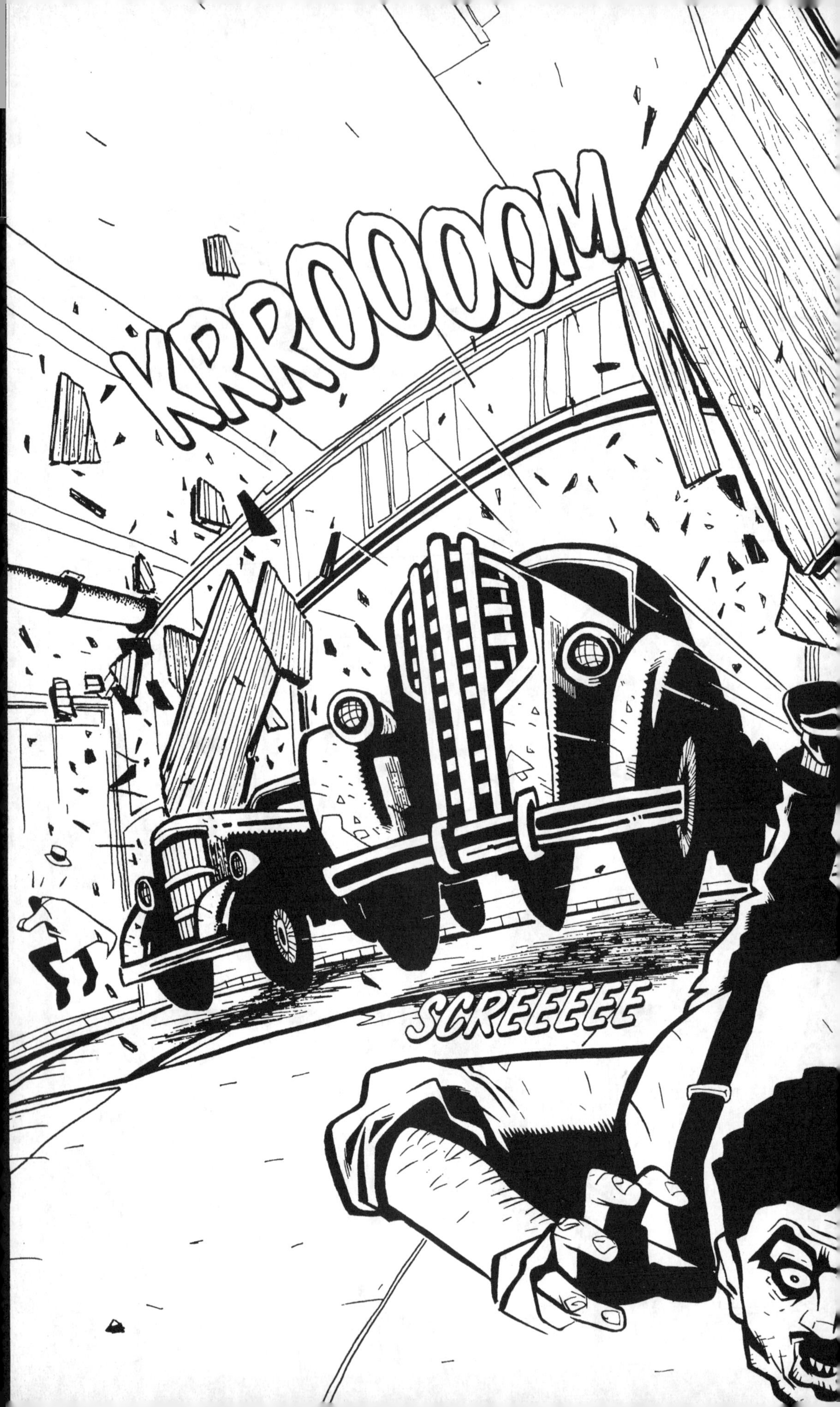
KRROOOOOM
SCREEEEEE

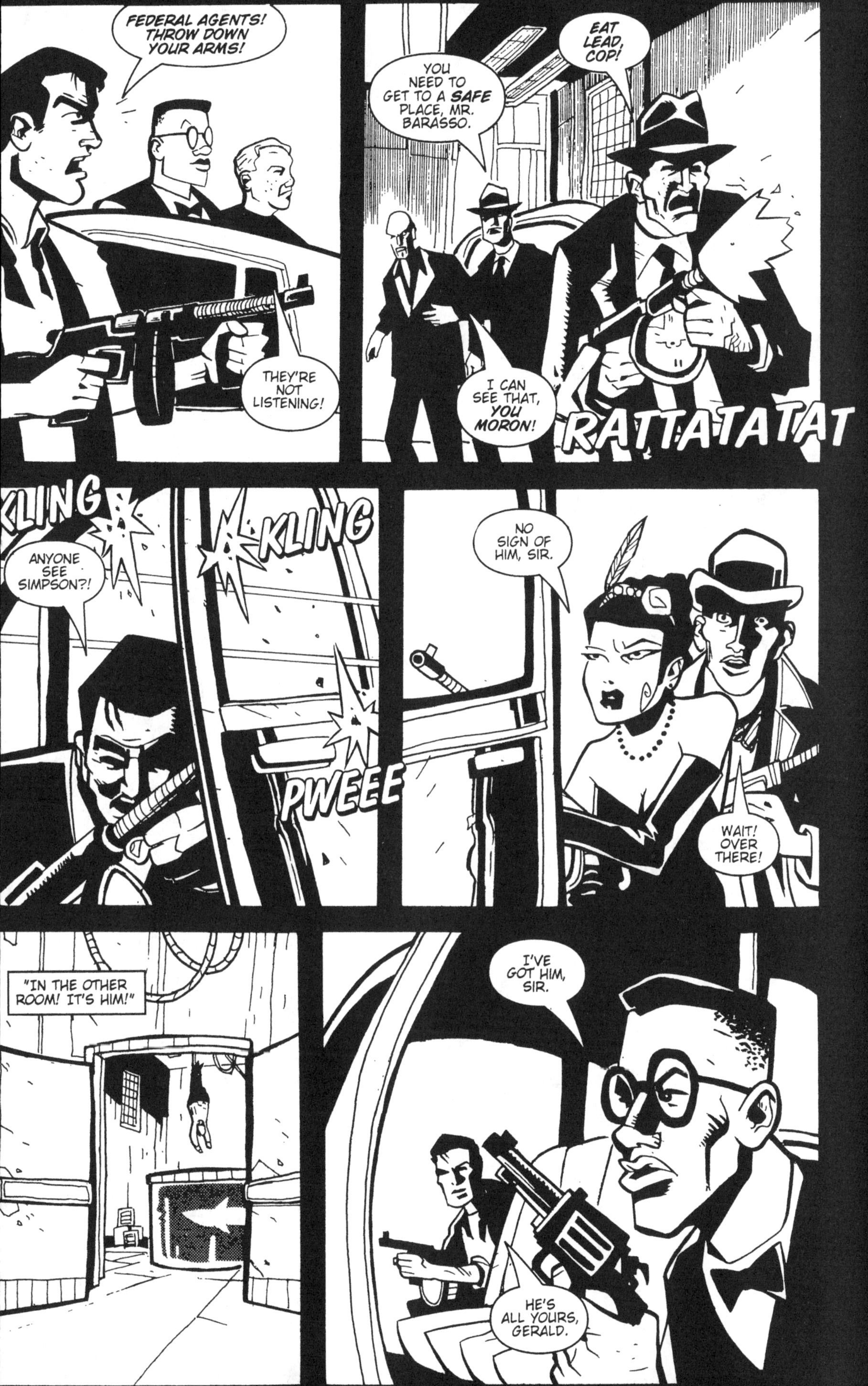
FEDERAL AGENTS! THROW DOWN YOUR ARMS!
THEY'RE NOT LISTENING!
YOU NEED TO GET TO A SAFE PLACE, MR. BARASSO.
EAT LEAD, COP!
I CAN SEE THAT, YOU MORON!
RATTATATAT
KLING
ANYONE SEE SIMPSON?!
KLING
PWEEE
NO SIGN OF HIM, SIR.
WAIT! OVER THERE!
"IN THE OTHER ROOM! IT'S HIM!"
I'VE GOT HIM, SIR.
HE'S ALL YOURS, GERALD.

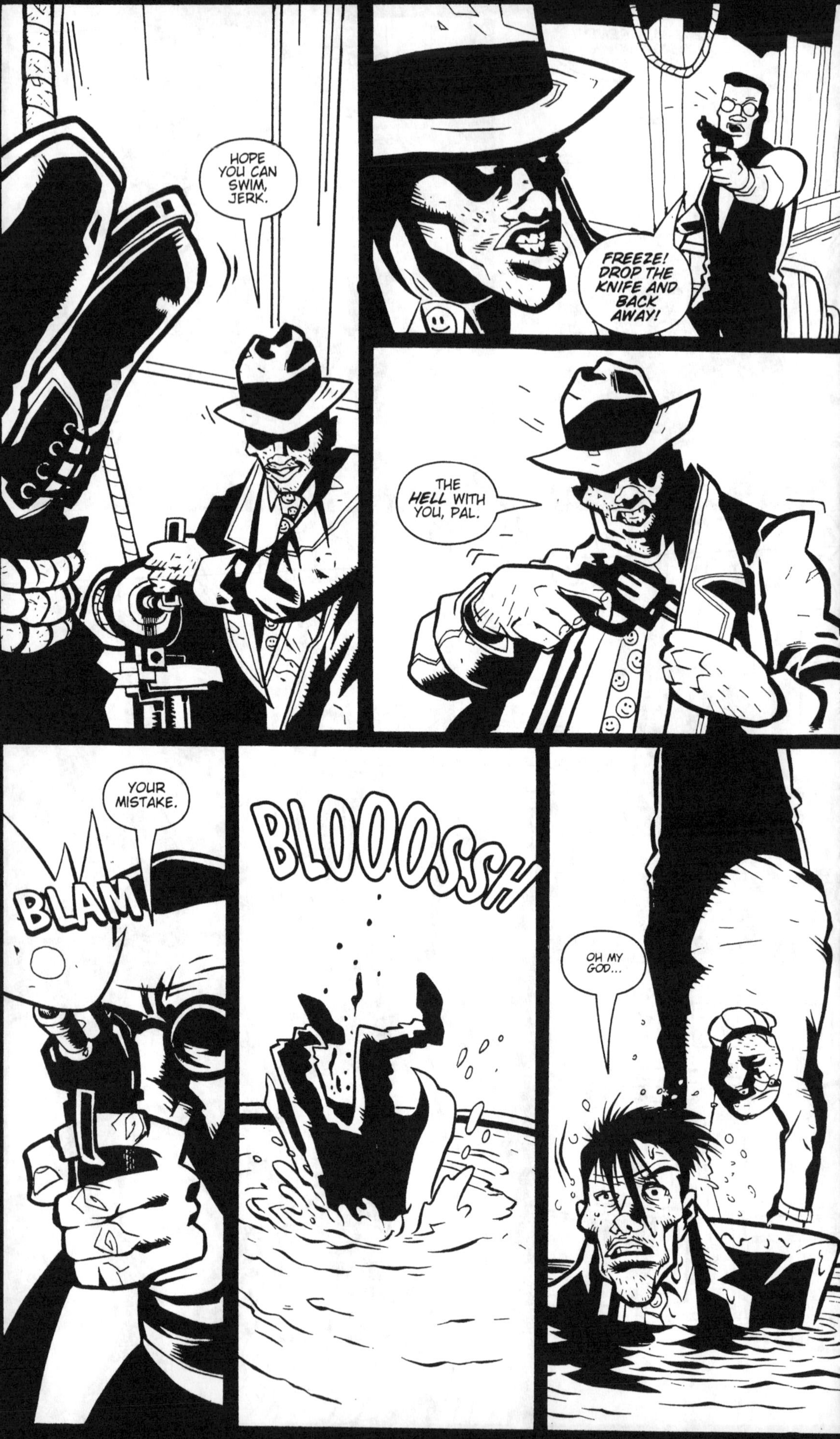
HOPE YOU CAN SWIM, JERK.
FREEZE! DROP THE KNIFE AND BACK AWAY!
THE HELL WITH YOU, PAL.
YOUR MISTAKE.
BLAM
BLOOOSSH
OH MY GOD...

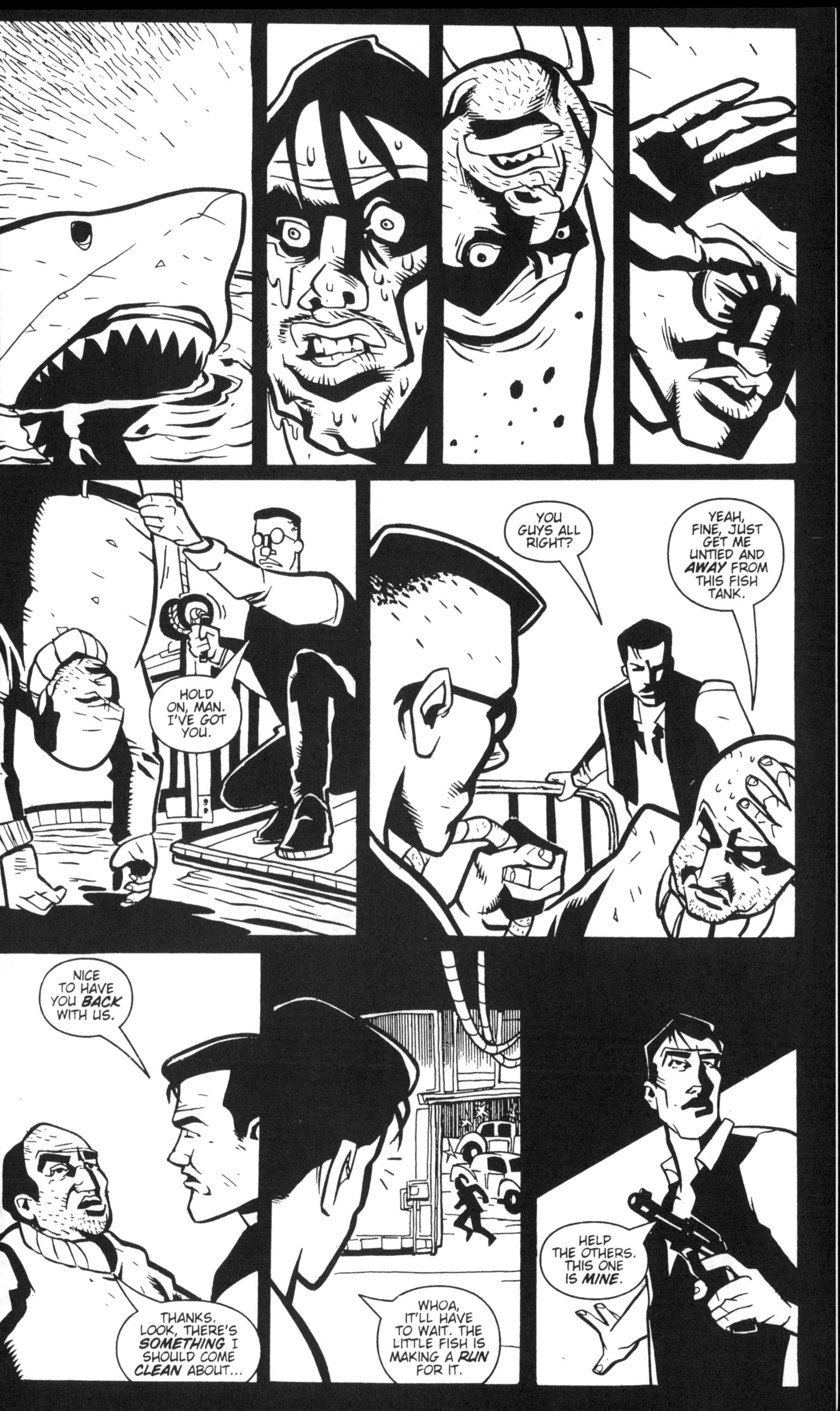
HOLD ON, MAN. I'VE GOT YOU.
YOU GUYS ALL RIGHT?
YEAH, FINE, JUST GET ME UNTIED AND *AWAY* FROM THIS FISH TANK.
NICE TO HAVE YOU *BACK* WITH US.
THANKS. LOOK, THERE'S *SOMETHING* I SHOULD COME *CLEAN* ABOUT...
WHOA, IT'LL HAVE TO WAIT. THE LITTLE FISH IS MAKING A *RUN* FOR IT.
HELP THE OTHERS. THIS ONE IS *MINE*.

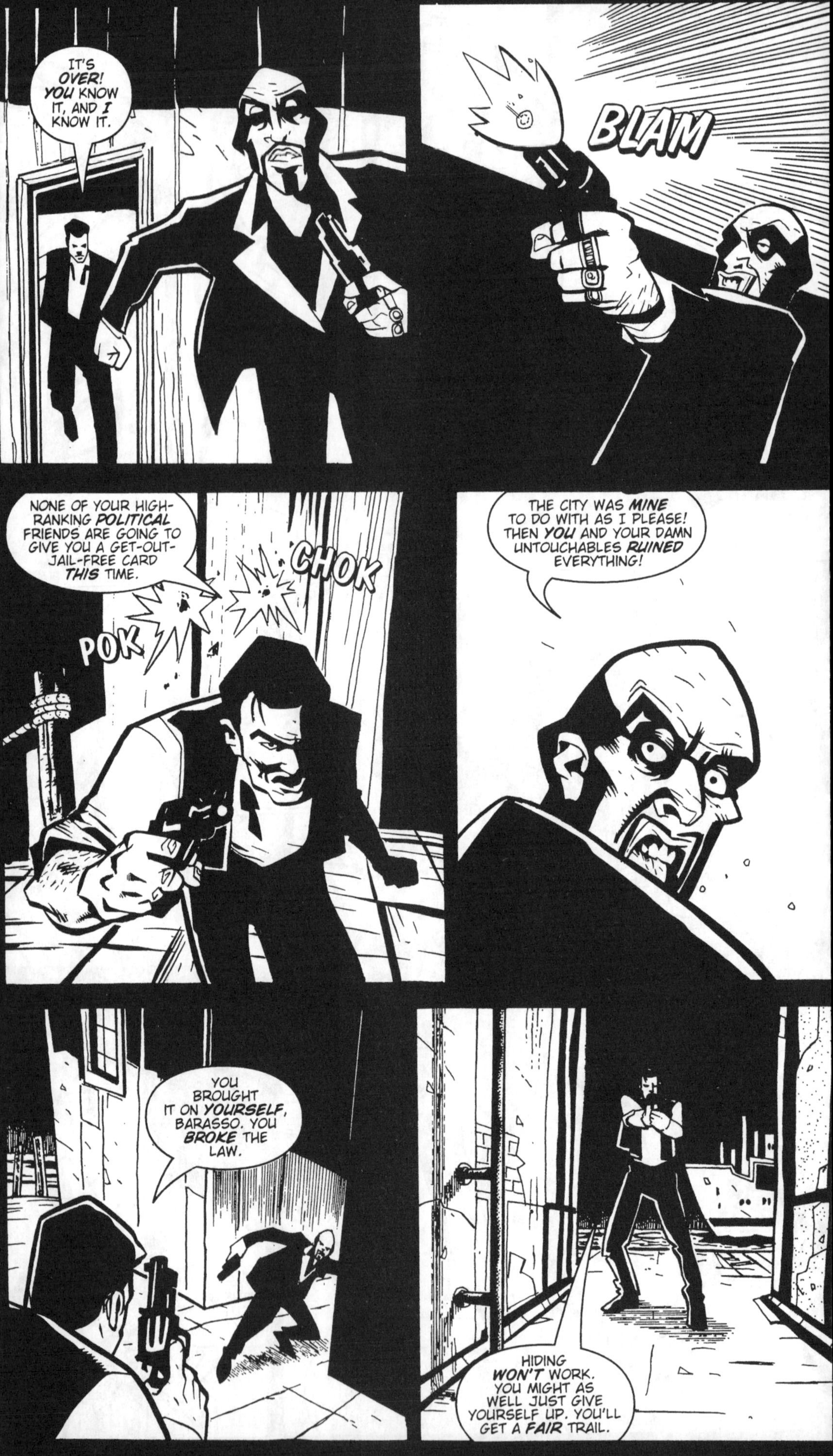

IT'S OVER! YOU KNOW IT, AND I KNOW IT.
BLAM
NONE OF YOUR HIGH-RANKING POLITICAL FRIENDS ARE GOING TO GIVE YOU A GET-OUT-JAIL-FREE CARD THIS TIME.
CHOK
POK
THE CITY WAS MINE TO DO WITH AS I PLEASE! THEN YOU AND YOUR DAMN UNTOUCHABLES RUINED EVERYTHING!
YOU BROUGHT IT ON YOURSELF, BARASSO. YOU BROKE THE LAW.
HIDING WON'T WORK. YOU MIGHT AS WELL JUST GIVE YOURSELF UP. YOU'LL GET A FAIR TRAIL.

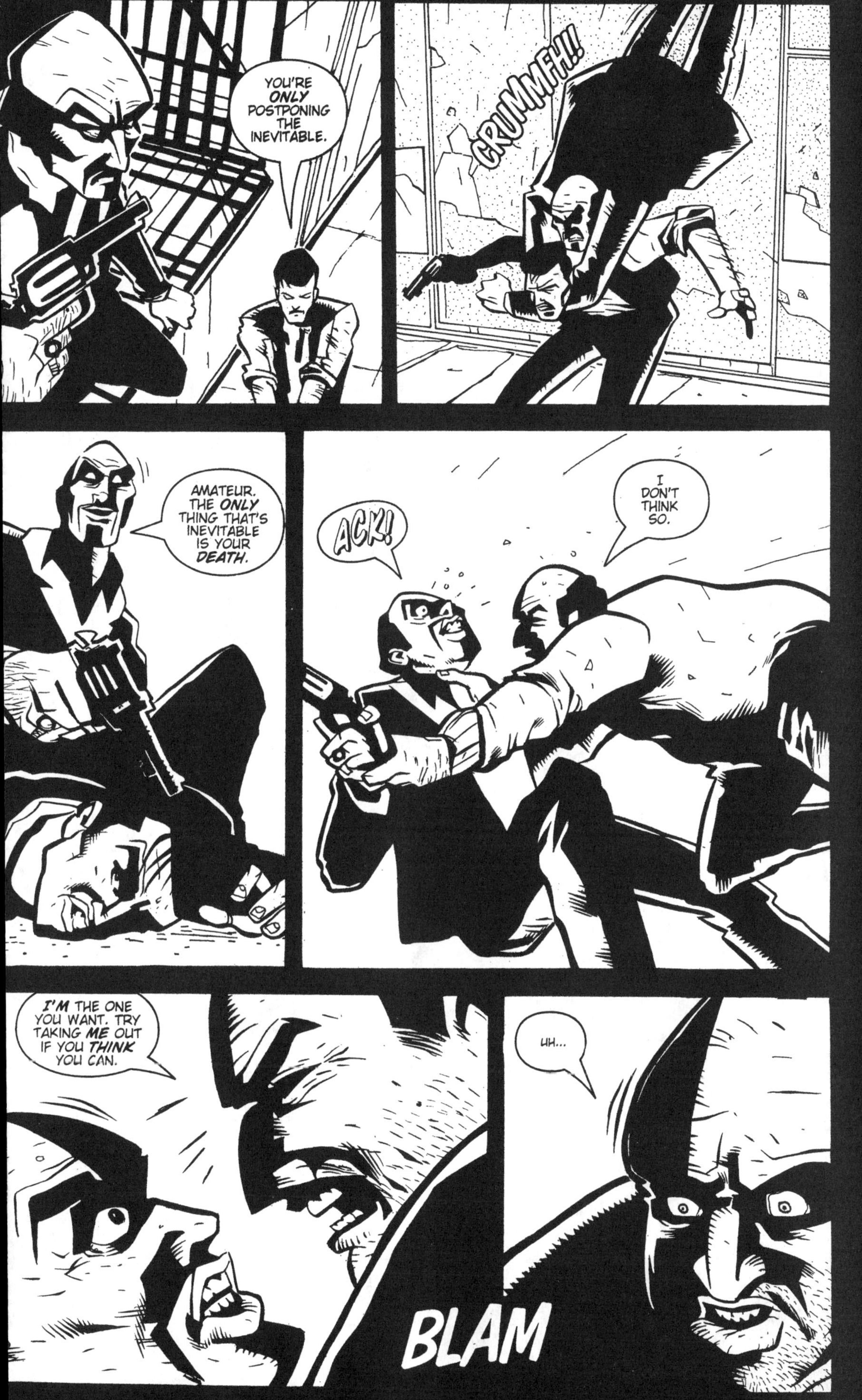
YOU'RE ONLY POSTPONING THE INEVITABLE.
CRUMMFH!!
AMATEUR. THE ONLY THING THAT'S INEVITABLE IS YOUR DEATH.
ACK!
I DON'T THINK SO.
I'M THE ONE YOU WANT. TRY TAKING ME OUT IF YOU THINK YOU CAN.
UH...
BLAM

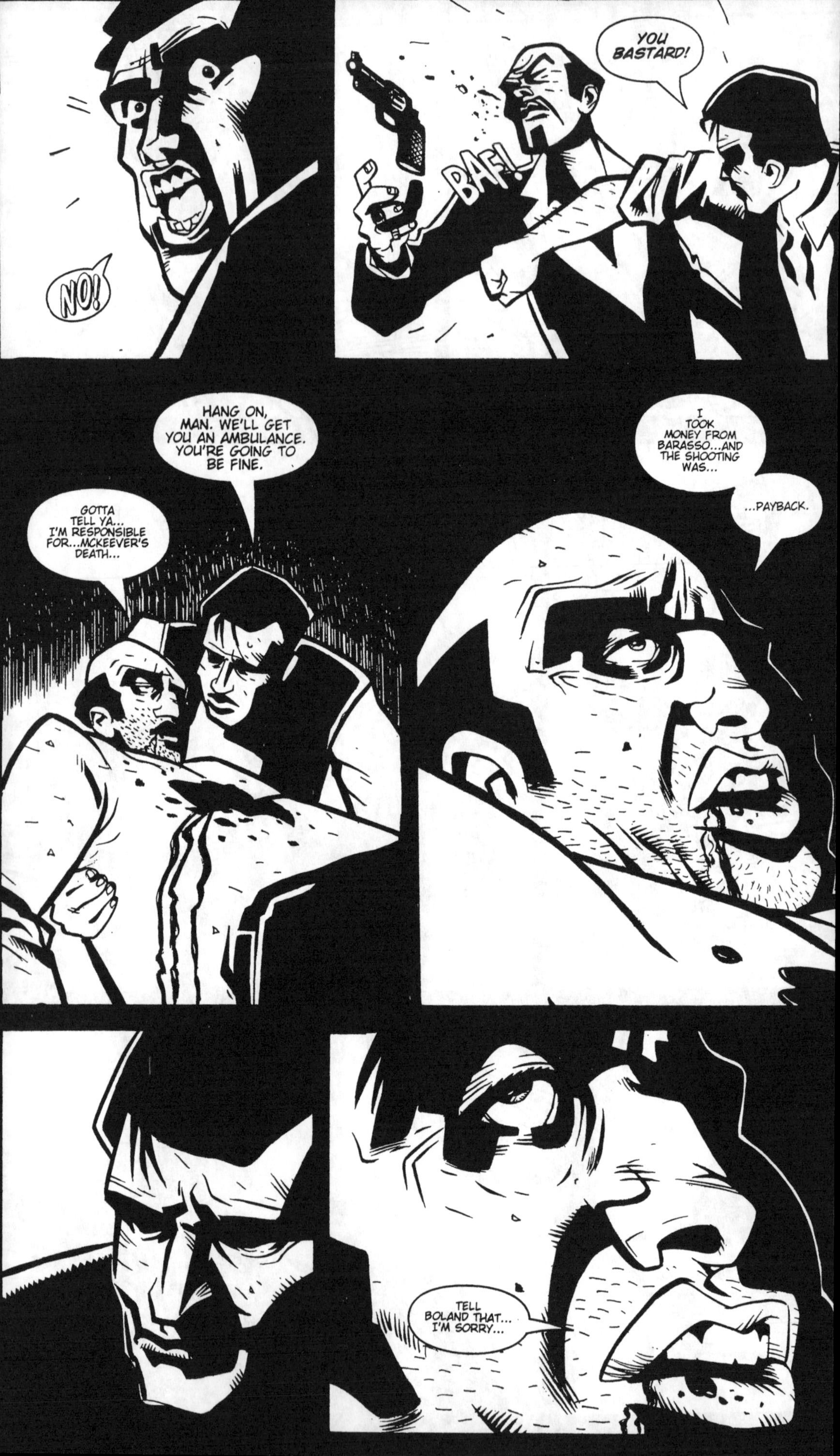
NO!
YOU BASTARD!
BAF!
HANG ON, MAN. WE'LL GET YOU AN AMBULANCE. YOU'RE GOING TO BE FINE.
GOTTA TELL YA... I'M RESPONSIBLE FOR...MCKEEVER'S DEATH...
I TOOK MONEY FROM BARASSO...AND THE SHOOTING WAS...
...PAYBACK.
TELL BOLAND THAT... I'M SORRY...

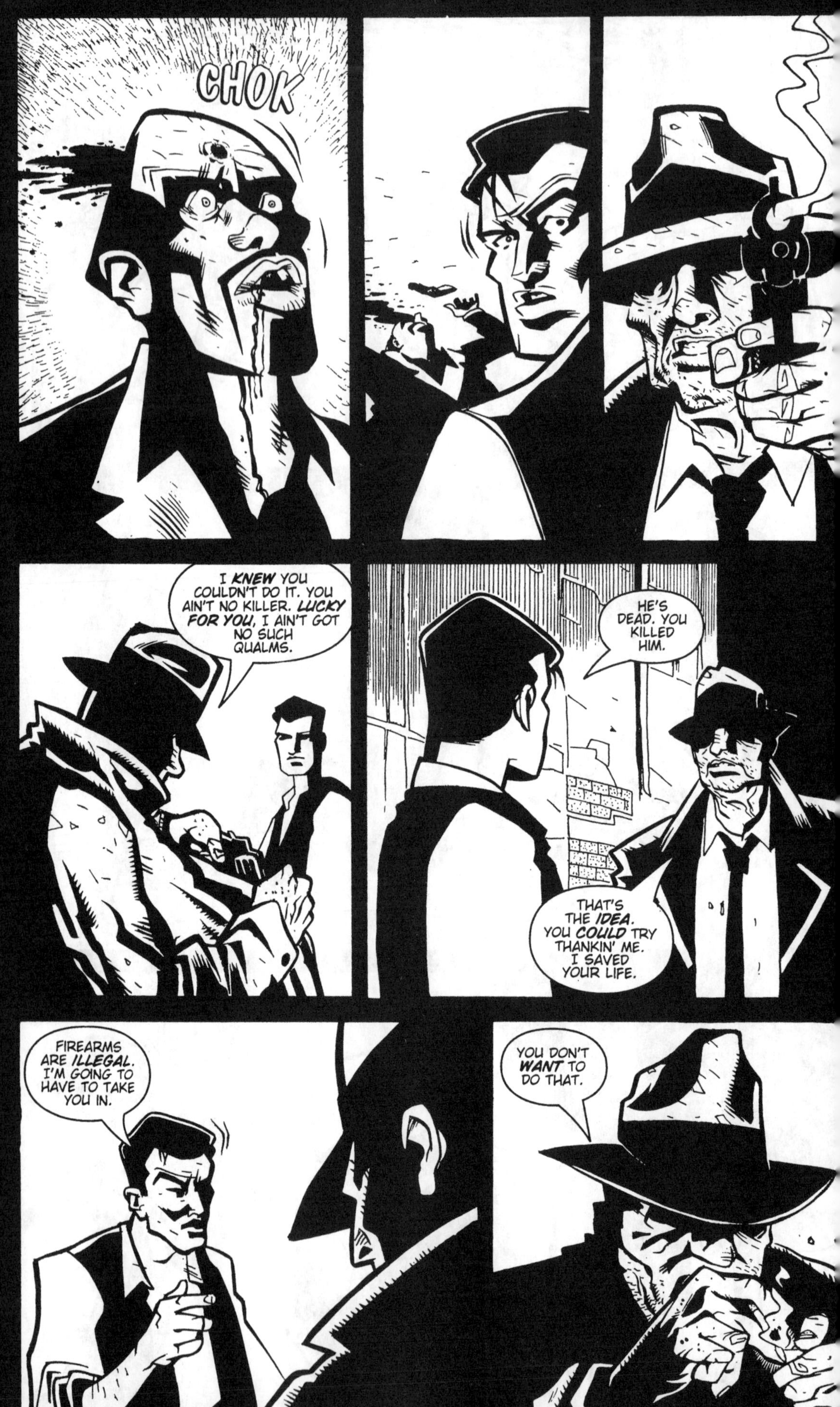
CHOK
I KNEW YOU COULDN'T DO IT. YOU AIN'T NO KILLER. LUCKY FOR YOU, I AIN'T GOT NO SUCH QUALMS.
HE'S DEAD. YOU KILLED HIM.
THAT'S THE IDEA. YOU COULD TRY THANKIN' ME. I SAVED YOUR LIFE.
FIREARMS ARE ILLEGAL. I'M GOING TO HAVE TO TAKE YOU IN.
YOU DON'T WANT TO DO THAT.

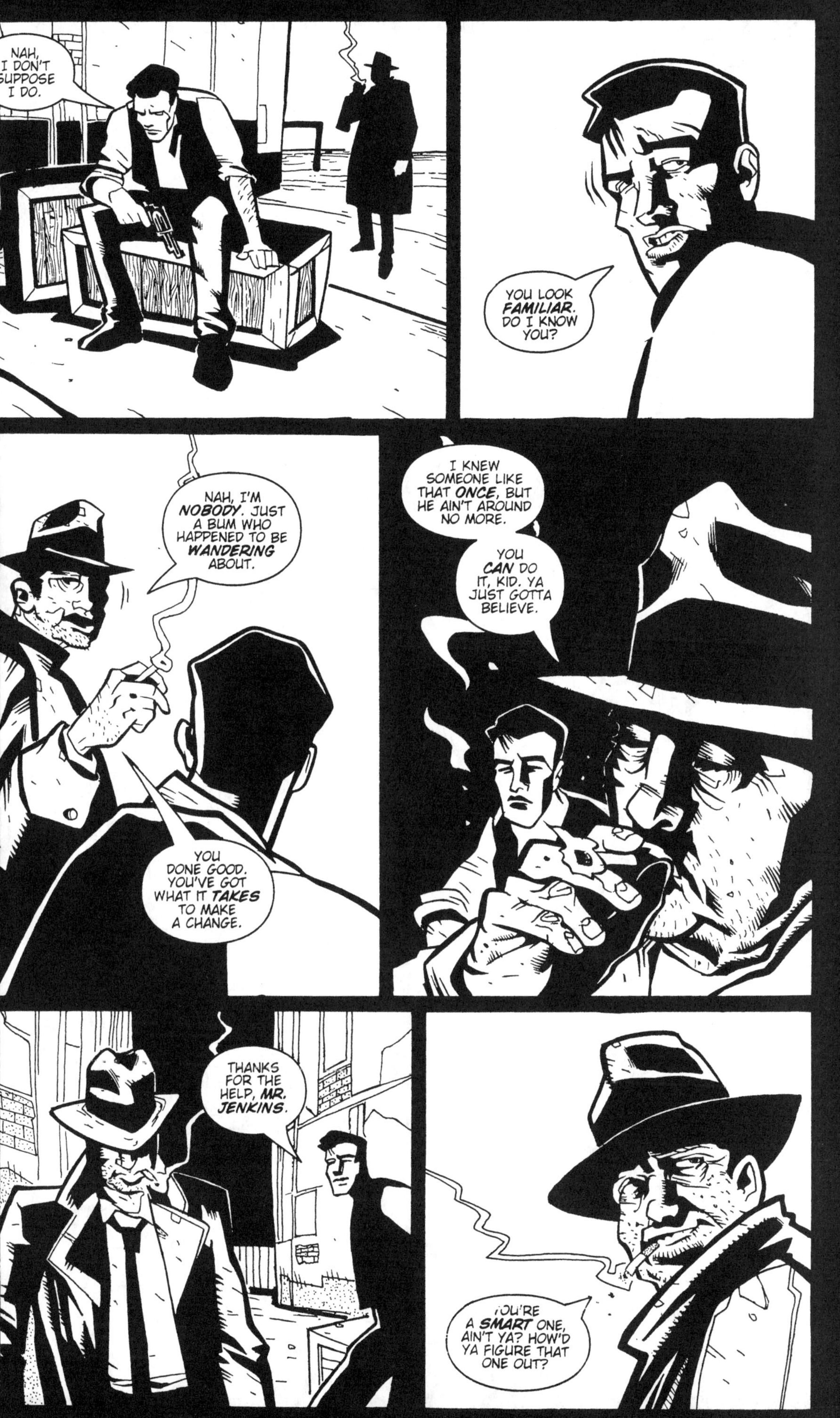
NAH, I DON'T SUPPOSE I DO.
YOU LOOK FAMILIAR. DO I KNOW YOU?
NAH, I'M NOBODY. JUST A BUM WHO HAPPENED TO BE WANDERING ABOUT.
YOU DONE GOOD. YOU'VE GOT WHAT IT TAKES TO MAKE A CHANGE.
I KNEW SOMEONE LIKE THAT ONCE, BUT HE AIN'T AROUND NO MORE.
YOU CAN DO IT, KID. YA JUST GOTTA BELIEVE.
THANKS FOR THE HELP, MR. JENKINS.
YOU'RE A SMART ONE, AIN'T YA? HOW'D YA FIGURE THAT ONE OUT?

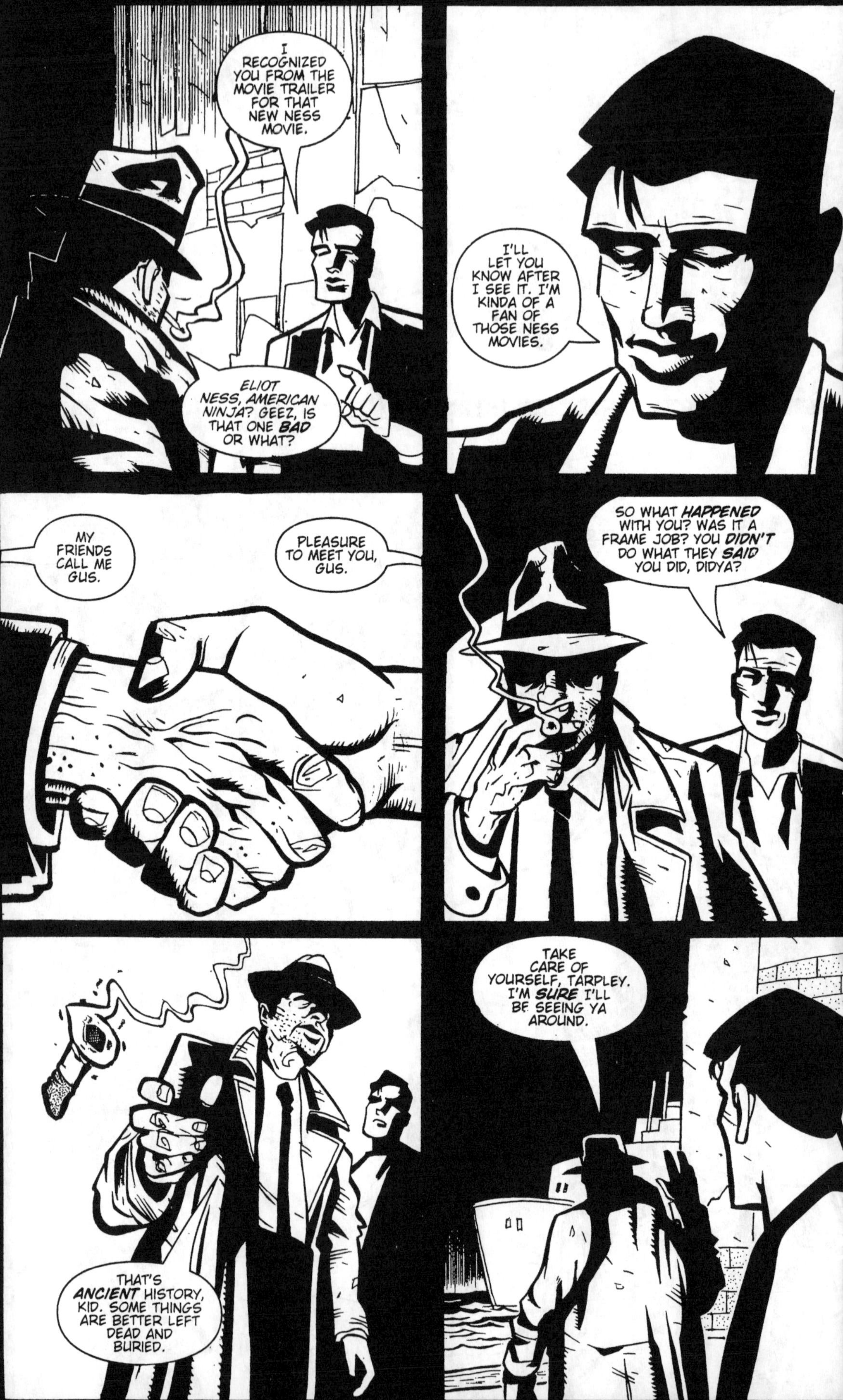
I RECOGNIZED YOU FROM THE MOVIE TRAILER FOR THAT NEW NESS MOVIE.
ELIOT NESS, AMERICAN NINJA? GEEZ, IS THAT ONE BAD OR WHAT?
I'LL LET YOU KNOW AFTER I SEE IT. I'M KINDA OF A FAN OF THOSE NESS MOVIES.
MY FRIENDS CALL ME GUS.
PLEASURE TO MEET YOU, GUS.
SO WHAT HAPPENED WITH YOU? WAS IT A FRAME JOB? YOU DIDN'T DO WHAT THEY SAID YOU DID, DIDYA?
THAT'S ANCIENT HISTORY, KID. SOME THINGS ARE BETTER LEFT DEAD AND BURIED.
TAKE CARE OF YOURSELF, TARPLEY. I'M SURE I'LL BE SEEING YA AROUND.

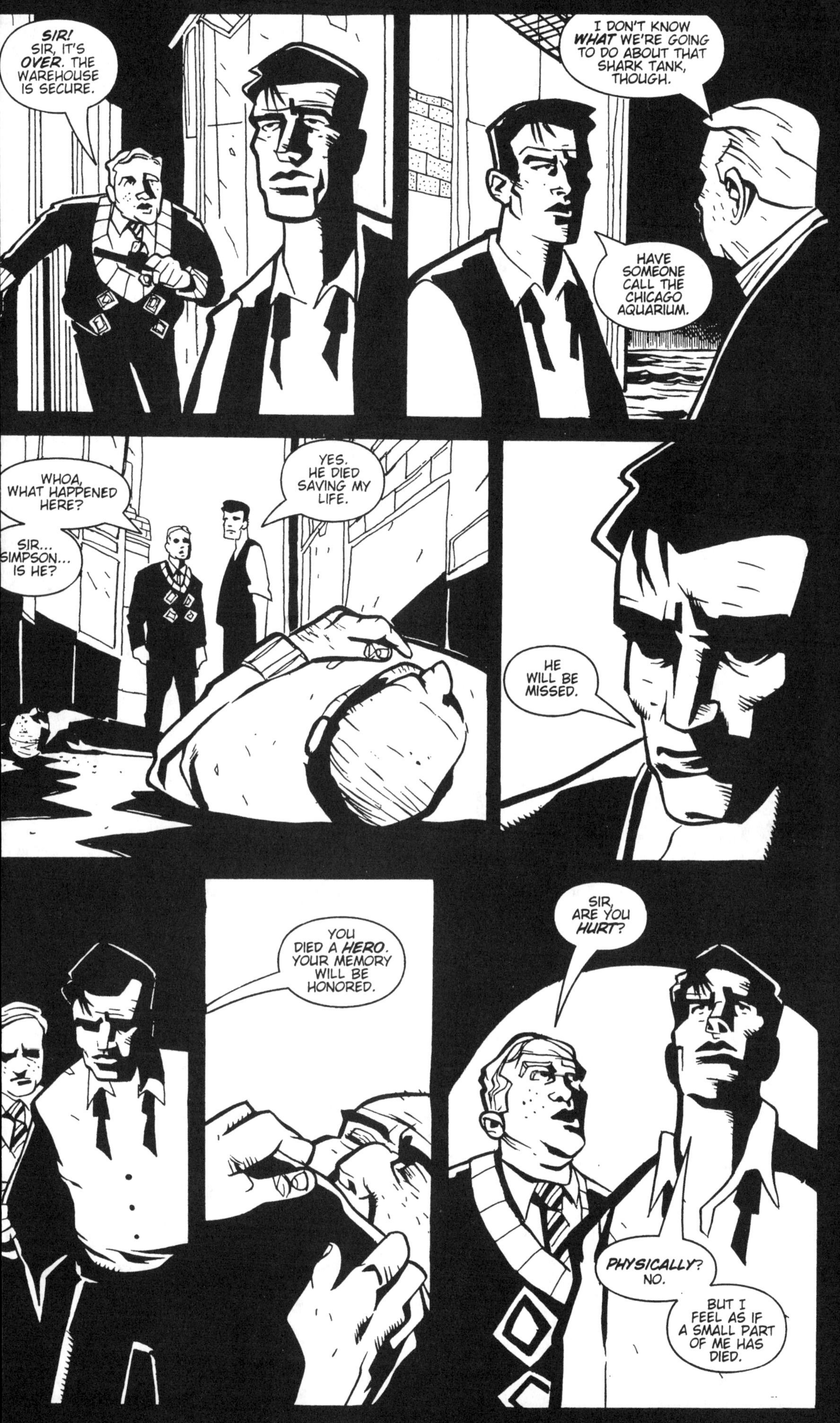
SIR! SIR, IT'S OVER. THE WAREHOUSE IS SECURE.
I DON'T KNOW WHAT WE'RE GOING TO DO ABOUT THAT SHARK TANK, THOUGH.
HAVE SOMEONE CALL THE CHICAGO AQUARIUM.
WHOA, WHAT HAPPENED HERE?
SIR... SIMPSON... IS HE?
YES. HE DIED SAVING MY LIFE.
HE WILL BE MISSED.
YOU DIED A HERO. YOUR MEMORY WILL BE HONORED.
SIR, ARE YOU HURT?
PHYSICALLY? NO.
BUT I FEEL AS IF A SMALL PART OF ME HAS DIED.

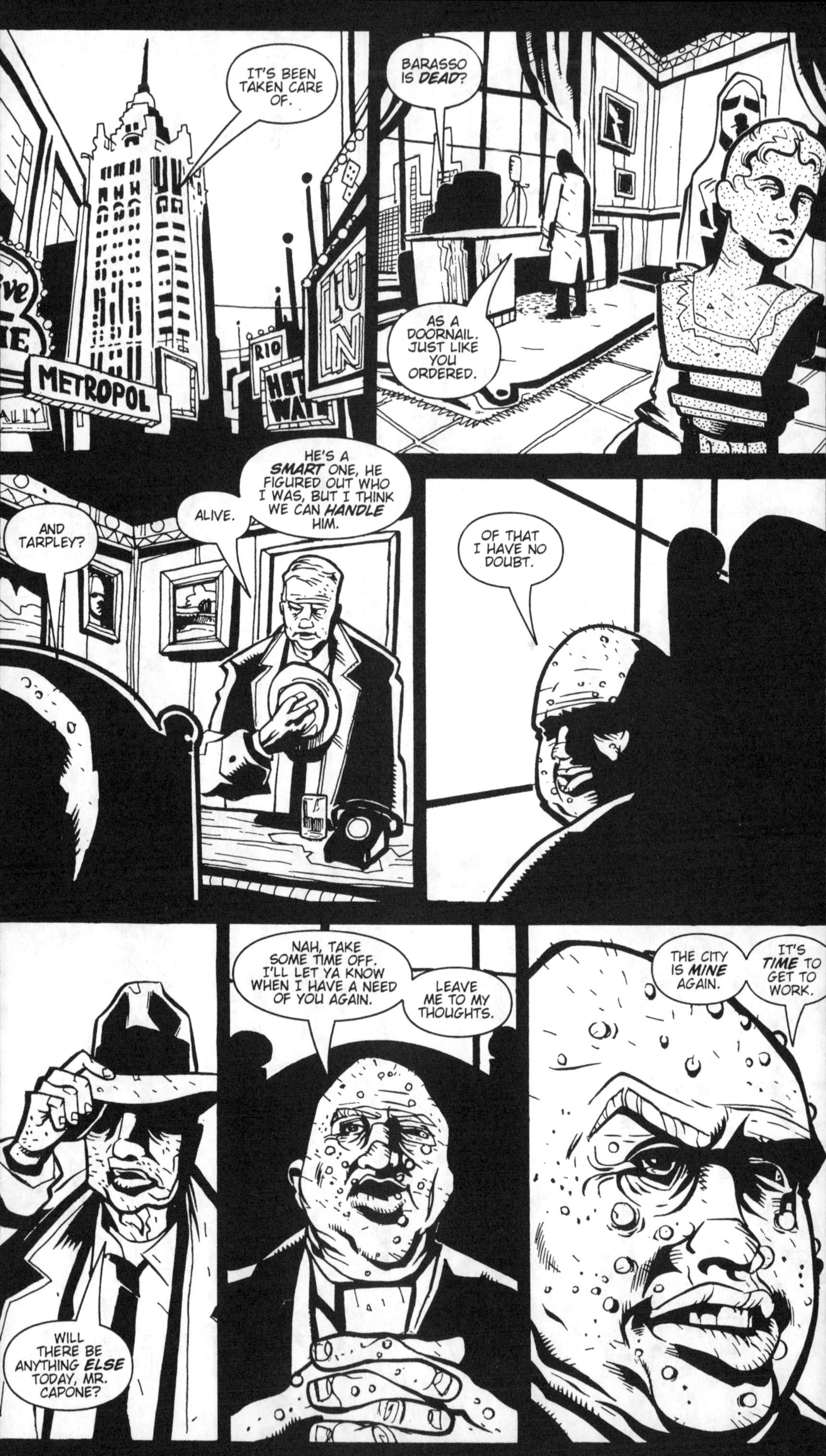
IT'S BEEN TAKEN CARE OF.
ive
IE
METROPOL
ALLY
RIO
LU
N
BARASSO IS *DEAD*?
AS A DOORNAIL. JUST LIKE YOU ORDERED.
AND TARPLEY?
ALIVE.
HE'S A *SMART* ONE, HE FIGURED OUT WHO I WAS, BUT I THINK WE CAN *HANDLE* HIM.
OF THAT I HAVE NO DOUBT.
WILL THERE BE ANYTHING *ELSE* TODAY, MR. CAPONE?
NAH, TAKE SOME TIME OFF. I'LL LET YA KNOW WHEN I HAVE A NEED OF YOU AGAIN.
LEAVE ME TO MY THOUGHTS.
THE CITY IS *MINE* AGAIN.
IT'S *TIME* TO GET TO WORK.

UNTOUCHABLES

"THE HIGH SOCIETY KILLER"

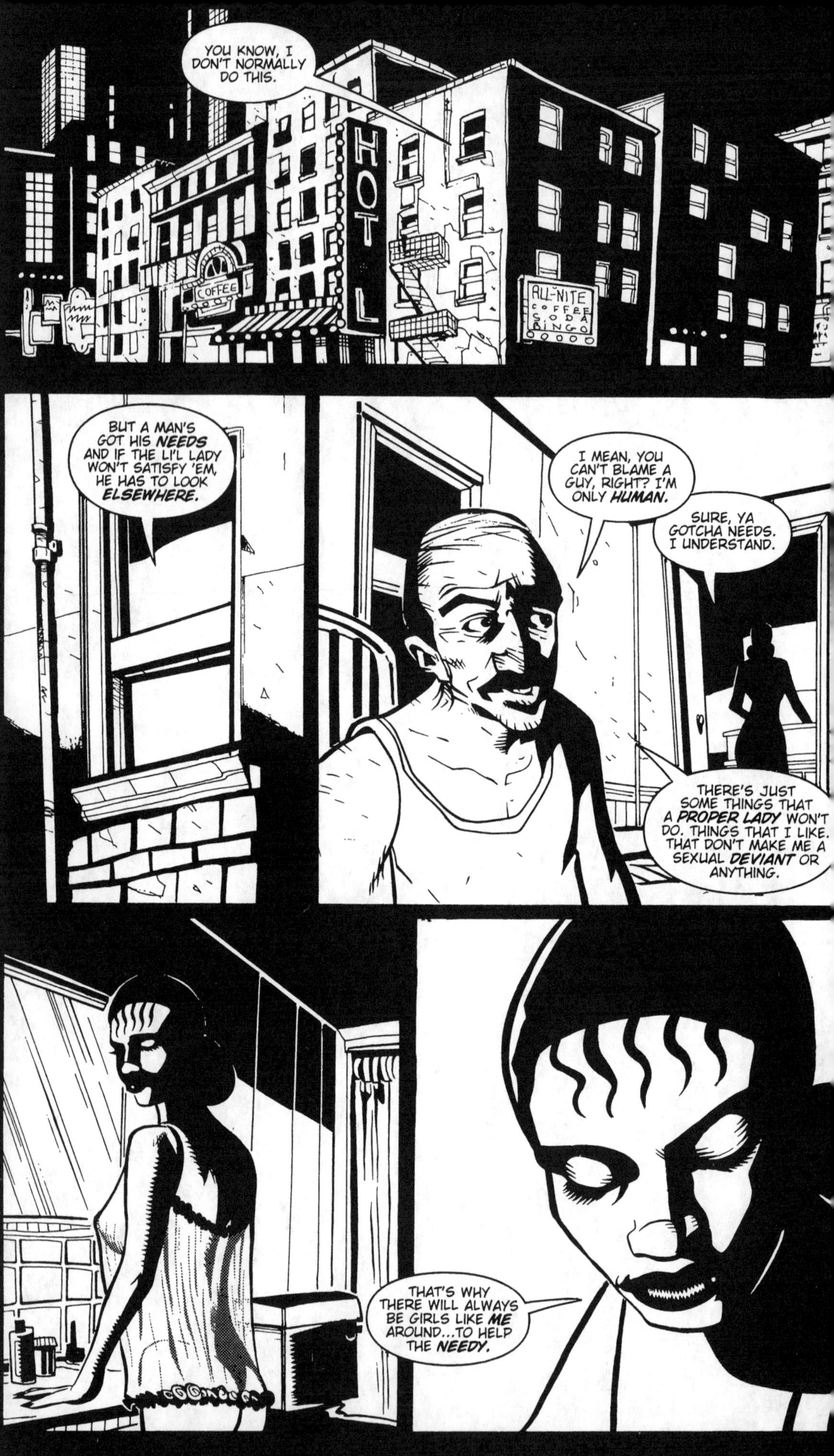
YOU KNOW, I DON'T NORMALLY DO THIS.
HOTEL
COFFEE
ALL-NITE COFFEE SODA BINGO
BUT A MAN'S GOT HIS NEEDS AND IF THE LI'L LADY WON'T SATISFY 'EM, HE HAS TO LOOK ELSEWHERE.
I MEAN, YOU CAN'T BLAME A GUY, RIGHT? I'M ONLY HUMAN.
SURE, YA GOTCHA NEEDS. I UNDERSTAND.
THERE'S JUST SOME THINGS THAT A PROPER LADY WON'T DO. THINGS THAT I LIKE. THAT DON'T MAKE ME A SEXUAL DEVIANT OR ANYTHING.
THAT'S WHY THERE WILL ALWAYS BE GIRLS LIKE ME AROUND...TO HELP THE NEEDY.

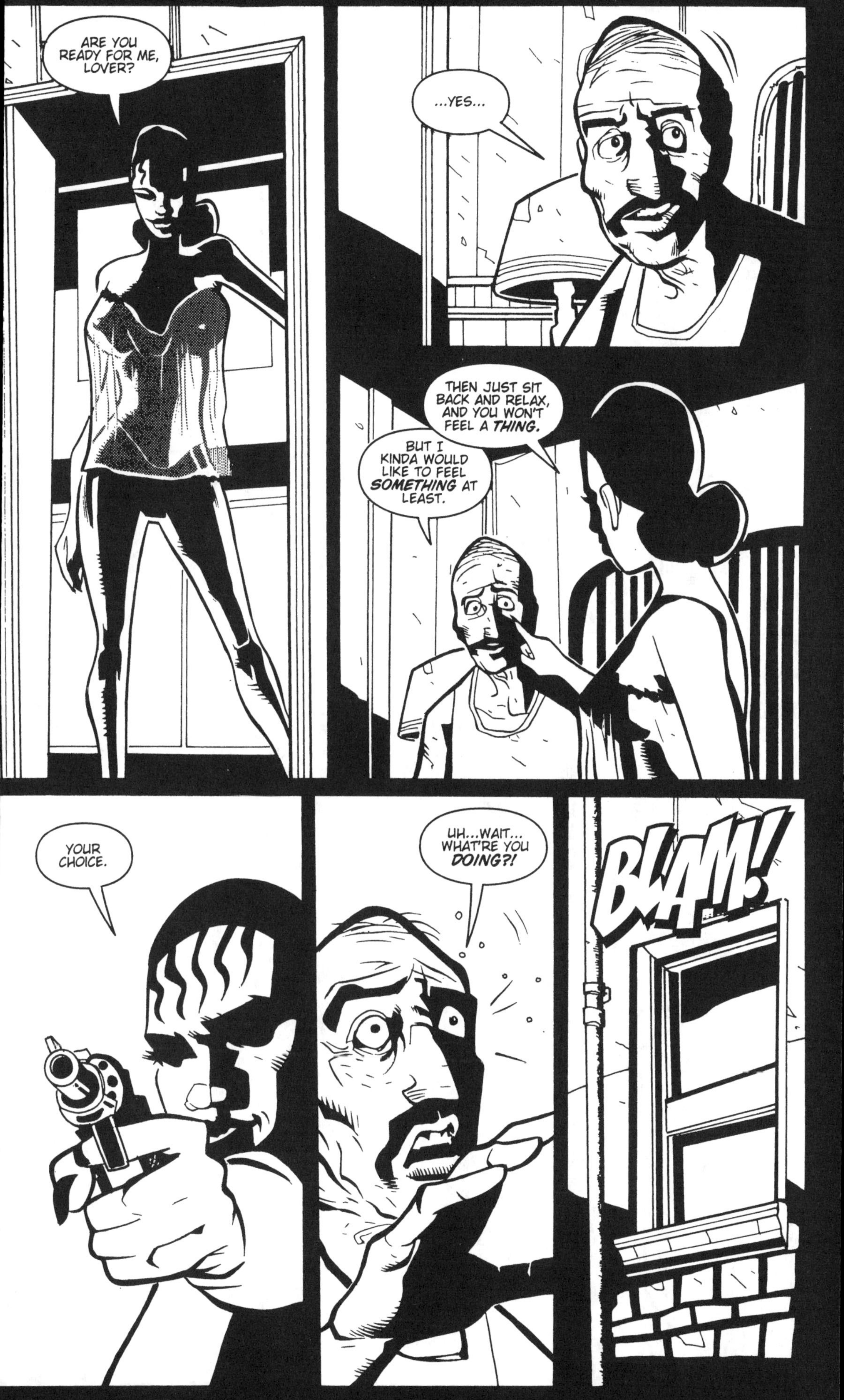

ARE YOU READY FOR ME, LOVER?
...YES...
THEN JUST SIT BACK AND RELAX, AND YOU WON'T FEEL A *THING.*
BUT I KINDA WOULD LIKE TO FEEL **SOMETHING** AT LEAST.
YOUR CHOICE.
UH...WAIT... WHAT'RE YOU **DOING?!**
BLAM!

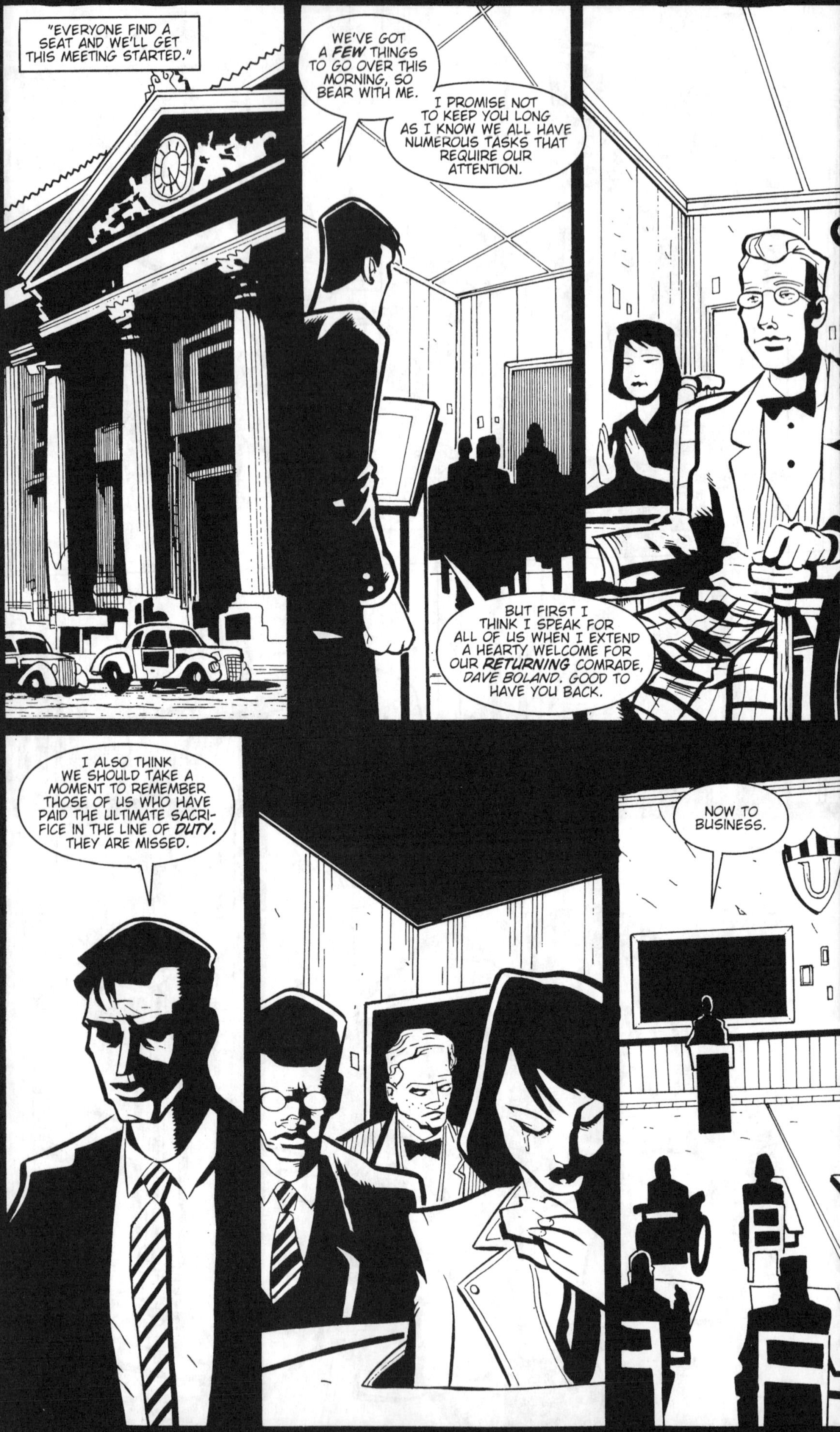
"EVERYONE FIND A SEAT AND WE'LL GET THIS MEETING STARTED."
WE'VE GOT A *FEW* THINGS TO GO OVER THIS MORNING, SO BEAR WITH ME.
I PROMISE NOT TO KEEP YOU LONG AS I KNOW WE ALL HAVE NUMEROUS TASKS THAT REQUIRE OUR ATTENTION.
BUT FIRST I THINK I SPEAK FOR ALL OF US WHEN I EXTEND A HEARTY WELCOME FOR OUR *RETURNING* COMRADE, *DAVE BOLAND*. GOOD TO HAVE YOU BACK.
I ALSO THINK WE SHOULD TAKE A MOMENT TO REMEMBER THOSE OF US WHO HAVE PAID THE ULTIMATE SACRIFICE IN THE LINE OF *DUTY*. THEY ARE MISSED.
NOW TO BUSINESS.

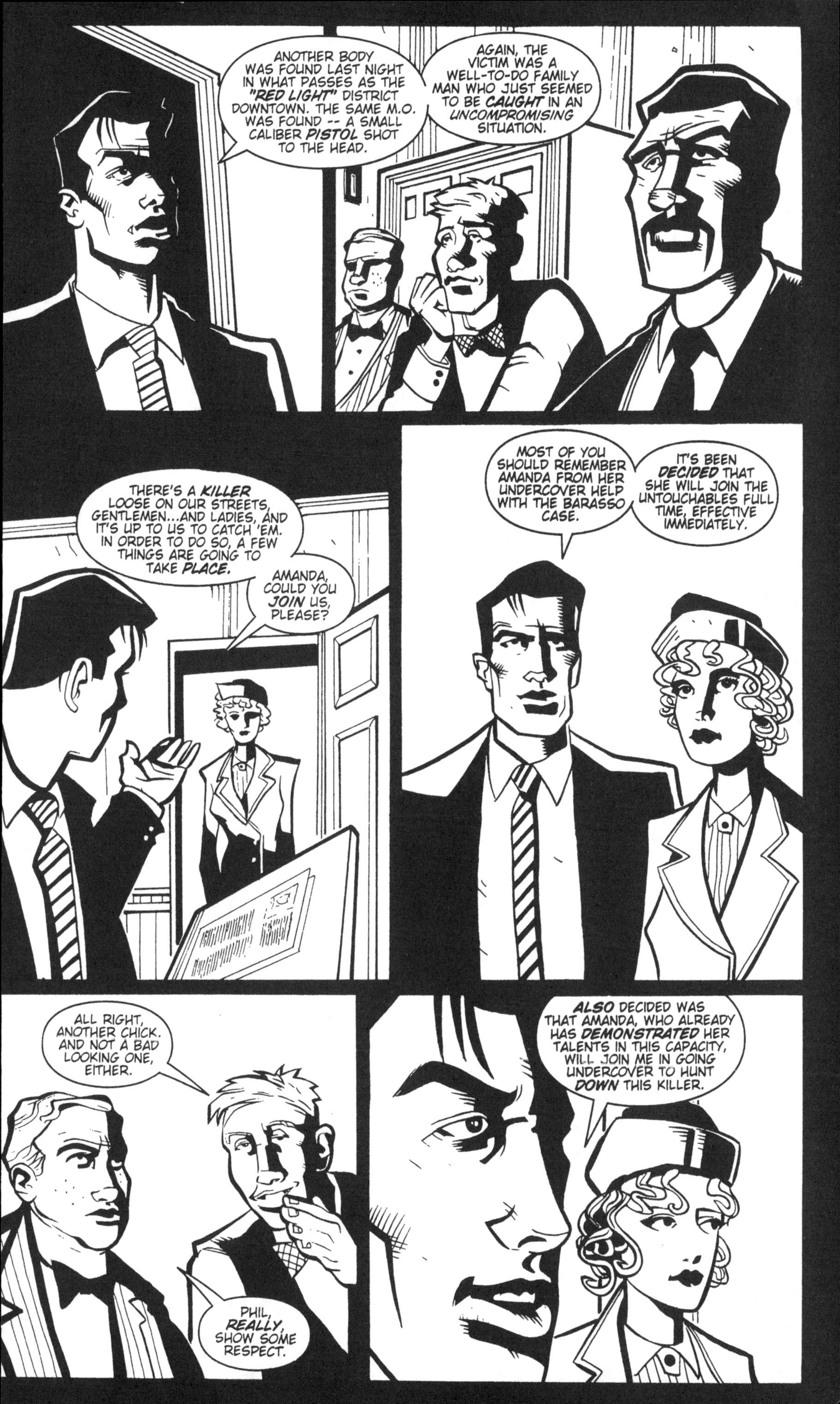
ANOTHER BODY WAS FOUND LAST NIGHT IN WHAT PASSES AS THE "RED LIGHT" DISTRICT DOWNTOWN. THE SAME M.O. WAS FOUND -- A SMALL CALIBER PISTOL SHOT TO THE HEAD.
AGAIN, THE VICTIM WAS A WELL-TO-DO FAMILY MAN WHO JUST SEEMED TO BE CAUGHT IN AN UNCOMPROMISING SITUATION.
THERE'S A KILLER LOOSE ON OUR STREETS, GENTLEMEN...AND LADIES, AND IT'S UP TO US TO CATCH 'EM. IN ORDER TO DO SO, A FEW THINGS ARE GOING TO TAKE PLACE.
AMANDA, COULD YOU JOIN US, PLEASE?
MOST OF YOU SHOULD REMEMBER AMANDA FROM HER UNDERCOVER HELP WITH THE BARASSO CASE.
IT'S BEEN DECIDED THAT SHE WILL JOIN THE UNTOUCHABLES FULL TIME, EFFECTIVE IMMEDIATELY.
ALL RIGHT, ANOTHER CHICK. AND NOT A BAD LOOKING ONE, EITHER.
PHIL, REALLY, SHOW SOME RESPECT.
ALSO DECIDED WAS THAT AMANDA, WHO ALREADY HAS DEMONSTRATED HER TALENTS IN THIS CAPACITY, WILL JOIN ME IN GOING UNDERCOVER TO HUNT DOWN THIS KILLER.

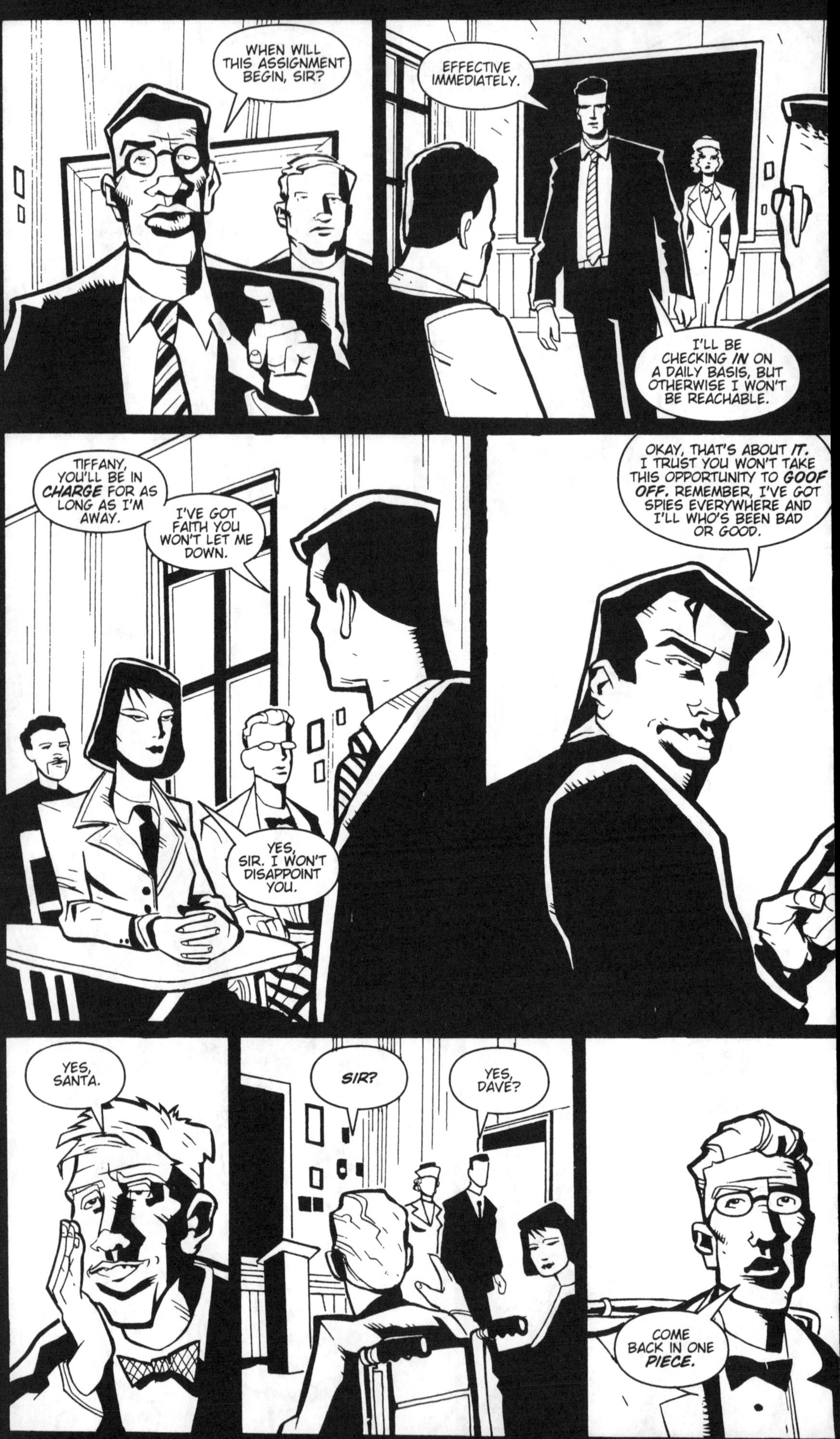
WHEN WILL THIS ASSIGNMENT BEGIN, SIR?
EFFECTIVE IMMEDIATELY.
I'LL BE CHECKING *IN* ON A DAILY BASIS, BUT OTHERWISE I WON'T BE REACHABLE.
TIFFANY, YOU'LL BE IN *CHARGE* FOR AS LONG AS I'M AWAY.
I'VE GOT FAITH YOU WON'T LET ME DOWN.
YES, SIR. I WON'T DISAPPOINT YOU.
OKAY, THAT'S ABOUT *IT.* I TRUST YOU WON'T TAKE THIS OPPORTUNITY TO *GOOF OFF.* REMEMBER, I'VE GOT SPIES EVERYWHERE AND I'LL WHO'S BEEN BAD OR GOOD.
YES, SANTA.
SIR?
YES, DAVE?
COME BACK IN ONE *PIECE.*

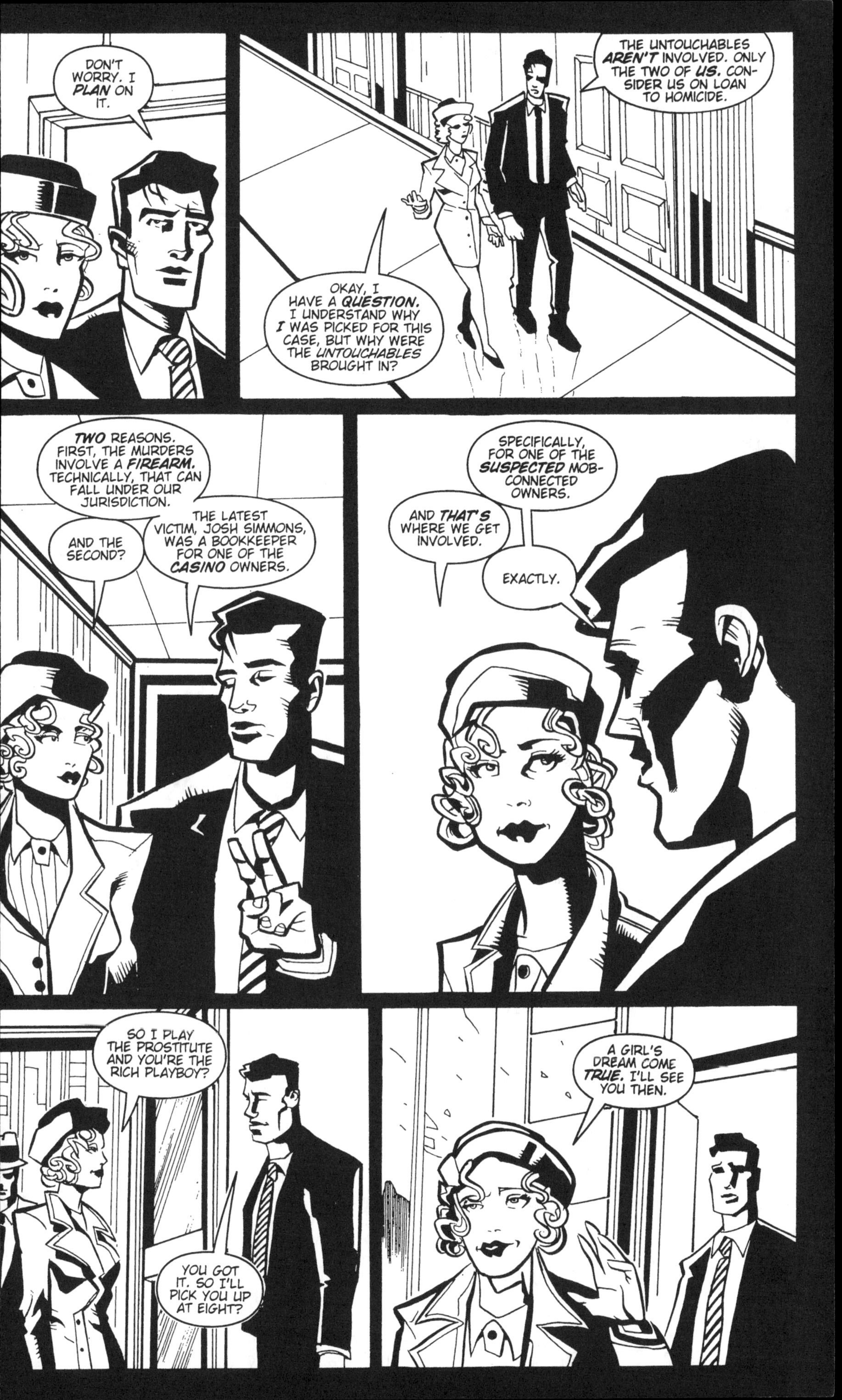
DON'T WORRY. I *PLAN* ON IT.
OKAY, I HAVE A **QUESTION.** I UNDERSTAND WHY *I* WAS PICKED FOR THIS CASE, BUT WHY WERE THE *UNTOUCHABLES* BROUGHT IN?
THE UNTOUCHABLES ***AREN'T*** INVOLVED. ONLY THE TWO OF ***US.*** CONSIDER US ON LOAN TO HOMICIDE.
TWO REASONS. FIRST, THE MURDERS INVOLVE A ***FIREARM.*** TECHNICALLY, THAT CAN FALL UNDER OUR JURISDICTION.
AND THE SECOND?
THE LATEST VICTIM, JOSH SIMMONS, WAS A BOOKKEEPER FOR ONE OF THE *CASINO* OWNERS.
SPECIFICALLY, FOR ONE OF THE ***SUSPECTED*** MOB-CONNECTED OWNERS.
AND ***THAT'S*** WHERE WE GET INVOLVED.
EXACTLY.
SO I PLAY THE PROSTITUTE AND YOU'RE THE RICH PLAYBOY?
YOU GOT IT. SO I'LL PICK YOU UP AT EIGHT?
A GIRL'S DREAM COME ***TRUE.*** I'LL SEE YOU THEN.

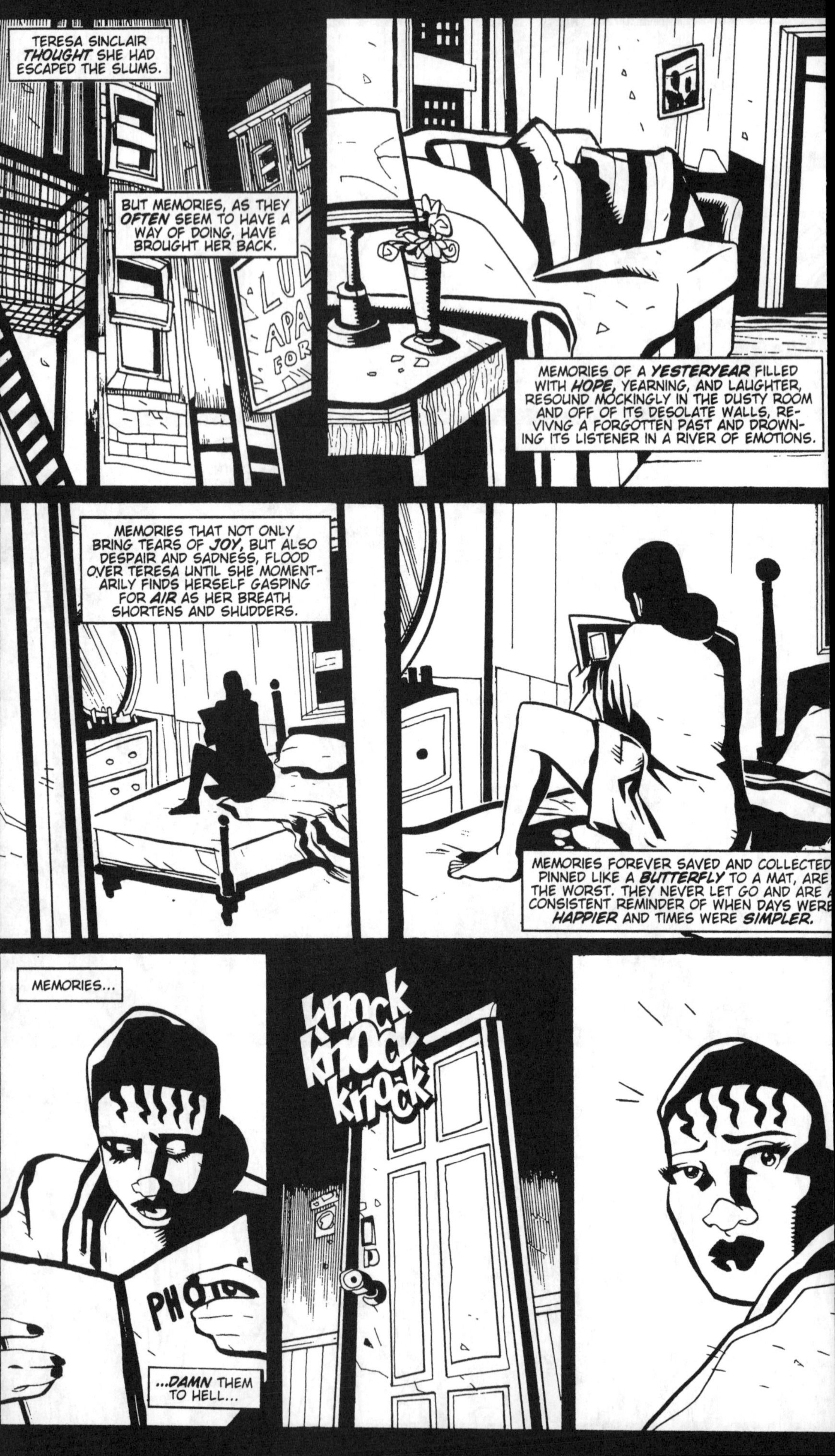

TERESA SINCLAIR THOUGHT SHE HAD ESCAPED THE SLUMS.
BUT MEMORIES, AS THEY OFTEN SEEM TO HAVE A WAY OF DOING, HAVE BROUGHT HER BACK.
MEMORIES OF A YESTERYEAR FILLED WITH HOPE, YEARNING, AND LAUGHTER, RESOUND MOCKINGLY IN THE DUSTY ROOM AND OFF OF ITS DESOLATE WALLS, RE-VIVNG A FORGOTTEN PAST AND DROWN-ING ITS LISTENER IN A RIVER OF EMOTIONS.
MEMORIES THAT NOT ONLY BRING TEARS OF JOY, BUT ALSO DESPAIR AND SADNESS, FLOOD OVER TERESA UNTIL SHE MOMENT-ARILY FINDS HERSELF GASPING FOR AIR AS HER BREATH SHORTENS AND SHUDDERS.
MEMORIES FOREVER SAVED AND COLLECTED PINNED LIKE A BUTTERFLY TO A MAT, ARE THE WORST. THEY NEVER LET GO AND ARE A CONSISTENT REMINDER OF WHEN DAYS WERE HAPPIER AND TIMES WERE SIMPLER.
MEMORIES...
PHOTO
...DAMN THEM TO HELL...
knock knock knock

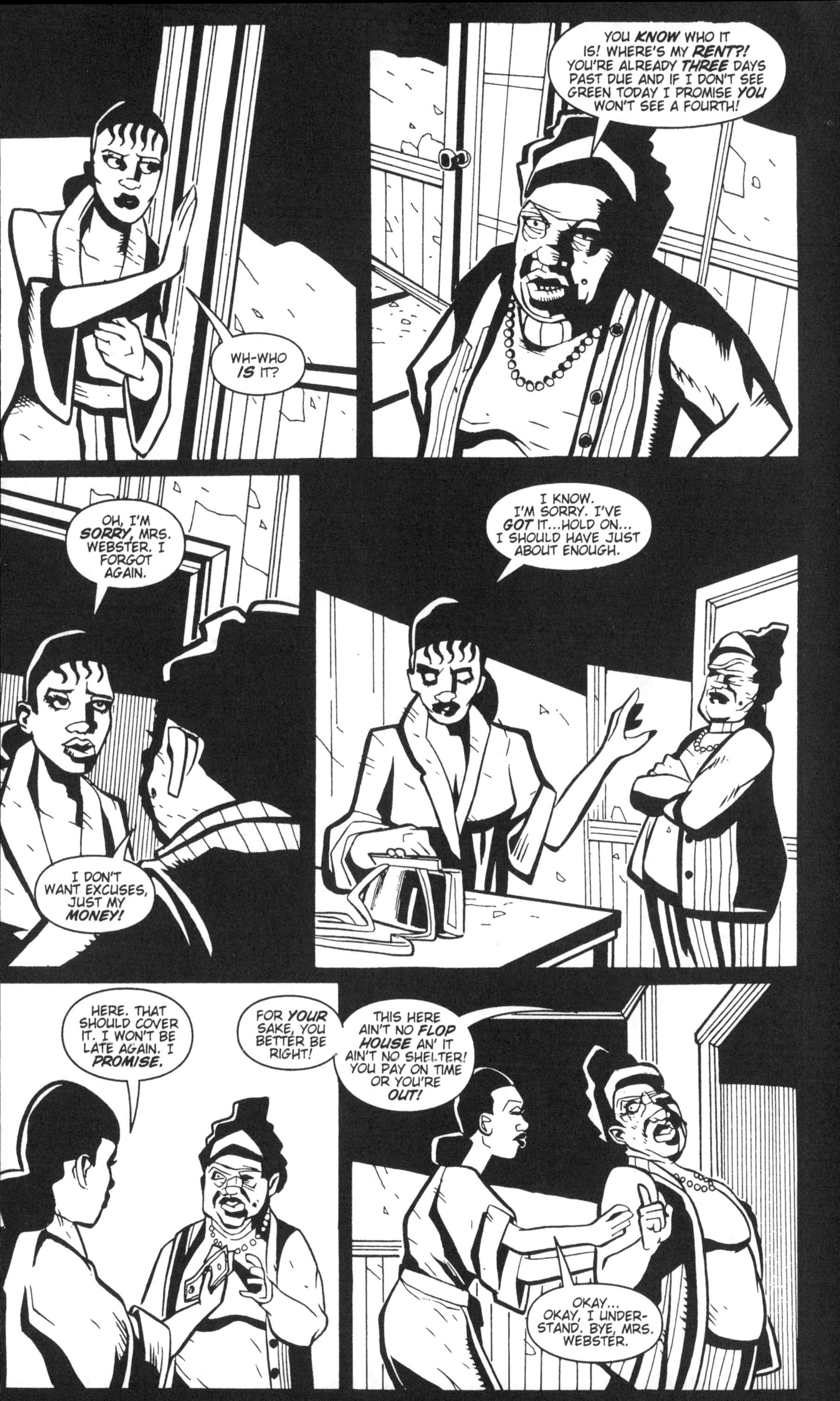
WH-WHO *IS* IT?
YOU *KNOW* WHO IT IS! WHERE'S MY *RENT?!* YOU'RE ALREADY *THREE* DAYS PAST DUE AND IF I DON'T SEE GREEN TODAY I PROMISE *YOU* WON'T SEE A FOURTH!
OH, I'M *SORRY,* MRS. WEBSTER. I FORGOT AGAIN.
I DON'T WANT EXCUSES, JUST MY *MONEY!*
I KNOW. I'M SORRY. I'VE *GOT* IT...HOLD ON... I SHOULD HAVE JUST ABOUT ENOUGH.
HERE. THAT SHOULD COVER IT. I WON'T BE LATE AGAIN. I *PROMISE.*
FOR *YOUR* SAKE, YOU BETTER BE RIGHT!
THIS HERE AIN'T NO *FLOP HOUSE* AN' IT AIN'T NO SHELTER! YOU PAY ON TIME OR YOU'RE *OUT!*
OKAY... OKAY, I UNDER-STAND. BYE, MRS. WEBSTER.

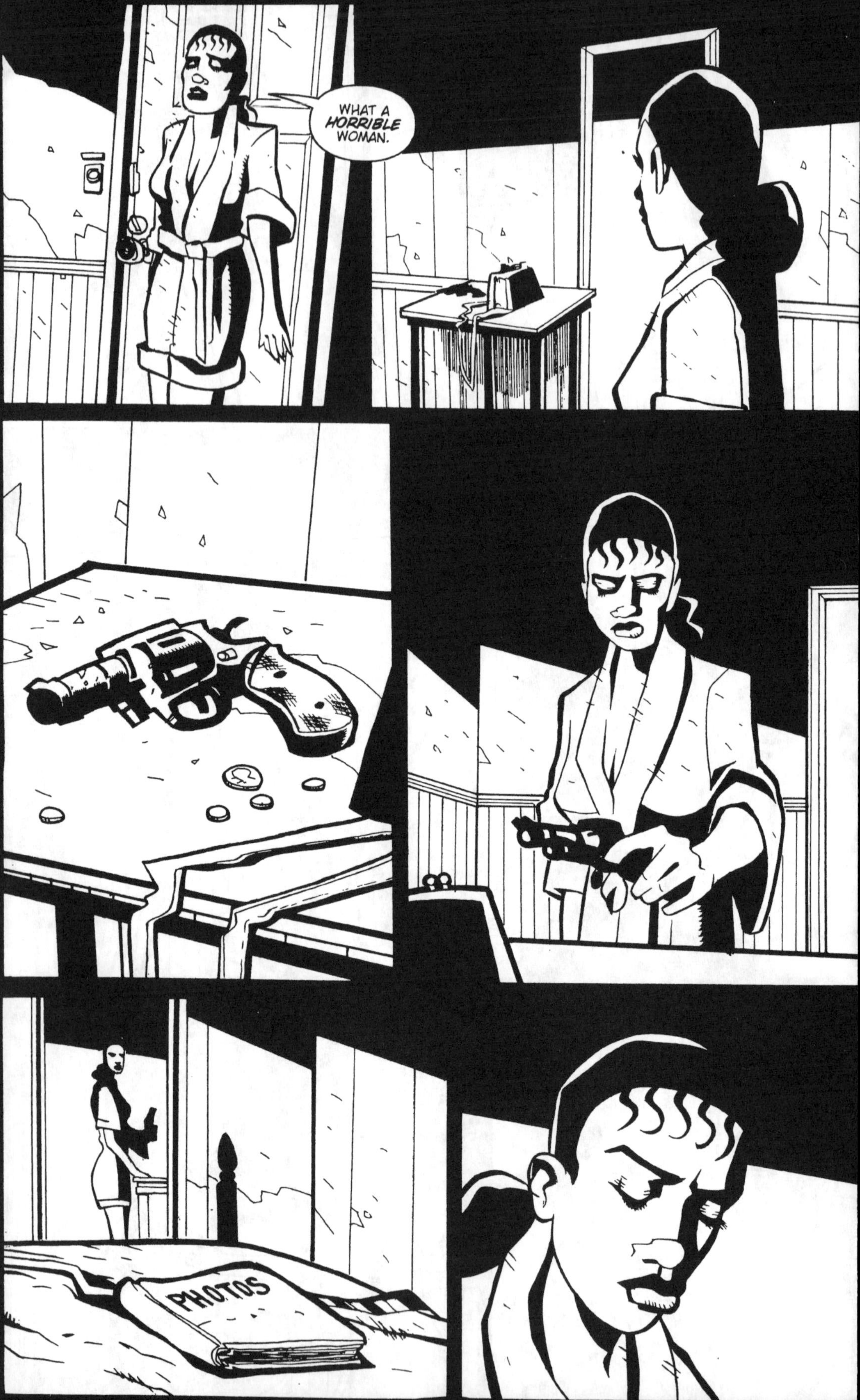
WHAT A HORRIBLE WOMAN.
PHOTOS

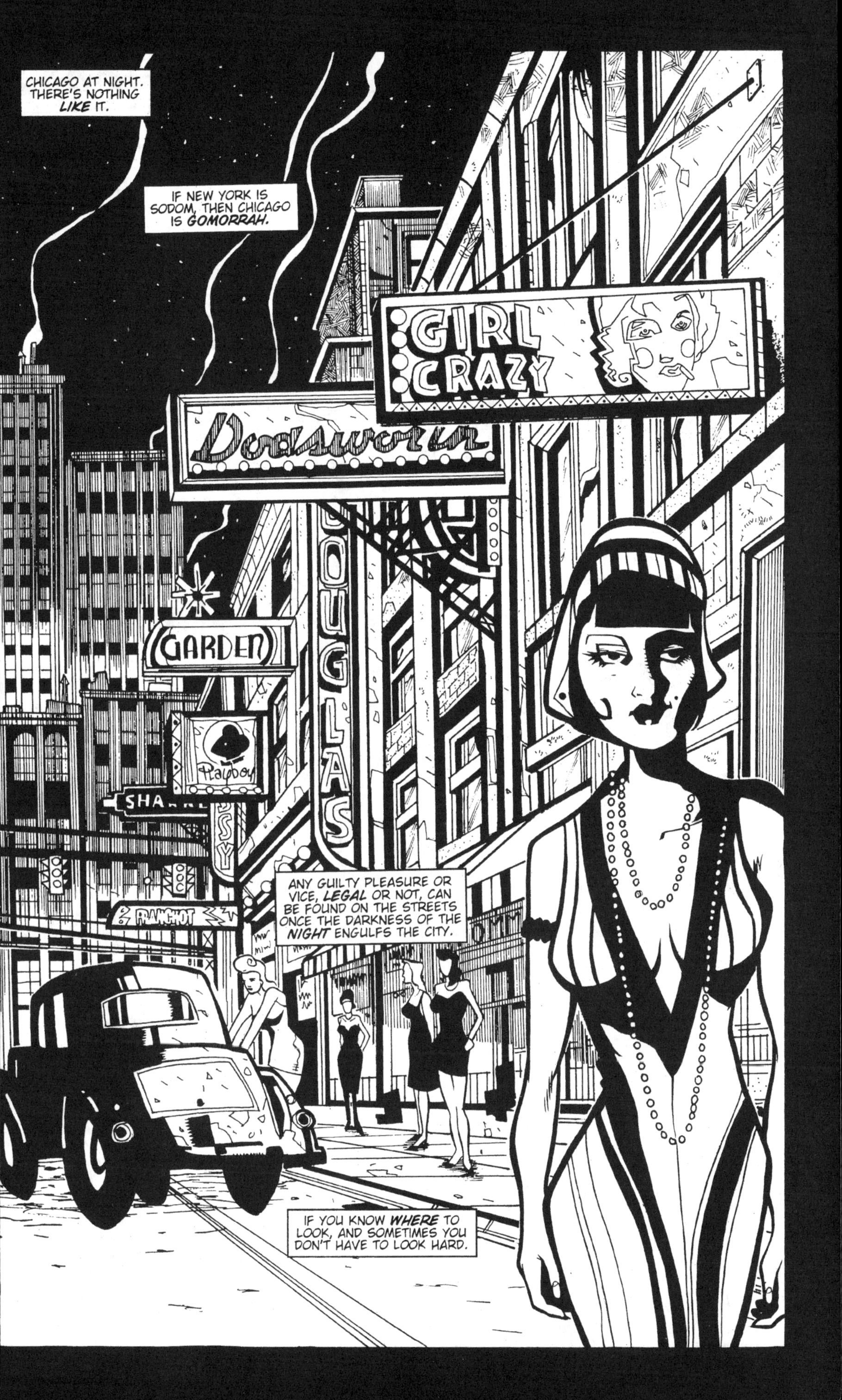
CHICAGO AT NIGHT. THERE'S NOTHING LIKE IT.
IF NEW YORK IS SODOM, THEN CHICAGO IS GOMORRAH.
GIRL CRAZY
GARDEN
DOUGLAS
Playboy
RANCHOT
ANY GUILTY PLEASURE OR VICE, LEGAL OR NOT, CAN BE FOUND ON THE STREETS ONCE THE DARKNESS OF THE NIGHT ENGULFS THE CITY.
IF YOU KNOW WHERE TO LOOK, AND SOMETIMES YOU DON'T HAVE TO LOOK HARD.

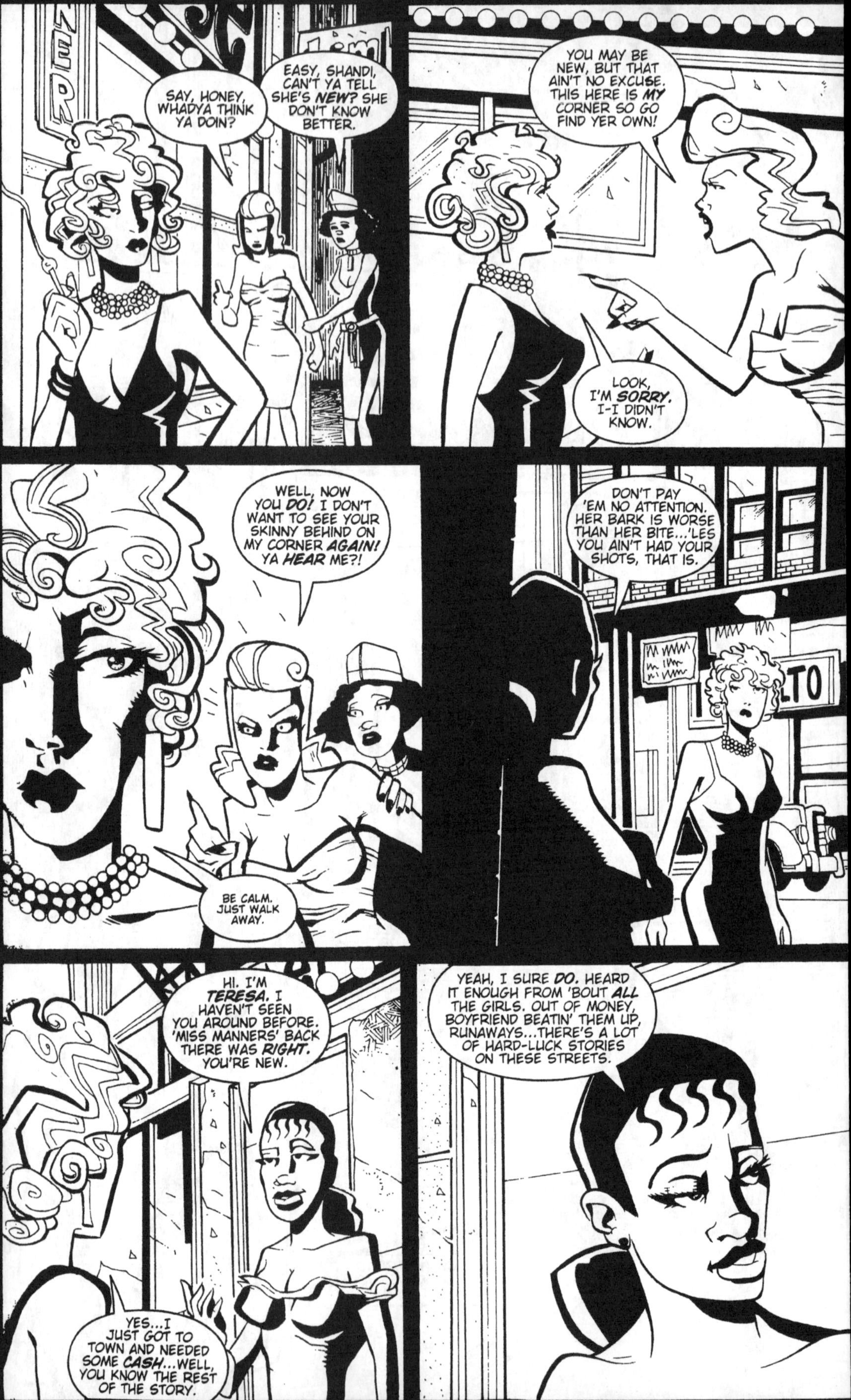
SAY, HONEY, WHADYA THINK YA DOIN?
EASY, SHANDI, CAN'T YA TELL SHE'S NEW? SHE DON'T KNOW BETTER.
YOU MAY BE NEW, BUT THAT AIN'T NO EXCUSE. THIS HERE IS MY CORNER SO GO FIND YER OWN!
LOOK, I'M SORRY. I-I DIDN'T KNOW.
WELL, NOW YOU DO! I DON'T WANT TO SEE YOUR SKINNY BEHIND ON MY CORNER AGAIN! YA HEAR ME?!
BE CALM. JUST WALK AWAY.
DON'T PAY 'EM NO ATTENTION. HER BARK IS WORSE THAN HER BITE...'LES YOU AIN'T HAD YOUR SHOTS, THAT IS.
LTO
HI. I'M TERESA. I HAVEN'T SEEN YOU AROUND BEFORE. 'MISS MANNERS' BACK THERE WAS RIGHT. YOU'RE NEW.
YES...I JUST GOT TO TOWN AND NEEDED SOME CASH...WELL, YOU KNOW THE REST OF THE STORY.
YEAH, I SURE DO. HEARD IT ENOUGH FROM 'BOUT ALL THE GIRLS. OUT OF MONEY, BOYFRIEND BEATIN' THEM UP, RUNAWAYS...THERE'S A LOT OF HARD-LUCK STORIES ON THESE STREETS.

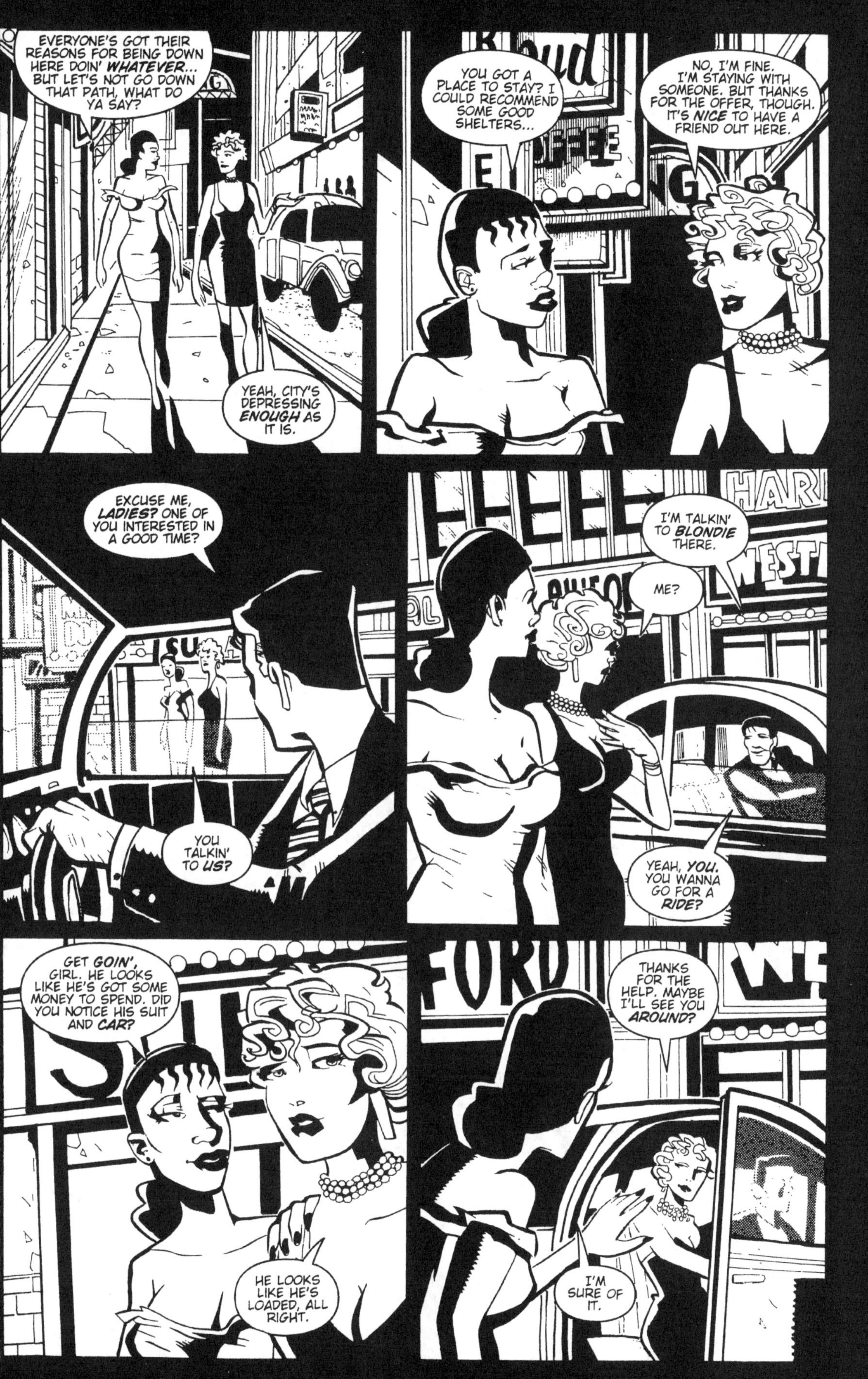
EVERYONE'S GOT THEIR REASONS FOR BEING DOWN HERE DOIN' WHATEVER... BUT LET'S NOT GO DOWN THAT PATH, WHAT DO YA SAY?
YEAH, CITY'S DEPRESSING ENOUGH AS IT IS.
YOU GOT A PLACE TO STAY? I COULD RECOMMEND SOME GOOD SHELTERS...
NO, I'M FINE. I'M STAYING WITH SOMEONE. BUT THANKS FOR THE OFFER, THOUGH. IT'S NICE TO HAVE A FRIEND OUT HERE.
COFFEE
EXCUSE ME, LADIES? ONE OF YOU INTERESTED IN A GOOD TIME?
YOU TALKIN' TO US?
I'M TALKIN' TO BLONDIE THERE.
ME?
YEAH, YOU. YOU WANNA GO FOR A RIDE?
GET GOIN', GIRL. HE LOOKS LIKE HE'S GOT SOME MONEY TO SPEND. DID YOU NOTICE HIS SUIT AND CAR?
HE LOOKS LIKE HE'S LOADED, ALL RIGHT.
THANKS FOR THE HELP. MAYBE I'LL SEE YOU AROUND?
I'M SURE OF IT.

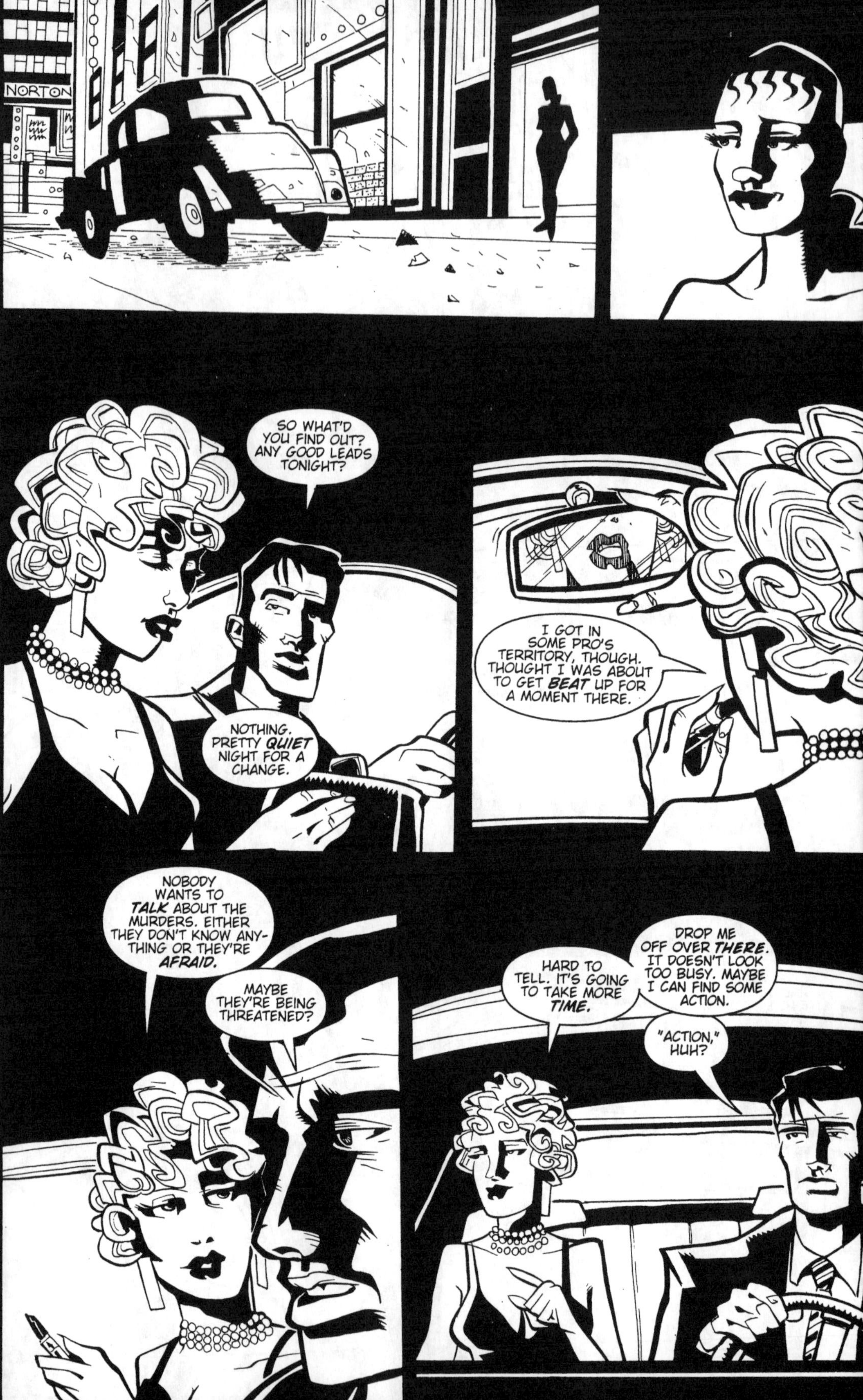
NORTON
SO WHAT'D YOU FIND OUT? ANY GOOD LEADS TONIGHT?
NOTHING. PRETTY QUIET NIGHT FOR A CHANGE.
I GOT IN SOME PRO'S TERRITORY, THOUGH. THOUGHT I WAS ABOUT TO GET BEAT UP FOR A MOMENT THERE.
NOBODY WANTS TO TALK ABOUT THE MURDERS. EITHER THEY DON'T KNOW ANY-THING OR THEY'RE AFRAID.
MAYBE THEY'RE BEING THREATENED?
HARD TO TELL. IT'S GOING TO TAKE MORE TIME.
DROP ME OFF OVER THERE. IT DOESN'T LOOK TOO BUSY. MAYBE I CAN FIND SOME ACTION.
"ACTION," HUH?

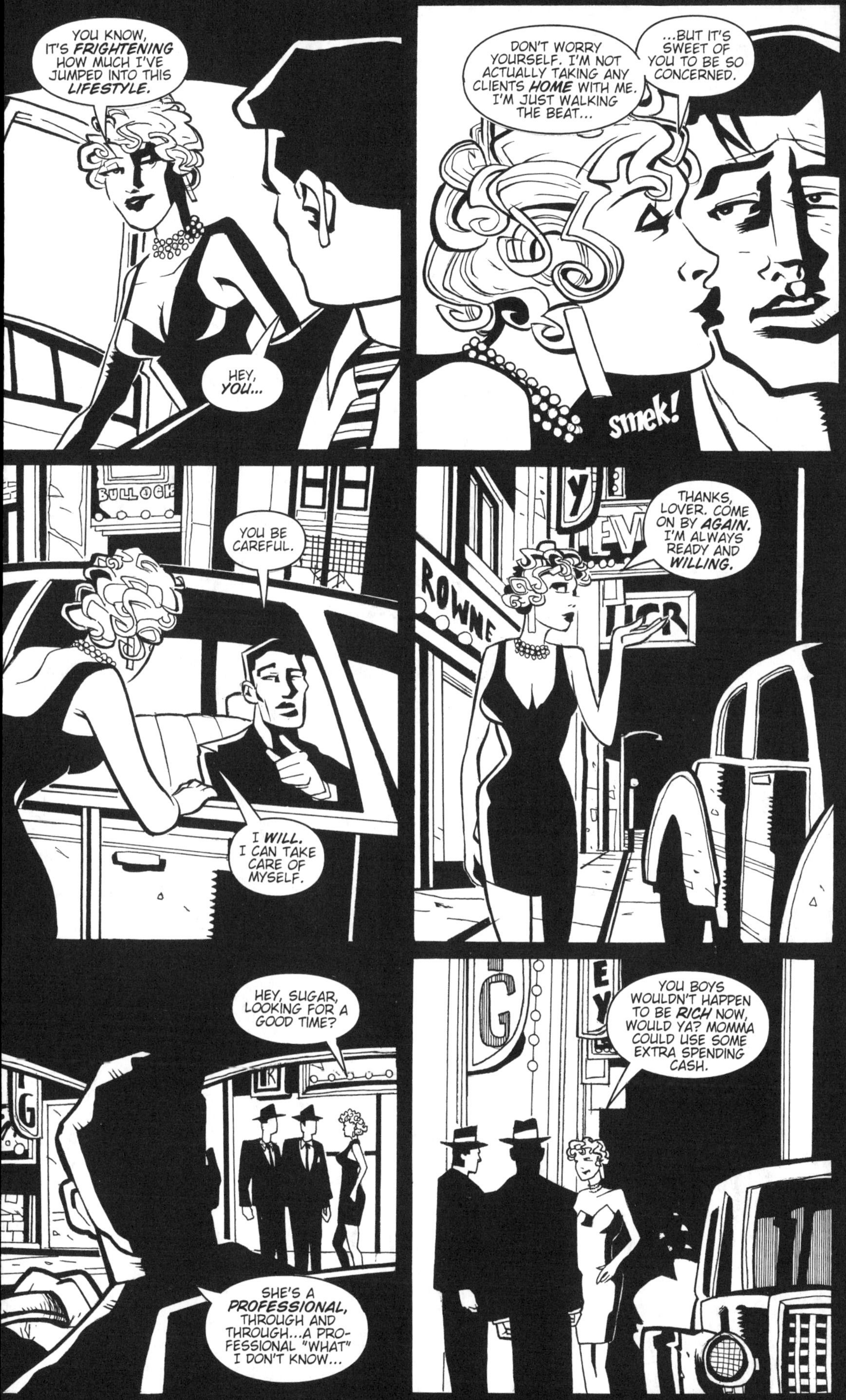
YOU KNOW, IT'S FRIGHTENING HOW MUCH I'VE JUMPED INTO THIS LIFESTYLE.
HEY, YOU...
DON'T WORRY YOURSELF. I'M NOT ACTUALLY TAKING ANY CLIENTS HOME WITH ME. I'M JUST WALKING THE BEAT...
...BUT IT'S SWEET OF YOU TO BE SO CONCERNED.
SMEK!
BULLOCH
YOU BE CAREFUL.
I WILL. I CAN TAKE CARE OF MYSELF.
THANKS, LOVER. COME ON BY AGAIN. I'M ALWAYS READY AND WILLING.
ROWNE
HEY, SUGAR, LOOKING FOR A GOOD TIME?
SHE'S A PROFESSIONAL, THROUGH AND THROUGH...A PROFESSIONAL "WHAT" I DON'T KNOW...
YOU BOYS WOULDN'T HAPPEN TO BE RICH NOW, WOULD YA? MOMMA COULD USE SOME EXTRA SPENDING CASH.

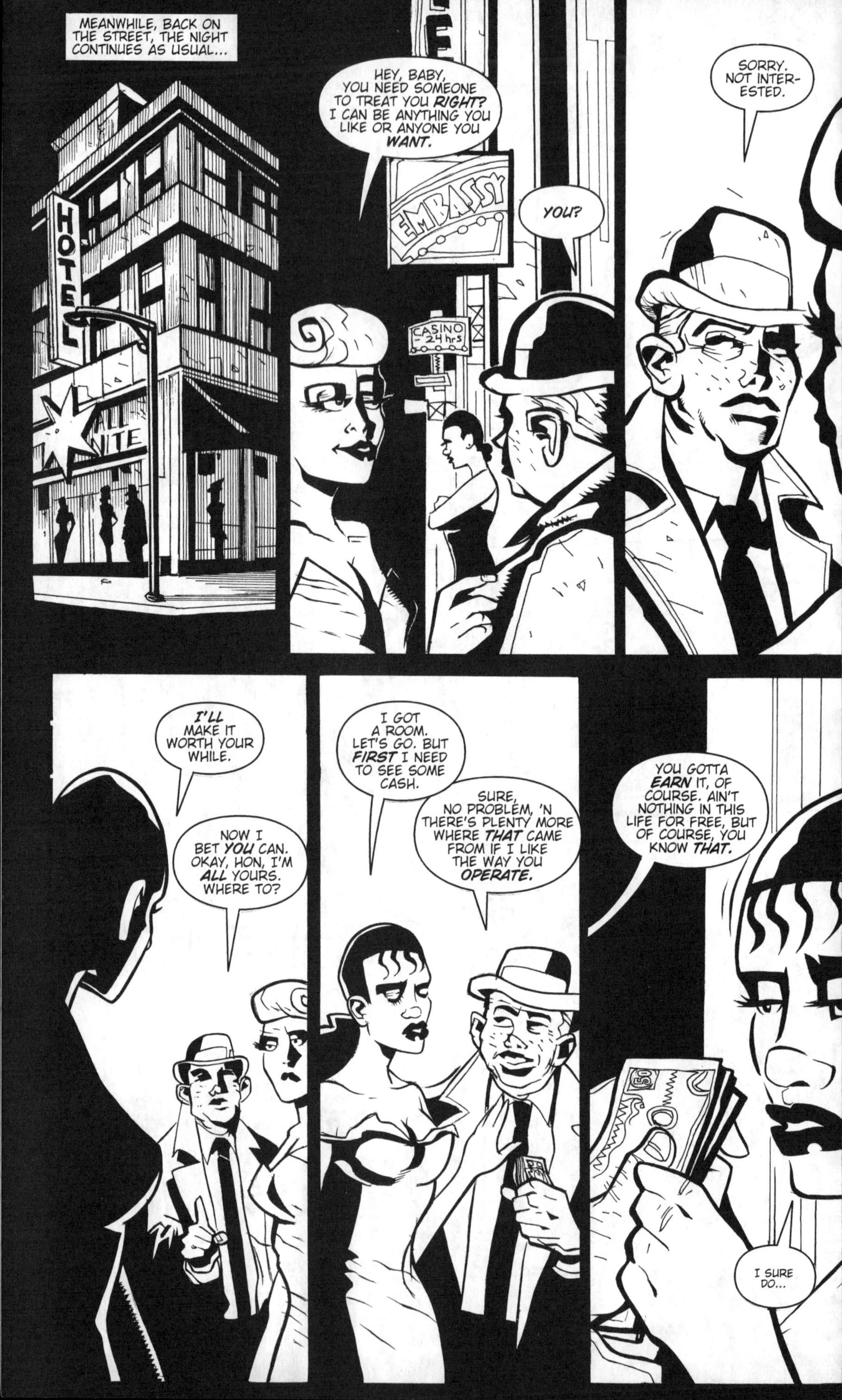

MEANWHILE, BACK ON THE STREET, THE NIGHT CONTINUES AS USUAL...
HOTEL
ALL NITE
HEY, BABY, YOU NEED SOMEONE TO TREAT YOU RIGHT? I CAN BE ANYTHING YOU LIKE OR ANYONE YOU WANT.
EMBASSY
CASINO - 24 hrs
YOU?
SORRY. NOT INTER-ESTED.
I'LL MAKE IT WORTH YOUR WHILE.
NOW I BET YOU CAN. OKAY, HON, I'M ALL YOURS. WHERE TO?
I GOT A ROOM. LET'S GO. BUT FIRST I NEED TO SEE SOME CASH.
SURE, NO PROBLEM, 'N THERE'S PLENTY MORE WHERE THAT CAME FROM IF I LIKE THE WAY YOU OPERATE.
YOU GOTTA EARN IT, OF COURSE. AIN'T NOTHING IN THIS LIFE FOR FREE, BUT OF COURSE, YOU KNOW THAT.
I SURE DO...

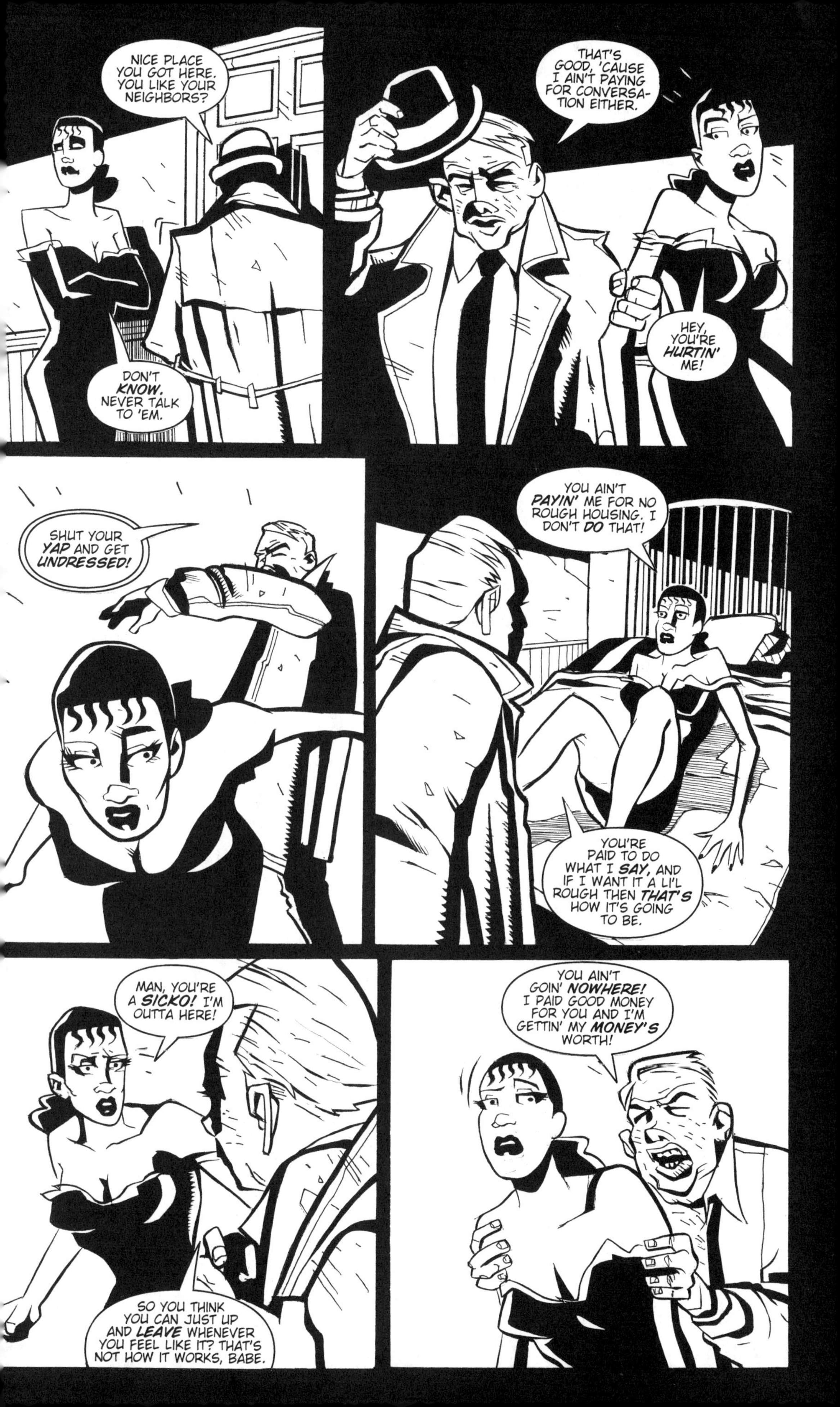
NICE PLACE YOU GOT HERE. YOU LIKE YOUR NEIGHBORS?
DON'T KNOW. NEVER TALK TO 'EM.
THAT'S GOOD, 'CAUSE I AIN'T PAYING FOR CONVERSATION EITHER.
HEY, YOU'RE HURTIN' ME!
SHUT YOUR YAP AND GET UNDRESSED!
YOU AIN'T PAYIN' ME FOR NO ROUGH HOUSING. I DON'T DO THAT!
YOU'RE PAID TO DO WHAT I SAY, AND IF I WANT IT A LI'L ROUGH THEN THAT'S HOW IT'S GOING TO BE.
MAN, YOU'RE A SICKO! I'M OUTTA HERE!
SO YOU THINK YOU CAN JUST UP AND LEAVE WHENEVER YOU FEEL LIKE IT? THAT'S NOT HOW IT WORKS, BABE.
YOU AIN'T GOIN' NOWHERE! I PAID GOOD MONEY FOR YOU AND I'M GETTIN' MY MONEY'S WORTH!

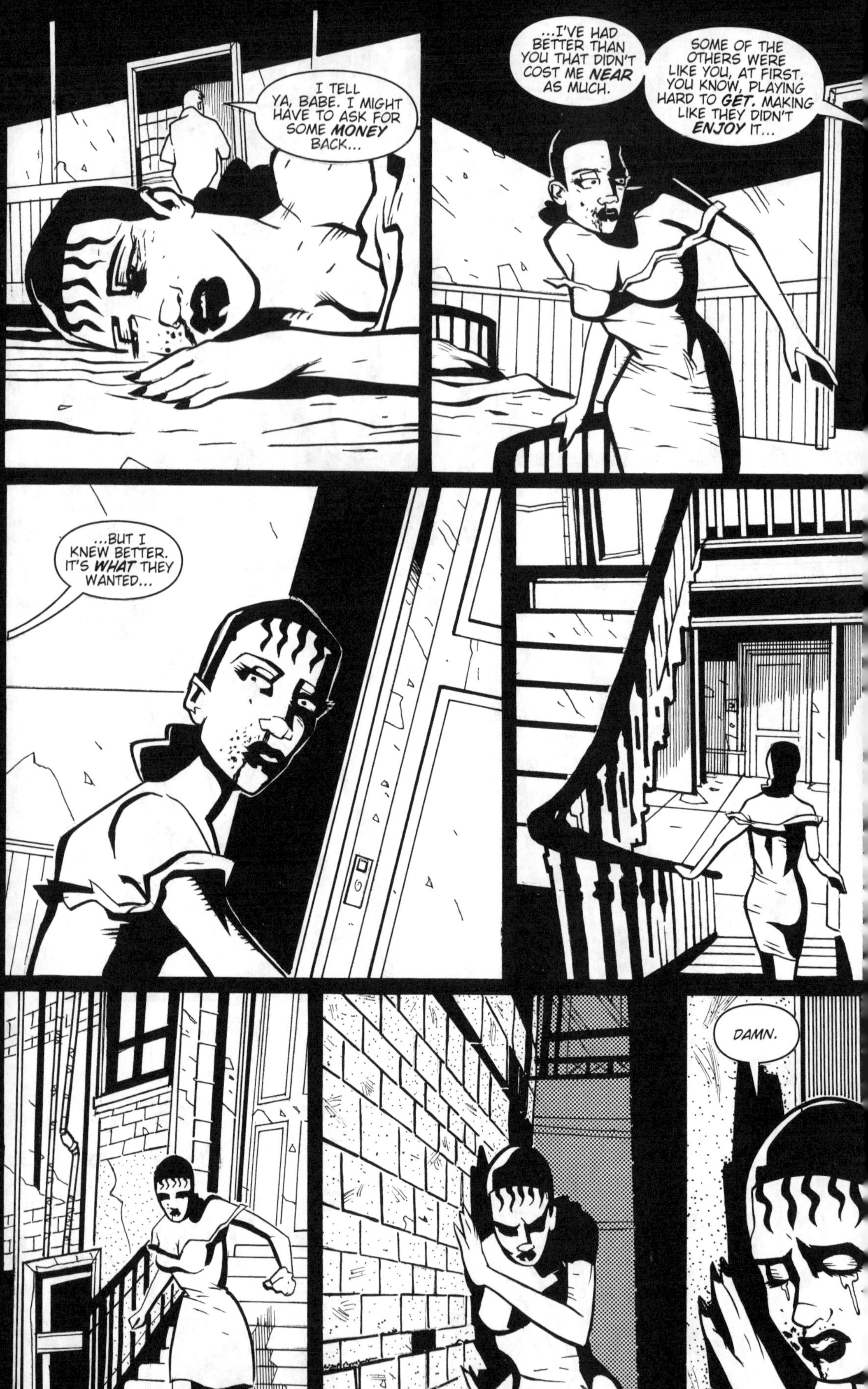

I TELL YA, BABE. I MIGHT HAVE TO ASK FOR SOME MONEY BACK...
...I'VE HAD BETTER THAN YOU THAT DIDN'T COST ME NEAR AS MUCH.
SOME OF THE OTHERS WERE LIKE YOU, AT FIRST. YOU KNOW, PLAYING HARD TO GET. MAKING LIKE THEY DIDN'T ENJOY IT...
...BUT I KNEW BETTER. IT'S WHAT THEY WANTED...
DAMN.

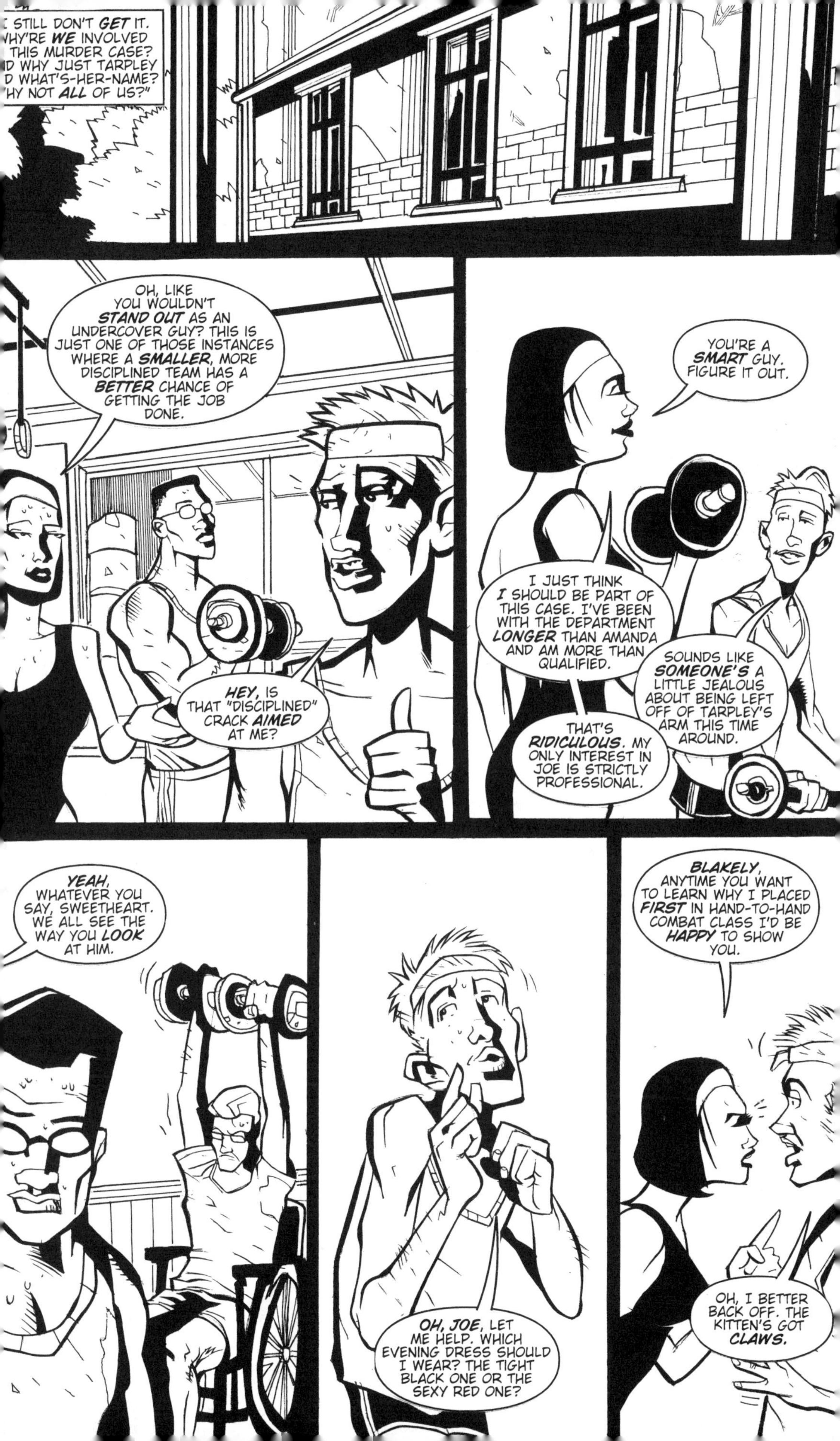

"I STILL DON'T GET IT. WHY'RE WE INVOLVED IN THIS MURDER CASE? AND WHY JUST TARPLEY AND WHAT'S-HER-NAME? WHY NOT ALL OF US?"
OH, LIKE YOU WOULDN'T STAND OUT AS AN UNDERCOVER GUY? THIS IS JUST ONE OF THOSE INSTANCES WHERE A SMALLER, MORE DISCIPLINED TEAM HAS A BETTER CHANCE OF GETTING THE JOB DONE.
HEY, IS THAT "DISCIPLINED" CRACK AIMED AT ME?
YOU'RE A SMART GUY. FIGURE IT OUT.
I JUST THINK I SHOULD BE PART OF THIS CASE. I'VE BEEN WITH THE DEPARTMENT LONGER THAN AMANDA AND AM MORE THAN QUALIFIED.
SOUNDS LIKE SOMEONE'S A LITTLE JEALOUS ABOUT BEING LEFT OFF OF TARPLEY'S ARM THIS TIME AROUND.
THAT'S RIDICULOUS. MY ONLY INTEREST IN JOE IS STRICTLY PROFESSIONAL.
YEAH, WHATEVER YOU SAY, SWEETHEART. WE ALL SEE THE WAY YOU LOOK AT HIM.
OH, JOE, LET ME HELP. WHICH EVENING DRESS SHOULD I WEAR? THE TIGHT BLACK ONE OR THE SEXY RED ONE?
BLAKELY, ANYTIME YOU WANT TO LEARN WHY I PLACED FIRST IN HAND-TO-HAND COMBAT CLASS I'D BE HAPPY TO SHOW YOU.
OH, I BETTER BACK OFF. THE KITTEN'S GOT CLAWS.

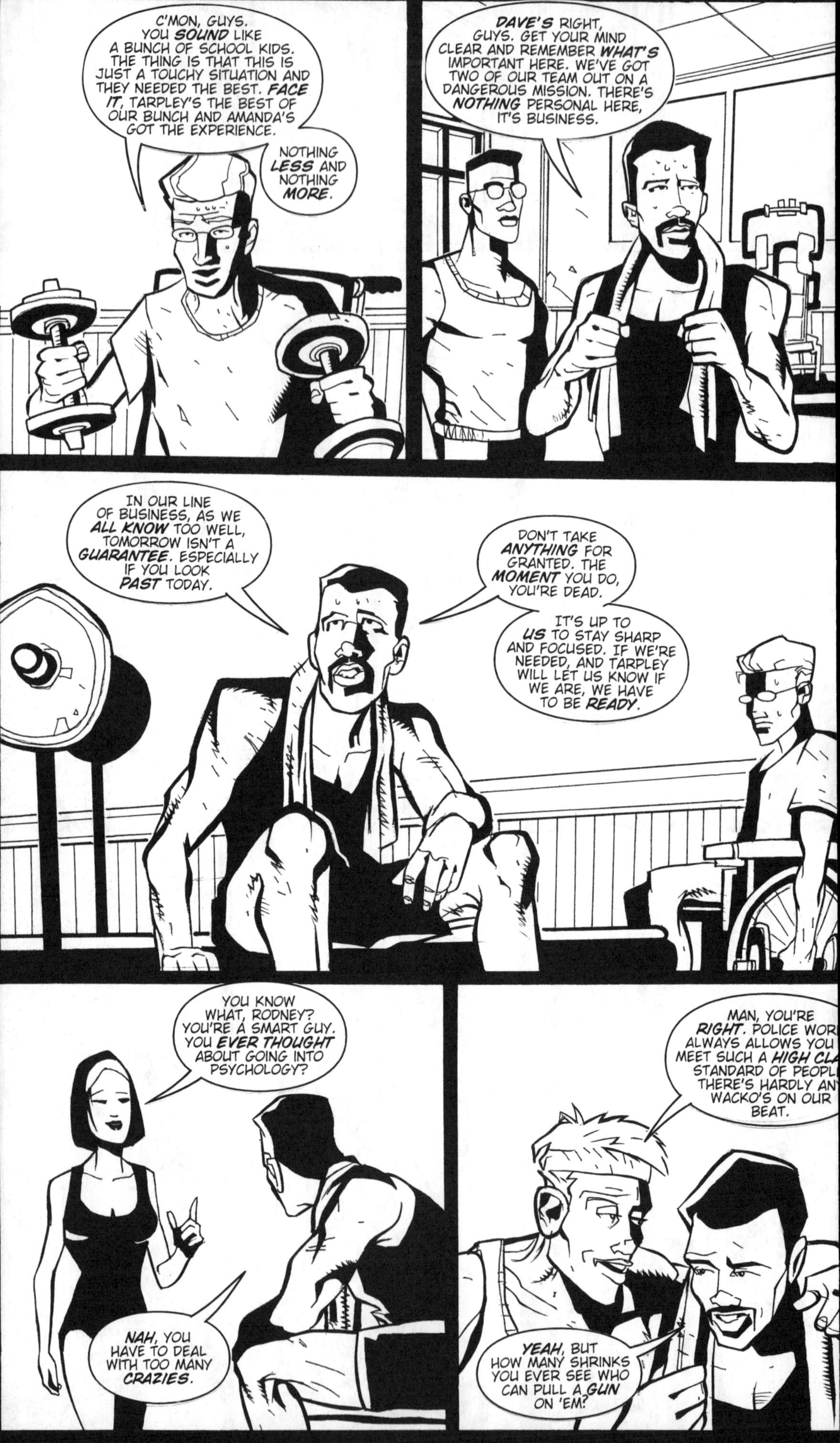
C'MON, GUYS. YOU SOUND LIKE A BUNCH OF SCHOOL KIDS. THE THING IS THAT THIS IS JUST A TOUCHY SITUATION AND THEY NEEDED THE BEST. FACE IT, TARPLEY'S THE BEST OF OUR BUNCH AND AMANDA'S GOT THE EXPERIENCE.
NOTHING LESS AND NOTHING MORE.
DAVE'S RIGHT, GUYS. GET YOUR MIND CLEAR AND REMEMBER WHAT'S IMPORTANT HERE. WE'VE GOT TWO OF OUR TEAM OUT ON A DANGEROUS MISSION. THERE'S NOTHING PERSONAL HERE, IT'S BUSINESS.
IN OUR LINE OF BUSINESS, AS WE ALL KNOW TOO WELL, TOMORROW ISN'T A GUARANTEE. ESPECIALLY IF YOU LOOK PAST TODAY.
DON'T TAKE ANYTHING FOR GRANTED. THE MOMENT YOU DO, YOU'RE DEAD.
IT'S UP TO US TO STAY SHARP AND FOCUSED. IF WE'RE NEEDED, AND TARPLEY WILL LET US KNOW IF WE ARE, WE HAVE TO BE READY.
YOU KNOW WHAT, RODNEY? YOU'RE A SMART GUY. YOU EVER THOUGHT ABOUT GOING INTO PSYCHOLOGY?
NAH, YOU HAVE TO DEAL WITH TOO MANY CRAZIES.
MAN, YOU'RE RIGHT. POLICE WOR ALWAYS ALLOWS YOU MEET SUCH A HIGH CLA STANDARD OF PEOPL THERE'S HARDLY AN WACKO'S ON OUR BEAT.
YEAH, BUT HOW MANY SHRINKS YOU EVER SEE WHO CAN PULL A GUN ON 'EM?

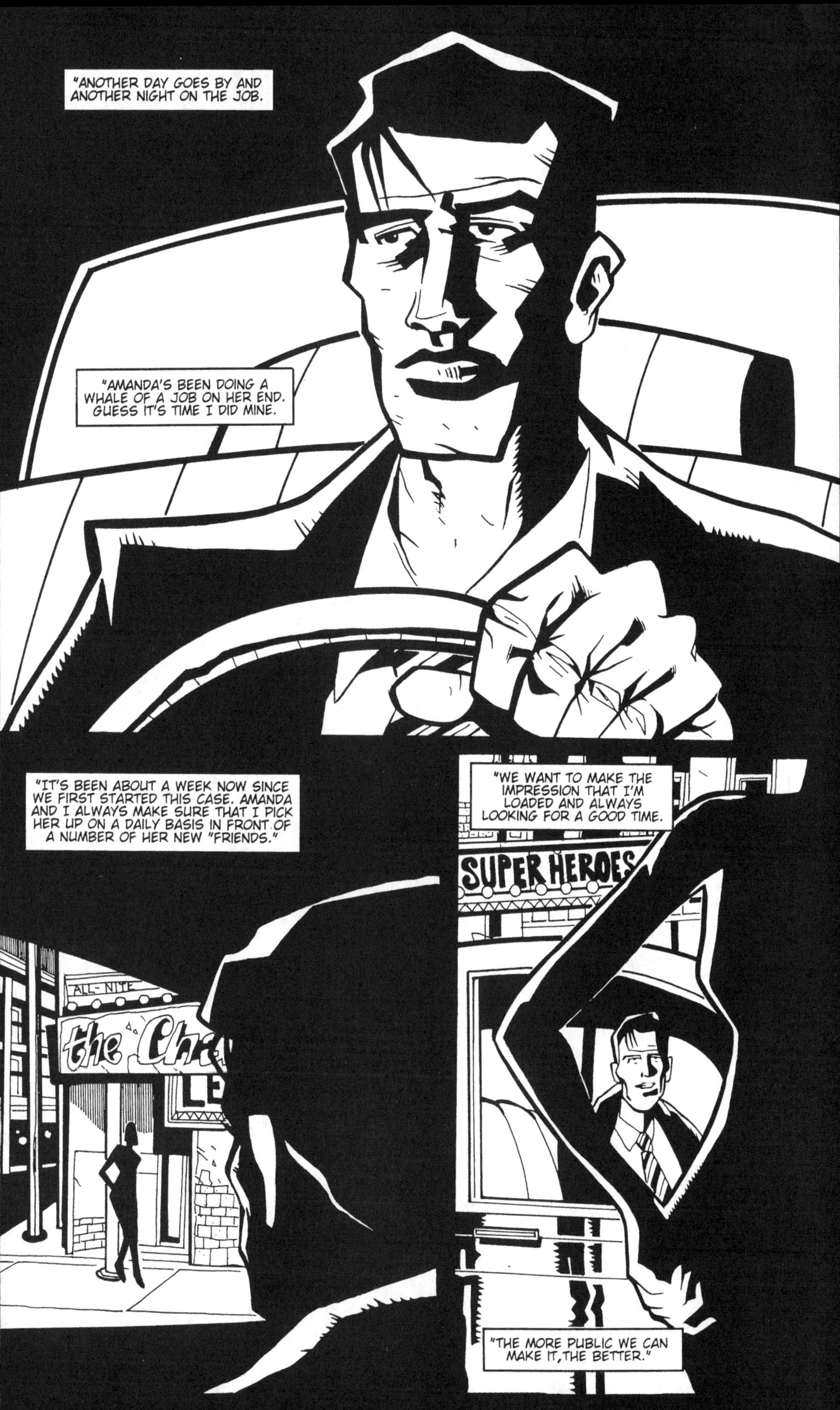

"ANOTHER DAY GOES BY AND ANOTHER NIGHT ON THE JOB.
"AMANDA'S BEEN DOING A WHALE OF A JOB ON HER END. GUESS IT'S TIME I DID MINE.
"IT'S BEEN ABOUT A WEEK NOW SINCE WE FIRST STARTED THIS CASE. AMANDA AND I ALWAYS MAKE SURE THAT I PICK HER UP ON A DAILY BASIS IN FRONT OF A NUMBER OF HER NEW "FRIENDS."
ALL-NITE
"WE WANT TO MAKE THE IMPRESSION THAT I'M LOADED AND ALWAYS LOOKING FOR A GOOD TIME.
SUPER HEROES
"THE MORE PUBLIC WE CAN MAKE IT, THE BETTER."

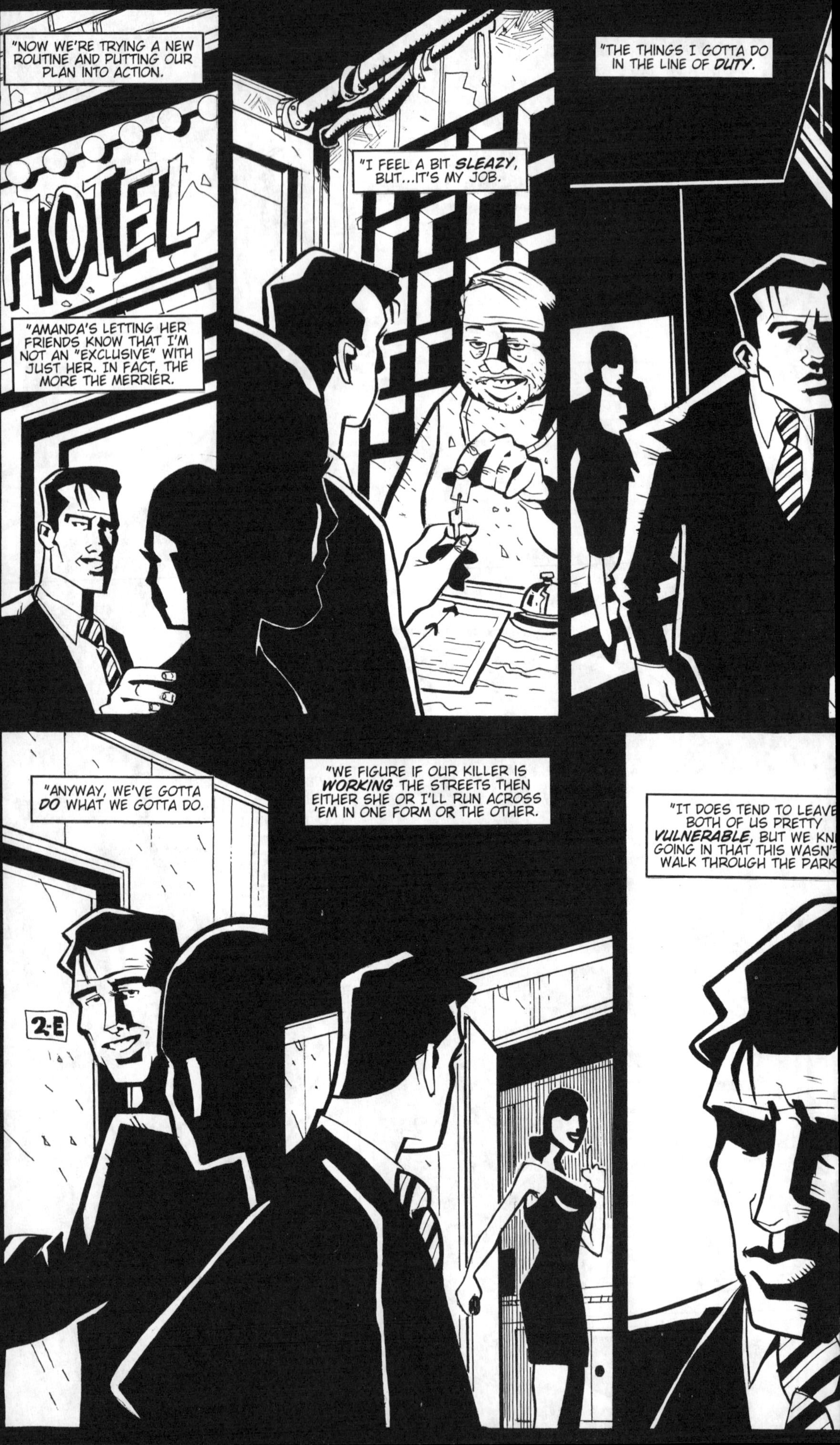
"NOW WE'RE TRYING A NEW ROUTINE AND PUTTING OUR PLAN INTO ACTION.
HOTEL
"AMANDA'S LETTING HER FRIENDS KNOW THAT I'M NOT AN "EXCLUSIVE" WITH JUST HER. IN FACT, THE MORE THE MERRIER.
"I FEEL A BIT SLEAZY, BUT...IT'S MY JOB.
"THE THINGS I GOTTA DO IN THE LINE OF DUTY.
"ANYWAY, WE'VE GOTTA DO WHAT WE GOTTA DO.
2-E
"WE FIGURE IF OUR KILLER IS WORKING THE STREETS THEN EITHER SHE OR I'LL RUN ACROSS 'EM IN ONE FORM OR THE OTHER.
"IT DOES TEND TO LEAVE BOTH OF US PRETTY VULNERABLE, BUT WE KN GOING IN THAT THIS WASN'T WALK THROUGH THE PARK

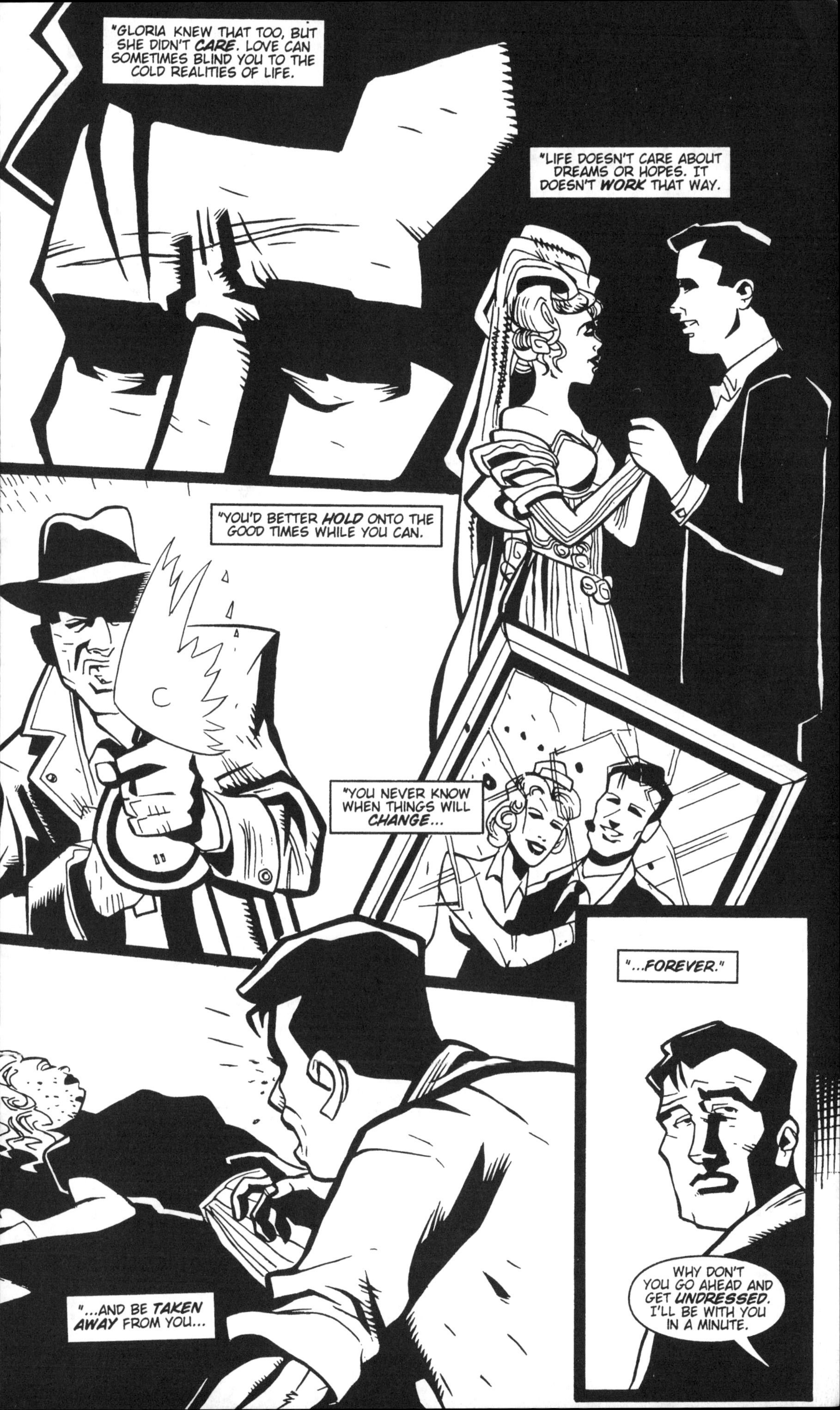
"GLORIA KNEW THAT TOO, BUT SHE DIDN'T CARE. LOVE CAN SOMETIMES BLIND YOU TO THE COLD REALITIES OF LIFE.
"LIFE DOESN'T CARE ABOUT DREAMS OR HOPES. IT DOESN'T WORK THAT WAY.
"YOU'D BETTER HOLD ONTO THE GOOD TIMES WHILE YOU CAN.
"YOU NEVER KNOW WHEN THINGS WILL CHANGE...
"...AND BE TAKEN AWAY FROM YOU...
"...FOREVER."
WHY DON'T YOU GO AHEAD AND GET UNDRESSED. I'LL BE WITH YOU IN A MINUTE.

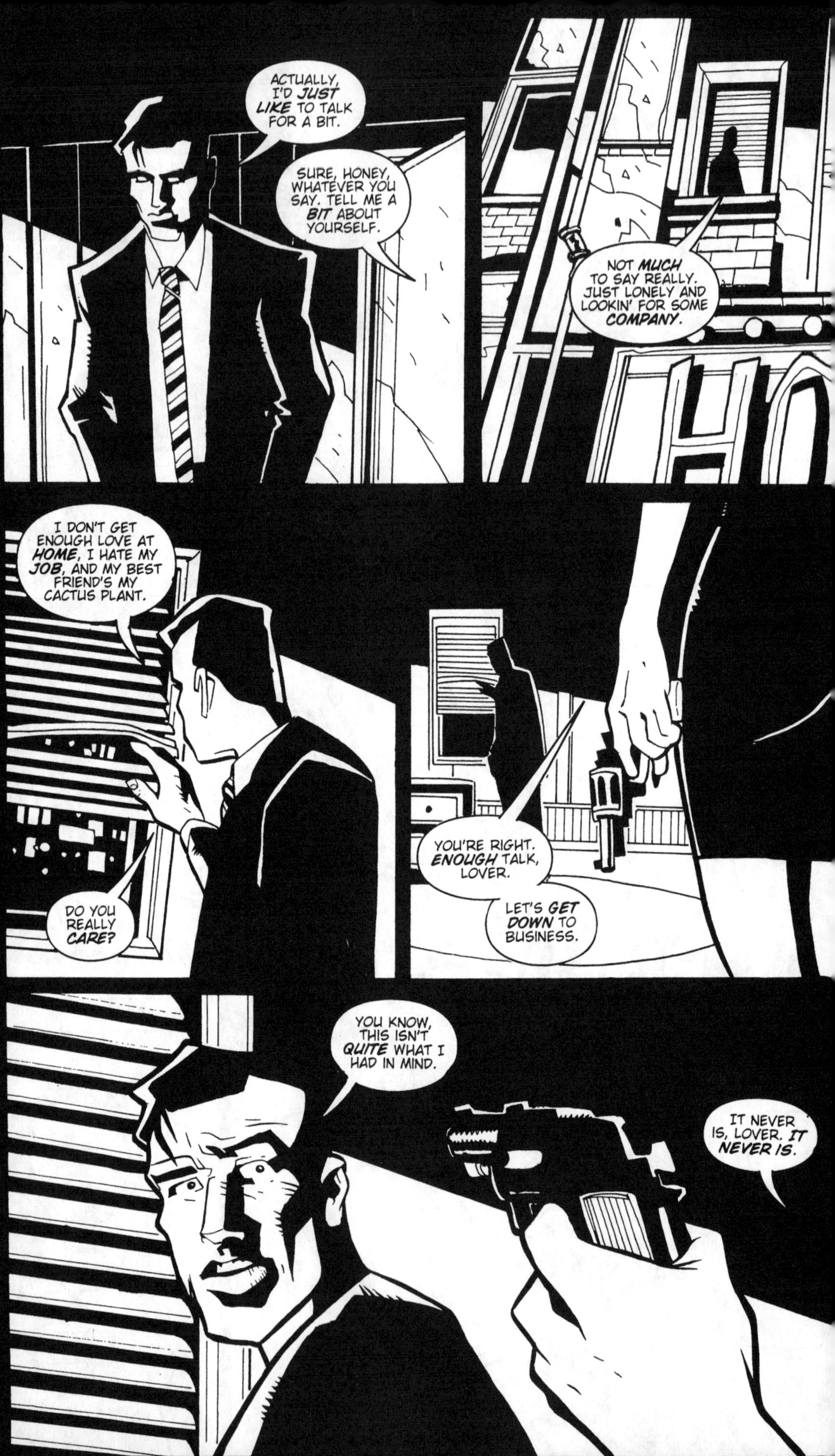

ACTUALLY, I'D JUST LIKE TO TALK FOR A BIT.
SURE, HONEY, WHATEVER YOU SAY. TELL ME A BIT ABOUT YOURSELF.
NOT MUCH TO SAY REALLY. JUST LONELY AND LOOKIN' FOR SOME COMPANY.
I DON'T GET ENOUGH LOVE AT HOME, I HATE MY JOB, AND MY BEST FRIEND'S MY CACTUS PLANT.
DO YOU REALLY CARE?
YOU'RE RIGHT. ENOUGH TALK, LOVER.
LET'S GET DOWN TO BUSINESS.
YOU KNOW, THIS ISN'T QUITE WHAT I HAD IN MIND.
IT NEVER IS, LOVER. IT NEVER IS.

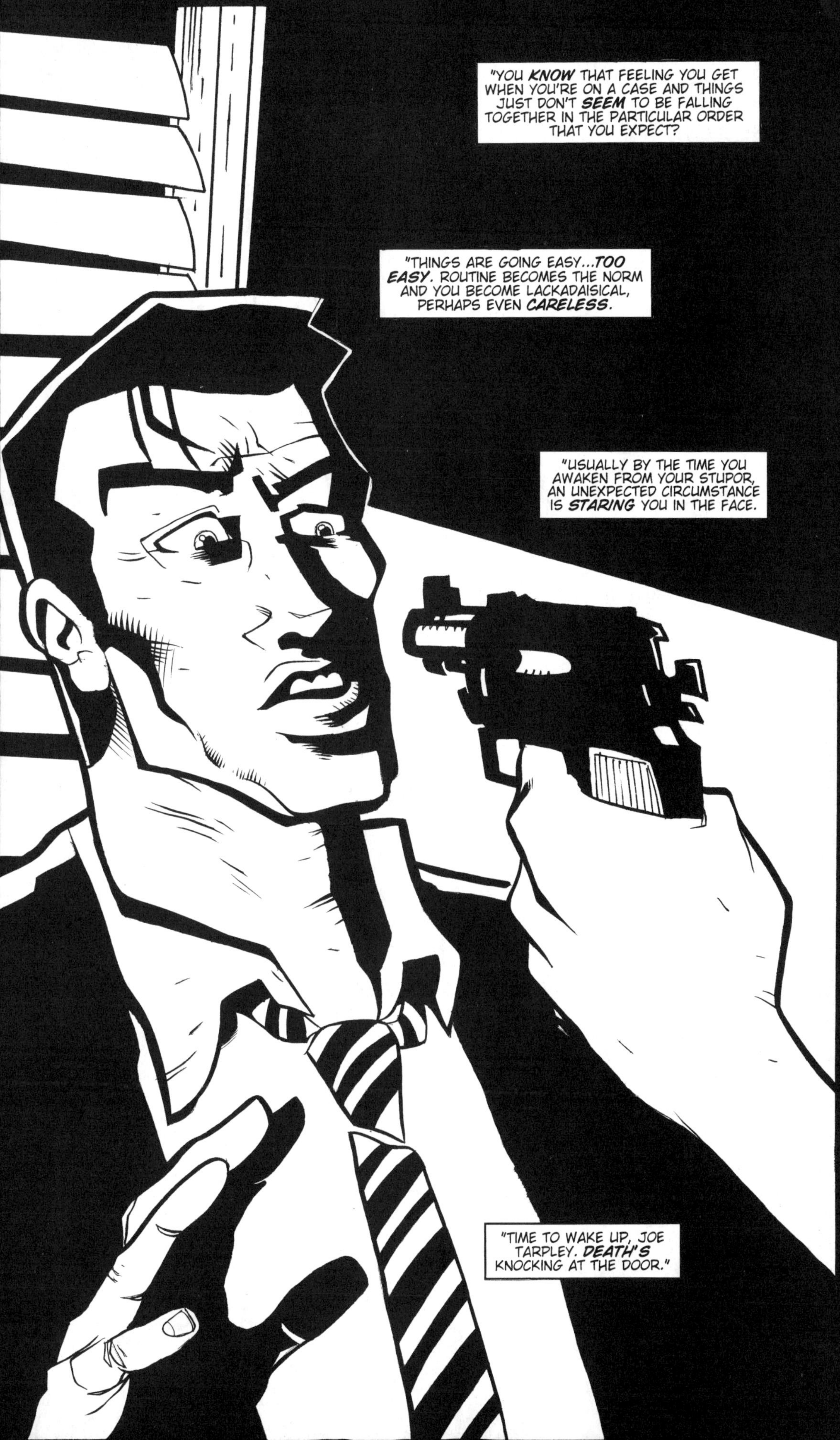
"YOU KNOW THAT FEELING YOU GET WHEN YOU'RE ON A CASE AND THINGS JUST DON'T SEEM TO BE FALLING TOGETHER IN THE PARTICULAR ORDER THAT YOU EXPECT?
"THINGS ARE GOING EASY...TOO EASY. ROUTINE BECOMES THE NORM AND YOU BECOME LACKADAISICAL, PERHAPS EVEN CARELESS.
"USUALLY BY THE TIME YOU AWAKEN FROM YOUR STUPOR, AN UNEXPECTED CIRCUMSTANCE IS STARING YOU IN THE FACE.
"TIME TO WAKE UP, JOE TARPLEY. DEATH'S KNOCKING AT THE DOOR."

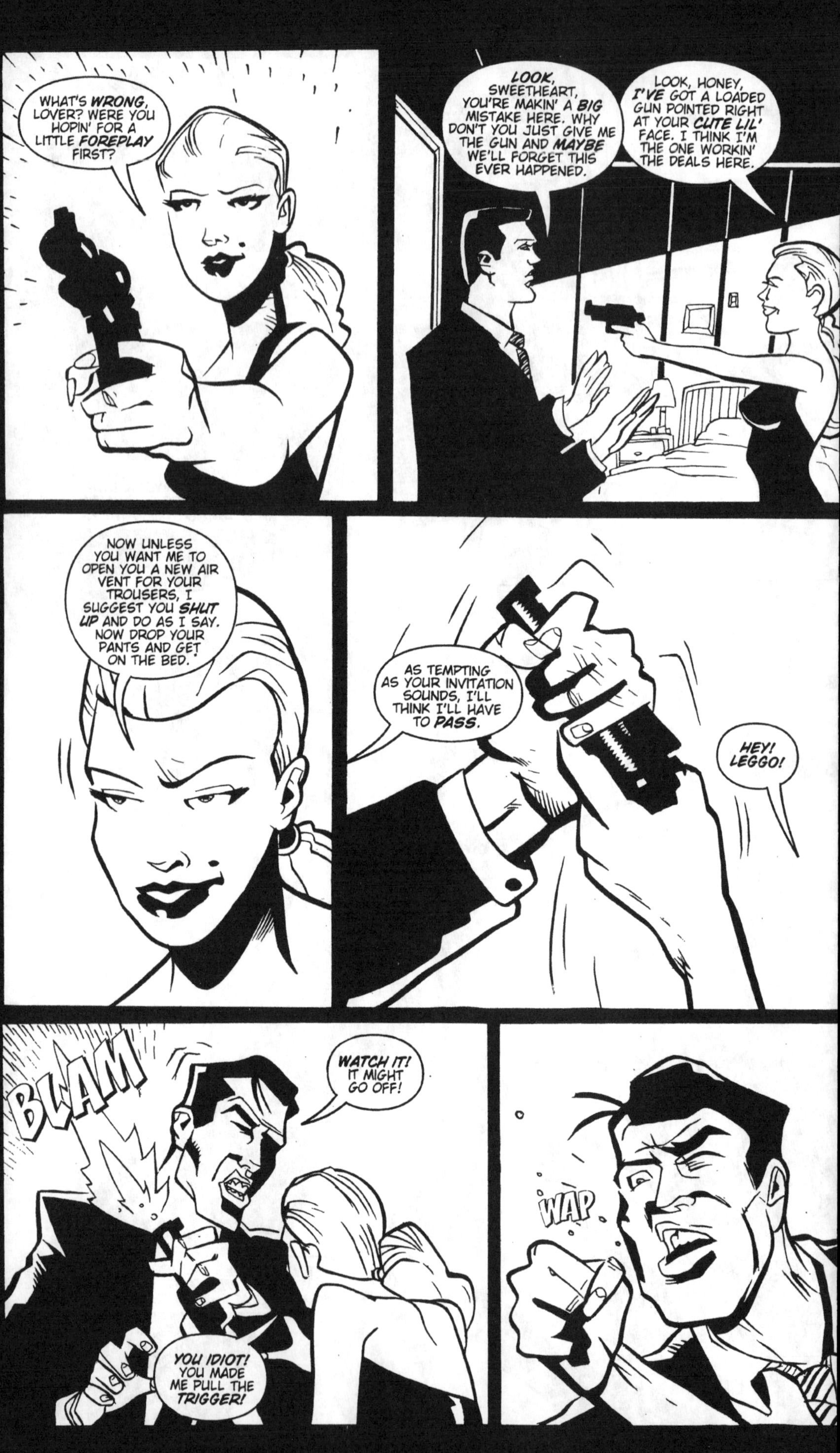
WHAT'S WRONG, LOVER? WERE YOU HOPIN' FOR A LITTLE FOREPLAY FIRST?
LOOK, SWEETHEART, YOU'RE MAKIN' A BIG MISTAKE HERE. WHY DON'T YOU JUST GIVE ME THE GUN AND MAYBE WE'LL FORGET THIS EVER HAPPENED.
LOOK, HONEY, I'VE GOT A LOADED GUN POINTED RIGHT AT YOUR CUTE LIL' FACE. I THINK I'M THE ONE WORKIN' THE DEALS HERE.
NOW UNLESS YOU WANT ME TO OPEN YOU A NEW AIR VENT FOR YOUR TROUSERS, I SUGGEST YOU SHUT UP AND DO AS I SAY. NOW DROP YOUR PANTS AND GET ON THE BED.
AS TEMPTING AS YOUR INVITATION SOUNDS, I'LL THINK I'LL HAVE TO PASS.
HEY! LEGGO!
BLAM
WATCH IT! IT MIGHT GO OFF!
YOU IDIOT! YOU MADE ME PULL THE TRIGGER!
WAP

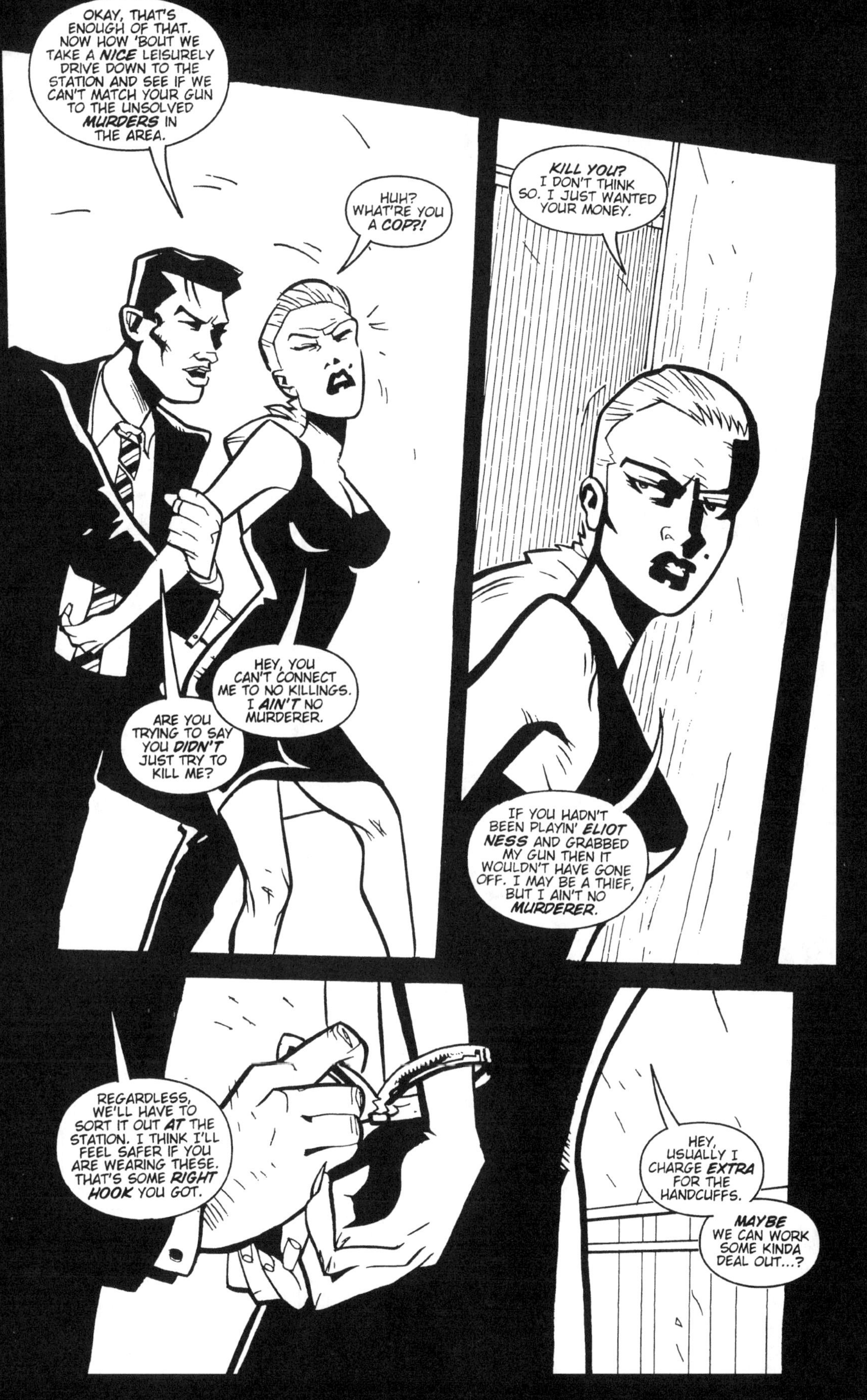
OKAY, THAT'S ENOUGH OF THAT. NOW HOW 'BOUT WE TAKE A NICE LEISURELY DRIVE DOWN TO THE STATION AND SEE IF WE CAN'T MATCH YOUR GUN TO THE UNSOLVED MURDERS IN THE AREA.
HUH? WHAT'RE YOU A COP?!
HEY, YOU CAN'T CONNECT ME TO NO KILLINGS. I AIN'T NO MURDERER.
ARE YOU TRYING TO SAY YOU DIDN'T JUST TRY TO KILL ME?
KILL YOU? I DON'T THINK SO. I JUST WANTED YOUR MONEY.
IF YOU HADN'T BEEN PLAYIN' ELIOT NESS AND GRABBED MY GUN THEN IT WOULDN'T HAVE GONE OFF. I MAY BE A THIEF, BUT I AIN'T NO MURDERER.
REGARDLESS, WE'LL HAVE TO SORT IT OUT AT THE STATION. I THINK I'LL FEEL SAFER IF YOU ARE WEARING THESE. THAT'S SOME RIGHT HOOK YOU GOT.
HEY, USUALLY I CHARGE EXTRA FOR THE HANDCUFFS.
MAYBE WE CAN WORK SOME KINDA DEAL OUT...?

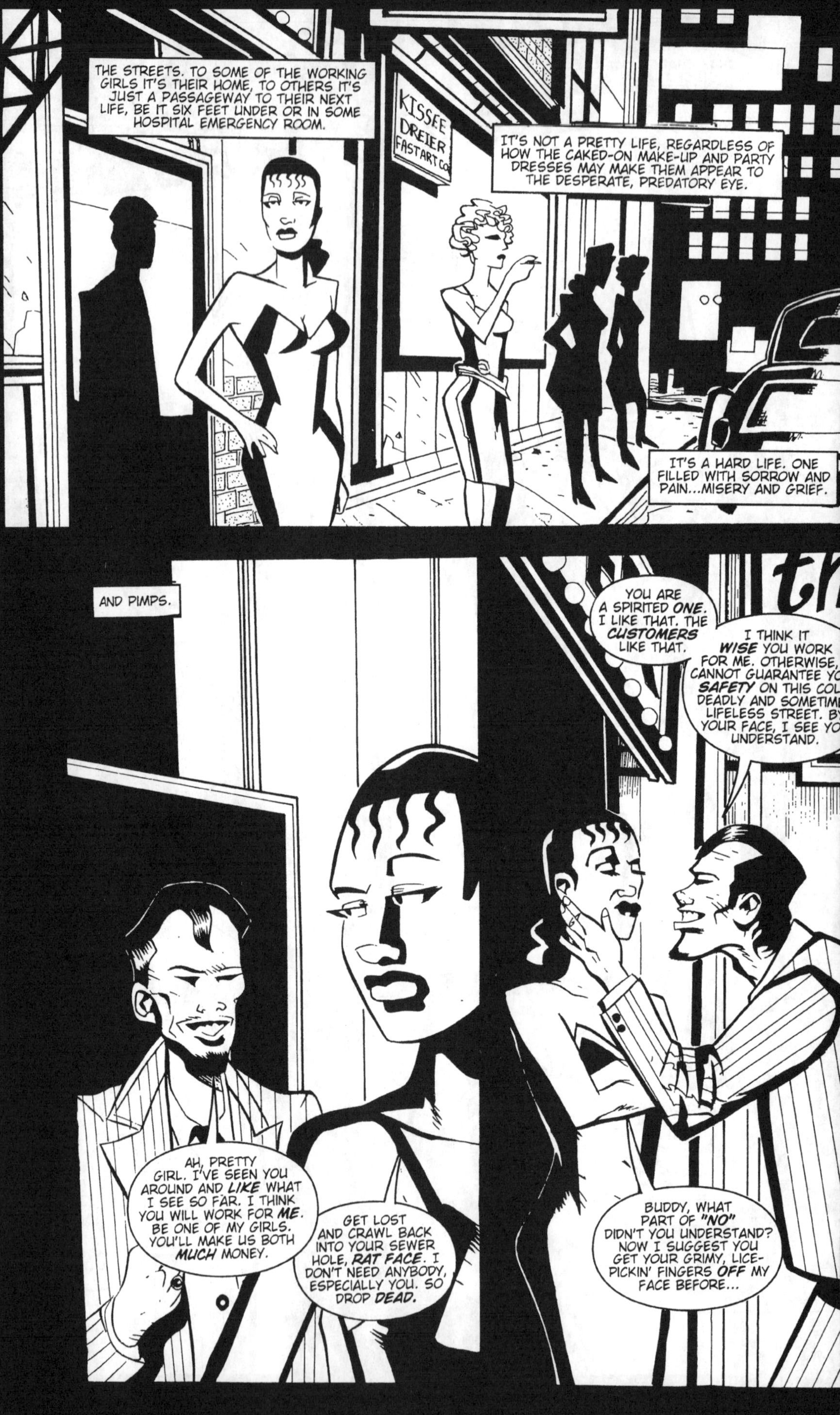

THE STREETS. TO SOME OF THE WORKING GIRLS IT'S THEIR HOME, TO OTHERS IT'S JUST A PASSAGEWAY TO THEIR NEXT LIFE, BE IT SIX FEET UNDER OR IN SOME HOSPITAL EMERGENCY ROOM.
KISSEE DREIER FASTART CO.
IT'S NOT A PRETTY LIFE, REGARDLESS OF HOW THE CAKED-ON MAKE-UP AND PARTY DRESSES MAY MAKE THEM APPEAR TO THE DESPERATE, PREDATORY EYE.
IT'S A HARD LIFE. ONE FILLED WITH SORROW AND PAIN...MISERY AND GRIEF.
AND PIMPS.
AH, PRETTY GIRL. I'VE SEEN YOU AROUND AND LIKE WHAT I SEE SO FAR. I THINK YOU WILL WORK FOR ME. BE ONE OF MY GIRLS. YOU'LL MAKE US BOTH MUCH MONEY.
GET LOST AND CRAWL BACK INTO YOUR SEWER HOLE, RAT FACE. I DON'T NEED ANYBODY, ESPECIALLY YOU. SO DROP DEAD.
YOU ARE A SPIRITED ONE. I LIKE THAT. THE CUSTOMERS LIKE THAT.
I THINK IT WISE YOU WORK FOR ME. OTHERWISE, CANNOT GUARANTEE YO SAFETY ON THIS COL DEADLY AND SOMETIM LIFELESS STREET. B YOUR FACE, I SEE YO UNDERSTAND.
BUDDY, WHAT PART OF "NO" DIDN'T YOU UNDERSTAND? NOW I SUGGEST YOU GET YOUR GRIMY, LICE-PICKIN' FINGERS OFF MY FACE BEFORE...

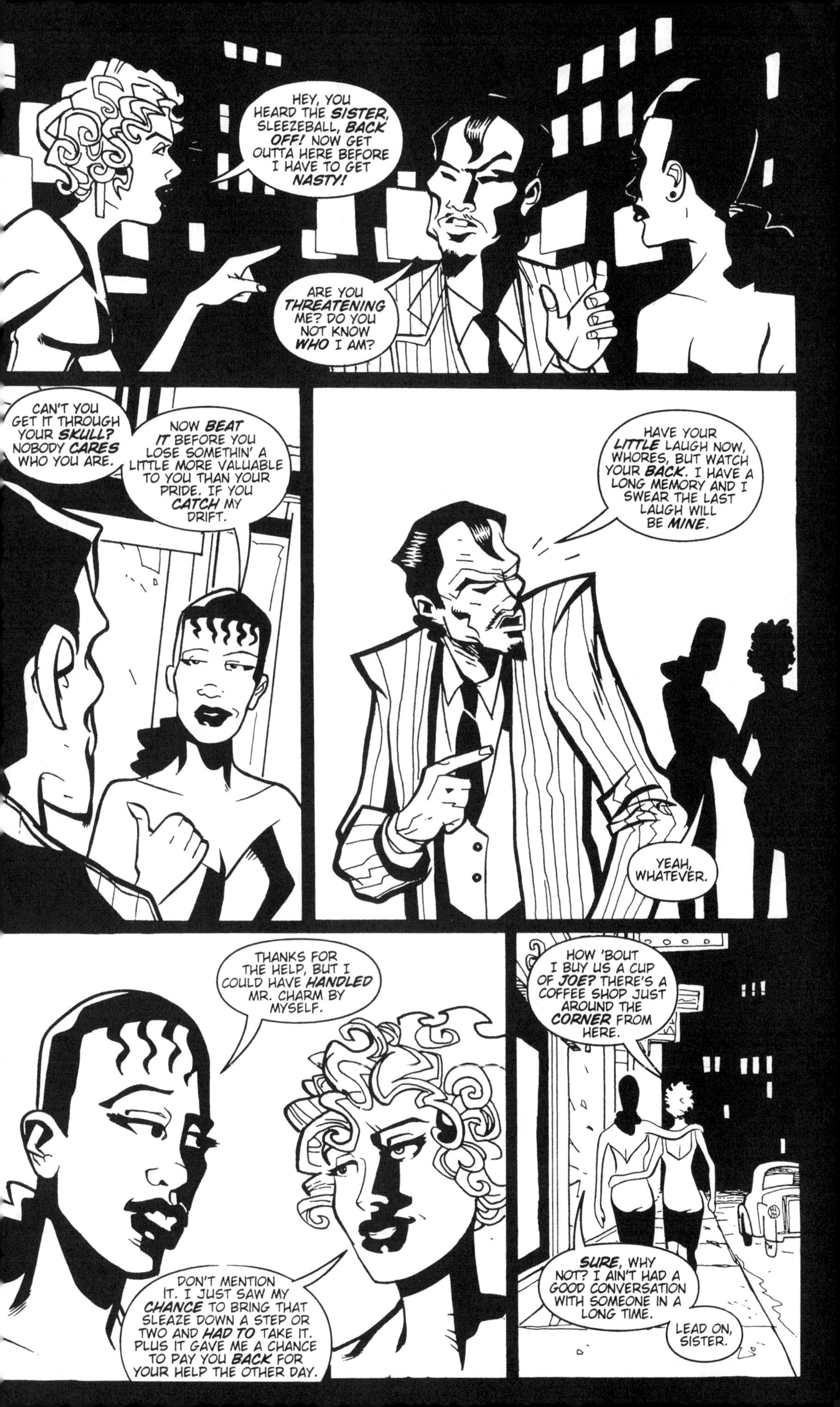
HEY, YOU HEARD THE SISTER, SLEEZEBALL, BACK OFF! NOW GET OUTTA HERE BEFORE I HAVE TO GET NASTY!
ARE YOU THREATENING ME? DO YOU NOT KNOW WHO I AM?
CAN'T YOU GET IT THROUGH YOUR SKULL? NOBODY CARES WHO YOU ARE.
NOW BEAT IT BEFORE YOU LOSE SOMETHIN' A LITTLE MORE VALUABLE TO YOU THAN YOUR PRIDE. IF YOU CATCH MY DRIFT.
HAVE YOUR LITTLE LAUGH NOW, WHORES, BUT WATCH YOUR BACK. I HAVE A LONG MEMORY AND I SWEAR THE LAST LAUGH WILL BE MINE.
YEAH, WHATEVER.
THANKS FOR THE HELP, BUT I COULD HAVE HANDLED MR. CHARM BY MYSELF.
DON'T MENTION IT. I JUST SAW MY CHANCE TO BRING THAT SLEAZE DOWN A STEP OR TWO AND HAD TO TAKE IT. PLUS IT GAVE ME A CHANCE TO PAY YOU BACK FOR YOUR HELP THE OTHER DAY.
HOW 'BOUT I BUY US A CUP OF JOE? THERE'S A COFFEE SHOP JUST AROUND THE CORNER FROM HERE.
SURE, WHY NOT? I AIN'T HAD A GOOD CONVERSATION WITH SOMEONE IN A LONG TIME.
LEAD ON, SISTER.

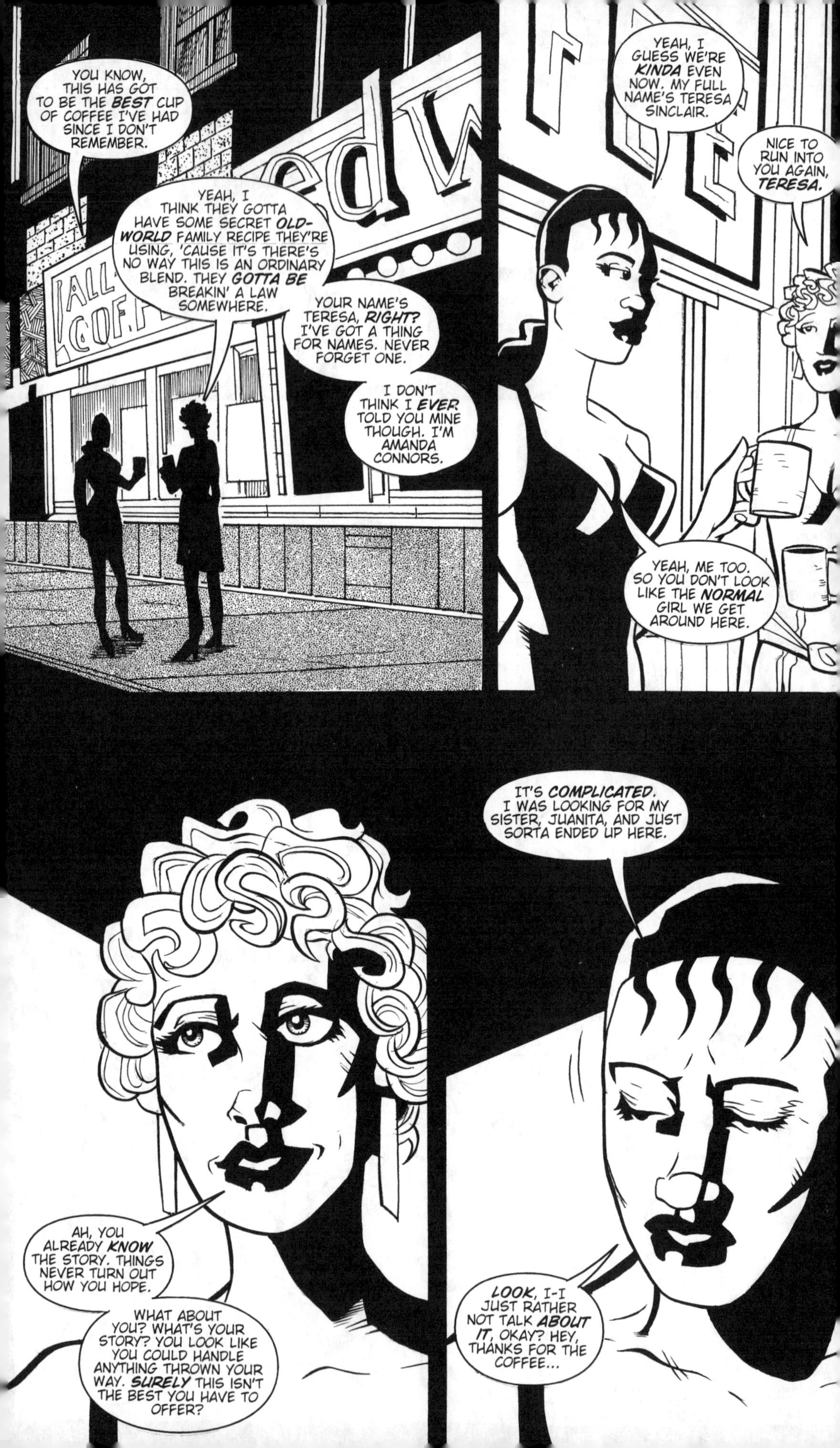
YOU KNOW, THIS HAS GOT TO BE THE BEST CUP OF COFFEE I'VE HAD SINCE I DON'T REMEMBER.
YEAH, I THINK THEY GOTTA HAVE SOME SECRET OLD-WORLD FAMILY RECIPE THEY'RE USING, 'CAUSE IT'S THERE'S NO WAY THIS IS AN ORDINARY BLEND. THEY GOTTA BE BREAKIN' A LAW SOMEWHERE.
YOUR NAME'S TERESA, RIGHT? I'VE GOT A THING FOR NAMES. NEVER FORGET ONE.
I DON'T THINK I EVER TOLD YOU MINE THOUGH. I'M AMANDA CONNORS.
YEAH, I GUESS WE'RE KINDA EVEN NOW. MY FULL NAME'S TERESA SINCLAIR.
NICE TO RUN INTO YOU AGAIN, TERESA.
YEAH, ME TOO. SO YOU DON'T LOOK LIKE THE NORMAL GIRL WE GET AROUND HERE.
AH, YOU ALREADY KNOW THE STORY. THINGS NEVER TURN OUT HOW YOU HOPE.
WHAT ABOUT YOU? WHAT'S YOUR STORY? YOU LOOK LIKE YOU COULD HANDLE ANYTHING THROWN YOUR WAY. SURELY THIS ISN'T THE BEST YOU HAVE TO OFFER?
IT'S COMPLICATED. I WAS LOOKING FOR MY SISTER, JUANITA, AND JUST SORTA ENDED UP HERE.
LOOK, I-I JUST RATHER NOT TALK ABOUT IT, OKAY? HEY, THANKS FOR THE COFFEE...

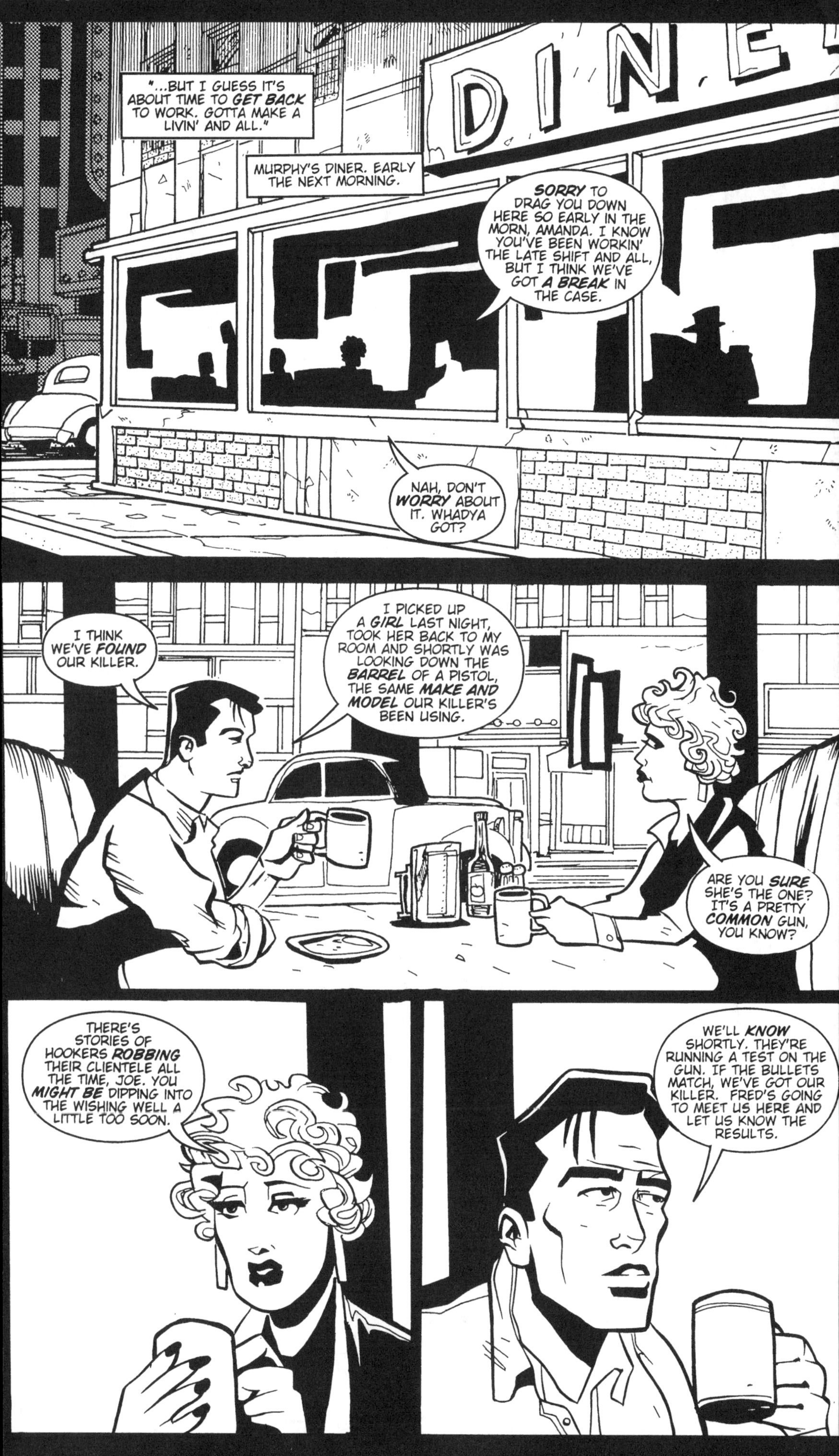
"...BUT I GUESS IT'S ABOUT TIME TO GET BACK TO WORK. GOTTA MAKE A LIVIN' AND ALL."
MURPHY'S DINER. EARLY THE NEXT MORNING.
DINE
SORRY TO DRAG YOU DOWN HERE SO EARLY IN THE MORN, AMANDA. I KNOW YOU'VE BEEN WORKIN' THE LATE SHIFT AND ALL, BUT I THINK WE'VE GOT A BREAK IN THE CASE.
NAH, DON'T WORRY ABOUT IT. WHADYA GOT?
I THINK WE'VE FOUND OUR KILLER.
I PICKED UP A GIRL LAST NIGHT, TOOK HER BACK TO MY ROOM AND SHORTLY WAS LOOKING DOWN THE BARREL OF A PISTOL, THE SAME MAKE AND MODEL OUR KILLER'S BEEN USING.
ARE YOU SURE SHE'S THE ONE? IT'S A PRETTY COMMON GUN, YOU KNOW?
THERE'S STORIES OF HOOKERS ROBBING THEIR CLIENTELE ALL THE TIME, JOE. YOU MIGHT BE DIPPING INTO THE WISHING WELL A LITTLE TOO SOON.
WE'LL KNOW SHORTLY. THEY'RE RUNNING A TEST ON THE GUN. IF THE BULLETS MATCH, WE'VE GOT OUR KILLER. FRED'S GOING TO MEET US HERE AND LET US KNOW THE RESULTS.

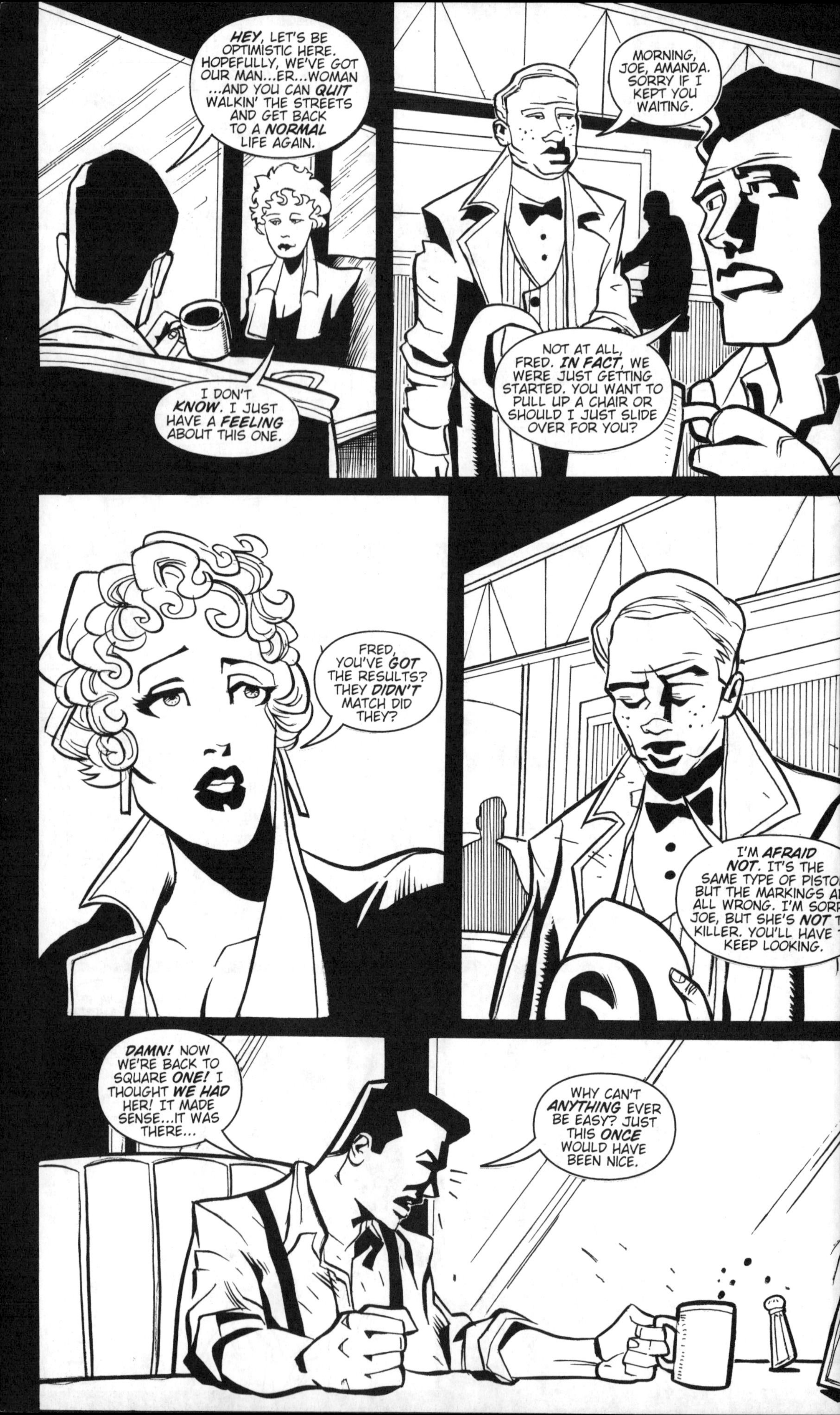
HEY, LET'S BE OPTIMISTIC HERE. HOPEFULLY, WE'VE GOT OUR MAN...ER...WOMAN ...AND YOU CAN QUIT WALKIN' THE STREETS AND GET BACK TO A NORMAL LIFE AGAIN.
I DON'T KNOW. I JUST HAVE A FEELING ABOUT THIS ONE.
MORNING, JOE, AMANDA. SORRY IF I KEPT YOU WAITING.
NOT AT ALL, FRED. IN FACT, WE WERE JUST GETTING STARTED. YOU WANT TO PULL UP A CHAIR OR SHOULD I JUST SLIDE OVER FOR YOU?
FRED, YOU'VE GOT THE RESULTS? THEY DIDN'T MATCH DID THEY?
I'M AFRAID NOT. IT'S THE SAME TYPE OF PISTO BUT THE MARKINGS A ALL WRONG. I'M SORR JOE, BUT SHE'S NOT T KILLER. YOU'LL HAVE T KEEP LOOKING.
DAMN! NOW WE'RE BACK TO SQUARE ONE! I THOUGHT WE HAD HER! IT MADE SENSE...IT WAS THERE...
WHY CAN'T ANYTHING EVER BE EASY? JUST THIS ONCE WOULD HAVE BEEN NICE.

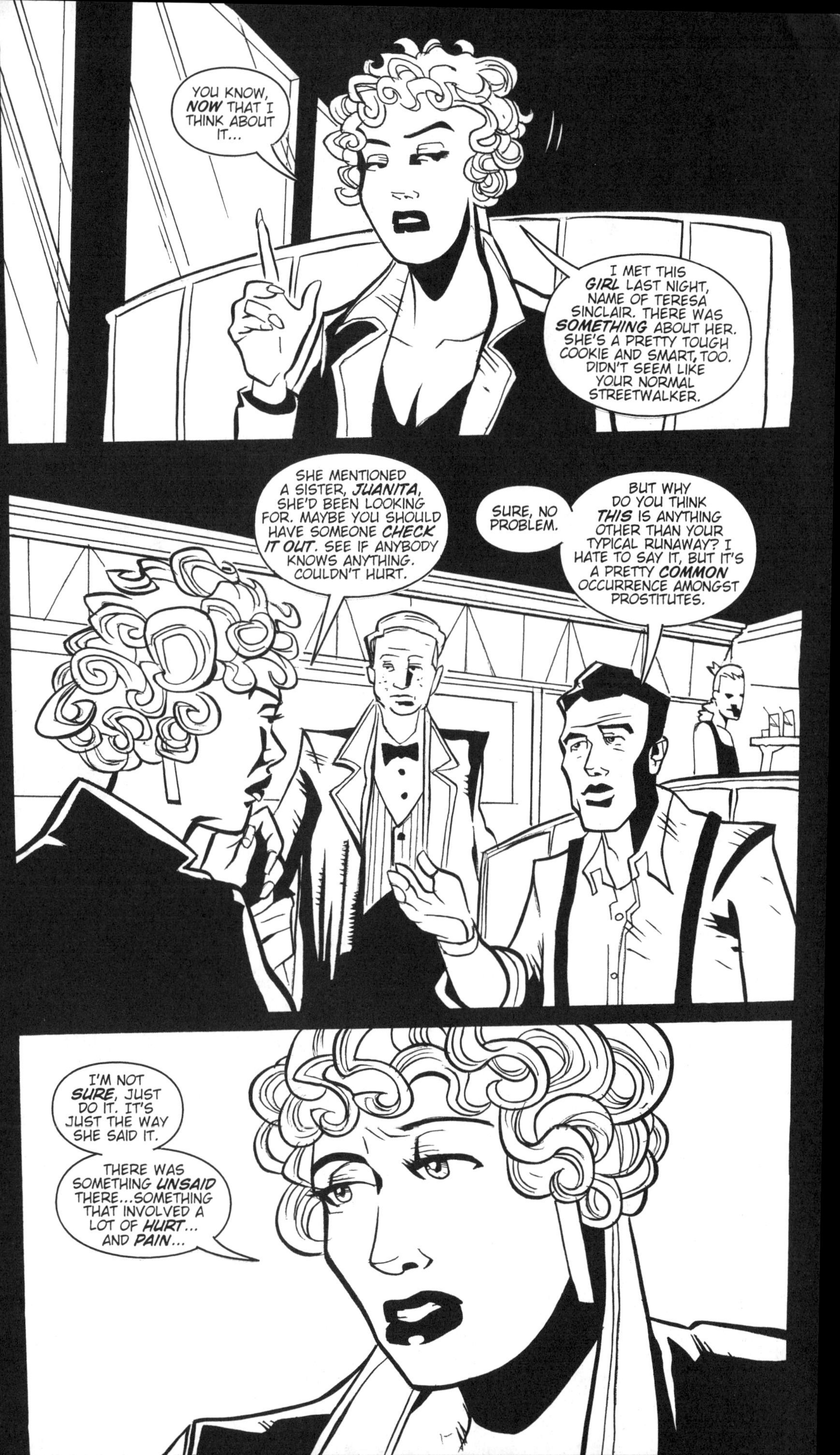

YOU KNOW, NOW THAT I THINK ABOUT IT...
I MET THIS GIRL LAST NIGHT, NAME OF TERESA SINCLAIR. THERE WAS SOMETHING ABOUT HER. SHE'S A PRETTY TOUGH COOKIE AND SMART, TOO. DIDN'T SEEM LIKE YOUR NORMAL STREETWALKER.
SHE MENTIONED A SISTER, JUANITA, SHE'D BEEN LOOKING FOR. MAYBE YOU SHOULD HAVE SOMEONE CHECK IT OUT. SEE IF ANYBODY KNOWS ANYTHING. COULDN'T HURT.
SURE, NO PROBLEM.
BUT WHY DO YOU THINK THIS IS ANYTHING OTHER THAN YOUR TYPICAL RUNAWAY? I HATE TO SAY IT, BUT IT'S A PRETTY COMMON OCCURRENCE AMONGST PROSTITUTES.
I'M NOT SURE, JUST DO IT. IT'S JUST THE WAY SHE SAID IT.
THERE WAS SOMETHING UNSAID THERE...SOMETHING THAT INVOLVED A LOT OF HURT... AND PAIN...

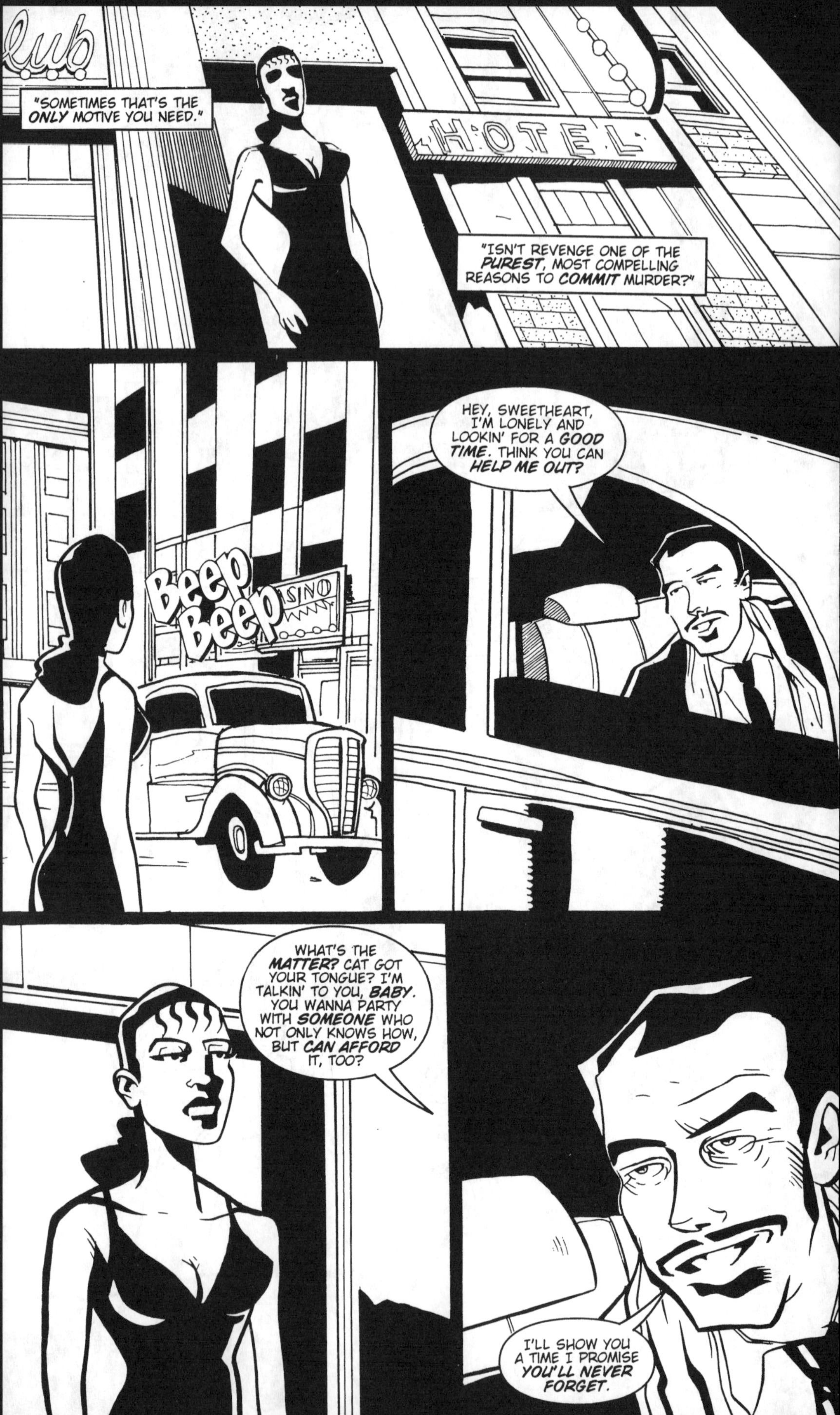

LUB
"SOMETIMES THAT'S THE ONLY MOTIVE YOU NEED."
HOTEL
"ISN'T REVENGE ONE OF THE PUREST, MOST COMPELLING REASONS TO COMMIT MURDER?"
BEEP BEEP
ASINO
HEY, SWEETHEART, I'M LONELY AND LOOKIN' FOR A GOOD TIME. THINK YOU CAN HELP ME OUT?
WHAT'S THE MATTER? CAT GOT YOUR TONGUE? I'M TALKIN' TO YOU, BABY. YOU WANNA PARTY WITH SOMEONE WHO NOT ONLY KNOWS HOW, BUT CAN AFFORD IT, TOO?
I'LL SHOW YOU A TIME I PROMISE YOU'LL NEVER FORGET.

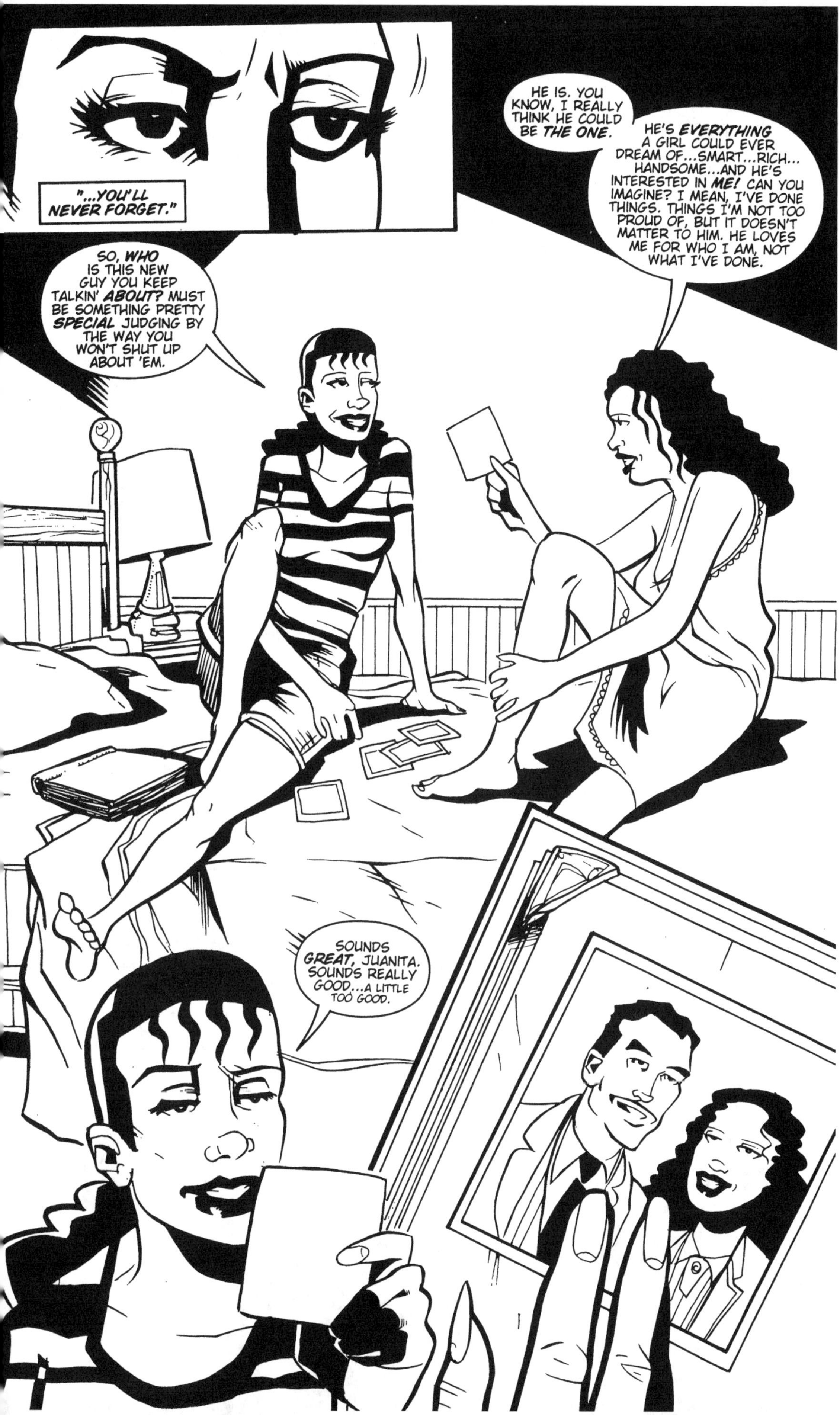
"...YOU'LL NEVER FORGET."
SO, WHO IS THIS NEW GUY YOU KEEP TALKIN' ABOUT? MUST BE SOMETHING PRETTY SPECIAL JUDGING BY THE WAY YOU WON'T SHUT UP ABOUT 'EM.
HE IS. YOU KNOW, I REALLY THINK HE COULD BE THE ONE.
HE'S EVERYTHING A GIRL COULD EVER DREAM OF...SMART...RICH... HANDSOME...AND HE'S INTERESTED IN ME! CAN YOU IMAGINE? I MEAN, I'VE DONE THINGS. THINGS I'M NOT TOO PROUD OF, BUT IT DOESN'T MATTER TO HIM. HE LOVES ME FOR WHO I AM, NOT WHAT I'VE DONE.
SOUNDS GREAT, JUANITA. SOUNDS REALLY GOOD...A LITTLE TOO GOOD.

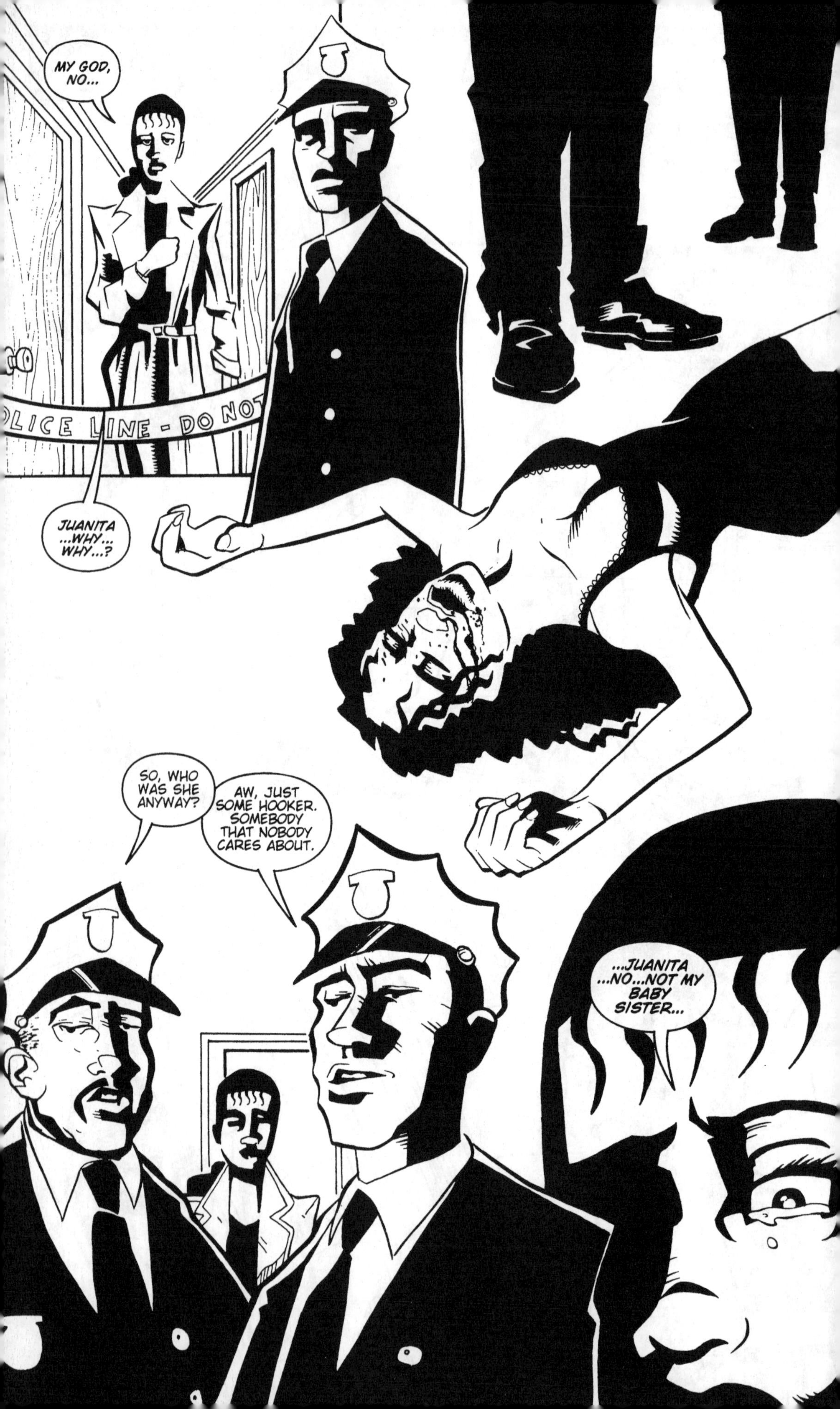
MY GOD, NO...
OLICE LINE - DO NOT
JUANITA ...WHY... WHY...?
SO, WHO WAS SHE ANYWAY?
AW, JUST SOME HOOKER. SOMEBODY THAT NOBODY CARES ABOUT.
...JUANITA ...NO...NOT MY BABY SISTER...

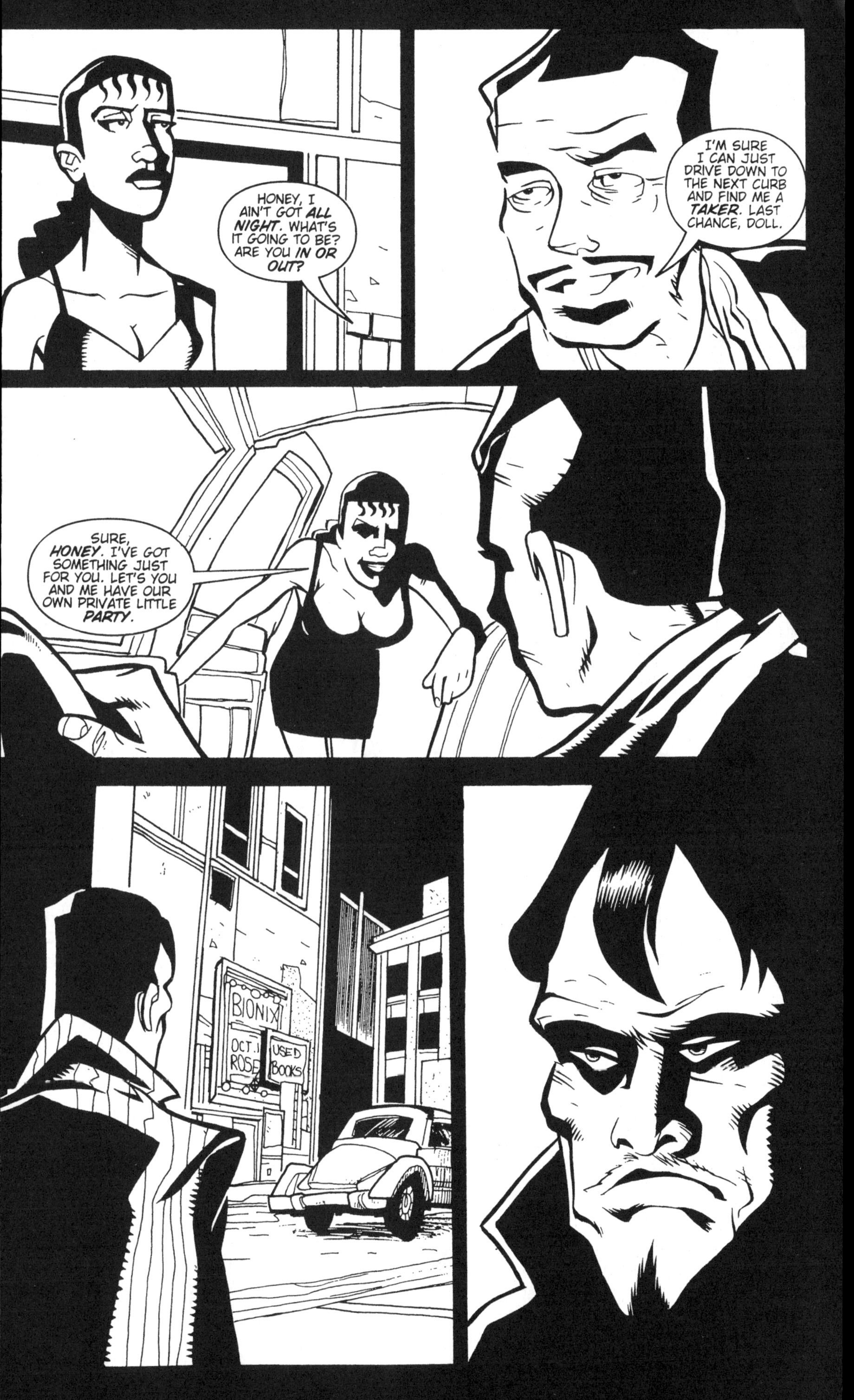
HONEY, I AIN'T GOT **ALL NIGHT**. WHAT'S IT GOING TO BE? ARE YOU **IN OR OUT?**
I'M SURE I CAN JUST DRIVE DOWN TO THE NEXT CURB AND FIND ME A **TAKER**. LAST CHANCE, DOLL.
SURE, **HONEY**. I'VE GOT SOMETHING JUST FOR YOU. LET'S YOU AND ME HAVE OUR OWN PRIVATE LITTLE **PARTY**.
BIONIX
OCT. 1
ROSE
USED BOOKS

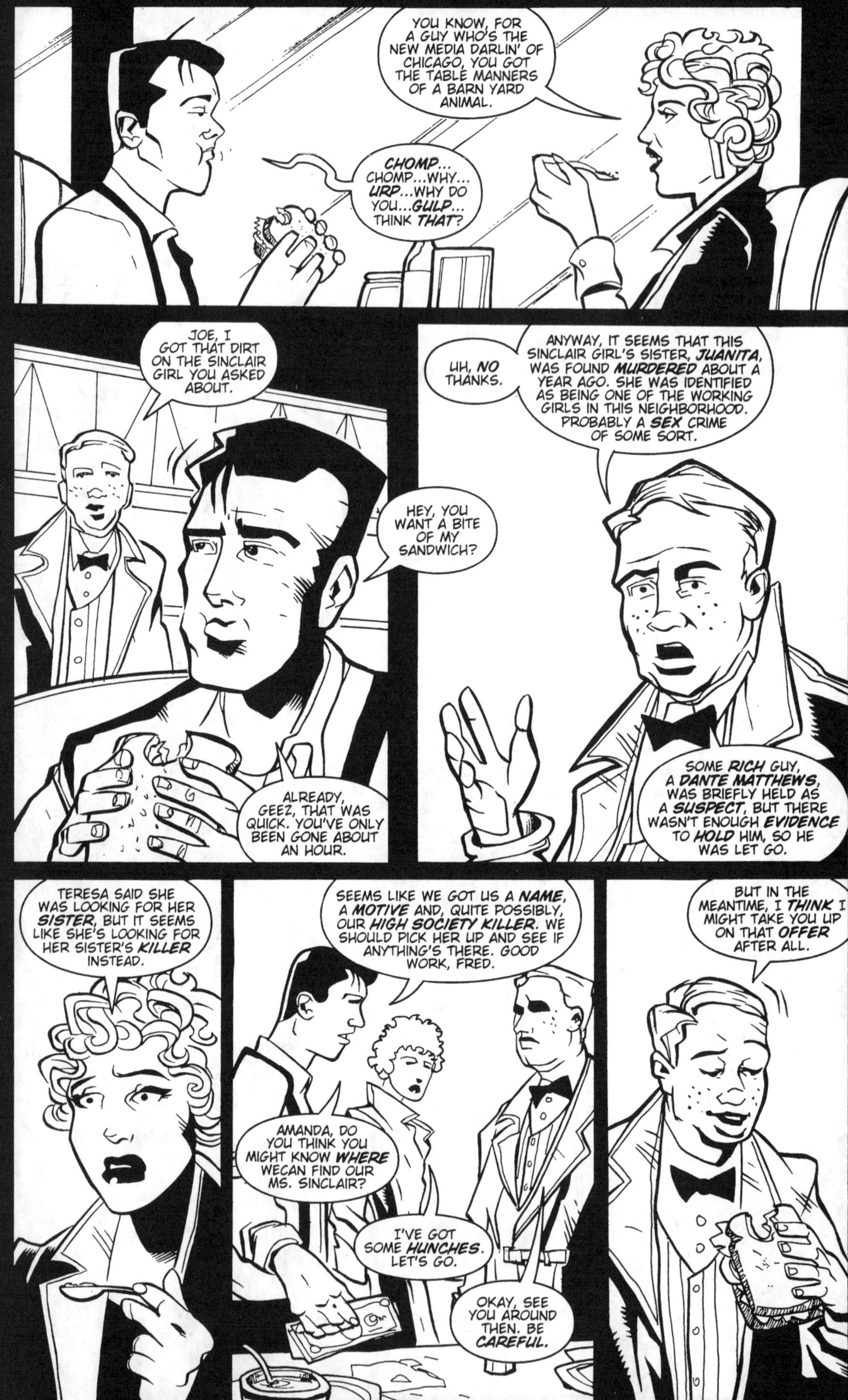
YOU KNOW, FOR A GUY WHO'S THE NEW MEDIA DARLIN' OF CHICAGO, YOU GOT THE TABLE MANNERS OF A BARN YARD ANIMAL.
CHOMP... CHOMP...WHY... URP...WHY DO YOU...GULP... THINK THAT?
JOE, I GOT THAT DIRT ON THE SINCLAIR GIRL YOU ASKED ABOUT.
HEY, YOU WANT A BITE OF MY SANDWICH?
ALREADY, GEEZ, THAT WAS QUICK. YOU'VE ONLY BEEN GONE ABOUT AN HOUR.
UH, NO THANKS.
ANYWAY, IT SEEMS THAT THIS SINCLAIR GIRL'S SISTER, JUANITA, WAS FOUND MURDERED ABOUT A YEAR AGO. SHE WAS IDENTIFIED AS BEING ONE OF THE WORKING GIRLS IN THIS NEIGHBORHOOD. PROBABLY A SEX CRIME OF SOME SORT.
SOME RICH GUY, A DANTE MATTHEWS, WAS BRIEFLY HELD AS A SUSPECT, BUT THERE WASN'T ENOUGH EVIDENCE TO HOLD HIM, SO HE WAS LET GO.
TERESA SAID SHE WAS LOOKING FOR HER SISTER, BUT IT SEEMS LIKE SHE'S LOOKING FOR HER SISTER'S KILLER INSTEAD.
SEEMS LIKE WE GOT US A NAME, A MOTIVE AND, QUITE POSSIBLY, OUR HIGH SOCIETY KILLER. WE SHOULD PICK HER UP AND SEE IF ANYTHING'S THERE. GOOD WORK, FRED.
AMANDA, DO YOU THINK YOU MIGHT KNOW WHERE WECAN FIND OUR MS. SINCLAIR?
I'VE GOT SOME HUNCHES. LET'S GO.
OKAY, SEE YOU AROUND THEN. BE CAREFUL.
BUT IN THE MEANTIME, I THINK I MIGHT TAKE YOU UP ON THAT OFFER AFTER ALL.

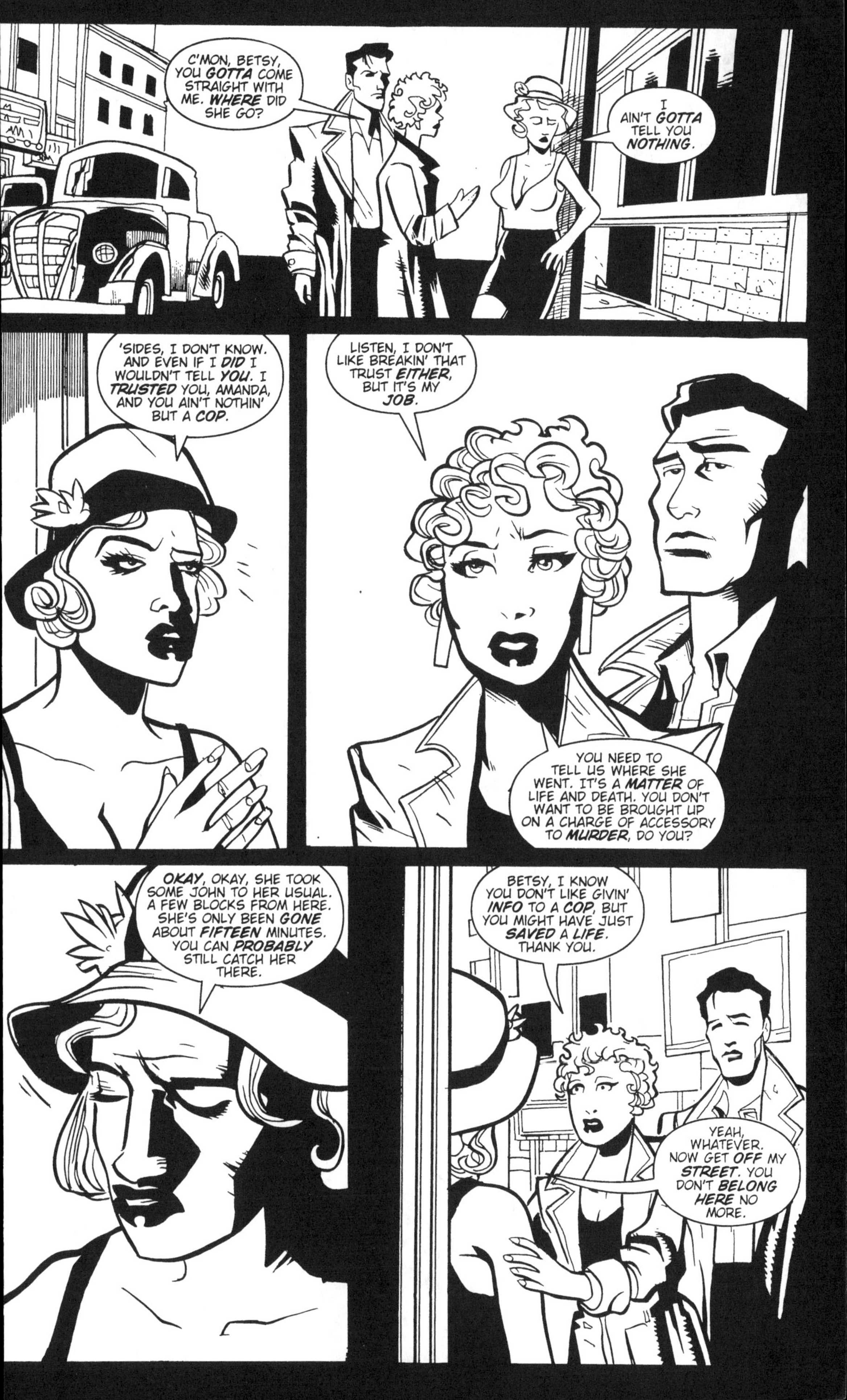
C'MON, BETSY, YOU GOTTA COME STRAIGHT WITH ME. WHERE DID SHE GO?
I AIN'T GOTTA TELL YOU NOTHING.
'SIDES, I DON'T KNOW. AND EVEN IF I DID I WOULDN'T TELL YOU. I TRUSTED YOU, AMANDA, AND YOU AIN'T NOTHIN' BUT A COP.
LISTEN, I DON'T LIKE BREAKIN' THAT TRUST EITHER, BUT IT'S MY JOB.
YOU NEED TO TELL US WHERE SHE WENT. IT'S A MATTER OF LIFE AND DEATH. YOU DON'T WANT TO BE BROUGHT UP ON A CHARGE OF ACCESSORY TO MURDER, DO YOU?
OKAY, OKAY, SHE TOOK SOME JOHN TO HER USUAL. A FEW BLOCKS FROM HERE. SHE'S ONLY BEEN GONE ABOUT FIFTEEN MINUTES. YOU CAN PROBABLY STILL CATCH HER THERE.
BETSY, I KNOW YOU DON'T LIKE GIVIN' INFO TO A COP, BUT YOU MIGHT HAVE JUST SAVED A LIFE. THANK YOU.
YEAH, WHATEVER. NOW GET OFF MY STREET. YOU DON'T BELONG HERE NO MORE.

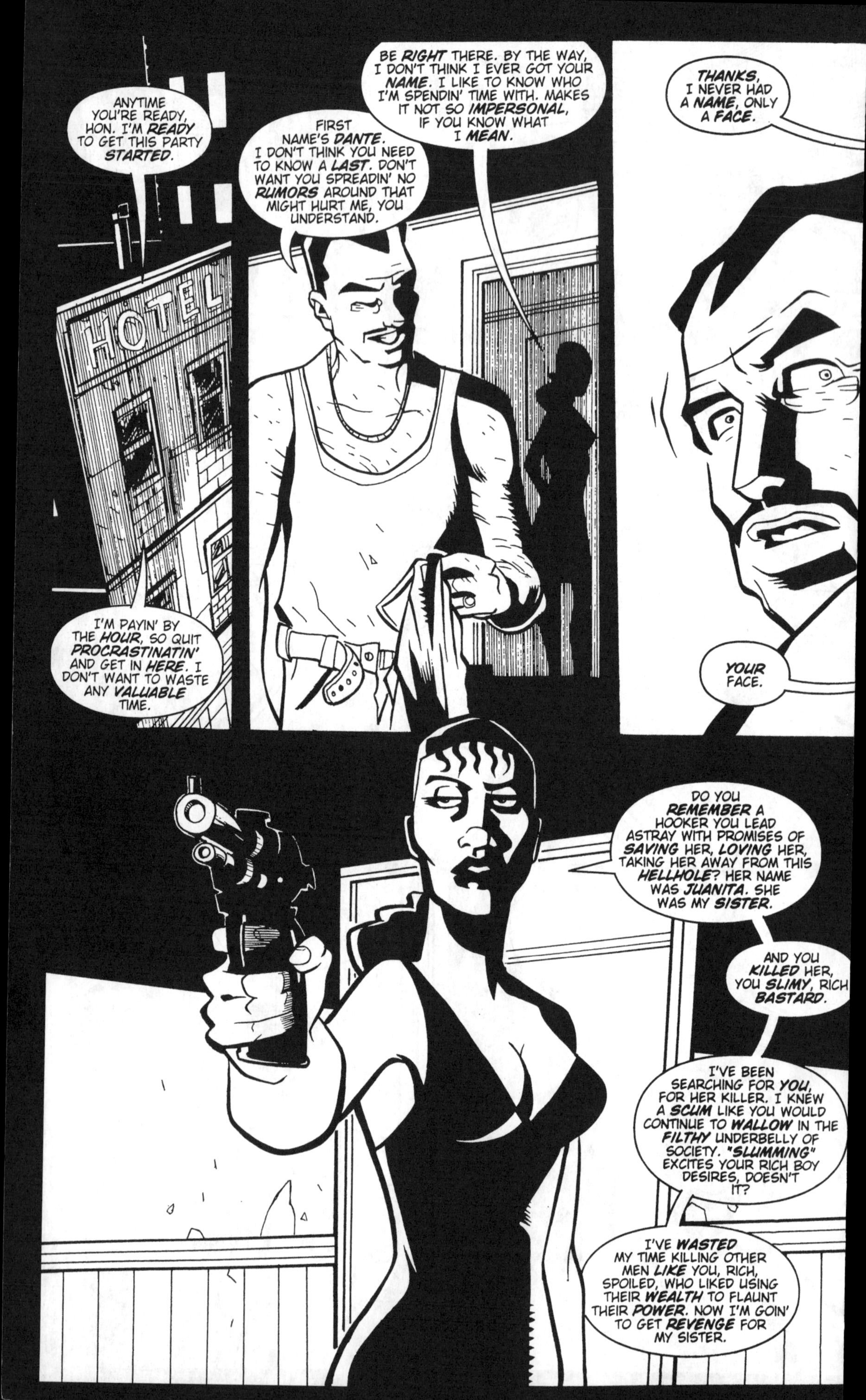
ANYTIME YOU'RE READY, HON. I'M READY TO GET THIS PARTY STARTED.
I'M PAYIN' BY THE HOUR, SO QUIT PROCRASTINATIN' AND GET IN HERE. I DON'T WANT TO WASTE ANY VALUABLE TIME.
BE RIGHT THERE. BY THE WAY, I DON'T THINK I EVER GOT YOUR NAME. I LIKE TO KNOW WHO I'M SPENDIN' TIME WITH. MAKES IT NOT SO IMPERSONAL, IF YOU KNOW WHAT I MEAN.
FIRST NAME'S DANTE. I DON'T THINK YOU NEED TO KNOW A LAST. DON'T WANT YOU SPREADIN' NO RUMORS AROUND THAT MIGHT HURT ME, YOU UNDERSTAND.
THANKS, I NEVER HAD A NAME, ONLY A FACE.
YOUR FACE.
DO YOU REMEMBER A HOOKER YOU LEAD ASTRAY WITH PROMISES OF SAVING HER, LOVING HER, TAKING HER AWAY FROM THIS HELLHOLE? HER NAME WAS JUANITA. SHE WAS MY SISTER.
AND YOU KILLED HER, YOU SLIMY, RICH BASTARD.
I'VE BEEN SEARCHING FOR YOU, FOR HER KILLER. I KNEW A SCUM LIKE YOU WOULD CONTINUE TO WALLOW IN THE FILTHY UNDERBELLY OF SOCIETY. "SLUMMING" EXCITES YOUR RICH BOY DESIRES, DOESN'T IT?
I'VE WASTED MY TIME KILLING OTHER MEN LIKE YOU, RICH, SPOILED, WHO LIKED USING THEIR WEALTH TO FLAUNT THEIR POWER. NOW I'M GOIN' TO GET REVENGE FOR MY SISTER.
HOTEL

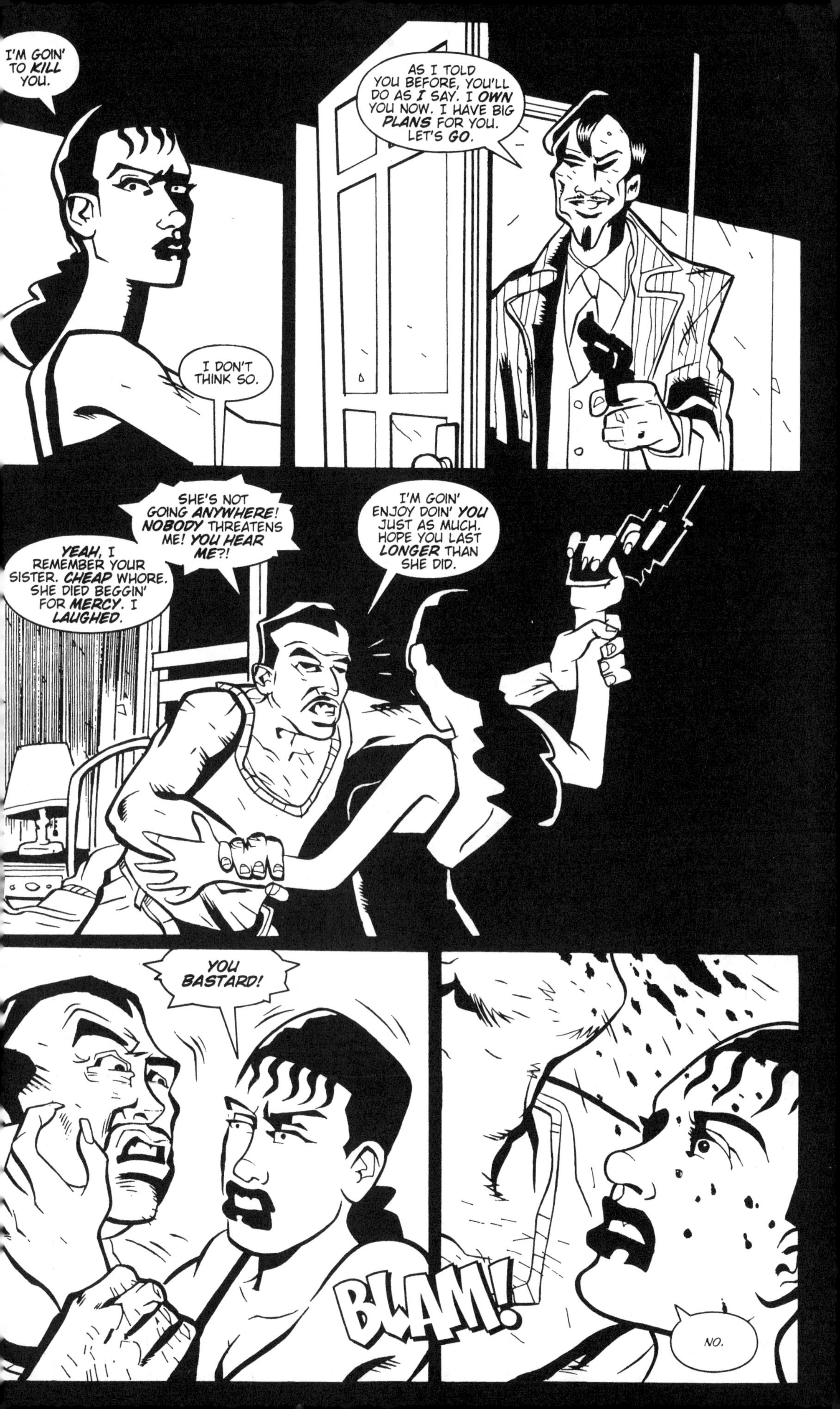
I'M GOIN' TO KILL YOU.
I DON'T THINK SO.
AS I TOLD YOU BEFORE, YOU'LL DO AS I SAY. I OWN YOU NOW. I HAVE BIG PLANS FOR YOU. LET'S GO.
YEAH, I REMEMBER YOUR SISTER. CHEAP WHORE. SHE DIED BEGGIN' FOR MERCY. I LAUGHED.
SHE'S NOT GOING ANYWHERE! NOBODY THREATENS ME! YOU HEAR ME?!
I'M GOIN' ENJOY DOIN' YOU JUST AS MUCH. HOPE YOU LAST LONGER THAN SHE DID.
YOU BASTARD!
BLAM!
NO.

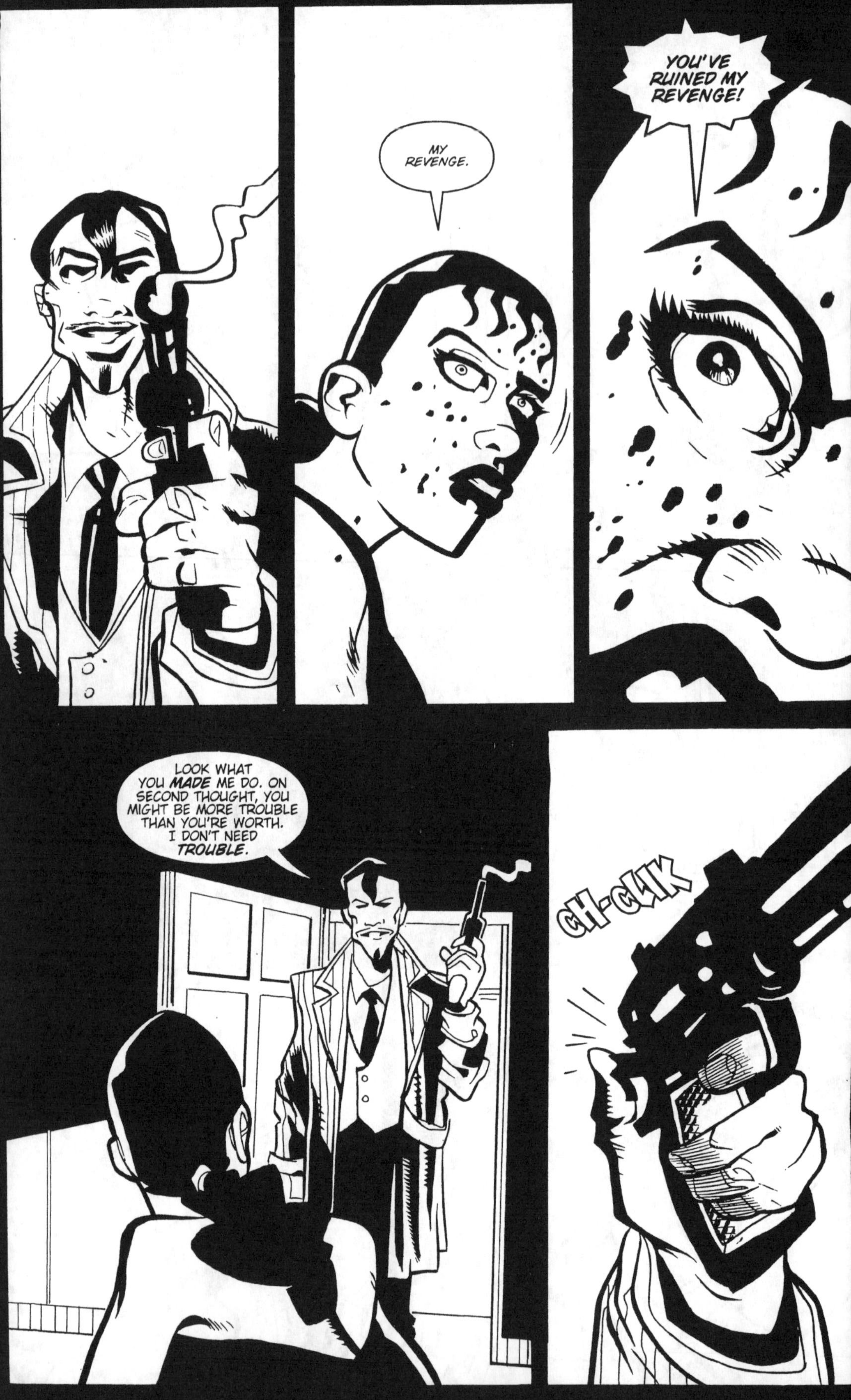
MY REVENGE.
YOU'VE RUINED MY REVENGE!
LOOK WHAT YOU MADE ME DO. ON SECOND THOUGHT, YOU MIGHT BE MORE TROUBLE THAN YOU'RE WORTH. I DON'T NEED TROUBLE.
CH-CLIK

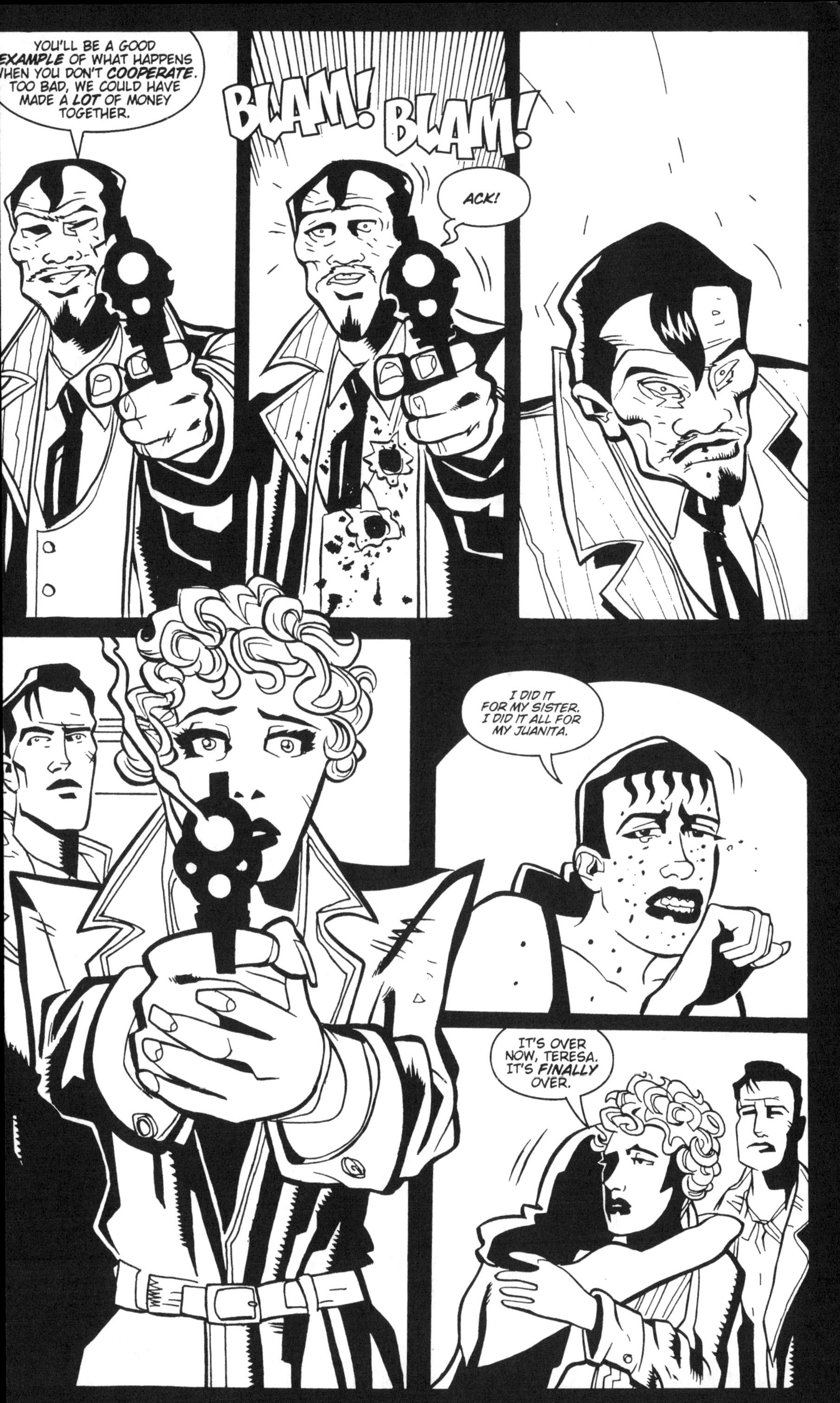
YOU'LL BE A GOOD EXAMPLE OF WHAT HAPPENS WHEN YOU DON'T COOPERATE. TOO BAD, WE COULD HAVE MADE A LOT OF MONEY TOGETHER.
BLAM! BLAM!
ACK!
I DID IT FOR MY SISTER. I DID IT ALL FOR MY JUANITA.
IT'S OVER NOW, TERESA. IT'S FINALLY OVER.

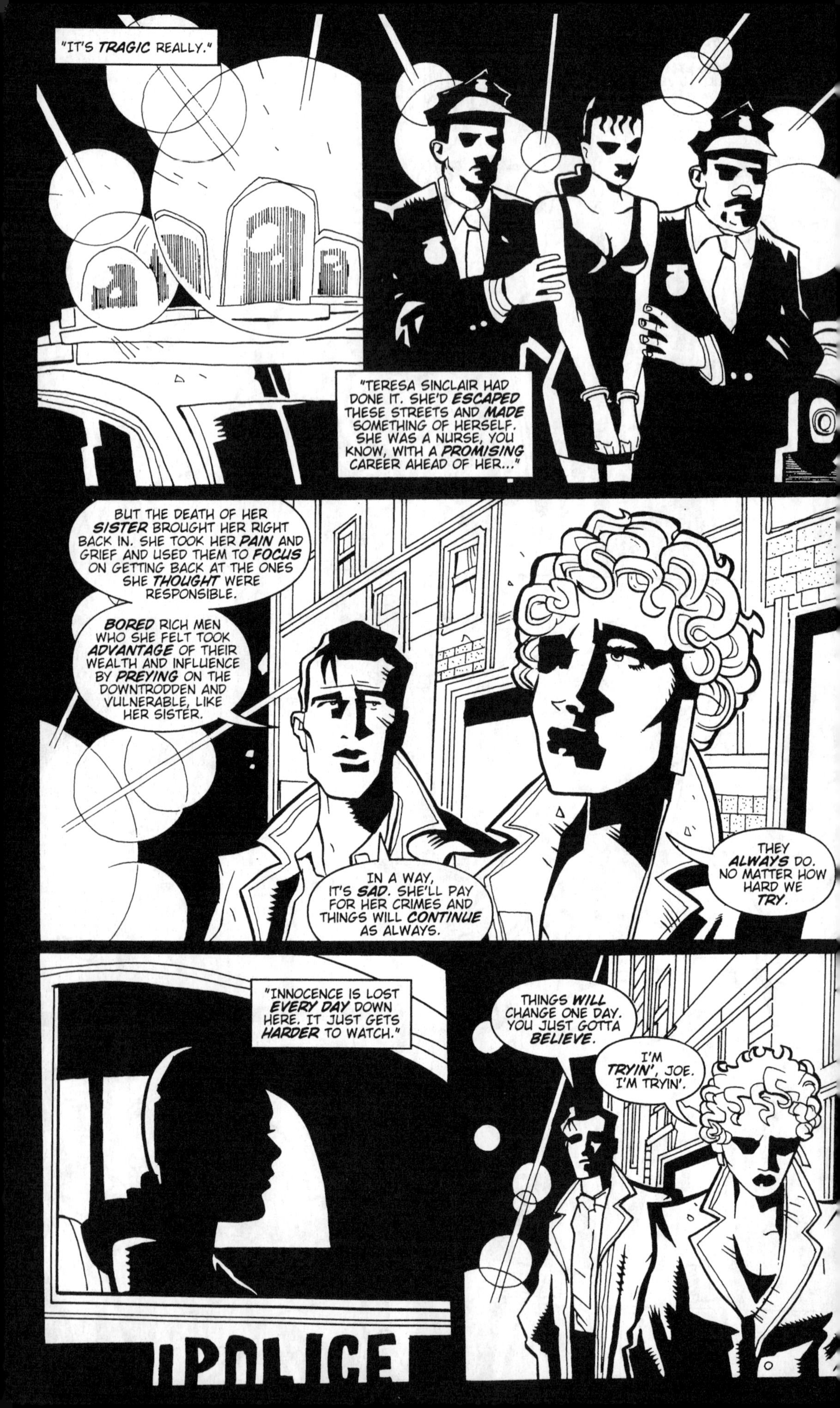
"IT'S TRAGIC REALLY."
"TERESA SINCLAIR HAD DONE IT. SHE'D ESCAPED THESE STREETS AND MADE SOMETHING OF HERSELF. SHE WAS A NURSE, YOU KNOW, WITH A PROMISING CAREER AHEAD OF HER..."
BUT THE DEATH OF HER SISTER BROUGHT HER RIGHT BACK IN. SHE TOOK HER PAIN AND GRIEF AND USED THEM TO FOCUS ON GETTING BACK AT THE ONES SHE THOUGHT WERE RESPONSIBLE.
BORED RICH MEN WHO SHE FELT TOOK ADVANTAGE OF THEIR WEALTH AND INFLUENCE BY PREYING ON THE DOWNTRODDEN AND VULNERABLE, LIKE HER SISTER.
IN A WAY, IT'S SAD. SHE'LL PAY FOR HER CRIMES AND THINGS WILL CONTINUE AS ALWAYS.
THEY ALWAYS DO. NO MATTER HOW HARD WE TRY.
"INNOCENCE IS LOST EVERY DAY DOWN HERE. IT JUST GETS HARDER TO WATCH."
THINGS WILL CHANGE ONE DAY. YOU JUST GOTTA BELIEVE.
I'M TRYIN', JOE. I'M TRYIN'.
POLICE

FIN

BIOGRAPHIES

JOE PRUETT

Joe Pruett has been in the comics industry since 1989, where he's served as an art assistant, a writer, a letterer, an editor, a creative director, and a publisher. His work has earned numerous Harvey, Eagle and Eisner Award nominations through the years. As a freelance writer, his stories have graced the pages of *X-Men Unlimited*, *Wolverine*, *Cable*, *Magneto Rex*, *Domino*, *Gen 13*, *Weird Western Tales*, among others. in 2004 he formed Desperado Publishing, fulfilling a life-long dream of becoming a publishing home for today's top creative talent.

JOHN KISSEE

John Kissee is an illustrator and graphic designer living in FortLauderdale, Florida. His work has appeared in *Mad Magazine*, *Instinct*, and *New Times LA*. His comics work includes *Raven Chronicles*, *Untouchables*, *Crime Wave*, and *Rib* for Caliber Comics and *The Dark Fringe* for Brainstorm comics. Check out more of John's work at *johnkissee.com*.

MORE GREAT BOOKS FROM IMAGE COMICS

POWERS
Who Killed Retro Girl?
BRIAN MICHAEL BENDIS
MICHAEL AVON OEMING

POWERS, VOL. 1: WHO KILLED RETRO GIRL? TP
ISBN# 1-58240-669-3
$21.99

POWERS
ROLEPLAY
BRIAN MICHAEL BENDIS
MICHAEL AVON OEMING

POWERS, VOL. 2: ROLEPLAY TP
ISBN# 1-58240-695-2
$13.99

COSTUMED CONSPIRACIES TAKE FLIGHT
POWERS

POWERS, VOL. 3: LITTLE DEATHS TP
ISBN# 1-58240-670-7
$19.99

POWERS
SUPERGROUP
BRIAN MICHAEL BENDIS
MICHAEL AVON OEMING

POWERS, VOL. 4: SUPERGROUP TP
ISBN# 1-58240-671-5
$21.99

POWERS
ANARCHY
BENDIS
OEMING

POWERS, VOL. 5: ANARCHY TP
ISBN# 1-58240-331-7
$14.95

goldfish
a crime graphic novel
by brian michael bendis

GOLDFISH: THE DEFINITIVE COLLECTION TP
ISBN# 1-58240-195-0
$19.95

jinx
brian michael bendis

JINX: THE DEFINITIVE COLLECTION TP
ISBN# 1-58240-179-9
$24.95

fire
a spy graphic novel
brian michael bendis

FIRE: THE DEFINITIVE COLLECTION TP
ISBN# 1-58240-071-7
$9.95

torso
a true crime graphic novel
brian michael bendis
marc andreyko

TORSO: THE DEFINITIVE COLLECTION TP
ISBN# 1-58240-174-8
$21.95

BRIAN MICHAEL BEND
TOTAL SELL OUT

TOTAL SELL OUT TP
ISBN# 1-58240-287-6
$14.95

ALSO AVAILABLE

40 OZ. COLLECTED TP
ISBN# 1-58240-329-5
$9.95

BAD IDEAS: COLLECTED! TP
ISBN# 1-58240-531-X
$12.99

CLASSIC 40 OZ.: TALES FROM THE BROWN BAG TP
ISBN# 1-58240-438-0
$14.95

DIORAMAS, A LOVE STORY GN
ISBN# 1-58240-359-7
$12.95

BLOOD RIVER GN
ISBN# 1-58240-509-3
$7.99

WINGS OF ANASI GN
$6.99

KABUKI

VOL. 1: CIRCLE OF BLOOD TP
ISBN# 1-88727-980-6
$19.95

VOL. 2: DREAMS TP
ISBN# 1-58240-277-9
$12.95

VOL. 3: MASKS OF NOH TP
ISBN# 1-58240-108-X
$12.95

VOL. 4: SKIN DEEP TP
ISBN# 1-58240-000-8
$12.95

VOL. 5: METAMORPHOSIS TP
ISBN# 1-58240-203-5
$24.99

VOL. 6: SCARAB TP
ISBN# 1-58240-258-2
$19.95

NIGHT TRIPPERS GN
ISBN# 1-58240-606-5
$16.99

NOWHERESVILLE TP
ISBN# 1-58240-241-8
$14.95

THE FURTHER ADVENTURES OF ONE PAGE FILLER MAN TP
ISBN# 1-58240-535-2
$11.99

GIRLS

VOL. 1: CONCEPTION TP
ISBN# 1-58240-529-8
$14.99

VOL. 2: EMERGENCE TP
ISBN# 1-58240-608-1
$14.99

GRRL SCOUTS

VOL. 1: TP
ISBN# 1-58240-316-3
$12.95

VOL. 2: WORK SUCKS TP
ISBN# 1-58240-343-0
$12.95

HAMMER OF THE GODS, VOL. 1: MORTAL ENEMY TP
ISBN# 1-58240-271-X
$18.95

POWERS SCRIPTBOOK
ISBN# 1-58240-233-7
$19.95

PUTTIN THE BACKBONE BACK TP
ISBN# 1-58240-402-X
$9.95

QUIXOTE NOVEL
ISBN# 1-58240-434-8
$9.95

SAN AND TWITCH: THE BRIAN MICHAEL BENDIS COLLECTION, VOL. 1 TP
ISBN# 1-58240-583-2
$24.95

SIX GN
ISBN# 1-58240-398-8
$5.95

STUPID COMICS, VOL. 1 TP
ISBN# 1-58240-611-1
$12.99

ULTRA: SEVEN DAYS TP
ISBN# 1-58240-483-6
$17.95

WHISKEY DICKEL, INTERNATIONAL COWGIRL GN
ISBN# 1-58240-318-X
$12.95

For a comic shop near you carrying graphic novels from Image Comics, please call toll free: 1-888-COMIC-BOOK

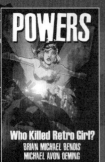

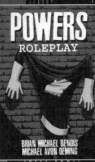

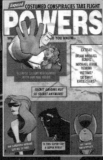

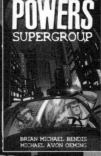

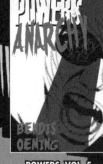

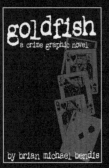

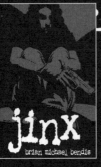

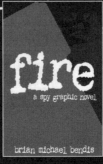

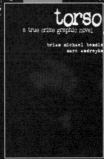

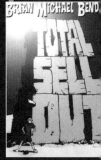